HARPER'S

PORTABLE

BOOK

OF

B·I·B·L·E

SELECTIONS

with the complete Psalms

THOUSANDS OF QUOTATIONS
FOR PRACTICAL HELP ON
OVER 300 TOPICS

compiled by
MARTIN H. MANSER

1817

HARPER & ROW, PUBLISHERS, SAN FRANCISCO
Cambridge, Hagerstown, New York, Philadelphia,
London, Mexico City, São Paulo, Sydney

To my grandmother, for her support in prayer,
and to David C. K. Watson, who told me about Jesus Christ.

Harper's Portable Book of Bible Selections.
Copyright © 1982 by Lion Publishing.
All rights reserved. No part of this book may be used or
reproduced in any manner whatsoever without written permission
except in the case of brief quotations embodied in critical articles
and reviews. For information address Harper & Row, Publishers,
Inc., 10 East 53rd Street, New York, NY 10022. Published
simultaneously in Canada by Fitzhenry & Whiteside, Limited,
Toronto.

FIRST U.S. EDITION

Illustrations by Simon Bull

Printed in Italy by International Publishing Enterprises

Library of Congress Cataloging in Publication Data

Bible. English. Selections. 1983.
  HARPER'S PORTABLE BOOK OF BIBLE SELECTIONS WITH THE COMPLETE
PSALMS.

  British ed. published as: The Lion concise book of Bible
quotations. Tring, Hertfordshire: Lion Pub., c1982.
  1. Bible—Indexes. I. Manser, Martin H. II. Bible. O.T. Psalms.
English. Revised Standard. 1983. III. Title, IV. Title: Portable
book of Bible selections with the complete Psalms.
BS391.2.M36 1983   220.5'2   83–47728
ISBN 0–06–065256–X

83 84 85 86 87 10 9 8 7 6 5 4 3 2 1

How to use this book

Part One
Verses appear **under nearly 300 themes arranged in alphabetical order.** This part is useful if you want to know what the Bible says about a particular subject. It is also helpful for finding a specific quotation: look up the main idea of the verse to discover its reference. Under each entry, the references are arranged in Bible order, so the verses can be looked up—and the content checked— in the Bible itself. A number of detailed entries may be found especially useful: 'God', 'Jesus Christ', 'Holy Spirit'; also subjects such as 'Faith', 'Comfort', 'Prayer', to find help on living the Christian life or meeting a particular need.

Part Two
The book of Psalms has long been a favorite source of comfort and inspiration for Christians. Here are some of the best-known and best-loved words of the Old Testament.

Contents

Introduction

Quotations from the Bible are among the best-known of all quotations in the English language. This book has been compiled both for reference and for those who like to browse. In Part One, quotations are listed according to themes; in Part Two, the full text of the Psalms is provided.

The quotations have been taken from a number of different translations. Often they are most familiar in the words of the *Authorized* or *King James Version* and so this has been quoted. The words of the *Revised Standard Version* and the more recent *New International Version* echo the older language but are more easily understood today. Others, such as the 'common-language' *Good News Bible* or more formal *New English Bible*, have been quoted where appropriate or where the fresh renderings have been recently taken up and become well-known. The Psalms are in the *Revised Standard Version* to retain their original poetry.

The aim throughout has been to try to be as faithful as possible to the Bible itself. 'All Scripture is God-breathed and is useful for teaching, rebuking, correcting and training in righteousness', wrote the apostle Paul to Timothy, 'so that the man of God may be thoroughly equipped for every good work.' So it is hoped that the book will help the reader enjoy something of the riches of the Bible, and that the quotations will lead to the discovery of passages which may not have been noticed before.

In addition it is hoped that the first part will serve as a valuable reference tool and source of help, for following up studies of words and themes and simply discovering where to find passages to meet a particular need.

This book has been compiled with the desire that it may lead to a greater reading of the Bible, and response to its message.

Martin H. Manser

BOOKS OF THE BIBLE

OLD TESTAMENT

Genesis
Exodus
Leviticus
Numbers
Deuteronomy
Joshua
Judges
Ruth
1 Samuel
2 Samuel
1 Kings
2 Kings
1 Chronicles
2 Chronicles
Ezra
Nehemiah
Esther
Job
Psalms
Proverbs
Ecclesiastes
Song of Solomon
Isaiah
Jeremiah
Lamentations
Ezekiel
Daniel
Hosea
Joel
Amos
Obadiah
Jonah
Micah
Nahum
Habakkuk
Zephaniah
Haggai
Zechariah
Malachi

NEW TESTAMENT

Matthew
Mark
Luke
John
Acts
Romans
1 Corinthians
2 Corinthians
Galatians
Ephesians
Philippians
Colossians
1 Thessalonians
2 Thessalonians
1 Timothy
2 Timothy
Titus
Philemon
Hebrews
James
1 Peter
2 Peter
1 John
2 John
3 John
Jude
Revelation

Abbreviations used for Bible versions

BCP	The Book of Common Prayer
GNB	Good News Bible
JB	The Jerusalem Bible
JBP	J. B. Phillips, New Testament in Modern English
KJV	King James Version (Authorized)
LB	The Living Bible
NEB	The New English Bible
NIV	Holy Bible, New International Version
RSV	Revised Standard Version

PART

1

Accepting the will of God

Moses said, 'No, Lord, don't send me. I have never been a good speaker, and I haven't become one since you began to speak to me. I am a poor speaker, slow and hesitant.' The Lord said to him, 'Who gives man his mouth? Who makes him deaf or dumb? Who gives him sight or makes him blind? It is I, the Lord. Now, go! I will help you to speak, and I will tell you what to say.' Exodus 4:10-12 GNB

Though he slay me, yet will I trust in him: but I will maintain mine own ways before him. Job 13:15 KJV

It is good for me that I was afflicted, that I might learn thy statutes. Psalm 119:71 RSV

My son, do not despise the Lord's discipline or be weary of his reproof, for the Lord reproves him whom he loves, as a father the son in whom he delights. Proverbs 3:11-12 RSV

Thy kingdom come. Thy will be done, in earth as it is in heaven. Matthew 6:10 BCP

And going a little farther he fell on his face and prayed, 'My Father, if it be possible, let this cup pass from me; nevertheless, not as I will, but as thou wilt.' Matthew 26:39 RSV

But one of you will say to me, 'If this is so, how can God find fault with anyone? Who can resist God's will?' But who are you, my friend, to answer God back? A clay pot does not ask the man who made it, 'Why did you make me like this?' After all, the man who makes the pots has the right to use the clay as he wishes, and to make two pots from the same lump of clay, one for special occasions and the other for ordinary use. Romans 9:19-21 GNB

He said to me, 'My grace is sufficient for you, for my power is made perfect in weakness.' I will all the more gladly boast of my weaknesses, that the power of Christ may rest upon me. 2 Corinthians 12:9 RSV

Beloved, do not be surprised at the fiery ordeal which comes upon you to prove you, as though something strange were happening to you. But rejoice in so far as you share Christ's sufferings, that you may also rejoice and be glad when his glory is revealed. 1 Peter 4:12-13 RSV

See also *Comfort; Contentment; Submission.*

Access

Who shall ascend the hill of the Lord? And who shall stand in his holy place? He who has clean hands and a pure heart, who does not lift up his soul to what is false, and does not swear deceitfully. Psalm 24:3-4 RSV

Jesus saith unto him, I am the way, the truth, and the life: no man cometh unto the Father, but by me. John 14:6 KJV

'Father, I desire that they also, whom thou hast given me, may be with me where I am, to behold my glory which thou hast given me in thy love for me before the foundation of the world.' John 17:24 RSV

By whom [Jesus Christ] also we have access by faith into this grace wherein we stand, and rejoice in hope of the glory of God. Romans 5:2 KJV

But now in Christ Jesus you who once were far off have been brought near in the blood of Christ . . . for through him we both have access in one Spirit to the Father. Ephesians 2:13, 18 RSV

In union with Christ and through our faith in him we have the boldness to go into God's presence with all confidence. Ephesians 3:12 GNB

Therefore, brethren, since we have confidence to enter the sanctuary by the blood of Jesus, by the new and living way which he opened for us through the curtain, that is, through his flesh, and since we have a great priest over the house of God, let us draw near with a true heart in full assurance of faith, with our hearts sprinkled clean from an evil conscience and our bodies washed with pure water. Hebrews 10:19-22 RSV

Draw near to God and he will draw near to you. James 4:8 RSV

For Christ also died for sins once for all, the righteous for the unrighteous, that he might bring us to God, being put to death in the flesh but made alive in the spirit. 1 Peter 3:18 RSV

See also *Adoption; Assurance; Prayer.*

Adam

So God created man in his own image, in the image of God created he him; male and female created he them. Genesis 1:27 KJV

And the Lord God formed man of the dust of the ground, and breathed into his nostrils the breath of life; and man became a living soul . . . And the Lord God said, It is not good that the man should be alone; I will make him an help meet for him. Genesis 2:7, 18 KJV

As by one man sin entered into the world, and death by sin . . . so death passed upon all men, for that all have sinned. Romans 5:12 KJV

Then as one man's trespass led to condemnation for all men, so one man's act of righteousness leads to acquittal and life for all men. For as by one man's disobedience many were made sinners, so by one man's obedience many will be made righteous. Law came in, to increase the trespass; but where sin increased, grace abounded all the more, so that, as sin reigned in death, grace also might reign through righteousness to eternal life through Jesus Christ our Lord. Romans 5:18-19 RSV

For as in Adam all die, so also in Christ shall all be made alive. 1 Corinthians 15:22 RSV

Thus it is written, 'The first man Adam became a living being'; the last Adam became a life-giving spirit. 1 Corinthians 15:45 RSV

See also *Eden, garden of; Fall, the; Man.*

Adoption

'But now I tell you: love your enemies and pray for those who persecute you, so that you may become the sons of your Father in heaven.' Matthew 5:44-45 GNB

Our Father, which art in heaven . . . Matthew 6:9 BCP

Therefore take no thought, saying, What shall we eat? or, What shall we drink? or, Wherewithal shall we be clothed? (For after all these things do the Gentiles seek:) for your heavenly Father knoweth that ye have need of all these things. But seek ye first the kingdom of God, and his righteousness; and all these things shall be added unto you. Matthew 6:31-33 KJV

But as many as received him, to them gave he power to become the sons of God, even to them that believe on his name. John 1:12 KJV

For all who are led by the Spirit of God are sons of God. For you did not receive the spirit of slavery to fall back into fear, but you have received the spirit of sonship. When we cry, 'Abba! Father!' it is the Spirit himself bearing witness with our spirit that we are children of God, and if children, then heirs, heirs of God and fellow heirs with Christ, provided we suffer with

him in order that we may also be glorified with him. Romans 8:14-17 RSV

'I will be your father, and you shall be my sons and daughters, says the Lord Almighty.' 2 Corinthians 6:18 GNB

[God sent his Son] to redeem those who were under the law, so that we might receive adoption as sons. And because you are sons, God has sent the Spirit of his Son into our hearts, crying, 'Abba! Father!' Galatians 4:5-6 RSV

He destined us in love to be his sons through Jesus Christ, according to the purpose of his will. Ephesians 1:5 RSV

See what love the Father has given us, that we should be called children of God; and so we are. The reason why the world does not know us is that it did not know him. Beloved, we are God's children now; it does not yet appear what we shall be, but we know that when he appears we shall be like him, for we shall see him as he is. 1 John 3:1-2 RSV

See also *Access; Assurance; Confidence.*

Adultery
See *Marriage.*

Advice
See *Counsel.*

Angels

For he will give his angels charge of you to guard you in all your ways. Psalm 91:11 RSV

Nebuchadnezzar said, 'Blessed be the God of Shadrach, Meshach, and Abednego, who has sent his angel and delivered his servants, who trusted in him, and set at naught the king's command, and yielded up their bodies rather than serve and worship any god except their own God.' Daniel 3:28 RSV

'At that time shall arise Michael, the great prince who has charge of your people. And there shall be a time of trouble, such as never has been since there was a nation till that time; but at that time your people shall be delivered, every one whose name shall be found written in the book.' Daniel 12:1 RSV

'See that you don't despise any of these little ones. Their angels in heaven, I tell you, are always in the presence of my Father in heaven.' Matthew 18:10 GNB

When the Son of man shall come in his glory, and all the holy angels with him, then shall he sit upon the throne of his glory. Matthew 25:31 KJV

In the sixth month the angel Gabriel was sent from God to a city of Galilee named Nazareth. Luke 1:26 RSV

'Just so, I tell you, there is joy before the angels of God over one sinner who repents.' Luke 15:10 RSV

'You who received the law as delivered by angels and did not keep it.' Acts 7:53 RSV

Do you not know that we are to judge angels? How much more, matters pertaining to this life! 1 Corinthians 6:3 RSV

To make all men see . . . that through the church the manifold wisdom of God might now be made known to the principalities and powers in the heavenly places. Ephesians 3:9-10 RSV

What are the angels, then? They are spirits who serve God and are sent by him to help those who are to receive salvation. Hebrews 1:14 GNB

Then I looked, and I heard around the throne and the living creatures and the elders the voice of many angels, numbering myriads of myriads and thousands of thousands, saying with a loud voice, 'Worthy is the Lamb who was slain, to receive power and wealth and wisdom and might and honour and glory and blessing!' Revelation 5:11-12 RSV

Anger
of God
The Lord is merciful and gracious, slow to anger, and plenteous in mercy. He will not always chide: neither will he keep his anger for ever. Psalm 103:8-9 KJV

They have rejected the law of the Lord of hosts, and have despised the word of the Holy One of Israel. Therefore the anger of the Lord was kindled against his people, and he stretched out his hand against them and smote them, and the mountains quaked; and their corpses were as refuse in the midst of the streets. For all this his anger is not turned away and his hand is stretched out still. Isaiah 5:24-25 RSV

O Lord, revive thy work in the midst of the years, in the midst of the years make known; in wrath remember mercy. Habakkuk 3:2 KJV

But when he [John the Baptist] saw many of the Pharisees and Sadducees coming for baptism, he said to them, 'You brood of vipers! Who warned you to

flee from the wrath to come?' Matthew 3:7 RSV

And he looked around at them with anger, grieved at their hardness of heart. Mark 3:5 RSV

He that believeth on the Son hath everlasting life: and he that believeth not the Son shall not see life; but the wrath of God abideth on him. John 3:36 KJV

For the wrath of God is revealed from heaven against all ungodliness and unrighteousness of men, who hold the truth in unrighteousness. Romans 1:18 KJV

Among these we all once lived in the passions of our flesh, following the desires of body and mind, and so we were by nature children of wrath, like the rest of mankind. Ephesians 2:3 RSV

Jesus who delivers us from the wrath to come. 1 Thessalonians 1:10 RSV

[They] said to the mountains and rocks, Fall on us, and hide us from the face of him that sitteth on the throne, and from the wrath of the Lamb. For the great day of his wrath is come; and who shall be able to stand? Revelation 6:16 KJV

See also *Propitiation; Punishment.*

of man
If you stay calm, you are wise, but if you have a hot temper, you only show how stupid you are. Proverbs 14:29 GNB

Hot tempers cause arguments, but patience brings peace. Proverbs 15:18 GNB

He who is slow to anger is better than the mighty, and he who rules his spirit than he who takes a city. Proverbs 16:32 RSV

'You have heard that people were told in the past, "Do not commit murder; anyone who does will be brought to trial." But now I tell you: whoever is angry with his brother will be brought to trial.' Matthew 5:21-22 GNB

[Love] is not touchy. 1 Corinthians 13:5 JBP

Now the works of the flesh are plain: . . . anger . . . Galatians 5:19-20 RSV

Be angry but do not sin; do not let the sun go down on your anger, and give no opportunity to the devil . . . Let all bitterness and wrath and anger and clamour and slander be put away from

you, with all malice. Ephesians
4:26-27, 31 RSV

Know this, my beloved brethren. Let
every man be quick to hear, slow to
speak, slow to anger, for the anger of
man does not work the righteousness of
God. James 1:19-20 RSV

Antichrist

'While I was thinking about the horns,
there before me was another horn, a
little one, which came up among them;
and three of the first horns were
uprooted before it. This horn had eyes
like the eyes of a man and a mouth that
spoke boastfully.' Daniel 7:8 NIV

'He shall speak words against the Most
High, and shall wear out the saints of
the Most High, and shall think to
change the times and the law; and they
shall be given into his hand for a time,
two times, and half a time.' Daniel 7:25
RSV

'For many will come in my name,
saying, "I am the Christ," and they will
lead many astray . . . For false Christs
and false prophets will arise and show
great signs and wonders, so as to lead
astray, if possible, even the elect.'
Matthew 24:5, 24 RSV

Let no one deceive you in any way; for
that day [the day of the Lord] will not
come, unless the rebellion comes first,
and the man of lawlessness is revealed,
the son of perdition, who opposes and
exalts himself against every so-called
god or object of worship, so that he
takes his seat in the temple of God,
proclaiming himself to be God.
2 Thessalonians 2:3-4 RSV

And now you know what is holding him
back, so that he may be revealed at the
proper time. For the secret power of
lawlessness is already at work; but the
one who now holds it back will
continue to do so till he is taken out of
the way. And then the lawless one will
be revealed, whom the Lord Jesus will
overthrow with the breath of his mouth
and destroy by the splendour of his
coming. The coming of the lawless one
will be in accordance with the work of
Satan displayed in all kinds of
counterfeit miracles, signs and
wonders, and in every sort of evil that
deceives those who are perishing. They
perish because they refused to love the
truth and so be saved. 2 Thessalonians
2:6-10 NIV

My children, this is the last hour! You
were told that Antichrist was to come,
and now many antichrists have
appeared; which proves to us that this

is indeed the last hour. 1 John 2:18 NEB

Who is the liar? Who but he that denies
that Jesus is the Christ? He is
Antichrist, for he denies both the
Father and the Son. 1 John 2:22 NEB

Every spirit which does not confess
Jesus is not of God. This is the spirit of
antichrist, of which you heard that it
was coming, and now it is in the world
already. 1 John 4:3 RSV

Apostles

And he called to him his twelve
disciples and gave them authority over
unclean spirits, to cast them out, and to
heal every disease and every infirmity.
The names of the twelve apostles are
these: first, Simon, who is called Peter,
and Andrew his brother; James the son
of Zebedee, and John his brother;
Philip and Bartholomew; Thomas and
Matthew the tax collector; James the
son of Alphaeus, and Thaddaeus;
Simon the Cananaean, and Judas
Iscariot, who betrayed him. Matthew
10:1-4 RSV

'So one of the men who have
accompanied us during all the time that
the Lord Jesus went in and out among
us, beginning from the baptism of John
until the day when he was taken up
from us—one of these men must
become with us a witness to his
resurrection.' Acts 1:21-22 RSV

But when the apostles Barnabas and
Paul heard of it, they tore their
garments and rushed out among the
multitude . . . Acts 14:14 RSV

Am I not free? Am I not an apostle?
Have I not seen Jesus our Lord? Are
not you my workmanship in the Lord?
If to others I am not an apostle, at least
I am to you; for you are the seal of my
apostleship in the Lord. 1 Corinthians
9:1-2 RSV

Now you are the body of Christ and
individually members of it. And God
has appointed in the church first
apostles . . . 1 Corinthians 12:28 RSV

So then you are no longer strangers and
sojourners, but you are fellow citizens
with the saints and members of the
household of God, built upon the
foundation of the apostles and
prophets, Christ Jesus himself being
the cornerstone. Ephesians 2:19-20
RSV

Therefore, holy brethren, who share in
a heavenly call, consider Jesus, the
apostle and high priest of our
confession. Hebrews 3:1 RSV

[To the church in Ephesus] ' " I know your

works, your toil and your patient endurance, and how you cannot bear evil men but have tested those who call themselves apostles but are not, and found them to be false."' Revelation 2:2 RSV

Ascension

See *Jesus Christ, Ascension.*

Assurance

All that the Father giveth me shall come to me; and him that cometh to me I will in no wise cast out. John 6:37 KJV

And I give unto them [my sheep] eternal life; and they shall never perish, neither shall any man pluck them out of my hand. John 10:28 KJV

Therefore being justified by faith, we have peace with God through our Lord Jesus Christ: by whom also we have access by faith into this grace wherein we stand, and rejoice in hope of the glory of God. And not only so, but we glory in tribulations also: knowing that tribulation worketh patience; and patience, experience; and experience, hope: and hope maketh not ashamed; because the love of God is shed abroad in our hearts by the Holy Ghost which is given unto us. Romans 5:1-5 KJV

Since, therefore, we are now justified by his blood, much more shall we be saved by him from the wrath of God. For if while we were enemies we were reconciled to God by the death of his Son, much more, now that we are reconciled, shall we be saved by his life. Romans 5:9-10 RSV

There is therefore now no condemnation for those who are in Christ Jesus. Romans 8:1 RSV

What then shall we say to this? If God is for us, who is against us? He who did not spare his own Son but gave him up for us all, will he not also give us all things with him? Who shall bring any charge against God's elect? It is God who justifies; who is to condemn? Is it Christ Jesus, who died, yes, who was raised from the dead, who is at the right hand of God, who indeed intercedes for us? Who shall separate us from the love of Christ? Shall tribulation, or distress, or persecution, or famine, or nakedness, or peril, or sword? . . . No, in all these things we are more than conquerors through him who loved us. For I am sure that neither death, nor life, nor angels, nor principalities, nor things present, nor things to come, nor powers, nor height, nor depth, nor anything else in all creation, will be able to separate us from the love of God in Christ Jesus our Lord. Romans 8:31-35, 37-39 RSV

And so I am sure that God, who began this good work in you, will carry it on until it is finished on the Day of Christ Jesus. Philippians 1:6 GNB

But I am not ashamed, for I know whom I have believed, and I am sure that he is able to guard until that Day what has been entrusted to me. 2 Timothy 1:12 RSV

Let us draw near with a true heart in full assurance of faith, with our hearts sprinkled clean from an evil conscience and our bodies washed with pure water. Hebrews 10:22 RSV

If we walk in the light, as he is in the light, we have fellowship with one another, and the blood of Jesus his Son cleanses us from all sin . . . If we confess our sins, he is faithful and just and will forgive our sins and cleanse us from all unrighteousness. 1 John 1:7, 9 RSV

By this we know that we abide in him and he in us, because he has given us of his own Spirit. 1 John 4:13 RSV

He that hath the Son hath life; and he that hath not the Son of God hath not life. 1 John 5:12 KJV

See also *Adoption; Comfort; Victory.*

Atonement

And he shall put his hand upon the head of the burnt offering; and it shall be accepted for him to make atonement for him. Leviticus 1:4 KJV

Surely he hath borne our griefs, and carried our sorrows: yet we did esteem him stricken, smitten of God, and afflicted. But he was wounded for our transgressions, he was bruised for our iniquities: the chastisement of our peace was upon him; and with his stripes we are healed. All we like sheep have gone astray; we have turned every one to his own way; and the Lord hath laid on him the iniquity of us all . . . Yet it pleased the Lord to bruise him; he hath put him to grief: when thou shalt make his soul an offering for sin, he shall see his seed, he shall prolong his days, and the pleasure of the Lord shall prosper in his hand. He shall see of the travail of his soul, and shall be satisfied: by his knowledge shall my righteous servant justify many; for he shall bear their iniquities. Therefore will I divide him a portion with the great, and he shall divide the spoil with the strong;

because he hath poured out his soul unto death; and he was numbered with the transgressors; and he bare the sin of many, and made intercession for the transgressors. Isaiah 53:4-6, 10-12 KJV

'For the Son of man also came not to be served but to serve, and to give his life as a ransom for many.' Mark 10:45 RSV

But God shows his love for us in that while we were yet sinners Christ died for us. Romans 5:8 RSV

For the love of Christ constraineth us; because we thus judge, that if one died for all, then were all dead. 2 Corinthians 5:14 KJV

For our sake he made him to be sin who knew no sin, so that in him we might become the righteousness of God. 2 Corinthians 5:21 RSV

And walk in love, as Christ loved us and gave himself up for us, a fragrant offering and sacrifice to God. Ephesians 5:2 RSV

The Son is the radiance of God's glory and the exact representation of his being, sustaining all things by his powerful word. After he had provided purification for sins, he sat down at the right hand of the Majesty in heaven. Hebrews 1:3 NIV

He himself bore our sins in his body on the tree, that we might die to sin and live to righteousness. By his wounds you have been healed. 1 Peter 2:24 RSV

For Christ also died for sins once for all, the righteous for the unrighteous, that he might bring us to God, being put to death in the flesh but made alive in the spirit. 1 Peter 3:18 RSV

See also *Blood; Jesus Christ, Death; Redemption.*

Authority

'For the lips of a priest should guard knowledge, and men should seek instruction from his mouth, for he is the messenger of the Lord of hosts.' Malachi 2:7 RSV

He [Jesus] taught . . . as one who had authority, and not as their scribes. Matthew 7:29 RSV

[A centurion] 'I, too, am a man under the authority of superior officers, and I have soldiers under me.' Matthew 8:9 GNB

'But that you may know that the Son of man has authority on earth to forgive sins'—he then said to the paralytic— 'Rise, take up your bed and go home.' Matthew 9:6 RSV

And he called to him his twelve disciples and gave them authority over unclean spirits, to cast them out, and to heal every disease and every infirmity. Matthew 10:1 RSV

And when they saw him they worshipped him; but some doubted. And Jesus came and said to them, 'All authority in heaven and on earth has been given to me . . .' Matthew 28:18 RSV

And they were all amazed, so that they questioned among themselves, saying, 'What is this? A new teaching! With authority he commands even the unclean spirits, and they obey him.' Mark 1:27 RSV

'I will warn you whom to fear: fear him who, after he has killed, has authority to cast into hell. Believe me, he is the one to fear.' Luke 12:5 NEB

But as many as received him, to them gave he power to become the sons of God, even to them that believe on his name. John 1:12 KJV

'For as the Father has life in himself, so he has granted the Son to have life in himself. And he has given him authority to judge because he is the Son of Man.' John 5:27 NIV

'No-one takes it [my life] from me, but I lay it down of my own accord. I have authority to lay it down and authority to take it up again. This command I received from my Father.' John 10:18 NIV

'For you [the Father] gave him [the Son] authority over all mankind, so that he might give eternal life to all those you gave him.' John 17:2 GNB

Everyone must obey the state authorities, because no authority exists without God's permission, and the existing authorities have been put there by God. Romans 13:1 GNB

See also *Power*.

Backsliding

See *Falling away*.

Baptism

[John the Baptist] 'I baptize you with water for repentance, but he who is coming after me is mightier than I, whose sandals I am not worthy to carry; he will baptize you with the Holy Spirit and with fire.' Matthew 3:11 RSV

And when Jesus was baptized, he went up immediately from the water, and behold, the heavens were opened and he saw the Spirit of God descending like a dove, and alighting on him. Matthew 3:16 RSV

'Go therefore and make disciples of all nations, baptizing them in the name of the Father and of the Son and of the Holy Spirit . . .' Matthew 28:19 RSV

And Peter said to them, 'Repent, and be baptized every one of you in the name of Jesus Christ for the forgiveness of your sins; and you shall receive the gift of the Holy Spirit' . . . So those who

received his word were baptized, and there were added that day about three thousand souls. Acts 2:38, 41 RSV

And as they went along the road they came to some water, and the eunuch said, 'See, here is water! What is to prevent my being baptized?' And he commanded the chariot to stop, and they both went down into the water, Philip and the eunuch, and he baptized him. Acts 8:36, 38 RSV

And he [the Philippian jailer] took them the same hour of the night, and washed their wounds, and he was baptized at once, with all his family. Acts 16:33 RSV

Paul said, 'The baptism of John was for those who turned from their sins; and he told the people of Israel to believe in the one who was coming after him— that is, in Jesus.' When they [disciples in Ephesus] heard this, they were baptized in the name of the Lord Jesus. Acts 19:4-5 GNB

Know ye not, that so many of us as were baptized into Jesus Christ were baptized into his death? Therefore we are buried with him by baptism into death: that like as Christ was raised up from the dead by the glory of the Father, even so we also should walk in newness of life. Romans 6:3-4 KJV

For by one Spirit we were all baptized into one body—Jews or Greeks, slaves or free—and all were made to drink of one Spirit. 1 Corinthians 12:13 RSV

Beatitudes

See Matthew 5:1-12.

Benedictus

See *Prayer, Prayers of the Bible*.

Bereavement

See *Comfort, in bereavement and sorrow*.

Bible

For as the rain cometh down, and the snow from heaven, and returneth not thither, but watereth the earth, and maketh it bring forth and bud, that it may give seed to the sower, and bread to the eater: so shall my word be that goeth forth out of my mouth: it shall not return unto me void, but it shall accomplish that which I please, and it shall prosper in the thing whereto I sent it. Isaiah 55:10-11 KJV

'It is written, "Man shall not live by bread alone, but by every word that proceeds from the mouth of God."' Matthew 4:4 RSV

[To the Jews] 'You search the scriptures,

because you think that in them you have eternal life; and it is they that bear witness to me; yet you refuse to come to me that you may have life.' John 5:39-40 RSV

'But the Counsellor, the Holy Spirit, whom the Father will send in my name, he will teach you all things, and bring to your remembrance all that I have said to you.' John 14:26 RSV

[The Jews at Berea] These were more noble than those in Thessalonica, in that they received the word with all readiness of mind, and searched the scriptures daily, whether those things were so. Acts 17:11 KJV

The Jews are entrusted with the oracles of God. Romans 3:2 RSV

And take the helmet of salvation, and the sword of the Spirit, which is the word of God. Ephesians 6:17 KJV

Let the word of Christ dwell in you richly in all wisdom; teaching and admonishing one another in psalms and hymns and spiritual songs, singing with grace in your hearts to the Lord. Colossians 3:16 KJV

And we also thank God constantly for this, that when you received the word of God which you heard from us, you accepted it not as the word of men but as what it really is, the word of God, which is at work in you believers. 1 Thessalonians 2:13 RSV

Do your best to present yourself to God as one approved, a workman who has no need to be ashamed, rightly handling the word of truth. 2 Timothy 2:15 RSV

How from childhood you have been acquainted with the sacred writings which are able to instruct you for salvation through faith in Christ Jesus. All scripture is inspired by God and profitable for teaching, for reproof, for correction, and for training in righteousness, that the man of God may be complete, equipped for every good work. 2 Timothy 3:15-17 RSV

For the word of God is living and active, sharper than any two-edged sword, piercing to the division of soul and spirit, of joints and marrow, and discerning the thoughts and intentions of the heart. Hebrews 4:12 RSV

First of all you must understand this, that no prophecy of scripture is a matter of one's own interpretation, because no prophecy ever came by the impulse of man, but men moved by the Holy Spirit spoke from God. 2 Peter 1:20-21 RSV

See also *Law; Revelation; Will of God.*

Bishops

See *Elders.*

Blasphemy

Thou shalt not take the name of the Lord thy God in vain; for the Lord will not hold him guiltless that taketh his name in vain. Exodus 20:7 KJV

'For my people have been taken away for nothing, and those who rule them mock,' declares the Lord. 'And all day long my name is constantly blasphemed.' Isaiah 52:5 NIV

'Therefore, son of man, speak to the people of Israel and say to them, "This is what the Sovereign Lord says: In this also your fathers blasphemed me by forsaking me."' Ezekiel 20:27 NIV

'Therefore I tell you, every sin and blasphemy will be forgiven men, but the blasphemy against the Spirit will not be forgiven.' Matthew 12:31 RSV

And the high priest said to him, 'I adjure you by the living God, tell us if you are the Christ, the Son of God.' Jesus said to him, 'You have said so. But I tell you, hereafter you will see the Son of man seated at the right hand of Power, and coming on the clouds of heaven.' Then the high priest tore his robes, and said, 'He has uttered blasphemy. Why do we still need witnesses? You have now heard his blasphemy.' Matthew 26:63-65 RSV

[In the last days] Men shall be lovers of their own selves, covetous, boasters, proud, blasphemers . . . 2 Timothy 3:2 KJV

Is it not they [the rich] who blaspheme that honourable name which was invoked over you? James 2:7 RSV

See also *Vow.*

Blessing

Now the Lord had said unto Abram, Get thee out of thy country, and from thy kindred, and from thy father's house, unto a land that I will shew thee: and I will make of thee a great nation, and I will bless thee, and make thy name great; and thou shalt be a blessing: and I will bless them that bless thee, and curse him that curseth thee: and in thee shall all families of the earth be blessed. Genesis 12:1-3 KJV

And he [Jacob] said, Let me go, for the day breaketh. And he said, I will not let thee go, except thou bless me. Genesis 32:26 KJV

The Lord bless thee, and keep thee: the Lord make his face shine upon thee, and be gracious unto thee: the Lord lift up his countenance upon thee, and give thee peace. Numbers 6:24-26 KJV

'And all these blessings shall come upon you and overtake you, if you obey the voice of the Lord your God . . .' Deuteronomy 28:2 RSV

'Bring the full tithes into the storehouse, that there may be food in my house; and thereby put me to the test, says the Lord of hosts, if I will not open the windows of heaven for you and pour down for you an overflowing blessing.' Malachi 3:10 RSV

[Jesus and young children] And he took them up in his arms, put his hands upon them, and blessed them. Mark 10:16 KJV

Bless those who persecute you; bless and do not curse. Romans 12:14 NIV

You also must help us by prayer, so that many will give thanks on our behalf for the blessing granted us in answer to many prayers. 2 Corinthians 1:11 RSV

Blessed be the God and Father of our Lord Jesus Christ, who has blessed us in Christ with every spiritual blessing in the heavenly places. Ephesians 1:3 RSV

Do not return evil for evil or reviling for reviling; but on the contrary bless, for to this you have been called, that you may obtain a blessing. 1 Peter 3:9 RSV

See also *Christian life, Character of the Christian.*

Blood

'For the life of the flesh is in the blood; and I have given it for you upon the altar to make atonement for your souls; for it is the blood that makes atonement, by reason of the life.' Leviticus 17:11 RSV

'This is my blood of the covenant, which is poured out for many for the forgiveness of sins.' Matthew 26:28 RSV

[Christ Jesus] whom God hath set forth to be a propitiation through faith in his blood. Romans 3:25 KJV

Since, therefore, we are now justified by his blood, much more shall we be saved by him from the wrath of God. Romans 5:9 RSV

In him [Christ] we have redemption through his blood, the forgiveness of our trespasses, according to the riches of his grace which he lavished upon us. Ephesians 1:7 RSV

Making peace by the blood of his cross. Colossians 1:20 RSV

Indeed, under the law almost everything is purified with blood, and without the shedding of blood there is no forgiveness of sins. Hebrews 9:22 RSV

Therefore, brethren, since we have confidence to enter the sanctuary by the blood of Jesus . . . Hebrews 10:19 RSV

Now the God of peace, that brought again from the dead our Lord Jesus, that great shepherd of the sheep, through the blood of the everlasting covenant . . . Hebrews 13:20 KJV

You know that you were ransomed from the futile ways inherited from your fathers, not with perishable things such as silver or gold, but with the precious blood of Christ, like that of a lamb without blemish or spot. 1 Peter 1:18-19 RSV

If we walk in the light, as he is in the light, we have fellowship with one another, and the blood of Jesus his Son cleanses us from all sin. 1 John 1:7 RSV

To him who loves us and freed us from our sins by his blood and made us a kingdom, priests to his God and Father, to him be glory and dominion for ever and ever. Amen. Revelation 1:5-6 RSV

'And they have conquered him by the blood of the Lamb and by the word of their testimony, for they loved not their lives even unto death.' Revelation 12:11 RSV

Body

Now as they were eating, Jesus took bread, and blessed, and broke it, and gave it to the disciples and said, 'Take, eat; this is my body.' Matthew 26:26 RSV

I beseech you therefore, brethren, by the mercies of God, that ye present your bodies a living sacrifice, holy, acceptable unto God, which is your reasonable service. Romans 12:1 KJV

Do you not know that your body is a temple of the Holy Spirit within you, which you have from God? You are not your own; you were bought with a price. So glorify God in your body. 1 Corinthians 6:19-20 RSV

Now you are the body of Christ and individually members of it. 1 Corinthians 12:27 RSV

It is sown a physical body, it is raised a spiritual body. If there is a physical body, there is also a spiritual body. 1 Corinthians 15:44 RSV

[Jesus] He is the head of the body, the church; he is the beginning, the first-born from the dead, that in everything he might be pre-eminent. Colossians 1:18 RSV

Boldness

See *Confidence*.

Bribe

'Moreover choose able men from all the people, such as fear God, men who are trustworthy and who hate a bribe; and place such men over the people as rulers of thousands, of hundreds, of fifties, and of tens.' Exodus 18:21 RSV

'Do not accept a bribe, for a bribe makes people blind to what is right and ruins the cause of those who are innocent.' Exodus 23:8 GNB

If you try to make a profit dishonestly, you will get your family into trouble. Don't take bribes and you will live longer. Proverbs 15:27 GNB

Corrupt judges accept secret bribes, and then justice is not done. Proverbs 17.23 GNB

They are all experts at doing evil. Officials and judges ask for bribes. The influential man tells them what he wants, and so they scheme together. Micah 7:3 GNB

Celibacy

His disciples said to him, 'If this is how it is between a man and his wife, it is better not to marry.' Jesus answered, 'This teaching does not apply to everyone, but only to those to whom God has given it. For there are different reasons why men cannot marry: some, because they were born that way; others, because men made them that way; and others do not marry for the sake of the Kingdom of heaven. Let him who can accept this teaching do so.' Matthew 19:10-12 GNB

I wish that all were as I myself am. But each has his own special gift from God, one of one kind and one of another. 1 Corinthians 7:7 RSV

I would like you to be free from worry. An unmarried man concerns himself with the Lord's work, because he is

trying to please the Lord. 1 Corinthians 7:32 GNB

Children

See *Family*.

Christian life

Calling of the Christian

But now thus saith the Lord that created thee, O Jacob, and he that formed thee, O Israel, Fear not: for I have redeemed thee, I have called thee by thy name; thou art mine. Isaiah 43:1 KJV

Ye are the salt of the earth: but if the salt have lost his savour, wherewith shall it be salted? It is thenceforth good for nothing, but to be cast out, and to be trodden under foot of men. Ye are the light of the world. A city that is set on an hill cannot be hid. Neither do men light a candle, and put it under a bushel, but on a candlestick; and it giveth light unto all that are in the house. Let your light so shine before men, that they may see your good works, and glorify your Father which is in heaven. Matthew 5:13-16 KJV

'But you shall receive power when the Holy Spirit has come upon you; and you shall be my witnesses in Jerusalem and in all Judea and Samaria and to the end of the earth.' Acts 1:8 RSV

We know that in everything God works for good with those who love him, who are called according to his purpose . . . And those whom he predestined he also called; and those whom he called he also justified; and those whom he justified he also glorified. Romans 8:28, 30 RSV

God is faithful, by whom you were called into the fellowship of his Son, Jesus Christ our Lord. 1 Corinthians 1:9 RSV

I therefore, a prisoner for the Lord, beg you to lead a life worthy of the calling to which you have been called. Ephesians 4:1 RSV

God, who saved us and called us with a holy calling, not in virtue of our works but in virtue of his own purpose and the grace which he gave us in Christ Jesus ages ago. 2 Timothy 1:8-9 RSV

Be holy in all that you do, just as God who called you is holy. 1 Peter 1:15 GNB

But you are a chosen race, a royal priesthood, a holy nation, God's own people, that you may declare the wonderful deeds of him who called you out of darkness into his marvellous light. 1 Peter 2:9 RSV

For what credit is there if you endure the beatings you deserve for having done wrong? But if you endure suffering even when you have done right, God will bless you for it. It was to this that God called you, for Christ himself suffered for you and left you an example, so that you would follow in his steps. 1 Peter 2:20-21 GNB

See what love the Father has given us, that we should be called children of God; and so we are. 1 John 3:1 RSV

To those who are called, beloved in God the Father and kept for Jesus Christ. Jude 1 RSV

See also *Church; Disciples; Election.*

Character of the Christian

Blessed is the man who walks not in the counsel of the wicked, nor stands in the way of sinners, nor sits in the seat of scoffers; but his delight is in the law of the Lord, and on his law he meditates day and night. He is like a tree planted by streams of water, that yields its fruit in its season, and its leaf does not wither. In all that he does, he prospers. Psalm 1:1-3 RSV

And seeing the multitudes, he went up into a mountain: and when he was set, his disciples came unto him: and he opened his mouth, and taught them, saying, Blessed are the poor in spirit: for theirs is the kingdom of heaven. Blessed are they that mourn: for they shall be comforted. Blessed are the meek: for they shall inherit the earth. Blessed are they which do hunger and thirst after righteousness: for they shall be filled. Blessed are the merciful: for they shall obtain mercy. Blessed are the pure in heart: for they shall see God. Blessed are the peacemakers: for they shall be called the children of God. Blessed are they which are persecuted for righteousness' sake: for theirs is the kingdom of heaven. Blessed are ye, when men shall revile you, and persecute you, and shall say all manner of evil against you falsely, for my sake. Matthew 5:3-11 KJV

But the fruit of the Spirit is love, joy, peace, patience, kindness, goodness, faithfulness, gentleness, self-control; against such there is no law. Galatians 5:22-23 RSV

His [God] divine power has given us everything we need for life and godliness through our knowledge of him who called us by his own glory and goodness. Through these he has given

us his very great and precious promises, so that through them you may participate in the divine nature and escape the corruption in the world caused by evil desires. For this very reason, make every effort to add to your faith goodness; and to goodness, knowledge; and to knowledge, self-control; and to self-control, perseverance; and to perseverance, godliness; and to godliness, brotherly kindness; and to brotherly kindness, love. For if you possess these qualities in increasing measure, they will keep you from being ineffective and unproductive in your knowledge of our Lord Jesus Christ. 2 Peter 1:3-8 NIV

Coming to faith

Seek ye the Lord while he may be found, call ye upon him while he is near. Let the wicked forsake his way, and the unrighteous man his thoughts: and let him return unto the Lord, and he will have mercy upon him; and to our God, for he will abundantly pardon. Isaiah 55:6-7 KJV

'Come to me, all who labour and are heavy-laden, and I will give you rest.' Matthew 11:28 RSV

Now great multitudes accompanied him; and he turned and said to them, 'If any one comes to me and does not hate his own father and mother and wife and children and brothers and sisters, yes, and even his own life, he cannot be my disciple. Whoever does not bear his own cross and come after me, cannot be my disciple.' Luke 14:25-27 RSV

But as many as received him, to them gave he power to become the sons of God, even to them that believe on his name. John 1:12 KJV

For God so loved the world, that he gave his only begotten Son, that whosoever believeth in him should not perish, but have everlasting life. John 3:16 KJV

All that the Father giveth me shall come to me; and him that cometh to me I will in no wise cast out. John 6:37 KJV

Jesus saith unto him, I am the way, the truth, and the life: no man cometh unto the Father, but by me. John 14:6 KJV

Now when they heard this they were cut to the heart, and said to Peter and the rest of the apostles, 'Brethren, what shall we do?' And Peter said to them, 'Repent, and be baptized every one of you in the name of Jesus Christ for the forgiveness of your sins; and you shall receive the gift of the Holy Spirit.' Acts 2:37-38 RSV

'Men, what must I do to be saved?' And they said, 'Believe in the Lord Jesus, and you will be saved, you and your household.' Acts 16:30-31 RSV

'The times of ignorance God overlooked, but now he commands all men everywhere to repent, because he has fixed a day on which he will judge the world in righteousness by a man whom he has appointed, and of this he has given assurance to all men by raising him from the dead.' Acts 17:30-31 RSV

For whosoever shall call upon the name of the Lord shall be saved. Romans 10:13 KJV

So we are ambassadors for Christ, God making his appeal through us. We beseech you on behalf of Christ, be reconciled to God. For our sake he made him to be sin who knew no sin, so that in him we might become the righteousness of God. 2 Corinthians 5:20-21 RSV

For Christ also died for sins once for all, the righteous for the unrighteous, that he might bring us to God, being put to death in the flesh but made alive in the spirit. 1 Peter 3:18 RSV·

See also *Conversion*.

Continuing in the faith
Jesus then said to the Jews who had believed in him, 'If you continue in my word, you are truly my disciples.' ... 'Truly, truly, I say to you, if any one keeps my word, he will never see death.' John 8:31, 51 RSV

'I am the vine, you are the branches. He who abides in me, and I in him, he it is that bears much fruit, for apart from me you can do nothing ... As the Father has loved me, so have I loved you; abide in my love.' John 15:5, 9 RSV

'And now I am no more in the world, but they are in the world, and I am coming to thee. Holy Father, keep them in thy name which thou hast given me, that they may be one, even as we are one.' John 17:11 RSV

And they continued stedfastly in the apostles' doctrine and fellowship, and in breaking of bread, and in prayers. Acts 2:42 KJV

[Paul and Barnabas] Strengthening the souls of the disciples, exhorting them to continue in the faith, and saying that through many tribulations we must enter the kingdom of God. Acts 14:22 RSV

And so I am sure that God, who began this good work in you, will carry it on until it is finished on the Day of Christ Jesus. Philippians 1:6 GNB

Him we proclaim, warning every man and teaching every man in all wisdom, that we may present every man mature in Christ. Colossians 1:28 RSV

Let us hold fast the confession of our hope without wavering, for he who promised is faithful. Hebrews 10:23 RSV

Therefore, since we are surrounded by so great a cloud of witnesses, let us also lay aside every weight, and sin which clings so closely, and let us run with perseverance the race that is set before us, looking to Jesus the pioneer and perfecter of our faith, who for the joy that was set before him endured the cross, despising the shame, and is seated at the right hand of the throne of God. Hebrews 12:1-2 RSV

[We] who by God's power are guarded through faith for a salvation ready to be revealed in the last time. 1 Peter 1:5 RSV

Therefore, brethren, be the more zealous to confirm your call and election, for if you do this you will never fall. 2 Peter 1:10 RSV

Keep yourselves in the love of God, looking for the mercy of our Lord Jesus Christ unto eternal life ... Now unto him that is able to keep you from falling, and to present you faultless before the presence of his glory with exceeding joy ... Jude 21, 24 KJV

'"I am coming soon; hold fast what you have, so that no one may seize your crown."' Revelation 3:11 RSV

See also *Endurance*.

Longing for God
Moses said, 'I pray thee, show me thy glory.' Exodus 33:18 RSV

One thing have I desired of the Lord, that will I seek after; that I may dwell in the house of the Lord all the days of my life, to behold the beauty of the Lord, and to inquire in his temple. Psalm 27:4 KJV

As the hart panteth after the water brooks, so panteth my soul after thee, O God. My soul thirsteth for God, for the living God: when shall I come and appear before God? Psalm 42:1-2 KJV

'O God . . . I seek thee early with a heart that
thirsts for thee . . . like a dry and thirsty land that
has no water.'

O God, thou art my God, I seek thee
early with a heart that thirsts for thee
and a body wasted with longing for
thee, like a dry and thirsty land that has
no water. So longing, I come before
thee in the sanctuary to look upon thy
power and glory. Psalm 63:1-2 NEB

Whom have I in heaven but thee? And
there is none upon earth that I desire
beside thee. Psalm 73:25 KJV

I pine, I faint with longing for the
courts of the Lord's temple; my whole
being cries out with joy to the living
God. Psalm 84:2 NEB

[Some Greeks] came therefore to Philip,
which was of Bethsaida of Galilee, and
desired him, saying, Sir, we would see
Jesus. John 12:21 KJV

For I delight in the law of God, in my
inmost self . . . Romans 7:22 RSV

Unto you therefore which believe he is
precious. 1 Peter 2:7 KJV

See also *Worship.*

Church

And I say also unto thee, That thou art
Peter, and upon this rock I will build
my church; and the gates of hell shall
not prevail against it. Matthew 16:18
KJV

'If he [a fellow Christian] refuses to listen
to them [witnesses], tell it to the church;
and if he refuses to listen even to the
church, let him be to you as a Gentile
and a tax collector.' Matthew 18:17 RSV

And they continued stedfastly in the
apostles' doctrine and fellowship, and
in breaking of bread, and in prayers.
Acts 2:42 KJV

And so it was that the church
throughout Judaea, Galilee, and
Samaria had a time of peace. Through
the help of the Holy Spirit it was
strengthened and grew in numbers, as
it lived in reverence for the Lord. Acts
9:31 GNB

And when they had appointed elders
for them in every church, with prayer
and fasting, they committed them to
the Lord in whom they believed. Acts
14:23 RSV

'Take heed to yourselves and to all the
flock, in which the Holy Spirit has
made you overseers, to care for the
church of God which he obtained with
the blood of his own Son.' Acts 20:28
RSV

For the husband is the head of the wife
as Christ is the head of the church, his
body, and is himself its Saviour . . .
Husbands, love your wives, as Christ
loved the church and gave himself up
for her, that he might sanctify her,
having cleansed her by the washing of
water with the word, that he might
present the church to himself in
splendour, without spot or wrinkle or
any such thing, that she might be holy
and without blemish. Ephesians
5:23, 25-27 RSV

Not neglecting to meet together, as is
the habit of some, but encouraging one
another, and all the more as you see the
Day drawing near. Hebrews 10:25 RSV

Circumcision

'This is my covenant, which you shall
keep, between me and you and your
descendants after you: Every male
among you shall be circumcised. You
shall be circumcised in the flesh of your
foreskins, and it shall be a sign of the
covenant between me and you. He that
is eight days old among you shall be
circumcised; every male throughout
your generations, whether born in your
house, or bought with your money
from any foreigner who is not of your

Five portraits of the church

Body of Christ
All of you are **Christ's body**, and each one is a part of it. 1 Corinthians 12:27; see also Romans 12:4-5; 1 Corinthians 12:12-28; Ephesians 1:22-23, 4:1-16.

Bride
And I saw the Holy City, the new Jerusalem, coming down out of heaven from God, prepared and ready, like a **bride** dressed to meet her husband. Revelation 21:2; see also Ephesians 5:23-27.

Building or temple
Christ Jesus . . . is the one who holds the whole **building** together and makes it grow into a sacred **temple** dedicated to the Lord. Ephesians 2:21; see also 1 Corinthians 3:9-17; 1 Peter 2:4-8.

Family or household
. . . God's **household**, which is the church of the living God, the pillar and support of the truth. 1 Timothy 3:15; see also Galatians 6:10; Ephesians 2:19.

People of God
You are the chosen race, the King's priests, the holy nation, **God's own people** . . . At one time you were not God's people, but now you are his people . . . 1 Peter 2:9-10

offspring . . . shall be circumcised.' Genesis 17:10-13 RSV

The Lord says, 'The time is coming when I will punish the people of Egypt, Judah, Edom, Ammon, Moab, and the desert people, who have their hair cut short. All these people are circumcised, but have not kept the covenant it symbolizes. None of these people and none of the people of Israel have kept my covenant.' Jeremiah 9:25-26 GNB

For he is not a real Jew who is one outwardly, nor is true circumcision something external and physical. He is a Jew who is one inwardly, and real circumcision is a matter of the heart, spiritual and not literal. His praise is not from men but from God. Romans 2:28-29 RSV

For whether or not a man is circumcised means nothing; what matters is to obey God's commandments. 1 Corinthians 7:19 GNB

For when we are in union with Christ Jesus, neither circumcision nor the lack of it makes any difference at all; what matters is faith that works through love. Galatians 5:6 GNB

For we are the true circumcision, who worship God in spirit, and glory in Christ Jesus, and put no confidence in the flesh. Philippians 3:3 RSV

Comfort
when afraid
After these things the word of the Lord came unto Abram in a vision, saying, Fear not, Abram: I am thy shield, and thy exceeding great reward. Genesis 15:1 KJV

The Lord is my light and my salvation; whom shall I fear? The Lord is the strength of my life; of whom shall I be afraid? Psalm 27:1 KJV

I sought the Lord, and he answered me, and delivered me from all my fears. Psalm 34:4 RSV

God is our refuge and strength, a very present help in trouble. Therefore will not we fear, though the earth be removed, and though the mountains be carried into the midst of the sea. Psalm 46:1-2 KJV

The name of the Lord is a strong tower; the righteous man runs into it and is safe. Proverbs 18:10 RSV

But now thus saith the Lord that created thee, O Jacob, and he that formed thee, O Israel, Fear not: for I have redeemed thee, I have called thee by thy name; thou art mine. When thou passest through the waters, I will be with thee; and through the rivers, they shall not overflow thee: when thou walkest through the fire, thou shalt not be burned; neither shall the flame kindle upon thee. Isaiah 43:1-2 KJV

But when the disciples saw him walking on the sea, they were terrified, saying, 'It is a ghost!' And they cried out for fear. But immediately he spoke to them, saying, 'Take heart, it is I; have no fear.' Matthew 14:26-27 RSV

And the angel said unto them [the shepherds], Fear not: for, behold, I bring you good tidings of great joy, which shall be to all people. Luke 2:10 KJV

Fear not, little flock; for it is your Father's good pleasure to give you the kingdom. Luke 12:32 KJV

'Peace I leave with you; my peace I give to you; not as the world gives do I give to you. Let not your hearts be troubled, neither let them be afraid.' John 14:27 RSV

'[Christ] himself . . . partook of the same nature, that through death he might destroy him who has the power of death, that is, the devil, and deliver all those who through fear of death were subject to lifelong bondage. Hebrews 2:14-15 RSV

when anxious

Therefore I say unto you, Take no thought for your life, what ye shall eat, or what ye shall drink; nor yet for your body, what ye shall put on. Is not the life more than meat, and the body than raiment? Behold the fowls of the air: for they sow not, neither do they reap, nor gather into barns; yet your heavenly Father feedeth them. Are ye not much better than they? Which of you by taking thought can add one cubit unto his stature? And why take ye thought for raiment? Consider the lilies of the field, how they grow; they toil not, neither do they spin: and yet I say unto you, That even Solomon in all his glory was not arrayed like one of these. Wherefore, if God so clothe the grass of the field, which to day is, and to morrow is cast into the oven, shall he not much more clothe you, O ye of little faith? Therefore take no thought, saying, What shall we eat? or, What shall we drink? or, Wherewithal shall we be clothed? (For after all these things do the Gentiles seek:) for your heavenly Father knoweth that ye have need of all these things. But seek ye first the kingdom of God, and his righteousness; and all these things shall be added unto you. Matthew 6:25-33 KJV

'When they deliver you up, do not be anxious how you are to speak or what you are to say; for what you are to say will be given to you in that hour.' Matthew 10:19 RSV

'Come to me, all who labour and are heavy-laden, and I will give you rest.' Matthew 11:28 RSV

Bear one another's burdens, and so fulfil the law of Christ. Galatians 6:2 RSV

Have no anxiety about anything, but in everything by prayer and supplication with thanksgiving let your requests be made known to God. And the peace of God, which passes all understanding, will keep your hearts and your minds in Christ Jesus. Philippians 4:6-7 RSV

Cast all your anxieties on him, for he cares about you. 1 Peter 5:7 RSV

in bereavement and sorrow

'The Lord gave, and the Lord has taken away; blessed be the name of the Lord.' Job 1:21 RSV

Yea, though I walk through the valley of the shadow of death, I will fear no evil: for thou art with me; thy rod and thy staff they comfort me. Psalm 23:4 KJV

Blessed are they that mourn: for they shall be comforted. Matthew 5:4 KJV

Jesus said unto her [Martha], I am the resurrection, and the life: he that believeth in me, though he were dead, yet shall he live. And whosoever liveth and believeth in me shall never die. Believest thou this? John 11:25-26 KJV

And if I go and prepare a place for you, I will come again, and receive you unto myself; that where I am, there ye may be also. John 14:3 KJV

Rejoice with those who rejoice; mourn with those who mourn. Romans 12:15 NIV

But in fact Christ has been raised from the dead, the first fruits of those who have fallen asleep. 1 Corinthians 15:20 RSV

For this corruptible must put on incorruption, and this mortal must put on immortality. 1 Corinthians 15:53 KJV

But I would not have you to be ignorant, brethren, concerning them which are asleep, that ye sorrow not, even as others which have no hope . . . For the Lord himself shall descend from heaven with a shout, with the voice of the archangel, and with the trump of God: and the dead in Christ shall rise first. Then we which are alive and remain shall be caught up together with them in the clouds, to meet the Lord in the air: and so shall we ever be with the Lord. Wherefore comfort one another with these words. 1 Thessalonians 4:13, 16-18 KJV

in despair

The Lord is near to those who are discouraged; he saves those who have lost all hope. Psalm 34:18 GNB

I waited patiently for the Lord; he inclined to me and heard my cry. He drew me up from the desolate pit, out of the miry bog, and set my feet upon a rock, making my steps secure. Psalm 40:1-2 RSV

Why art thou cast down, O my soul? and why art thou disquieted in me?

Hope thou in God: for I shall yet praise him for the help of his countenance. O my God, my soul is cast down within me: therefore will I remember thee . . . Psalm 42:5-6 KJV

Cast me not away from thy presence; and take not thy holy spirit from me. Restore unto me the joy of thy salvation; and uphold me with thy free spirit. Psalm 51:11-12 KJV

A bruised reed shall he [the Lord's servant] not break, and the smoking flax shall he not quench: he shall bring forth judgment unto truth. Isaiah 42:3 KJV

But this I call to mind, and therefore I have hope: The steadfast love of the Lord never ceases, his mercies never come to an end; they are new every morning; great is thy faithfulness. Lamentations 3:21-23 RSV

We are afflicted in every way, but not crushed; perplexed, but not driven to despair . . . 2 Corinthians 4:8 RSV

when lonely

Turn to me, Lord, and be merciful to me, because I am lonely and weak. Psalm 25:16 GNB

I lie awake, I am like a lonely bird on the housetop. Psalm 102:7 RSV

Fear thou not; for I am with thee: be not dismayed; for I am thy God: I will strengthen thee; yea, I will help thee; yea, I will uphold thee with the right hand of my righteousness. Isaiah 41:10 KJV

But Zion said, The Lord hath forsaken me, and my Lord hath forgotten me. Can a woman forget her sucking child, that she should not have compassion on the son of her womb? Yea, they may forget, yet will I not forget thee. Behold, I have graven thee upon the palms of my hands; thy walls are continually before me. Isaiah 49:14-16 KJV

I will not leave you comfortless: I will come to you. John 14:18 KJV

No one stood by me the first time I defended myself; all deserted me. May God not count it against them! But the Lord stayed with me and gave me strength, so that I was able to proclaim the full message for all the Gentiles to hear. 2 Timothy 4:16-17 GNB

in suffering

And God heard their groaning, and God remembered his covenant with Abraham, with Isaac, and with Jacob. And God saw the people of Israel, and God knew their condition. Exodus 2:24-25 RSV

The eternal God is thy refuge, and underneath are the everlasting arms. Deuteronomy 33:27 KJV

Though he slay me, yet will I trust in him: but I will maintain mine own ways before him. Job 13:15 KJV

My flesh and my heart faileth: but God is the strength of my heart, and my portion for ever. Psalm 73:26 KJV

Comfort ye, comfort ye my people, saith your God. Speak ye comfortably to Jerusalem, and cry unto her, that her warfare is accomplished, that her iniquity is pardoned: for she hath received of the Lord's hand double for all her sins. Isaiah 40:1-2 KJV

Surely he hath borne our griefs, and carried our sorrows: yet we did esteem him stricken, smitten of God, and afflicted. Isaiah 53:4 KJV

Though the fig tree do not blossom, nor fruit be on the vines, the produce of the olive fail and the fields yield no food, the flock be cut off from the fold and there be no herd in the stalls, yet I will rejoice in the Lord, I will joy in the God of my salvation. Habakkuk 3:17-18 RSV

We know that in everything God works for good with those who love him, who are called according to his purpose . . . Who shall separate us from the love of Christ? Shall tribulation, or distress, or persecution, or famine, or nakedness, or peril, or sword? As it is written, 'For thy sake we are being killed all the day long; we are regarded as sheep to be slaughtered.' No, in all these things we are more than conquerors through him who loved us. For I am sure that neither death, nor life, nor angels, nor principalities, nor things present, nor things to come, nor powers, nor height, nor depth, nor anything else in all creation, will be able to separate us from the love of God in Christ Jesus our Lord. Romans 8:28, 35-39 RSV

Rejoice in your hope, be patient in tribulation, be constant in prayer. Romans 12:12 RSV

No temptation has overtaken you that is not common to man. God is faithful, and he will not let you be tempted beyond your strength, but with the temptation will also provide the way of escape, that you may be able to endure it. 1 Corinthians 10:13 RSV

Praise be to the God and Father of our Lord Jesus Christ, the Father of compassion and the God of all comfort, who comforts us in all our troubles, so that we can comfort those in any trouble with the comfort we ourselves have received from God. 2 Corinthians 1:3-4 NIV

So we do not lose heart. Though our outer nature is wasting away, our inner nature is being renewed every day. For this slight momentary affliction is preparing for us an eternal weight of glory beyond all comparison, because we look not to the things that are seen but to the things that are unseen; for the things that are seen are transient, but the things that are unseen are eternal. 2 Corinthians 4:16-18 RSV

He said to me, 'My grace is sufficient for you, for my power is made perfect in weakness.' I will all the more gladly boast of my weaknesses, that the power of Christ may rest upon me. 2 Corinthians 12:9 RSV

Let us then with confidence draw near to the throne of grace, that we may receive mercy and find grace to help in time of need. Hebrews 4:16 RSV

Looking unto Jesus the author and finisher of our faith; who for the joy that was set before him endured the cross, despising the shame, and is set down at the right hand of the throne of God. Hebrews 12:2 KJV

Beloved, do not be surprised at the fiery ordeal which comes upon you to prove you, as though something strange were happening to you. But rejoice in so far as you share Christ's sufferings, that you may also rejoice and be glad when his glory is revealed. 1 Peter 4:12-13 RSV

And God shall wipe away all tears from their eyes; and there shall be no more death, neither sorrow, nor crying, neither shall there be any more pain: for the former things are passed away. Revelation 21:4 KJV

Commitment

See *Covenant; Disciples; Obedience.*

Communion

Now as they were eating, Jesus took bread, and blessed, and broke it, and gave it to the disciples and said, 'Take, eat; this is my body.' And he took a cup, and when he had given thanks he gave it to them, saying, 'Drink of it, all of you; for this is my blood of the covenant, which is poured out for many for the forgiveness of sins.' Matthew 26:26-28 RSV

And they continued stedfastly in the

'For as often as you eat this bread and drink the cup, you proclaim the Lord's death until he comes.'

apostles' doctrine and fellowship, and in breaking of bread, and in prayers. Acts 2:42 KJV

The cup of blessing which we bless, is it not a participation in the blood of Christ? The bread which we break, is it not a participation in the body of Christ? Because there is one bread, we who are many are one body, for we all partake of the one bread. 1 Corinthians 10:16-17 RSV

For I received from the Lord what I also delivered to you, that the Lord Jesus on the night when he was betrayed took bread, and when he had given thanks, he broke it, and said, 'This is my body which is for you. Do this in remembrance of me.' In the same way also the cup, after supper, saying, 'This cup is the new covenant in my blood. Do this, as often as you drink it, in remembrance of me.' For as often as you eat this bread and drink the cup, you proclaim the Lord's death until he comes. Whoever, therefore, eats the bread or drinks the cup of the Lord in an unworthy manner will be guilty of profaning the body and blood of the Lord. Let a man examine himself, and so eat of the bread and drink of the cup. For any one who eats and drinks without discerning the body eats and drinks judgment upon himself. That is why many of you are weak and ill, and some have died. 1 Corinthians 11:23-30 RSV

See also *Fellowship.*

Compassion

See *Mercy.*

Confession

'If anyone declares publicly that he belongs to me, I will do the same for him before my Father in heaven.' Matthew 10:32 GNB

That if thou shalt confess with thy mouth the Lord Jesus, and shalt believe in thine heart that God hath raised him from the dead, thou shalt be saved. For with the heart man believeth unto righteousness; and with the mouth confession is made unto salvation. Romans 10:9-10 KJV

Every tongue [should] confess that Jesus Christ is Lord, to the glory of God the Father. Philippians 2:11 RSV

Whoever confesses that Jesus is the Son of God, God abides in him, and he in God. 1 John 4:15 RSV

of sin

'When a man is guilty in any of these [sins], he shall confess the sin he has committed.' Leviticus 5:5 RSV

Blessed is the man to whom the Lord imputes no iniquity, and in whose spirit there is no deceit. When I declared not my sin, my body wasted away through my groaning all day long. For day and night thy hand was heavy upon me; my strength was dried up as by the heat of summer. I acknowledged my sin to thee, and I did not hide my iniquity; I said, 'I will confess my transgressions to the Lord'; then thou didst forgive the guilt of my sin. Psalm 32:3-5 RSV

You will never succeed in life if you try to hide your sins. Confess them and give them up; then God will show mercy to you. Proverbs 28:13 GNB

Confess your faults one to another, and pray one for another, that ye may be healed. The effectual fervent prayer of a righteous man availeth much. James 5:16 KJV

If we confess our sins, he is faithful and just and will forgive our sins and cleanse us from all unrighteousness. 1 John 1:9 RSV

See also *Repentance.*

Confidence

Though an host should encamp against me, my heart shall not fear: though war should rise against me, in this will I be confident. One thing have I desired of the Lord, that will I seek after; that I may dwell in the house of the Lord all the days of my life, to behold the beauty of the Lord, and to inquire in his temple. Psalm 27:3-4 KJV

In the fear of the Lord one has strong confidence. Proverbs 14:6 RSV

The righteous are bold as a lion. Proverbs 28:1 RSV

Now when they saw the boldness of Peter and John, and perceived that they were uneducated, common men,

they wondered; and they recognised that they had been with Jesus. Acts 4:13 RSV

For we have not a high priest who is unable to sympathize with our weaknesses, but one who in every respect has been tempted as we are, yet without sin. Let us then with confidence draw near to the throne of grace, that we may receive mercy and find grace to help in time of need. Hebrews 4:15-16 RSV

Therefore, brethren, since we have confidence to enter the sanctuary by the blood of Jesus . . . Hebrews 10:19 RSV

Hence we can confidently say, 'The Lord is my helper, I will not be afraid; what can man do to me?' Hebrews 13:6 RSV

And now, little children, abide in him, so that when he appears we may have confidence and not shrink from him in shame at his coming. 1 John 2:28 RSV

Beloved, if our hearts do not condemn us, we have confidence before God. 1 John 3:21 RSV

In this is love perfected with us, that we may have confidence for the day of judgment, because as he is so are we in this world. 1 John 4.17 RSV

And this is the confidence which we have in him, that if we ask anything according to his will he hears us. 1 John 5:14 RSV

See also *Access; Assurance; Courage.*

Conscience

He [David] . . . got up stealthily and cut off a piece of Saul's cloak; but when he had cut it off, his conscience smote him. 1 Samuel 24:5 NEB

'So I always take pains to have a clear conscience toward God and toward men.' Acts 24:16 RSV

When Gentiles who have not the law do by nature what the law requires, they are a law to themselves, even though they do not have the law. They show that what the law requires is written on their hearts, while their conscience also bears witness and their conflicting thoughts accuse or perhaps excuse them. Romans 2:14-15 RSV

I am speaking the truth in Christ, I am not lying; my conscience bears me witness in the Holy Spirit. Romans 9:1 RSV

Some people are still so accustomed to idols that when they eat such food they think of it as having been sacrificed to an idol, and since their conscience is weak, it is defiled. 1 Corinthians 8:7 NIV

To the pure, all things are pure, but to the corrupt and unbelieving nothing is pure; their very minds and consciences are corrupted. Titus 1:15 RSV

Let us draw near with a true heart in full assurance of faith, with our hearts sprinkled clean from an evil conscience and our bodies washed with pure water. Hebrews 10:22 RSV

God is greater than our hearts, and he knows everything. Beloved, if our hearts do not condemn us, we have confidence before God. 1 John 3:20-21 RSV

See also *Guilt*.

Contentment

Trust in the Lord, and do good; so you will dwell in the land, and enjoy security. Psalm 37:3 RSV

'If you pour yourself out for the hungry and satisfy the desire of the afflicted, then shall your light rise in the darkness and your gloom be as the noonday. And the Lord will guide you continually, and satisfy your desire with good things, and make your bones strong; and you shall be like a watered garden, like a spring of water, whose waters fail not.' Isaiah 58:10-11 RSV

Soldiers also asked him [John the Baptist], 'And we, what shall we do?' And he said to them, 'Rob no one by violence or by false accusation, and be content with your wages.' Luke 3:14 RSV

And Jesus said unto them, I am the bread of life: he that cometh to me shall never hunger; and he that believeth on me shall never thirst. John 6:35 KJV

And do not grumble, as some of them [children of Israel] did—and were killed by the destroying angel. 1 Corinthians 10:10 NIV

Not that I complain of want; for I have learned, in whatever state I am, to be content. I know how to be abased, and I know how to abound; in any and all circumstances I have learned the secret of facing plenty and hunger, abundance and want. I can do all things in him who strengthens me. Philippians 4:11-13 RSV

There is great gain in godliness with contentment; for we brought nothing into the world, and we cannot take anything out of the world; but if we have food and clothing, with these we shall be content. 1 Timothy 6:6-8 RSV

Keep your life free from love of money, and be content with what you have; for he has said, 'I will never fail you nor forsake you.' Hebrews 13:5 RSV

See also *Joy*.

Conversion

All the ends of the earth shall remember and turn to the Lord; and all the families of the nations shall worship before him. Psalm 22:27 RSV

Verily I say unto you, Except ye be converted, and become as little children, ye shall not enter into the kingdom of heaven. Matthew 18:3 KJV

[The purpose of parables] 'That they may indeed see but not perceive, and may indeed hear but not understand; lest they should turn again, and be forgiven.' Mark 4:12 RSV

[The Lord Jesus to Simon Peter] I have prayed for thee, that thy faith fail not: and when thou art converted, strengthen thy brethren. Luke 22:32 KJV

'We . . . bring you good news, that you should turn from these vain things to a living God who made the heaven and the earth and the sea and all that is in them.' Acts 14:15 RSV

'"That they may turn from darkness to light and from the power of Satan to God, that they may receive forgiveness of sins and a place among those who are sanctified by faith in me."' Acts 26:18 RSV

For they themselves report concerning us what a welcome we had among you, and how you turned to God from idols, to serve a living and true God. 1 Thessalonians 1:9 RSV

For you were straying like sheep, but have now returned to the Shepherd and Guardian of your souls. 1 Peter 2:25 RSV

See also *Faith; New birth; Repentance*.

Conviction of sin

For I acknowledge my transgressions: and my sin is ever before me. Against thee, thee only, have I sinned, and done this evil in thy sight: that thou mightest be justified when thou speakest, and be clear when thou judgest. Psalm 51:3-4 KJV

And I said: 'Woe is me! For I am lost; for I am a man of unclean lips, and I dwell in the midst of a people of unclean lips; for my eyes have seen the King, the Lord of hosts!' Isaiah 6:5 RSV

When Simon Peter saw it, he fell down

at Jesus' knees, saying, Depart from me; for I am a sinful man, O Lord. Luke 5:8 KJV

And when he [the Holy Spirit] comes, he will convince the world concerning sin and righteousness and judgment: concerning sin, because they do not believe in me.' John 16:8-9 RSV

Now when they heard this they were cut to the heart, and said to Peter and the rest of the apostles, 'Brethren, what shall we do?' Acts 2:37 RSV

Counsel

Blessed is the man who walks not in the counsel of the wicked, nor stands in the way of sinners, nor sits in the seat of scoffers. Psalm 1:1 RSV

I will instruct you and teach you the way you should go; I will counsel you with my eye upon you. Be not like a horse or a mule, without understanding, which must be curbed with bit and bridle. Psalm 32:8-9 RSV

The Lord brings the counsel of the nations to naught; he frustrates the plans of the peoples. The counsel of the Lord stands for ever, the thoughts of his heart to all generations. Psalm 33:10-11 RSV

The way of a fool is right in his own eyes, but a wise man listens to advice. Proverbs 12:15 RSV

Listen to advice and accept instruction, that you may gain wisdom for the future. Proverbs 19:20 RSV

For unto us a child is born, unto us a son is given: and the government shall be upon his shoulder: and his name shall be called Wonderful, Counsellor, The mighty God, The everlasting Father, The Prince of Peace. Isaiah 9:6 KJV

O Lord, thou art my God; I will exalt thee, I will praise thy name; for thou hast done wonderful things; thy counsels of old are faithfulness and truth. Isaiah 25:1 KJV

[Paul to the elders at Ephesus] 'For I did not shrink from declaring to you the whole counsel of God.' Acts 20:27 RSV

See also *Guidance; Way.*

Courage

[God to Joshua] 'Be strong and of good courage; for you shall cause this people to inherit the land which I swore to their fathers to give them. Only be strong and very courageous, being careful to do according to all the law which Moses my servant commanded

you; turn not from it to the right hand or to the left, that you may have good success wherever you go. This book of the law shall not depart out of your mouth, but you shall meditate on it day and night, that you may be careful to do according to all that is written in it; for then you shall make your way prosperous, and then you shall have good success. Have I not commanded you? Be strong and of good courage; be not frightened, neither be dismayed; for the Lord your God is with you wherever you go.' Joshua 1:6-9 RSV

[Hezekiah's encouragement] 'Be strong and courageous. Do not be afraid or discouraged because of the king of Assyria and the vast army with him, for there is a greater power with us than with him. With him is only the arm of flesh, but with us is the Lord our God to help us fight our battles.' 2 Chronicles 32:7-8 NIV

Wait for the Lord; be strong, and let your heart take courage; yea, wait for the Lord! Psalm 27:14 RSV

They brought to him a paralytic, lying on his bed; and when Jesus saw their faith he said to the paralytic, 'Take heart, my son; your sins are forgiven.' Matthew 9:2 RSV

Jesus turned, and seeing her he said, 'Take heart, daughter; your faith has made you well.' And instantly the woman was made well. Matthew 9:22 RSV

These things I have spoken unto you, that in me ye might have peace. In the world ye shall have tribulation: but be of good cheer; I have overcome the world. John 16:33 KJV

'And now, Lord, look upon their threats, and grant to thy servants to speak thy word with all boldness . . .' Acts 4:29 RSV

I will know that you stand firm in one spirit, contending as one man for the faith of the gospel without being frightened in any way by those who oppose you. Philippians 1:27-28 NIV

For God hath not given us the spirit of fear; but of power, and of love, and of a sound mind. 2 Timothy 1:7 KJV

See also *Comfort; Confidence.*

Covenant

'And I will establish my covenant between me and you and your descendants after you throughout their generations for an everlasting covenant, to be God to you and to your

descendants after you. And I will give to you, and to your descendants after you, the land of your sojournings, all the land of Canaan, for an everlasting possession; and I will be their God . . . This is my covenant, which you shall keep, between me and you and your descendants after you: Every male among you shall be circumcised.'
Genesis 17:7-10 RSV

And Moses took the blood, and sprinkled it on the people, and said, Behold the blood of the covenant, which the Lord hath made with you concerning all these words. Exodus 24:8 KJV

The friendship of the Lord is for those who fear him, and he makes known to them his covenant. Psalm 25:14 RSV

'This is my blood of the covenant, which is poured out for many for the forgiveness of sins.' Matthew 26:28 RSV

[The Gentiles] Strangers to the covenants of promise . . . Ephesians 2:12 RSV

It follows that it is a greater covenant for which Jesus has become our guarantee. Hebrews 7:22 JB

'This is the covenant that I will make with the house of Israel after those days, says the Lord: I will put my laws into their minds, and write them on their hearts, and I will be their God, and they shall be my people.' Hebrews 8:10 RSV

Therefore he is the mediator of a new covenant, so that those who are called may receive the promised eternal inheritance, since a death has occurred which redeems them from the transgressions under the first covenant. Hebrews 9:15 RSV

Now the God of peace, that brought again from the dead our Lord Jesus, that great shepherd of the sheep, through the blood of the everlasting covenant . . . Hebrews 13:20 KJV

And I heard a great voice out of heaven saying, Behold, the tabernacle of God is with men, and he will dwell with them, and they shall be his people, and God himself shall be with them, and be their God. Revelation 21:3 KJV

Covetousness

See *Desire, wrong.*

Creation

In the beginning God created the heaven and the earth. Genesis 1:1 KJV

So God created man in his own image, in the image of God created he him;

male and female created he them.
Genesis 1:27 KJV

When I consider thy heavens, the work of thy fingers, the moon and the stars, which thou hast ordained; what is man, that thou art mindful of him? and the son of man, that thou visitest him?
Psalm 8:3-4 KJV

O come, let us worship, and fall down, and kneel before the Lord our Maker.
Psalm 95:6 BCP

Lift up your eyes on high, and behold who hath created these things, that bringeth out their host by number: he calleth them all by names by the greatness of his might, for that he is strong in power; not one faileth . . . Hast thou not known? hast thou not heard, that the everlasting God, the Lord, the Creator of the ends of the earth, fainteth not, neither is weary? There is no searching of his understanding. Isaiah 40:26, 28 KJV

And he said to them, 'Go into all the world and preach the gospel to the whole creation.' Mark 16:15 RSV

Ever since the creation of the world his invisible nature, namely, his eternal power and deity, has been clearly perceived in the things that have been made. Romans 1:20 RSV

For the creation waits with eager longing for the revealing of the sons of God; for the creation was subjected to futility, not of its own will but by the will of him who subjected it in hope; because the creation itself will be set free from its bondage to decay and obtain the glorious liberty of the children of God. We know that the whole creation has been groaning in travail together until now; and not only the creation, but we ourselves, who have the first fruits of the Spirit, groan inwardly as we wait for adoption as sons, the redemption of our bodies.
Romans 8:19-23 RSV

Therefore, if any one is in Christ, he is a new creation; the old has passed away, behold, the new has come.
2 Corinthians 5:17 RSV

For we are his workmanship, created in Christ Jesus unto good works, which God hath before ordained that we should walk in them. Ephesians 2:10 KJV

[Christ] He is the image of the invisible God, the first-born of all creation; for in him all things were created, in heaven and on earth, visible and invisible, whether thrones or

'God saw every thing that he had made, and ... it was very good.'

dominions or principalities or authorities—all things were created through him and for him. Colossians 1:15-16 RSV

Thou art worthy, O Lord, to receive glory and honour and power: for thou hast created all things, and for thy pleasure they are and were created. Revelation 4:11 KJV

See also *Providence; Revelation; World.*

Cross

See *Jesus Christ, Death.*

Deacon

Now in these days when the disciples were increasing in number, the Hellenists murmured against the Hebrews because their widows were neglected in the daily distribution. And the twelve summoned the body of the disciples and said, 'It is not right that we should give up preaching the word of God to serve tables. Therefore, brethren, pick out from among you seven men of good repute, full of the Spirit and of wisdom, whom we may appoint to this duty. But we will devote ourselves to prayer and to the ministry of the word.' Acts 6:1-4 RSV

Deacons likewise must be serious, not double-tongued, not addicted to much wine, not greedy for gain; they must hold the mystery of the faith with a clear conscience. And let them also be tested first; then if they prove themselves blameless let them serve as deacons. The women likewise must be serious, no slanderers, but temperate, faithful in all things. Let deacons be the husband of one wife, and let them manage their children and their households well; for those who serve well as deacons gain a good standing for themselves and also great confidence in the faith which is in Christ Jesus. 1 Timothy 3:8-13 RSV

See also *Elders; Service.*

Death

But of the tree of the knowledge of good and evil, thou shalt not eat of it: for in the day that thou eatest thereof thou shalt surely die. Genesis 2:17 KJV

In the sweat of thy face shalt thou eat bread, till thou return unto the ground; for out of it wast thou taken: for dust thou art, and unto dust shalt thou return. Genesis 3:19 KJV

Precious in the sight of the Lord is the death of his saints. Psalm 116:15 RSV

There is a way which seemeth right unto a man, but the end thereof are the ways of death. Proverbs 14:12 KJV

'For I have no pleasure in the death of any one, says the Lord God; so turn, and live.' Ezekiel 18:32 RSV

'Truly, truly, I say to you, if any one

keeps my word, he will never see death.' John 8:51 RSV

For he who has died is freed from sin. But if we have died with Christ, we believe that we shall also live with him ... So you also must consider yourselves dead to sin and alive to God in Christ Jesus. Romans 6:7-8, 11 RSV

For the wages of sin is death; but the gift of God is eternal life through Jesus Christ our Lord. Romans 6:23 KJV

But if Christ is in you, although your bodies are dead because of sin, your spirits are alive because of righteousness. If the Spirit of him who raised Jesus from the dead dwells in you, he who raised Christ Jesus from the dead will give life to your mortal bodies also through his Spirit which dwells in you. Romans 8:10-11 RSV

If we live, we live to the Lord, and if we die, we die to the Lord; so then, whether we live or whether we die, we are the Lord's. For to this end Christ died and lived again, that he might be Lord both of the dead and of the living. Romans 14:8-9 RSV

For as in Adam all die, so also in Christ shall all be made alive. 1 Corinthians 15:22 RSV

The last enemy that shall be destroyed is death. 1 Corinthians 15:26 KJV

So when this corruptible shall have put on incorruption, and this mortal shall have put on immortality, then shall be brought to pass the saying that is written, Death is swallowed up in victory. O death, where is thy sting? O grave, where is thy victory?
1 Corinthians 15:54-55 KJV

We are of good courage, and we would rather be away from the body and at home with the Lord. 2 Corinthians 5:8 RSV

As for you, you were dead in your transgressions and sins ... Ephesians 2:1 NIV

For me to live is Christ, and to die is gain. Philippians 1:21 KJV

I am pulled in two directions. I want very much to leave this life and be with Christ, which is a far better thing . . Philippians 1:23 GNB

You must put to death, then, the earthly desires at work in you, such as sexual immorality, indecency, lust, evil passions, and greed (for greed is a form of idolatry). Colossians 3:5 GNB

The Lord himself shall descend from heaven with a shout, with the voice of the archangel, and with the trump of God: and the dead in Christ shall rise first. Then we which are alive and remain shall be caught up together with them in the clouds, to meet the Lord in the air: and so shall we ever be with the Lord. Wherefore comfort one another with these words. 1 Thessalonians 4:16-18 KJV

Our Saviour Christ Jesus, who abolished death and brought life and immortality to light through the gospel. 2 Timothy 1:10 RSV

'Christ has been raised from the dead.'

The saying is sure: If we have died with him, we shall also live with him; if we endure, we shall also reign with him. 2 Timothy 2:11 RSV

Since therefore the children share in flesh and blood, he himself likewise partook of the same nature, that through death he might destroy him who has the power of death, that is, the devil. Hebrews 2:14 RSV

It is appointed unto men once to die, but after this the judgment. Hebrews 9:27 KJV

Then desire when it has conceived gives birth to sin; and sin when it is full-grown brings forth death. James 1:15 RSV

Be thou faithful unto death, and I will give thee a crown of life. Revelation 2:10 KJV

And God shall wipe away all tears from their eyes; and there shall be no more death, neither sorrow, nor crying, neither shall there be any more pain: for the former things are passed away. Revelation 21:4 KJV

See also *Comfort; Last things, Resurrection; Life.*

Deliverance

See *Redemption; Salvation and Saviour.*

Demons

When evening came, people brought to Jesus many who had demons in them. Jesus drove out the evil spirits with a word and healed all who were sick. Matthew 8:16 GNB

The demons begged Jesus, 'If you are going to drive us out, send us into that herd of pigs.' Matthew 8:31 GNB

Then shall he say also unto them on the left hand, Depart from me, ye cursed, into everlasting fire, prepared for the devil and his angels. Matthew 25:41 KJV

And whenever the unclean spirits beheld him, they fell down before him and cried out, 'You are the Son of God.' Mark 3:11 RSV

Some teachers of the Law who had come from Jerusalem were saying, 'He has Beelzebul in him! It is the chief of the demons who gives him the power to drive them out.' Mark 3:22 GNB

As Jesus stepped ashore, he was met by a man from the town who had demons in him. For a long time this man had gone without clothes and would not stay at home, but spent his time in the burial caves. Luke 8:27 GNB

And he called the twelve together and gave them power and authority over all demons and to cure diseases . . . Luke 10:17 RSV

Now he was casting out a demon that was dumb; when the demon had gone out, the dumb man spoke, and the people marvelled. Luke 11:14 RSV

For we wrestle not against flesh and blood, but against principalities, against powers, against the rulers of the darkness of this world, against spiritual wickedness in high places. Ephesians 6:12 KJV

He disarmed the principalities and powers and made a public example of them, triumphing over them in him. Colossians 2:15 RSV

Thou believest that there is one God; thou doest well: the devils also believe, and tremble. James 2:19 KJV

See also *Devil; Occult.*

Depression

And Job spake, and said, Let the day perish wherein I was born. Job 3:2-3 KJV

I am worn out with grief; every night my bed is damp from my weeping; my pillow is soaked with tears. I can hardly see; my eyes are so swollen from the weeping caused by my enemies. Psalm 6:6-7 GNB

How much longer will you forget me, Lord? For ever? How much longer will you hide yourself from me? How long must I endure trouble? How long will sorrow fill my heart day and night? How long will my enemies triumph over me? Psalm 13:1-2 GNB

For day and night thy hand was heavy upon me; my strength was dried up as by the heat of summer. Psalm 32:4 RSV

My tears have been my meat day and night, while they continually say unto me, Where is thy God? . . all thy waves and thy billows are gone over me. Psalm 42:3, 7 KJV

A man's spirit will endure sickness; but a broken spirit who can bear? Proverbs 18:14 RSV

My soul is bereft of peace, I have forgotten what happiness is . . . Remember my affliction and my bitterness, the wormwood and the gall! My soul continually thinks of it and is bowed down within me. But this I call to mind, and therefore I have hope: The steadfast love of the Lord never ceases, his mercies never come to an end; they are new every morning; great is thy faithfulness. 'The Lord is my portion,' says my soul, 'therefore I will hope in him.' Lamentations 3:17, 19-24 RSV

See also *Comfort*.

Desire
See *Christian life, Longing for God*.

Desire, wrong
Thou shalt not covet thy neighbour's house, thou shalt not covet thy neighbour's wife, nor his manservant, nor his maidservant, nor his ox, nor his ass, nor any thing that is thy neighbour's. Exodus 20:17 KJV

Give me the desire to obey your laws rather than to get rich. Keep me from paying attention to what is worthless; be good to me, as you have promised. Psalm 119:36-37 GNB

If you try to make a profit dishonestly, you will get your family into trouble. Proverbs 15:27 GNB

'For from the least to the greatest of them, every one is greedy for unjust gain; and from prophet to priest, every one deals falsely.' Jeremiah 6:13 RSV

And he said to them, 'Take heed, and beware of all covetousness; for a man's life does not consist in the abundance of his possessions.' Luke 12:15 RSV

You may be sure that no one who is immoral, indecent, or greedy (for greed is a form of idolatry) will ever receive a share in the Kingdom of Christ and of God. Ephesians 5:5 GNB

But those who want to get rich fall into temptation and are caught in the trap of many foolish and harmful desires, which pull them down to ruin and destruction. 1 Timothy 6:9 GNB

You desire and do not have; so you kill. And you covet and cannot obtain; so you fight and wage war. James 4:2 RSV

Love not the world, neither the things that are in the world. If any man love the world, the love of the Father is not in him. For all that is in the world, the lust of the flesh, and the lust of the eyes, and the pride of life, is not of the Father, but is of the world. 1 John 2:15-16 KJV

Devil
Now the serpent was more subtil than any beast of the field which the Lord God had made. And he said unto the woman, Yea, hath God said, Ye shall not eat of every tree of the garden? Genesis 3:1 KJV

So Satan went forth from the presence of the Lord, and afflicted Job with loathsome sores from the sole of his foot to the crown of his head. Job 2:7 RSV

Then Jesus was led up by the Spirit into the wilderness to be tempted by the devil. Matthew 4:1 RSV

'When any one hears the word of the kingdom and does not understand it, the evil one comes and snatches away what is sown in his heart; this is what was sown along the path.' Matthew 13:19 RSV

'You are of your father the devil, and your will is to do your father's desires. He was a murderer from the beginning, and has nothing to do with the truth, because there is no truth in him. When he lies, he speaks according to his own nature, for he is a liar and the father of lies.' John 8:44 RSV

'"That they may turn from darkness to light and from the power of Satan to God, that they may receive forgiveness of sins and a place among those who are sanctified by faith in me."' Acts 26:18 RSV

Lest Satan should get an advantage of us: for we are not ignorant of his devices. 2 Corinthians 2:11 KJV

In their case the god of this world has blinded the minds of the unbelievers, to keep them from seeing the light of the gospel of the glory of Christ, who is the likeness of God. 2 Corinthians 4:4 RSV

Even Satan disguises himself as an angel of light. 2 Corinthians 11:14 RSV

As for you, you were dead in your transgressions and sins, in which you used to live when you followed the ways of this world and of the ruler of the kingdom of the air, the spirit who is now at work in those who are disobedient. Ephesians 2:2 NIV

Put on the whole armour of God, that ye may be able to stand against the wiles of the devil. Ephesians 6:11 KJV

Since therefore the children share in flesh and blood, he himself likewise partook of the same nature, that through death he might destroy him who has the power of death, that is, the devil. Hebrews 2:14 RSV

Be sober, be watchful. Your adversary the devil prowls around like a roaring lion, seeking some one to devour. Resist him, firm in your faith. 1 Peter 5:8-9 RSV

The reason the Son of God appeared

was to destroy the works of the devil.
1 John 3:8 RSV

We know that we are of God, and the whole world is in the power of the evil one. 1 John 5:19 RSV

And the great dragon was thrown down, that ancient serpent, who is called the Devil and Satan, the deceiver of the whole world—he was thrown down to the earth, and his angels were thrown down with him. And I heard a loud voice in heaven, saying, 'Now the salvation and the power and the kingdom of our God and the authority of his Christ have come, for the accuser of our brethren has been thrown down, who accuses them day and night before our God.' Revelation 12:9-10 RSV

Then the Devil, who deceived them, was thrown into the lake of fire and sulphur, where the beast and the false prophet had already been thrown; and they will be tormented day and night for ever and ever. Revelation 20:10 GNB

See also *Demons; Victory.*

Diligence
See *Work.*

Discernment
[Solomon's prayer] 'Give thy servant therefore an understanding mind to govern thy people, that I may discern between good and evil; for who is able to govern this thy great people?' 1 Kings 3:9 RSV

And the spirit of the Lord shall rest upon him, the spirit of wisdom and understanding, the spirit of counsel and might, the spirit of knowledge and of the fear of the Lord. Isaiah 11:2 KJV

The man without the Spirit does not accept the things that come from the Spirit of God, for they are foolishness to him and he cannot understand them, because they are spiritually discerned. 1 Corinthians 2:14 NIV

To another the ability to distinguish between spirits . . . 1 Corinthians 12:10 RSV

Two or three prophets should speak, and the others should weigh carefully what is said. 1 Corinthians 14:29 NIV

And it is my prayer that your love may abound more and more, with knowledge and all discernment. Philippians 1:9 RSV

For the word of God is living and active, sharper than any two-edged sword, piercing to the division of soul and spirit, of joints and marrow, and discerning the thoughts and intentions of the heart. Hebrews 4:12 RSV

But solid food is for the mature, for those who have their faculties trained by practice to distinguish good from evil. Hebrews 5:14 RSV

See also *Examination; Self-examination; Wisdom.*

Disciples
And he called to him his twelve disciples and gave them authority over unclean spirits, to cast them out, and to heal every disease and every infirmity. Matthew 10:1 RSV

'Go therefore and make disciples of all nations, baptizing them in the name of the Father and of the Son and of the Holy Spirit, teaching them to observe all that I have commanded you; and lo, I am with you always, to the close of the age.' Matthew 28:19-20 RSV

'If any one comes to me and does not hate his own father and mother and wife and children and brothers and sisters, yes, and even his own life, he cannot be my disciple. Whoever does not bear his own cross and come after me, cannot be my disciple . . . So therefore, whoever of you does not renounce all that he has cannot be my disciple.' Luke 14:26-27, 33 RSV

Jesus then said to the Jews who had believed in him, 'If you continue in my word, you are truly my disciples.' John 8:31 RSV

By this shall all men know that ye are my disciples, if ye have love one to another. John 13:35 KJV

'By this my Father is glorified, that you bear much fruit, and so prove to be my disciples.' John 15:8 RSV

Discipline
My son, do not despise the Lord's discipline or be weary of his reproof, for the Lord reproves him whom he loves, as a father the son in whom he delights. Proverbs 3:11-12 RSV

'If your brother sins against you, go and tell him his fault, between you and him alone. If he listens to you, you have gained your brother. But if he does not listen, take one or two others along with you, that every word may be confirmed by the evidence of two or three witnesses. If he refuses to listen to them, tell it to the church; and if he refuses to listen even to the church, let him be to you as a Gentile and a tax collector. Truly, I say to you, whatever you bind on earth shall be bound in

heaven, and whatever you loose on earth shall be loosed in heaven.'
Matthew 18:15-18 RSV

Preach the word, be urgent in season and out of season, convince, rebuke, and exhort, be unfailing in patience and in teaching. 2 Timothy 4:2 RSV

It is for discipline that you have to endure. God is treating you as sons; for what son is there whom his father does not discipline? If you are left without discipline, in which all have participated, then you are illegitimate children and not sons. Besides this, we have had earthly fathers to discipline us and we respected them. Shall we not much more be subject to the Father of spirits and live? For they disciplined us for a short time at their pleasure, but he disciplines us for our good, that we may share his holiness. For the moment all discipline seems painful rather than pleasant; later it yields the peaceful fruit of righteousness to those who have been trained by it. Hebrews 12:7-11 RSV

'"Those whom I love, I reprove and chasten; so be zealous and repent."'
Revelation 3:19 RSV

See also Family, Children and the whole family.

Disobedience

'But if you will not obey the voice of the Lord your God or be careful to do all his commandments and his statutes which I command you this day, then all these curses shall come upon you and overtake you.' Deuteronomy 28:15 RSV

'But they did not obey or incline their ear, but walked in their own counsels and the stubbornness of their evil hearts, and went backward and not forward. From the day that your fathers came out of the land of Egypt to this day, I have persistently sent all my servants the prophets to them, day after day; yet they did not listen to me, or incline their ear, but stiffened their neck. They did worse than their fathers . . . And you shall say to them, "This is the nation that did not obey the voice of the Lord their God, and did not accept discipline; truth has perished; it is cut off from their lips."' Jeremiah 7:24-26, 28 RSV

For as by one man's disobedience many were made sinners, so by one man's obedience many will be made righteous. Romans 5:19 RSV

The ruler of the kingdom of the air, the spirit who is now at work in those who are disobedient. Ephesians 2:2 NIV

[Jesus will appear] with a flaming fire, to punish those who reject God and who do not obey the Good News about our Lord Jesus. 2 Thessalonians 1:8 GNB

[In the last days] Men will be lovers of self, lovers of money, proud, arrogant, abusive, disobedient to their parents, ungrateful, unholy. 2 Timothy 3:2 RSV

See also Obedience; Punishment; Submission.

Divorce

See Marriage.

Doubt

So Sarah laughed to herself, saying, 'After I have grown old, and my husband is old, shall I have pleasure?' The Lord said to Abraham, 'Why did Sarah laugh, and say, "Shall I indeed bear a child, now that I am old?" Is anything too hard for the Lord? At the appointed time I will return to you, in the spring, and Sarah shall have a son.' Genesis 18:12-14 RSV

I was afraid and thought that he had driven me out of his presence. But he heard my cry, when I called to him for help. Psalm 31:22 GNB

Why sayest thou, O Jacob, and speakest, O Israel, My way is hid from the Lord, and my judgment is passed over from my God? Hast thou not . known? hast thou not heard, that the everlasting God, the Lord, the Creator of the ends of the earth, fainteth not, neither is weary? There is no searching of his understanding. Isaiah 40:27-28 KJV

Now when John heard in prison about the deeds of the Christ, he sent word by his disciples and said to him, 'Are you he who is to come, or shall we look for another?' Matthew 11:2-3 RSV

Jesus immediately reached out his hand and caught him [Peter], saying to him, 'O man of little faith, why did you doubt?' Matthew 14:31 RSV

And Jesus answered them, 'Truly, I say to you, if you have faith and never doubt, you will not only do what has been done to the fig tree, but even if you say to this mountain, "Be taken up and cast into the sea," it will be done.' Matthew 21:21 RSV

And when they saw him they worshipped him; but some doubted. Matthew 28:17 RSV

But he [Thomas] said to them, 'Unless I

see in his hands the print of the nails, and place my finger in the mark of the nails, and place my hand in his side, I will not believe.' John 20:25 RSV

But let him ask in faith, with no doubting, for he who doubts is like a wave of the sea that is driven and tossed by the wind. James 1:6 RSV

And I heard a loud voice in heaven, saying, 'Now the salvation and the power and the kingdom of our God and the authority of his Christ have come, for the accuser of our brethren has been thrown down, who accuses them day and night before our God.' Revelation 12:10 RSV

See also *Assurance; Comfort; Unbelief.*

Dreams

And he [Jacob] dreamed, and behold a ladder set up on the earth, and the top of it reached to heaven: and behold the angels of God ascending and descending on it. Genesis 28:12 KJV

Now Joseph had a dream, and when he told it to his brothers they only hated him the more. Genesis 37:5 RSV

'A prophet or an interpreter of dreams may promise a miracle or a wonder, in order to lead you to worship and serve gods that you have not worshipped before. Even if what he promises comes true, do not pay any attention to him. The Lord your God is using him to test you, to see if you love the Lord with all your heart. Follow the Lord and fear him; obey him and keep his commands; worship him and be faithful to him. But put to death any interpreter of dreams or prophet that tells you to rebel against the Lord, who rescued you from Egypt, where you were slaves. Such a man is evil and is trying to lead you away from the life that the Lord has commanded you to live. He must be put to death, in order to rid yourselves of this evil.' Deuteronomy 13:1-5 GNB

When the Lord brought us back to Jerusalem, it was like a dream! Psalm 126:1 GNB

I am against the prophets, says the Lord, who dream lies and retail them, misleading my people with wild and reckless falsehoods. It was not I who sent them or commissioned them, and they will do this people no good. Jeremiah 23:32 NEB

Daniel answered the king, 'No wise men, enchanters, magicians, or astrologers can show to the king the mystery which the king has asked, but there is a God in heaven who reveals mysteries, and he has made known to King Nebuchadnezzar what will be in the latter days. Your dream and the visions of your head as you lay in bed are these . . .' Daniel 2:27-28 RSV

'And it shall come to pass afterward, that I will pour out my spirit on all flesh; your sons and your daughters shall prophesy, your old men shall dream dreams, and your young men shall see visions.' Joel 2:28 RSV

But as he considered this, behold, an angel of the Lord appeared to him in a dream, saying, 'Joseph, son of David, do not fear to take Mary your wife, for that which is conceived in her is of the Holy Spirit.' Matthew 1:20 RSV

That night Paul had a vision in which he saw a Macedonian standing and begging him, 'Come over to Macedonia and help us!' Acts 16:9 GNB

Drunkenness

Show me someone who drinks too much, who has to try out some new drink, and I will show you someone miserable and sorry for himself, always causing trouble and always complaining. His eyes are bloodshot, and he has bruises that could have been avoided. Proverbs 23:29-30 GNB

You are doomed! You get up early in the morning to start drinking, and you spend long evenings getting drunk. Isaiah 5:11 GNB

'Let us eat and drink, for tomorrow we die.' Isaiah 22:13 RSV

These also reel with wine and stagger with strong drink; the priest and the prophet reel with strong drink, they are confused with wine, they stagger with strong drink; they err in vision, they stumble in giving judgment. Isaiah 28:7 RSV

Let us conduct ourselves properly, as people who live in the light of day—no orgies or drunkenness . . . Romans 13:13 GNB

Now the works of the flesh are plain: . . . drunkenness, carousing, and the like. Galatians 5:19, 21 RSV

And be not drunk with wine, wherein is excess; but be filled with the Spirit. Ephesians 5:18 KJV

See also *Temperance.*

Eden, *garden of*

And the Lord God planted a garden eastward in Eden; and there he put the man whom he had formed. And out of the ground made the Lord God to grow every tree that is pleasant to the sight, and good for food; the tree of life also in the midst of the garden, and the tree of knowledge of good and evil . . . And the Lord God took the man, and put him into the garden of Eden to dress it and to keep it. And the Lord God commanded the man, saying, Of every tree of the garden thou mayest freely eat: but of the tree of the knowledge of good and evil, thou shalt not eat of it: for in the day that thou eatest thereof thou shalt surely die. Genesis 2:8-9, 15-17 KJV

Therefore the Lord God sent him forth from the garden of Eden, to till the ground from whence he was taken. So he drove out the man; and he placed at the east of the garden of Eden Cherubims, and a flaming sword which turned every way, to keep the way of the tree of life. Genesis 3:23-24 KJV

Education

See *Teachers and teaching.*

Elders

'Go and gather the elders of Israel together, and say to them, "The Lord, the God of your fathers, the God of Abraham, of Isaac, and of Jacob, has appeared to me."' Exodus 3:16 RSV

And the disciples determined, every one according to his ability, to send relief to the brethren who lived in Judea; and they did so, sending it to the elders by the hand of Barnabas and Saul. Acts 11:29-30 RSV

And when they had appointed elders for them in every church, with prayer and fasting, they committed them to the Lord in whom they believed. Acts 14:23 RSV

[Paul to the elders of the church at Ephesus] 'Take heed to yourselves and to all the flock, in which the Holy Spirit has made you overseers, to care for the church of God which he obtained with the blood of his own Son.' Acts 20:28 RSV

Now we ask you, brothers, to respect those who work hard among you, who are over you in the Lord and who admonish you. Hold them in the highest regard in love because of their work. 1 Thessalonians 5:12-13 NIV

This is a true saying: If a man is eager to be a church leader, he desires an excellent work. A church leader must be without fault; he must have only one wife, be sober, self-controlled, and orderly; he must welcome strangers in his home; he must be able to teach; he must not be a drunkard or a violent man, but gentle and peaceful; he must not love money; he must be able to manage his own family well and make his children obey him with all respect. 1 Timothy 3:1-4 GNB

Let the elders who rule well be considered worthy of double honour, especially those who labour in preaching and teaching. 1 Timothy 5:17 RSV

This is why I left you in Crete, that you might amend what was defective, and appoint elders in every town as I directed you. Titus 1:5 RSV

Remember your leaders, those who spoke to you the word of God; consider the outcome of their life, and imitate their faith. Hebrews 13:7 RSV

Obey your leaders and submit to them; for they are keeping watch over your souls, as men who will have to give account. Let them do this joyfully, and not sadly, for that would be of no advantage to you. Hebrews 13:17 RSV

Is any sick among you? Let him call for the elders of the church; and let them pray over him, anointing him with oil in the name of the Lord. James 5:14 KJV

I, who am an elder myself, appeal to the church elders among you. I am a witness of Christ's sufferings, and I will share in the glory that will be revealed. I appeal to you to be shepherds of the flock that God gave you and to take care of it willingly, as God wants you to, and not unwillingly. Do your work, not for mere pay, but from a real desire to serve. Do not try to rule over those who have been put in your care, but examples to the flock. 1 Peter 5:1-3 GNB

See also *Deacon; Pastor.*

Election

'All things have been delivered to me by my Father; and no one knows the Son except the Father, and no one knows the Father except the Son and any one to whom the Son chooses to reveal him.' Matthew 11:27 RSV

Then shall the King say unto them on his right hand, Come, ye blessed of my Father, inherit the kingdom prepared for you from the foundation of the world. Matthew 25:34 KJV

All that the Father giveth me shall come to me; and him that cometh to me I will in no wise cast out. John 6:37 KJV

'No one can come to me unless the Father who sent me draws him; and I will raise him up at the last day.' John 6:44 RSV

'You did not choose me, but I chose you and appointed you that you should go and bear fruit and that your fruit should abide.' John 15:16 RSV

'I have manifested thy name to the men whom thou gavest me out of the world; thine they were, and thou gavest them to me, and they have kept thy word.' John 17:6 RSV

And when the Gentiles heard this, they were glad and glorified the word of God; and as many as were ordained to eternal life believed. Acts 13:48 RSV

For those whom he foreknew he also predestined to be conformed to the image of his Son, in order that he might be the first-born among many brethren. And those whom he predestined he also called; and those whom he called he also justified; and those whom he justified he also glorified . . . Who shall bring any charge against God's elect? Romans 8:29-30, 33 RSV

For he says to Moses, 'I will have mercy on whom I have mercy, and I will have compassion on whom I have compassion.' So it depends not upon man's will or exertion, but upon God's mercy. Romans 9:15-16 RSV

Even before the world was made, God had already chosen us to be his through our union with Christ, so that we would be holy and without fault before him. Because of his love God had already decided that through Jesus Christ he would make us his sons—this was his pleasure and purpose. Ephesians 1:4-5 GNB

You are the people of God; he loved you and chose you for his own. So then, you must clothe yourselves with compassion, kindness, humility, gentleness, and patience. Colossians 3:12 GNB

But we are bound to give thanks to God always for you, brethren beloved by the Lord, because God chose you from the beginning to be saved, through sanctification by the Spirit and belief in the truth. 2 Thessalonians 2:13 RSV

Elect according to the foreknowledge of God the Father, through sanctification of the Spirit, unto obedience and sprinkling of the blood of Jesus Christ. 1 Peter 1:2 KJV

But you are a chosen race, a royal priesthood, a holy nation, God's own people, that you may declare the wonderful deeds of him who called y' out of darkness into his marvellous light. 1 Peter 2:9 RSV

Therefore, brethren, be the more zealous to confirm your call and election, for if you do this you will never fall. 2 Peter 1:10 RSV

See also *Christian life, Calling of the Christian; Grace.*

Encouragement

And he [Peter] testified with many other words and exhorted them, saying, 'Save yourselves from this crooked generation.' Acts 2:40 RSV

Joseph who was surnamed by the apostles Barnabas (which means, Son of encouragement), a Levite, a native of Cyprus. Acts 4:36 RSV

When he [Barnabas] came and saw the grace of God, he was glad; and he exhorted them all to remain faithful to the Lord with steadfast purpose. Acts 11:23 RSV

[Paul and Barnabas] Strengthening the souls of the disciples, exhorting them to continue in the faith, and saying that through many tribulations we must enter the kingdom of God. Acts 14:22 RSV

Judas and Silas, being themselves prophets, spoke for a long time, encouraging and strengthening the brothers. Acts 15:32 JB

If it [a man's gift] is encouraging, let him encourage. Romans 12:8 NIV

You know that we treated each one of you just as a father treats his own children. We encouraged you, we comforted you, and we kept urging you to live the kind of life that pleases God. 1 Thessalonians 2:11-12 GNB

And we urge you, brothers, warn those who are idle, encourage the timid, help the weak, be patient with everyone. 1 Thessalonians 5:14 NIV

Preach the word, be urgent in season and out of season, convince, rebuke, and exhort, be unfailing in patience and in teaching. 2 Timothy 4:2 RSV

But encourage one another daily, as

long as it is called Today, so that none of you may be hardened by sin's deceitfulness. Hebrews 3:13 NIV

Let us consider how to stir up one another to love and good works, not neglecting to meet together, as is the habit of some, but encouraging one another, and all the more as you see the Day drawing near. Hebrews 10:24-25 RSV

See also *Comfort; Fellowship.*

Endurance

'But he who endures to the end will be saved.' Matthew 10:22 RSV

'He has no root in himself, but endures for a while, and when tribulation or persecution arises on account of the word, immediately he falls away.' Matthew 13:21 RSV

Endurance produces character, and character produces hope. Romans 5:4 RSV

No temptation has overtaken you that is not common to man. God is faithful, and he will not let you be tempted beyond your strength, but with the temptation will also provide the way of escape, that you may be able to endure it. 1 Corinthians 10:13 RSV

Put on the whole armour of God, that ye may be able to stand against the wiles of the devil . . . praying always with all prayer and supplication in the Spirit, and watching thereunto with all perseverance and supplication for all saints. Ephesians 6:11, 18 KJV

May you be strengthened with all power, according to his glorious might, for all endurance and patience with joy. Colossians 1:11 RSV

Share in suffering as a good soldier of Christ Jesus. 2 Timothy 2:3 RSV

If we endure, we shall also reign with him; if we deny him, he also will deny us. 2 Timothy 2:12 RSV

Looking unto Jesus the author and finisher of our faith; who for the joy that was set before him endured the cross, despising the shame, and is set down at the right hand of the throne of God. Hebrews 12:2 KJV

Blessed is the man who endures trial, for when he has stood the test he will receive the crown of life which God has promised to those who love him. James 1:12 RSV

See also *Christian life, Continuing in the faith; Victory; Zeal.*

Enemy

'If you meet your enemy's ox or his ass going astray, you shall bring it back to him. If you see the ass of one who hates you lying under its burden, you shall refrain from leaving him with it, you shall help him to lift it up.' Exodus 23:4-5 RSV

When a man's ways please the Lord, he makes even his enemies to be at peace with him. Proverbs 16:7 RSV

Do not rejoice when your enemy falls, do not gloat when he is brought down. Proverbs 24:17 NEB

If your enemy is hungry, give him bread to eat; and if he is thirsty, give him water to drink; for you will heap coals of fire on his head, and the Lord will reward you. Proverbs 25:21-22 RSV

Ye have heard that it hath been said, Thou shalt love thy neighbour, and hate thine enemy. But I say unto you, Love your enemies, bless them that curse you, do good to them that hate you, and pray for them which despitefully use you, and persecute you. Matthew 5:43-44 KJV

For if while we were enemies we were reconciled to God by the death of his Son, much more, now that we are reconciled, shall we be saved by his life. Romans 5:10 RSV

Enjoyment

See *Joy.*

Envy

Fret not thyself because of evildoers, neither be thou envious against the workers of iniquity. Psalm 37:1 KJV

For I was envious of the arrogant, when I saw the prosperity of the wicked. Psalm 73:3 RSV

Then I saw that all toil and all skill in work come from a man's envy of his neighbour. Ecclesiastes 4:4 RSV

For he [Pontius Pilate] knew that it was out of envy that they had delivered him up. Matthew 27:18 RSV

Now the works of the flesh are plain: . . . anger, selfishness, dissension, party spirit, envy . . . Galatians 5:19, 21 RSV

So put away all malice and all guile and insincerity and envy and all slander. 1 Peter 2:1 RSV

See also *Jealousy.*

Eucharist

See *Communion.*

Evangelism

See *Witness*.

Evangelists

And on that day a great persecution arose against the church in Jerusalem; and they were all scattered throughout the region of Judea and Samaria, except the apostles . . . Now those who were scattered went about preaching the word. Philip went down to a city of Samaria, and proclaimed to them the Christ . . . When they believed Philip as he preached good news about the kingdom of God and the name of Jesus Christ, they were baptized, both men and women. Acts 8:1, 4-5, 12 RSV

Then Philip opened his mouth, and beginning with this scripture he told him the good news of Jesus. Acts 8:35 RSV

On the following day we left and arrived in Caesarea. There we stayed at the house of Philip the evangelist. Acts 21:8 GNB

And his gifts were that some should be apostles, some prophets, some evangelists . . . Ephesians 4:11 RSV

As for you, always be steady, endure suffering, do the work of an evangelist, fulfil your ministry. 2 Timothy 4:5 RSV

See also *Witness*.

Evil

For God doth know that in the day ye eat thereof, then your eyes shall be opened, and ye shall be as gods, knowing good and evil. Genesis 3:5 KJV

Shall there be evil in a city, and the Lord hath not done it? Amos 3:6 KJV

Thou who art of purer eyes than to behold evil and canst not look on wrong. Habakkuk 1:13 RSV

Take therefore no thought for the morrow: for the morrow shall take thought for the things of itself. Sufficient unto the day is the evil thereof. Matthew 6:34 KJV

And he [Pontius Pilate] said, 'Why, what evil has he done?' But they shouted all the more, 'Let him be crucified.' Matthew 27:23 RSV

And he said, 'What comes out of a man is what defiles a man. For from within, out of the heart of man, come evil thoughts . . .' Mark 7:21 RSV

And this is the judgment, that the light has come into the world, and men loved darkness rather than light, because their deeds were evil. John 3:19 RSV

For I do not do the good I want, but the evil I do not want is what I do. Romans 7:19 RSV

Let love be genuine; hate what is evil, hold fast to what is good. Romans 12:9 RSV

See that none of you repays evil for evil, but always seek to do good to one another and to all. 1 Thessalonians 5:15 RSV

Abstain from all appearance of evil. 1 Thessalonians 5:22 KJV

For the love of money is the root of all evil. 1 Timothy 6:10 KJV

I am writing to you, young men, because you have overcome the evil one. 1 John 2:13 RSV

Examination

Search me, O God, and know my heart: try me, and know my thoughts. And see if there be any wicked way in me, and lead me in the way everlasting. Psalm 139:23-24 KJV

[The Jews at Berea] These were more noble than those in Thessalonica, in that they received the word with all readiness of mind, and searched the scriptures daily, whether those things were so. Acts 17:11 KJV

And he who searches the hearts of men knows what is the mind of the Spirit. Romans 8:27 RSV

Prove all things; hold fast that which is good. 1 Thessalonians 5:21 KJV

Beloved, do not believe every spirit, but test the spirits to see whether they are of God. 1 John 4:1 RSV

See also *Discernment; Self-examination*.

Faith

And he [Abraham] believed in the Lord; and he counted it to him for righteousness. Genesis 15:6 KJV

The Lord is my rock, and my fortress, and my deliverer, my God, my rock, in whom I take refuge, my shield, and the horn of my salvation, my stronghold. Psalm 18:2 RSV

Trust in the Lord, and do good; so you will dwell in the land, and enjoy security. Take delight in the Lord, and he will give you the desires of your heart. Commit your way to the Lord; trust in him, and he will act. Psalm 37:3-5 RSV

Trust in the Lord with all thine heart; and lean not unto thine own understanding. Proverbs 3:5 KJV

The righteous shall live by his faith.' Habakkuk 2:4 RSV

And he said to them, 'Why are you afraid, O men of little faith?' Matthew 8:26 RSV

And Jesus said to him, '. . . All things are possible to him who believes.' Immediately the father of the child cried out and said, 'I believe; help my unbelief!' Mark 9:23-24 RSV

And Jesus answered them, 'Have faith in God . . . I tell you, whatever you ask in prayer, believe that you have received it, and it will be yours.' Mark 11:22, 24 RSV

But as many as received him, to them gave he power to become the sons of God, even to them that believe on his name. John 1:12 KJV

For God so loved the world, that he gave his only begotten Son, that whosoever believeth in him should not perish, but have everlasting life. John 3:16 KJV

He who believes in him is not condemned; he who does not believe is condemned already, because he has not believed in the name of the only Son of God. John 3:18 RSV

Jesus answered them, 'This is the work of God, that you believe in him whom he has sent.' John 6:29 RSV

Let not your heart be troubled: ye believe in God, believe also in me. John 14:1 KJV

These [signs] are written that you may believe that Jesus is the Christ, the Son of God, and that believing you may have life in his name. John 20:31 RSV

And what they said pleased the whole multitude, and they chose Stephen, a man full of faith and of the Holy Spirit. Acts 6:5 RSV

And they said, 'Believe in the Lord Jesus, and you will be saved, you and your household.' Acts 16:31 RSV

[Christ Jesus] whom God hath set forth to be a propitiation through faith in his blood. Romans 3:25 KJV

Therefore being justified by faith, we have peace with God through our Lord Jesus Christ. Romans 5:1 KJV

That if thou shalt confess with thy mouth the Lord Jesus, and shalt believe in thine heart that God hath raised him from the dead, thou shalt be saved. For with the heart man believeth unto righteousness; and with the mouth confession is made unto salvation. Romans 10:9-10 KJV

So faith comes from what is heard, and what is heard comes by the preaching of Christ. Romans 10:17 RSV

So faith, hope, love abide, these three; but the greatest of these is love. 1 Corinthians 13:13 RSV

We walk by faith, not by sight. 2 Corinthians 5:7 RSV

I have been crucified with Christ; it is no longer I who live, but Christ who lives in me; and the life I now live in the flesh I live by faith in the Son of God, who loved me and gave himself for me. Galatians 2:20 RSV

For by grace are ye saved through faith; and that not of yourselves: it is the gift of God. Ephesians 2:8 KJV

Above all, taking the shield of faith, wherewith ye shall be able to quench all the fiery darts of the wicked. Ephesians 6:16 KJV

Now faith is the substance of things hoped for, the evidence of things not seen. Hebrews 11:1 KJV

By faith we understand that the world was created by the word of God, so that what is seen was made out of things which do not appear. Hebrews 11:3 RSV

But without faith it is impossible to please him: for he that cometh to God must believe that he is, and that he is a rewarder of them that diligently seek him. Hebrews 11:6 KJV

What does it profit, my brethren, if a man says he has faith but has not works? Can his faith save him? James 2:14 RSV

You see that faith was active along with his works, and faith was completed by works . . . For as the body apart from the spirit is dead, so faith apart from works is dead. James 2:22, 26 RSV

Every one who believes that Jesus is the Christ is a child of God. 1 John 5:1 RSV

For whatever is born of God overcomes the world; and this is the victory that overcomes the world, our faith. 1 John 5:4 RSV

See also *Conversion; Repentance; Righteousness.*

'I will say of the Lord, "He is my refuge and my fortress."'

Faithfulness, faithful

'Know therefore that the Lord your God is God, the faithful God who keeps covenant and steadfast love with those who love him and keep his commandments, to a thousand generations.' Deuteronomy 7:9 RSV

Many a man proclaims his own loyalty, but a faithful man who can find? Proverbs 20:6 RSV

The steadfast love of the Lord never ceases, his mercies never come to an end; they are new every morning; great is thy faithfulness. Lamentations 3:22-23 RSV

'Who then is the faithful and wise servant, whom his master has set over his household, to give them their food at the proper time?' Matthew 24:45 RSV

His lord said unto him, Well done, thou good and faithful servant: thou hast been faithful over a few things, I will make thee ruler over many things: enter thou into the joy of thy lord. Matthew 25:21 KJV

'He who is faithful in a very little is faithful also in much; and he who is dishonest in a very little is dishonest also in much.' Luke 16:10 RSV

God is faithful, and he will not let you be tempted beyond your strength, but with the temptation will also provide the way of escape, that you may be able to endure it. 1 Corinthians 10:13 RSV

But the fruit of the Spirit is . . . faithfulness . . . Galatians 5:22 RSV

What you have heard from me before many witnesses entrust to faithful men who will be able to teach others also. 2 Timothy 2:2 RSV

If we are faithless, he remains faithful—for he cannot deny himself. 2 Timothy 2:13 RSV

For this reason he had to be made like his brothers in every way, in order that he might become a merciful and faithful high priest in service to God, and that he might make atonement for the sins of the people. Hebrews 2:17 NIV

Behold, the devil shall cast some of you into prison, that ye may be tried; and ye shall have tribulation ten days: be thou faithful unto death, and I will give thee a crown of life. Revelation 2:10 KJV

See also *Mercy*.

Fall, *the*

Now the serpent was more subtil than any beast of the field which the Lord God had made. And he said unto the woman, Yea, hath God said, Ye shall not eat of every tree of the garden? . . . And the serpent said unto the woman, Ye shall not surely die . . . And when the woman saw that the tree was good for food, and that it was pleasant to the eyes, and a tree to be desired to make one wise, she took of the fruit thereof, and did eat, and gave also unto her husband with her; and he did eat. And the eyes of them both were opened, and they knew that they were naked; and they sewed fig leaves together, and made themselves aprons . . . and Adam and his wife hid themselves from the presence of the Lord God amongst the trees of the garden. Genesis 3:1, 4, 6-8 KJV

Unto the woman he said, I will greatly multiply thy sorrow and thy conception; in sorrow thou shalt bring forth children; and thy desire shall be to thy husband, and he shall rule over thee. And unto Adam he said, Because thou hast hearkened unto the voice of thy wife, and hast eaten of the tree, of which I commanded thee, saying, Thou shalt not eat of it: cursed is the ground for thy sake; in sorrow shalt thou eat of it all the days of thy life . . . in the sweat of thy face shalt thou eat bread, till thou return unto the ground; for out of it wast thou taken: for dust thou art, and unto dust shalt thou return. Genesis 3:16-19 KJV

As by one man sin entered into the world, and death by sin . . . so death passed upon all men, for that all have sinned. Romans 5:12 KJV

But the free gift is not like the trespass. For if many died through one man's trespass, much more have the grace of God and the free gift in the grace of that one man Jesus Christ abounded for many. And the free gift is not like the effect of that one man's sin. For the judgment following one trespass brought condemnation, but the free gift following many trespasses brings justification. If, because of one man's trespass, death reigned through that one man, much more will those who receive the abundance of grace and the free gift of righteousness reign in life through the one man Jesus Christ. Then as one man's trespass led to condemnation for all men, so one man's act of righteousness leads to acquittal and life for all men. For as by one man's disobedience many were made sinners, so by one man's obedience many will be made righteous. Romans 5:15-19 RSV

See also *Adam; Eden, garden of.*

Falling away

The backslider in heart shall be filled with his own ways: and a good man shall be satisfied from himself. Proverbs 14:14 KJV

'But they did not obey or incline their ear, but walked in their own counsels and the stubbornness of their evil hearts, and went backward and not forward.' Jeremiah 7:24 RSV

'Though our iniquities testify against us, act, O Lord, for thy name's sake; for our backslidings are many, we have sinned against thee.' Jeremiah 14:7 RSV

'You, like your ancestors before you, have turned away from my laws and have not kept them. Turn back to me, and I will turn to you. But you ask, "What must we do to turn back to you?"' Malachi 3:7 GNB

Then Jesus said to them, 'You will all fall away because of me this night; for it is written, "I will strike the shepherd, and the sheep of the flock will be scattered."' Matthew 26:31 RSV

'If a man does not abide in me, he is cast forth as a branch and withers; and the branches are gathered, thrown into the fire and burned.' John 15:6 RSV

'I have said all this to you to keep you from falling away.' John 16:1 RSV

Now the Spirit expressly says that in later times some will depart from the faith by giving heed to deceitful spirits and doctrines of demons. 1 Timothy 4:1 RSV

For how can those who abandon their faith be brought back to repent again? They were once in God's light; they tasted heaven's gift and received their share of the Holy Spirit; they knew from experience that God's word is good, and they had felt the powers of the coming age. And then they abandoned their faith! It is impossible to bring them back to repent again, because they are again crucifying the Son of God and exposing him to public shame. Hebrews 6:4-6 GNB

For if we sin deliberately after receiving the knowledge of the truth, there no longer remains a sacrifice for sins. Hebrews 10:26 RSV

See also *Rejection; Repentance; Unbelief.*

Family

Husbands and wives

Therefore shall a man leave his father and his mother, and shall cleave unto his wife: and they shall be one flesh. Genesis 2:24 KJV

A good wife is the crown of her husband, but she who brings shame is like rottenness in his bones. Proverbs 12:4 RSV

He who finds a wife finds a good thing, and obtains favour from the Lord. Proverbs 18:22 RSV

A good wife who can find? She is far more precious than jewels. Proverbs 31:10 RSV

For the unbelieving husband is consecrated through his wife, and the unbelieving wife is consecrated through her husband. Otherwise, your children would be unclean, but as it is they are holy. 1 Corinthians 7:14 RSV

But I want you to understand that the head of every man is Christ, the head of a woman is her husband, and the head of Christ is God. 1 Corinthians 11:3 RSV

Be subject to one another out of reverence for Christ. Wives, be subject to your husbands, as to the Lord. For the husband is the head of the wife as Christ is the head of the church, his body, and is himself its Saviour. As the church is subject to Christ, so let wives also be subject in everything to their husbands. Husbands, love your wives, as Christ loved the church and gave himself up for her ... Even so husbands should love their wives as their own bodies. He who loves his wife loves himself. Ephesians 5:21-25, 28 RSV

In the same way you wives must submit to your husbands, so that if any of them do not believe God's word, your conduct will win them over to believe. It will not be necessary for you to say a word, because they will see how pure and reverent your conduct is. You should not use outward aids to make yourselves beautiful, such as the way you do your hair, or the jewellery you put on, or the dresses you wear. Instead, your beauty should consist of your true inner self, the ageless beauty of a gentle and quiet spirit, which is of the greatest value in God's sight. For the devout women of the past who placed their hope in God used to make themselves beautiful by submitting to their husbands. Sarah was like that; she obeyed Abraham and called him her master. You are now her daughters if you do good and are not afraid of anything. In the same way you husbands must live with your wives with the proper understanding that they are the weaker sex. Treat them with respect, because they also will receive, together with you, God's gift of life. Do this so that nothing will interfere with your prayers. 1 Peter 3:1-7 GNB

See also *Marriage*.

Children and the whole family

Honour thy father and thy mother: that thy days may be long upon the land which the Lord thy God giveth thee. Exodus 20:12 KJV

'You shall teach them [the words the Lord commands] diligently to your children, and shall talk of them when you sit in your house, and when you walk by the way, and when you lie down, and when you rise.' Deuteronomy 6:7 RSV

[Joshua] But as for me and my house, we will serve the Lord. Joshua 24:15 KJV

She [Hannah] vowed a vow and said, 'O Lord of hosts, if thou wilt indeed look on the affliction of thy maidservant, and remember me, and not forget thy maidservant, but wilt give to thy maidservant a son, then I will give him to the Lord all the days of his life, and no razor shall touch his head.' 1 Samuel 1:11 RSV

Lo, children are an heritage of the Lord: and the fruit of the womb is his reward. As arrows are in the hand of a mighty man; so are children of the youth. Happy is the man that hath his quiver full of them: they shall not be ashamed, but they shall speak with the enemies in the gate. Psalm 127:3-5 KJV

A father who spares the rod hates his son, but one who loves him keeps him in order. Proverbs 13:24 NEB

Children's children are a crown to the aged, and parents are the pride of their children. Proverbs 17:6 NIV

Train up a child in the way he should go: and when he is old, he will not depart from it. Proverbs 22:6 KJV

'Whoever loves his father or mother more than me is not fit to be my disciple; whoever loves his son or daughter more than me is not fit to be my disciple.' Matthew 10:37 GNB

'But you teach that if a person has something he could use to help his father or mother, but says, "This is

Corban" (which means, it belongs to God), he is excused from helping his father or mother.' Mark 7:11-12 GNB

And they brought young children to him, that he should touch them: and his disciples rebuked those that brought them. But when Jesus saw it, he was much displeased, and said unto them, Suffer the little children to come unto me, and forbid them not: for of such is the kingdom of God. Verily I say unto you, Whosoever shall not receive the kingdom of God as a little child, he shall not enter therein. And he took them up in his arms, put his hands upon them, and blessed them. Mark 10:13-16 KJV

[Jesus and his parents] And he went down with them and came to Nazareth, and was obedient to them; and his mother kept all these things in her heart. And Jesus increased in wisdom and in stature, and in favour with God and man. Luke 2:51-52 RSV

Children, obey your parents in the Lord, for this is right. 'Honour your father and mother' (this is the first commandment with a promise). Ephesians 6:1-2 RSV

Fathers, do not provoke your children to anger, but bring them up in the discipline and instruction of the Lord. Ephesians 6:4 RSV

Children, obey your parents in everything, for this pleases the Lord. Colossians 3:20 RSV

[A church leader] must be able to manage his own family well and make his children obey him with all respect. 1 Timothy 3:4 GNB

If any one does not provide for his relatives, and especially for his own family, he has disowned the faith and is worse than an unbeliever. 1 Timothy 5:8 RSV

See also *Teachers and teaching.*

Fasting

'The tenth day of this seventh month is the Day of Atonement. Hold a sacred assembly and deny yourselves, and present an offering made to the Lord by fire.' Leviticus 23:27 NIV

Then David took hold of his clothes, and rent them; and so did all the men who were with him; and they mourned and wept and fasted until evening for Saul and for Jonathan his son and for the people of the Lord and for the house of Israel, because they had fallen by the sword. 2 Samuel 1:11-12 RSV

The people ask, 'Why should we fast if the Lord never notices? Why should we go without food if he pays no attention?' The Lord says to them, 'The truth is that at the same time as you fast, you pursue your own interests and oppress your workers. Your fasting makes you violent, and you quarrel and fight. Do you think this kind of fasting will make me listen to your prayers? . . . The kind of fasting I want is this: Remove the chains of oppression and the yoke of injustice, and let the oppressed go free.' Isaiah 58:3-4, 6 GNB

'Yet even now,' says the Lord, 'return to me with all your heart, with fasting, with weeping, and with mourning; and rend your hearts and not your garments.' Joel 2:12-13 RSV

He [Jesus] fasted for forty days and forty nights, after which he was very hungry. Matthew 4:2 JB

'Suffer little children to come unto me, and forbid them not.'

'And when you fast, do not put on a sad face as the hypocrites do. They neglect their appearance so that everyone will see that they are fasting. I assure you, they have already been paid in full. When you go without food, wash your face and comb your hair, so that others cannot know that you are fasting—only your Father, who is unseen, will know. And your Father, who sees what you do in private, will reward you.' Matthew 6:16-18 GNB

Jesus answered, 'Do you expect the guests at a wedding party to be sad as long as the bridegroom is with them? Of course not! But the day will come when the bridegroom will be taken away from them, and then they will fast.' Matthew 9:15 GNB

[A Pharisee] '"I fast twice a week, I give tithes of all that I get."' Luke 18:12 RSV

While they were worshipping the Lord and fasting, the Holy Spirit said, 'Set apart for me Barnabas and Saul for the work to which I have called them.' Then after fasting and praying they laid their hands on them and sent them off. Acts 13:2-3 RSV

Father

See *Family; God, Names, titles and descriptions of God.*

Fear

And he [Adam] said, I heard thy voice in the garden, and I was afraid, because I was naked; and I hid myself. Genesis 3:10 KJV

And Moses hid his face; for he was afraid to look upon God. Exodus 3:6 KJV

And the hearts of the people melted, and became as water. Joshua 7:5 RSV

Fear and trembling come upon me, and horror overwhelms me. Psalm 55:5 RSV

'So do not be afraid of people. Whatever is now covered up will be uncovered, and every secret will be made known.' Matthew 10:26 GNB

'Do not be afraid of those who kill the body but cannot kill the soul; rather be afraid of God, who can destroy both body and soul in hell.' Matthew 10:28, 31 GNB

He said to them, 'Why are you afraid? Have you no faith?' Mark 4:40 RSV

'People will faint from fear as they wait for what is coming over the whole earth, for the powers in space will be driven from their courses.' Luke 21:26 GNB

Yet for fear of the Jews no one spoke openly of him. John 7:13 RSV

Christian fellowship: secrets of success

accept one another
Romans 15:7

bear one another's **burdens**
Galatians 6:2

be **concerned** for one another
Hebrews 10:24

confess your sins to one another
James 5:16

encourage one another
Hebrews 10:25

forgive one another
Ephesians 4:32

have fellowship with one another
1 John 1:7

honour one another
Romans 12:10

live in harmony with one another
Romans 15:5

love one another
Romans 12:10

offer hospitality to one another
1 Peter 4:9

pray for one another
James 5:16

serve one another
Galatians 5:13

stir up one another to love and good works
Hebrews 10:24

be **subject to** one another
Ephesians 5:21

teach and admonish one another
Colossians 3:16

For you did not receive the spirit of slavery to fall back into fear, but you have received the spirit of sonship. Romans 8:15 RSV

And I was with you in weakness and in much fear and trembling. 1 Corinthians 2:3 RSV

There is no fear in love, but perfect love casts out fear. For fear has to do with punishment, and he who fears is not perfected in love. 1 John 4:18 RSV

See also *Comfort*.

Fear of God

See *Reverence*.

Fellowship

And they continued stedfastly in the apostles' doctrine and fellowship, and in breaking of bread, and in prayers. Acts 2:42 KJV

And all who believed were together and had all things in common. Acts 2:44 RSV

God is faithful, by whom you were called into the fellowship of his Son, Jesus Christ our Lord. 1 Corinthians 1:9 RSV

The cup of blessing which we bless, is it not a participation in the blood of Christ? The bread which we break, is it not a participation in the body of Christ? Because there is one bread, we who are many are one body, for we all partake of the one bread. 1 Corinthians 10:16-17 RSV

The grace of the Lord Jesus Christ, the love of God, and the fellowship of the Holy Spirit be with you all. 2 Corinthians 13:13 GNB

James and Cephas and John, who were reputed to be pillars, gave to me and Barnabas the right hand of fellowship, that we should go to the Gentiles and they to the circumcised. Galatians 2:9 RSV

Your fellowship in the gospel. Philippians 1:5 KJV

No church entered into partnership with me in giving and receiving except you only. Philippians 4:15 RSV

But rejoice in so far as you share Christ's sufferings, that you may also rejoice and be glad when his glory is revealed. 1 Peter 4:13 RSV

That which we have seen and heard declare we unto you, that ye also may have fellowship with us: and truly our fellowship is with the Father, and with his Son Jesus Christ. 1 John 1:3 KJV

If we say we have fellowship with him while we walk in darkness, we lie and do not live according to the truth; but if we walk in the light, as he is in the light, we have fellowship with one another, and the blood of Jesus his Son cleanses us from all sin. 1 John 1:6-7 RSV

See also *Love; Unity*.

Fool, foolish

'Please, don't pay any attention to Nabal, that good-for-nothing! He is exactly what his name means—a fool!' 1 Samuel 25:25 GNB

The fool hath said in his heart, There is no God. Psalm 14:1 KJV

The way of a fool is right in his own eyes, but a wise man listens to advice. Proverbs 12:15 RSV

As a dog returneth to his vomit, so a fool returneth to his folly. Proverbs 26:11 KJV

A fool speaks foolishly and thinks up evil things to do. What he does and what he says are an insult to the Lord, and he never feeds the hungry or gives thirsty people anything to drink. Isaiah 32:6 GNB

'And every one who hears these words of mine and does not do them will be like a foolish man who built his house upon the sand.' Matthew 7:26 RSV

But God said unto him, Thou fool, this night thy soul shall be required of thee: then whose shall those things be, which thou hast provided? Luke 12:20 KJV

Claiming to be wise, they became fools, and exchanged the glory of the immortal God for images resembling mortal man or birds or animals or reptiles. Romans 1:22-23 RSV

For the word of the cross is folly to those who are perishing, but to us who are being saved it is the power of God. 1 Corinthians 1:18 RSV

But God hath chosen the foolish things of the world to confound the wise; and God hath chosen the weak things of the world to confound the things which are mighty. 1 Corinthians 1:27 KJV

The man without the Spirit does not accept the things that come from the Spirit of God, for they are foolishness to him and he cannot understand them, because they are spiritually discerned. 1 Corinthians 2:14 NIV

See also *Wisdom*.

Forgiveness

Blessed is he whose transgression is forgiven, whose sin is covered. Blessed is the man to whom the Lord imputes no iniquity, and in whose spirit there is no deceit. Psalm 32:1-2 RSV

Have mercy upon me, O God, according to thy lovingkindness: according unto the multitude of thy tender mercies blot out my transgressions. Wash me throughly from mine iniquity, and cleanse me from my sin. Psalm 51:1-2 KJV

As far as the east is from the west, so far hath he removed our transgressions from us. Psalm 103:12 KJV

If thou, O Lord, shouldst mark iniquities, Lord, who could stand? But there is forgiveness with thee, that thou mayest be feared. Psalm 130:3-4 RSV

'And no longer shall each man teach his neighbour and each his brother, saying, "Know the Lord," for they shall all know me, from the least of them to the greatest, says the Lord; for I will forgive their iniquity, and I will remember their sin no more.' Jeremiah 31:34 RSV

Who is a God like thee, pardoning iniquity and passing over transgression for the remnant of his inheritance? Micah 7:18 RSV

And forgive us our trespasses, as we forgive them that trespass against us. Matthew 6:12 BCP

'If you forgive others the wrongs they have done to you, your Father in heaven will also forgive you. But if you do not forgive others, then your Father will not forgive the wrongs you have done.' Matthew 6:14-15 GNB

'But that you may know that the Son of man has authority on earth to forgive sins'—he then said to the paralytic—'Rise, take up your bed and go home.' Matthew 9:6 RSV

'Therefore I tell you, every sin and blasphemy will be forgiven men, but the blasphemy against the Spirit will not be forgiven.' Matthew 12:31 RSV

And Peter said to them, 'Repent, and be baptized every one of you in the name of Jesus Christ for the forgiveness of your sins; and you shall receive the gift of the Holy Spirit.' Acts 2:38 RSV

'To him all the prophets bear witness that every one who believes in him receives forgiveness of sins through his name.' Acts 10:43 RSV

In him [Jesus Christ] we have redemption through his blood, the forgiveness of our trespasses, according to the riches of his grace. Ephesians 1:7 RSV

Be kind to one another, tenderhearted, forgiving one another, as God in Christ forgave you. Ephesians 4:32 RSV

Indeed, under the law almost everything is purified with blood, and without the shedding of blood there is no forgiveness of sins. Hebrews 9:22 RSV

If we confess our sins, he is faithful and just and will forgive our sins and cleanse us from all unrighteousness. 1 John 1:9 RSV

See also *Atonement; Repentance; Sin.*

Freedom, free

The Spirit of the Lord God is upon me; because the Lord hath anointed me to preach good tidings unto the meek; he hath sent me to bind up the brokenhearted, to proclaim liberty to the captives, and the opening of the prison to them that are bound ... Isaiah 61:1 KJV

Jesus then said to the Jews who had believed in him, 'If you continue in my word, you are truly my disciples, and you will know the truth, and the truth will make you free ... Truly, truly, I say to you, every one who commits sin is a slave to sin. The slave does not continue in the house for ever; the son continues for ever. So if the Son makes you free, you will be free indeed.' John 8:31-32, 34-36 RSV

But now that you have been set free from sin and have become slaves to God, the benefit you reap leads to holiness, and the result is eternal life. Romans 6:22 NIV

For the law of the Spirit of life in Christ Jesus has set me free from the law of sin and death. For God has done what the law, weakened by the flesh, could not do: sending his own Son in the likeness of sinful flesh and for sin, he condemned sin in the flesh, in order that the just requirement of the law might be fulfilled in us, who walk not according to the flesh but according to the Spirit. Romans 8:2-4 RSV

The creation itself will be set free from its bondage to decay and obtain the glorious liberty of the children of God. Romans 8:21 RSV

Be careful, however, not to let your freedom of action make those who are weak in the faith fall into sin. 1 Corinthians 8:9 GNB

Now the Lord is the Spirit, and where the Spirit of the Lord is, there is freedom. And we all, with unveiled face, beholding the glory of the Lord, are being changed into his likeness from one degree of glory to another; for this comes from the Lord who is the Spirit. 2 Corinthians 3:17-18 RSV

For freedom Christ has set us free; stand fast therefore, and do not submit again to a yoke of slavery. Galatians 5:1 RSV

As for you, my brothers, you are called to be free. But do not let this freedom become an excuse for letting your physical desires control you. Instead, let love make you serve one another. Galatians 5:13 GNB

Since therefore the children share in flesh and blood, he himself likewise partook of the same nature, that through death he might destroy him who has the power of death, that is, the devil, and deliver all those who through fear of death were subject to lifelong bondage. Hebrews 2:14-15 RSV

Friends

Thus the Lord used to speak to Moses face to face, as a man speaks to his friend. Exodus 33:11 RSV

The friendship of the Lord is for those who fear him, and he makes known to them his covenant. Psalm 25:14 RSV

A friend loves at all times, and a brother is born for adversity. Proverbs 17:17 RSV

There are friends who pretend to be friends, but there is a friend who sticks closer than a brother. Proverbs 18:24 RSV

Faithful are the wounds of a friend; but the kisses of an enemy are deceitful. Proverbs 27:6 KJV

'The Son of man came eating and drinking, and they say, "Behold, a glutton and a drunkard, a friend of tax collectors and sinners!" Yet wisdom is justified by her deeds.' Matthew 11:19 RSV

Jesus said to him [Judas], 'Friend, why are you here?' Matthew 26:50 RSV

'Greater love has no man than this, that a man lay down his life for his friends. You are my friends if you do what I command you. No longer do I call you servants, for the servant does not know what his master is doing; but I have called you friends, for all that I have heard from my Father I have made known to you.' John 15:13-15 RSV

The scripture was fulfilled which says,

'Abraham believed God, and it was reckoned to him as righteousness'; and he was called the friend of God. James 2:23 RSV

Fruit

He will bless the fruit of your womb. Deuteronomy 7:13 NIV

[John the Baptist to the Pharisees and Sadducees] 'Bear fruit that befits repentance.' Matthew 3:8 RSV

'You will know them by their fruits.' Matthew 7:16 RSV

'I am the vine, you are the branches. He who abides in me, and I in him, he it is that bears much fruit, for apart from me you can do nothing . . . By this my Father is glorified, that you bear much fruit, and so prove to be my disciples.' John 15:5, 8 RSV

'You did not choose me, but I chose you and appointed you that you should go and bear fruit and that your fruit should abide.' John 15:16 RSV

But the fruit of the Spirit is love, joy, peace, patience, kindness, goodness, faithfulness, gentleness, self-control; against such there is no law. Galatians 5:22-23 RSV

Fullness

The earth is the Lord's and the fullness thereof, the world and those who dwell therein. Psalm 24:1 RSV

And the Word was made flesh, and dwelt among us, (and we beheld his glory, the glory as of the only begotten of the Father,) full of grace and truth. John 1:14 KJV

And from his fullness have we all received, grace upon grace. John 1:16 RSV

[The church] which is his body, the fullness of him that filleth all in all. Ephesians 1:23 KJV

[Paul's prayer] That you may be filled with all the fullness of God. Ephesians 3:19 RSV

And be not drunk with wine, wherein is excess; but be filled with the Spirit. Ephesians 5:18 KJV

For in him [Christ] the whole fullness of deity dwells bodily, and you have come to fullness of life in him. Colossians 2:9-10 RSV

Gentiles

Ask of me, and I shall give thee the heathen for thine inheritance, and the uttermost parts of the earth for thy possession. Psalm 2:8 KJV

And in that day there shall be a root of Jesse, which shall stand for an ensign of the people; to it shall the Gentiles seek: and his rest shall be glorious. Isaiah 11:10 KJV

A light to lighten the Gentiles, and to be the glory of thy people Israel. Luke 2:32 BCP

The Lord said to him [Ananias], 'Go, because I have chosen him [Paul] to serve me, to make my name known to Gentiles and kings and to the people of Israel.' Acts 9:15 GNB

And the believers from among the circumcised who came with Peter were amazed, because the gift of the Holy Spirit had been poured out even on the Gentiles. Acts 10:45 RSV

And they glorified God, saying, 'Then to the Gentiles also God has granted repentance unto life.' Acts 11:18 RSV

When Gentiles who have not the law do by nature what the law requires, they are a law to themselves, even though they do not have the law. Romans 2:14 RSV

There is neither Jew nor Greek, there is neither bond nor free, there is neither male nor female: for ye are all one in Christ Jesus. Galatians 3:28 KJV

Therefore remember that at one time you Gentiles in the flesh, called the uncircumcision by what is called the circumcision, which is made in the flesh by hands—remember that you were at that time separated from Christ, alienated from the commonwealth of Israel, and strangers to the covenants of promise, having no hope and without God in the world. But now in Christ Jesus you who once were far off have been brought near in the blood of Christ. For he is our peace, who has made us both one, and has broken down the dividing wall of hostility, by abolishing in his flesh the law of commandments and ordinances, that he might create in himself one new man in place of the two, so making peace, and might reconcile us both to God in one body through the cross, thereby bringing the hostility to an end. And he came and preached peace to you who were far off and peace to those who were near; for through him we both have access in one Spirit to the Father. So then you are no longer strangers and sojourners, but you are fellow citizens with the saints and members of the household of God. Ephesians 2:11-19 RSV

After this I looked, and behold, a great multitude which no man could number, from every nation, from all tribes and peoples and tongues, standing before the throne and before the Lamb, clothed in white robes, with palm branches in their hands . . . Revelation 7:9 RSV

Gentleness

'Take my yoke upon you, and learn from me; for I am gentle and lowly in heart, and you will find rest for your souls.' Matthew 11:29 RSV

I, Paul, myself entreat you, by the meekness and gentleness of Christ—I who am humble when face to face with you, but bold to you when I am away!' 2 Corinthians 10:1 RSV

But the fruit of the Spirit is . . . gentleness . . . Galatians 5:22-23 RSV

Brethren, if a man is overtaken in any trespass, you who are spiritual should restore him in a spirit of gentleness. Galatians 6:1 RSV

But we were gentle among you, like a nurse taking care of her children. 1 Thessalonians 2:7 RSV

And the servant of the Lord must not strive; but be gentle unto all men, apt to teach, patient. 2 Timothy 2:24 KJV

But the wisdom from above is first pure, then peaceable, gentle, open to reason, full of mercy and good fruits, without uncertainty or insincerity. James 3:17 RSV

[Peter's instructions to wives] Your beauty should consist of your true inner self, the ageless beauty of a gentle and quiet spirit, which is of the greatest value in God's sight. 1 Peter 3:4 GNB

Gift

For God so loved the world, that he

gave his only begotten Son, that whosoever believeth in him should not perish, but have everlasting life. John 3:16 KJV

And Peter said to them, 'Repent, and be baptized every one of you in the name of Jesus Christ for the forgiveness of your sins; and you shall receive the gift of the Holy Spirit.' Acts 2:38 RSV

'God exalted him at his right hand as Leader and Saviour, to give repentance to Israel and forgiveness of sins.' Acts 5:31 RSV

For the wages of sin is death; but the gift of God is eternal life through Jesus Christ our Lord. Romans 6:23 KJV

We have different gifts, according to the grace given us. Romans 12:6 NIV

Now there are varieties of gifts, but the same Spirit; and there are varieties of service, but the same Lord; and there are varieties of working, but it is the same God who inspires them all in every one. To each is given the manifestation of the Spirit for the common good ... All these are inspired by one and the same Spirit, who apportions to each one individually as he wills. 1 Corinthians 12:4-7, 11 RSV

Make love your aim, and earnestly desire the spiritual gifts, especially that you may prophesy. 1 Corinthians 14:1 RSV

Thanks be to God for his inexpressible gift! 2 Corinthians 9:15 RSV

For by grace are ye saved through faith; and that not of yourselves: it is the gift of God. Ephesians 2:8 KJV

Do not neglect the gift you have, which was given you by prophetic utterance when the council of elders laid their hands upon you. 1 Timothy 4:14 RSV

Every good gift and every perfect gift is from above, and cometh down from the Father of lights, with whom is no variableness, neither shadow of turning. James 1:17 KJV

Giving

[Melchizedek] 'Blessed be Abram by God Most High, maker of heaven and earth; and blessed be God Most High, who has delivered your enemies into your hand!' And Abram gave him a tenth of everything. Genesis 14:20 RSV

For all things come of thee, and of thine own have we given thee. 1 Chronicles 29:14 KJV

'Bring the full tithes into the storehouse, that there may be food in my house; and thereby put me to the test, says the Lord of hosts, if I will not open the windows of heaven for you and pour down for you an overflowing blessing.' Malachi 3:10 RSV

'So when you give something to a needy person, do not make a big show of it, as the hypocrites do in the houses of worship and on the streets. They do it so that people will praise them ... But when you help a needy person, do it in such a way that even your closest friend will not know about it.' Matthew 6:2-3 GNB

And a poor widow came, and put in two copper coins, which make a penny. And he called his disciples to him, and said to them, 'Truly, I say to you, this poor widow has put in more than all those who are contributing to the treasury. For they all contributed out of their abundance; but she out of her poverty has put in everything she had, her whole living.' Mark 12:42-44 RSV

'Give, and it will be given to you; good measure, pressed down, shaken together, running over, will be put into your lap. For the measure you give will be the measure you get back.' Luke 6:38 RSV

On the first day of every week, each of you is to put something aside and store it up, as he may prosper, so that contributions need not be made when I come. 1 Corinthians 16:2 RSV

We want you to know, brethren, about the grace of God which has been shown in the churches of Macedonia, for in a severe test of affliction, their abundance of joy and their extreme poverty have overflowed in a wealth of liberality on their part. For they gave according to their means, as I can testify, and beyond their means, of their own free will, begging us earnestly for the favour of taking part in the relief of the saints—and this, not as we expected, but first they gave themselves to the Lord and to us by the will of God. 2 Corinthians 8:1-5 RSV

Each one must do as he has made up his mind, not reluctantly or under compulsion, for God loves a cheerful giver. 2 Corinthians 9:7 RSV

See also *Stewardship*.

Glory

Moses said, 'I pray thee, show me thy glory.' Exodus 33:18 RSV

But as truly as I live, all the earth shall

be filled with the glory of the Lord.
Numbers 14:21 KJV

She [the wife of Phinehas] named the child
Ichabod, saying, 'The glory has
departed from Israel!' because the ark
of God had been captured and because
of her father-in-law and her husband.
1 Samuel 4:21 RSV

And he [Jesus] was transfigured before
them, and his face shone like the sun,
and his garments became white as light.
Matthew 17:2 RSV

'For whoever is ashamed of me and of
my words in this adulterous and sinful
generation, of him will the Son of man
also be ashamed, when he comes in the
glory of his Father with the holy
angels.' Mark 8:38 RSV

Jesus performed this first miracle in
Cana in Galilee; there he revealed his
glory, and his disciples believed in him.
John 2:11 GNB

'And now, Father, glorify thou me in
thy own presence with the glory which I
had with thee before the world was
made.' John 17:5 RSV

For all have sinned, and come short of
the glory of God. Romans 3:23 KJV

I consider that the sufferings of this
present time are not worth comparing
with the glory that is to be revealed to
us. Romans 8:18 RSV

So, whether you eat or drink, or
whatever you do, do all to the glory of
God. 1 Corinthians 10:31 RSV

For a man ought not to cover his head,
since he is the image and glory of God;
but woman is the glory of man.
1 Corinthians 11:7 RSV

And we all, with unveiled face,
beholding the glory of the Lord, are
being changed into his likeness from
one degree of glory to another; for this
comes from the Lord who is the Spirit.
2 Corinthians 3:18 RSV

The Son is the radiance of God's glory
and the exact representation of his
being, sustaining all things by his
powerful word. Hebrews 1:3 NIV

God

All-knowing

O Lord, thou hast searched me and
known me! Thou knowest when I sit
down and when I rise up; thou
discernest my thoughts from afar. Thou
searchest out my path and my lying
down, and art acquainted with all my
ways. Even before a word is on my
tongue, lo, O Lord, thou knowest it

altogether. Thou dost beset me behind
and before, and layest thy hand upon
me. Such knowledge is too wonderful
for me; it is high, I cannot attain it.
Psalm 139:1-6 RSV

O the depth of the riches both of the
wisdom and knowledge of God! how
unsearchable are his judgments, and
his ways past finding out! Romans
11:33 KJV

Before him no creature is hidden, but
all are open and laid bare to the eyes of
him with whom we have to do.
Hebrews 4:13 RSV

All-present

Whither shall I go from thy Spirit? Or
whither shall I flee from thy presence?
If I ascend to heaven, thou art there! If
I make my bed in Sheol, thou art there!
If I take the wings of the morning and
dwell in the uttermost parts of the sea,
even there thy hand shall lead me, and
thy right hand shall hold me. Psalm
139:7-10 RSV

Almighty

[Job to the Lord] 'I know that thou canst
do all things, and that no purpose of
thine can be thwarted.' Job 42:2 RSV

'For with God nothing will be
impossible.' Luke 1:37 RSV

Alleluia: for the Lord God omnipotent
reigneth. Revelation 19:6 KJV

Eternal

Before the mountains were brought
forth, or ever thou hadst formed the
earth and the world, from everlasting
to everlasting thou art God. Psalm 90:2
RSV

Now unto the King eternal, immortal,
invisible, the only wise God, be honour
and glory for ever and ever. Amen.
1 Timothy 1:17 KJV

Faithful

'Know therefore that the Lord your
God is God, the faithful God who
keeps covenant and steadfast love with
those who love him and keep his
commandments, to a thousand
generations.' Deuteronomy 7:9 RSV

The steadfast love of the Lord never
ceases, his mercies never come to an
end; they are new every morning; great
is thy faithfulness. Lamentations
3:22-23 RSV

God is faithful, by whom you were
called into the fellowship of his Son,
Jesus Christ our Lord. 1 Corinthians 1:9
RSV

Names, titles and descriptions of God

Creator
Isaiah 40:28

Father
Malachi 2:10; Matthew 5:45, 6:9; John
14:6, 20:17; Romans 8:15

Father of lights
James 1:17

God almighty
Genesis 17:1

God most high'
Genesis 14:18

God of all flesh
Jeremiah 32:27

God of heaven
Nehemiah 2:4

God of hosts
Psalm 80:7, 14

God of Israel
Joshua 24:2

Holy One
Job 6:10

Holy One of Israel
Isaiah 1:4

I am
Exodus 3:14

Judge
Genesis 18:25

King
Jeremiah 10:7

King of kings
1 Timothy 6:15

Lord (Jehovah)
Exodus 6:3; Malachi 3:6

Lord of hosts
Jeremiah 32:18

Lord of lords
1 Timothy 6:15

Lord will provide
(Jehovah jireh) Genesis 22:14

Saviour
Isaiah 43:3

Good

O taste and see that the Lord is good!
Happy is the man who takes refuge in
him! Psalm 34:8 RSV

O give thanks to the Lord, for he is
good, for his steadfast love endures for
ever. Psalm 136:1 RSV

And Jesus said to him, 'Why do you
call me good? No one is good but God
alone.' Mark 10:18 RSV

Or do you presume upon the riches of
his kindness and forbearance and
patience? Do you not know that God's
kindness is meant to lead you to
repentance? Romans 2:4 RSV

Holy

'Holy, holy, holy is the Lord of hosts;
the whole earth is full of his glory.'
Isaiah 6:3 RSV

Thou who art of purer eyes than to
behold evil and canst not look on
wrong. Habakkuk 1:13 RSV

'Who shall not fear and glorify thy
name, O Lord? For thou alone art
holy. All nations shall come and
worship thee, for thy judgments have
been revealed.' Revelation 15:4 RSV

Infinite

[Solomon's prayer] 'Behold, heaven and
the highest heaven cannot contain thee;
how much less this house which I have
built!' 1 Kings 8:27 RSV

For thus saith the high and lofty One
that inhabiteth eternity, whose name is
Holy; I dwell in the high and holy
place, with him also that is of a contrite
and humble spirit. Isaiah 57:15 KJV

'Can a man hide himself in secret places
so that I cannot see him? says the Lord.
Do I not fill heaven and earth? says the
Lord.' Jeremiah 23:24 RSV

Just

[Abraham pleading for Sodom] 'Far be it
from thee to do such a thing, to slay the
righteous with the wicked, so that the
righteous fare as the wicked! Far be
that from thee! Shall not the Judge of
all the earth do right?' Genesis 18:25
RSV

'The Lord is your mighty defender,
perfect and just in all his ways; Your
God is faithful and true; he does what is
right and fair.' Deuteronomy 32:4 GNB

He has fixed a day on which he will

...dge the world in righteousness by a man whom he has appointed, and of this he has given assurance to all men by raising him from the dead.' Acts 17:31 RSV

If we confess our sins, he is faithful and just and will forgive our sins and cleanse us from all unrighteousness. 1 John 1:9 RSV

Loving

'It was not because you were more in number than any other people that the Lord set his love upon you and chose you, for you were the fewest of all peoples; but it is because the Lord loves you, and is keeping the oath which he swore to your fathers, that the Lord has brought you out with a mighty hand, and redeemed you from the house of bondage, from the hand of Pharaoh king of Egypt. Know therefore that the Lord your God is God, the faithful God who keeps covenant and steadfast love with those who love him and keep his commandments, to a thousand generations.' Deuteronomy 7:7-9 RSV

For God so loved the world, that he gave his only begotten Son, that whosoever believeth in him should not perish, but have everlasting life. John 3:16 KJV

Herein is love, not that we loved God, but that he loved us, and sent his Son to be the propitiation for our sins. 1 John 4:10 KJV

Merciful

The Lord passed before him, and proclaimed, 'The Lord, the Lord, a God merciful and gracious, slow to anger, and abounding in steadfast love and faithfulness, keeping steadfast love for thousands, forgiving iniquity and transgression and sin, but who will by no means clear the guilty, visiting the iniquity of the fathers upon the children and the children's children, to the third and the fourth generation.' Exodus 34:6-7 RSV

[The Lord] who crowneth thee with lovingkindness and tender mercies. Psalm 103:4 KJV

But because of his great love for us, God, who is rich in mercy, made us alive with Christ even when we were dead in transgressions—it is by grace you have been saved. Ephesians 2:4-5 NIV

Self-existent

God said to Moses, 'I am who I am.' Exodus 3:14 RSV

'For as the Father has life in himself, so he has granted the Son to have life in himself.' John 5:26 NIV

Spiritual

'But the hour is coming, and now is, when the true worshippers will worship the Father in spirit and truth, for such the Father seeks to worship him. God is spirit, and those who worship him must worship in spirit and truth.' John 4:23-24 RSV

Unchangeable

'God is not man, that he should lie, or a son of man, that he should repent. Has he said, and will he not do it? Or has he spoken, and will he not fulfil it?' Numbers 23:19 RSV

For I am the Lord, I change not; therefore ye sons of Jacob are not consumed. Malachi 3:6 KJV

Every good gift and every perfect gift is from above, and cometh down from the Father of lights, with whom is no variableness, neither shadow of turning. James 1:17 KJV

Wise

O Lord, how manifold are thy works! In wisdom hast thou made them all: the earth is full of thy riches. Psalm 104:24 KJV

Daniel said: 'Blessed be the name of God for ever and ever, to whom belong wisdom and might.' Daniel 2:20 RSV

Now unto the King eternal, immortal, invisible, the only wise God, be honour and glory for ever and ever. Amen. 1 Timothy 1:17 KJV

See also *Creation; Providence; Sovereignty of God.*

Godless

'The triumph of the wicked is short-lived, the glee of the godless lasts but a moment.' Job 20:5 NEB

What hope is there for godless men in the hour when God demands their life? Job 27:8 GNB

The kings of the earth stand up, and the rulers take counsel together, against the Lord, and against his anointed. Psalm 2:2 BCP

Let the godless be put to shame, because they have subverted me with guile; as for me, I will meditate on thy precepts. Psalm 119:78 RSV

With his mouth the godless man would destroy his neighbour, but by knowledge the righteous are delivered. Proverbs 11:9 RSV

Let the wicked forsake his way, and the unrighteous man his thoughts: and let him return unto the Lord, and he will have mercy upon him; and to our God, for he will abundantly pardon. Isaiah 55:7 KJV

For the wrath of God is revealed from heaven against all ungodliness and unrighteousness of men, who hold the truth in unrighteousness. Romans 1:18 KJV

While we were still weak, at the right time Christ died for the ungodly. Romans 5:6 RSV

See also *Unbeliever*.

Golden rule

See Matthew 7:12.

Good

And God saw every thing that he had made, and, behold, it was very good. Genesis 1:31 KJV

The song was raised, with trumpets and cymbals and other musical instruments, in praise to the Lord, 'For he is good, for his steadfast love endures for ever. 2 Chronicles 5:13 RSV

Do good in thy good pleasure unto Zion: build thou the walls of Jerusalem. Psalm 51:18 KJV

And Jesus said to him, 'Why do you call me good? No one is good but God alone.' Mark 10:18 RSV

'How he [Jesus] went about doing good and healing all that were oppressed by the devil, for God was with him.' Acts 10:38 RSV

So the law is holy, and the commandment is holy and just and good. Romans 7:12 RSV

For I know that nothing good dwells within me, that is, in my flesh. Romans 7:18 RSV

We know that in everything God works for good with those who love him, who are called according to his purpose. Romans 8:28 RSV

And be not conformed to this world: but be ye transformed by the renewing of your mind, that ye may prove what is that good, and acceptable, and perfect, will of God. Romans 12:2 KJV

Let love be genuine; hate what is evil, hold fast to what is good. Romans 12:9 RSV

Do not be overcome by evil, but overcome evil with good. Romans 12:21 RSV

But the fruit of the Spirit is love, joy, peace, patience, kindness, goodness, faithfulness, gentleness, self-control. Galatians 5:22 RSV

For we are his workmanship, created in Christ Jesus unto good works, which God hath before ordained that we should walk in them. Ephesians 2:10 KJV

For everything created by God is good, and nothing is to be rejected if it is received with thanksgiving; for then it is consecrated by the word of God and prayer. 1 Timothy 4:4 RSV

Good Samaritan

See *Jesus Christ, Parables of Jesus*.

Gospel

'And because wickedness is multiplied, most men's love will grow cold. But he who endures to the end will be saved. And this gospel of the kingdom will be preached throughout the whole world, as a testimony to all nations; and then the end will come.' Matthew 24:14 RSV

Now after John was arrested, Jesus came into Galilee, preaching the gospel of God, and saying, 'The time is fulfilled, and the kingdom of God is at hand; repent, and believe in the gospel.' Mark 1:14-15 RSV

And he said to them, 'Go into all the world and preach the gospel to the whole creation.' Mark 16:15 RSV

[Jesus reading the book of Isaiah] 'The Spirit of the Lord is upon me, because he has anointed me to preach good news to the poor. He has sent me to proclaim release to the captives and recovering of sight to the blind, to set at liberty those who are oppressed, to proclaim the acceptable year of the Lord.' And he closed the book, and gave it back to the attendant, and sat down; and the eyes of all in the synagogue were fixed on him. And he began to say to them, 'Today this scripture has been fulfilled in your hearing.' Luke 4:18-21 RSV

'But I do not account my life of any value nor as precious to myself, if only I may accomplish my course and the ministry which I received from the Lord Jesus, to testify to the gospel of the grace of God.' Acts 20:24 RSV

For I am not ashamed of the gospel of Christ: for it is the power of God unto salvation to every one that believeth; to the Jew first, and also to the Greek. For therein is the righteousness of God revealed from faith to faith: as it is written, The just shall live by faith. Romans 1:16-17 KJV

r necessity is laid upon me. Woe to me if I do not preach the gospel!
1 Corinthians 9:16 RSV

And now, my brothers, I must remind you of the gospel that I preached to you; the gospel which you received, on which you have taken your stand.
1 Corinthians 15:1 NEB

For I delivered to you as of first importance what I also received, that Christ died for our sins in accordance with the scriptures, that he was buried, that he was raised on the third day in accordance with the scriptures, and that he appeared to Cephas, then to the twelve. 1 Corinthians 15:3-5 RSV

Even if our gospel is veiled, it is veiled only to those who are perishing. In their case the god of this world has blinded the minds of the unbelievers, to keep them from seeing the light of the gospel of the glory of Christ, who is the likeness of God. 2 Corinthians 4:3-4 RSV

Let me tell you, my brothers, that the gospel I preach is not of human origin. I did not receive it from any man, nor did anyone teach it to me. It was Jesus Christ himself who revealed it to me.
Galatians 1:11-12 GNB

And the scripture, foreseeing that God would justify the Gentiles by faith, preached the gospel beforehand to Abraham, saying, 'In you shall all the nations be blessed.' Galatians 3:8 RSV

[Paul asks for prayer] That utterance may be given unto me, that I may open my mouth boldly, to make known the mystery of the gospel. Ephesians 6:19 KJV

Whatever happens, conduct yourselves in a manner worthy of the gospel of Christ. Then, whether I come and see you or only hear about you in my absence, I will know that you stand firm in one spirit, contending as one man for the faith of the gospel. Philippians 1:27 NIV

The glorious gospel of the blessed God, which was committed to my trust.
1 Timothy 1:11 KJV

Grace

'For you are a people holy to the Lord your God; the Lord your God has chosen you to be a people for his own possession, out of all the peoples that are on the face of the earth. It was not because you were more in number than any other people that the Lord set his love upon you and chose you, for you were the fewest of all peoples; but it is because the Lord loves you, and is keeping the oath which he swore to your fathers, that the Lord has brought you out with a mighty hand, and redeemed you from the house of bondage.' Deuteronomy 7:6-8 RSV

And the Word was made flesh, and dwelt among us, (and we beheld his glory, the glory as of the only begotten of the Father,) full of grace and truth.
John 1:14 KJV

And from his fullness have we all received, grace upon grace. For the law was given through Moses; grace and truth came through Jesus Christ. John 1:16-17 RSV

And with great power the apostles gave their testimony to the resurrection of the Lord Jesus, and great grace was upon them all. Acts 4:33 RSV

Paul and Barnabas . . . spoke to them and urged them to continue in the grace of God. Acts 13:43 RSV

Being justified freely by his grace through the redemption that is in Christ Jesus. Romans 3:24 KJV

By whom [the Lord Jesus Christ] also we have access by faith into this grace wherein we stand, and rejoice in hope of the glory of God. Romans 5:2 KJV

Law came in, to increase the trespass; but where sin increased, grace abounded all the more, so that, as sin reigned in death, grace also might reign through righteousness to eternal life through Jesus Christ our Lord. What shall we say then? Are we to continue in sin that grace may abound? By no means! Romans 5:20-6:2 RSV

But by the grace of God I am what I am, and his grace toward me was not in vain. On the contrary, I worked harder than any of them, though it was not I, but the grace of God which is with me.
1 Corinthians 15:10 RSV

For ye know the grace of our Lord Jesus Christ, that, though he was rich, yet for your sakes he became poor, that ye through his poverty might be rich.
2 Corinthians 8:9 KJV

'My grace is sufficient for you, for my power is made perfect in weakness.'
2 Corinthians 12:9 RSV

The grace of the Lord Jesus Chris love of God, and the fellowship Holy Spirit be with you all.
2 Corinthians 13:13 GNB

But because of his great lo God, who is rich in mercy

alive with Christ even when we were dead in transgressions—it is by grace you have been saved. Ephesians 2:4-5 NIV

For by grace are ye saved through faith; and that not of yourselves: it is the gift of God. Ephesians 2:8 KJV

[Because Jesus can sympathize with our weaknesses] Let us then with confidence draw near to the throne of grace, that we may receive mercy and find grace to help in time of need. Hebrews 4:16 RSV

But grow in the grace and knowledge of our Lord and Saviour Jesus Christ. To him be the glory both now and to the day of eternity. Amen. 2 Peter 3:18 RSV

Great commission
See Matthew 28:18-20.

Greed
See *Desire, wrong.*

Grief
For my life is spent with grief, and my years with sighing: my strength faileth because of mine iniquity, and my bones are consumed. Psalm 31:10 KJV

The sacrifices of God are a broken spirit: a broken and a contrite heart, O God, thou wilt not despise. Psalm 51:17 KJV

A time to weep, and a time to laugh; a time to mourn, and a time to dance. Ecclesiastes 3:4 KJV

And I said: 'Woe is me! For I am lost; for I am a man of unclean lips, and I dwell in the midst of a people of unclean lips; for my eyes have seen the King, the Lord of hosts!' Isaiah 6:5 RSV

He is despised and rejected of men; a man of sorrows, and acquainted with grief: and we hid as it were our faces from him; he was despised, and we esteemed him not. Surely he hath borne our griefs, and carried our sorrows: yet we did esteem him stricken, smitten of God, and afflicted. Isaiah 53:3-4 KJV

Is there no balm in Gilead; is there no physician there? Why then is not the health of the daughter of my people recovered? Jeremiah 8:22 KJV

the children of the kingdom shall be cast out into outer darkness: there shall be weeping and gnashing of teeth. 12 KJV

with him Peter and the two sons of Zebedee, he began to be sorrowful and troubled. Then he said to them, 'My soul is very sorrowful, even to death; remain here, and watch with me.' Matthew 26:37-38 RSV

He [Jesus] came closer to the city, and when he saw it, he wept over it, saying, 'If you only knew today what is needed for peace! But now you cannot see it!' Luke 19:41-42 GNB

And when he rose from prayer, he came to the disciples and found them sleeping for sorrow. Luke 22:45 RSV

And the Lord turned, and looked upon Peter. And Peter remembered the word of the Lord, how he had said unto him, Before the cock crow, thou shalt deny me thrice. And Peter went out, and wept bitterly. Luke 22:61-62 KJV

Jesus wept. John 11:35 KJV

Sorrowful, yet always rejoicing. 2 Corinthians 6:10 RSV

For godly grief produces a repentance that leads to salvation and brings no regret, but worldly grief produces death. 2 Corinthians 7:10 RSV

See also *Comfort; Repentance.*

Growth, *spiritual*
See *Christian life, Character of the Christian.*

Guidance
He leadeth me beside the still waters. He restoreth my soul: he leadeth me in the paths of righteousness for his name's sake. Psalm 23:2-3 KJV

Trust in the Lord, and do good; so you will dwell in the land, and enjoy security. Take delight in the Lord, and he will give you the desires of your heart. Commit your way to the Lord; trust in him, and he will act. Psalm 37:3-5 RSV

The steps of a man are from the Lord, and he establishes him in whose way he delights. Psalm 37:23 RSV

'If you pour yourself out for the hungry and satisfy the desire of the afflicted, then shall your light rise in the darkness and your gloom be as the noonday. And the Lord will guide you continually, and satisfy your desire with good things, and make your bones strong.' Isaiah 58:10-11 RSV

'When the Spirit of truth comes, he will guide you into all the truth; for he will not speak on his own authority, but whatever he hears he will speak, and he will declare to you the things that are to come.' John 16:13 RSV

Then it seemed good to the apostles and the elders, with the whole church, to choose men from among them and send them to Antioch with Paul and Barnabas. Acts 15:22 RSV

'For it has seemed good to the Holy Spirit and to us to lay upon you no greater burden than these necessary things . . .' Acts 15:28 RSV

And be not conformed to this world: but be ye transformed by the renewing of your mind, that ye may prove what is that good, and acceptable, and perfect, will of God. Romans 12:2 KJV

If any of you lacks wisdom, let him ask God, who gives to all men generously and without reproaching, and it will be given him. James 1:5 RSV

See also *Counsel; Sovereignty of God.*

Guilt

And they heard the voice of the Lord God walking in the garden in the cool of the day: and Adam and his wife hid themselves from the presence of the Lord God amongst the trees of the garden . . . And he [Adam] said, I heard thy voice in the garden, and I was afraid, because I was naked; and I hid myself. Genesis 3:8, 10 KJV

Thou shalt not take the name of the Lord thy God in vain; for the Lord will not hold him guiltless that taketh his name in vain. Exodus 20:7 KJV

I acknowledged my sin to thee, and I did not hide my iniquity; I said, 'I will confess my transgressions to the Lord'; then thou didst forgive the guilt of my sin. Psalm 32:5 RSV

Have mercy upon me, O God, according to thy lovingkindness: according unto the multitude of thy tender mercies blot out my transgressions. Wash me throughly from mine iniquity, and cleanse me from my sin. For I acknowledge my transgressions: and my sin is ever before me. Against thee, thee only, have I sinned, and done this evil in thy sight: that thou mightest be justified when thou speakest, and be clear when thou judgest. Psalm 51:1-4 KJV

And he touched my mouth, and said: 'Behold, this has touched your lips; your guilt is taken away, and your sin forgiven.' Isaiah 6:7 RSV

There is therefore now no condemnation for those who are in Christ Jesus. Romans 8:1 RSV

Whoever, therefore, eats the bread or drinks the cup of the Lord in an unworthy manner will be guilty of profaning the body and blood of the Lord. 1 Corinthians 11:27 RSV

For if a man keeps the whole law apart from one single point, he is guilty of breaking all of it. James 2:10 NEB

See also *Conscience; Conviction of sin; Forgiveness.*

Happiness
See *Joy.*

Hardness

And the Lord said to Moses, 'When you go back to Egypt, see that you do before Pharaoh all the miracles which I have put in your power; but I will harden his heart, so that he will not let the people go.' Exodus 4:21 RSV

'If there is among you a poor man, one of your brethren, in any of your towns within your land which the Lord your God gives you, you shall not harden your heart or shut your hand against your poor brother.' Deuteronomy 15:7 RSV

Always obey the Lord and you will be happy. If you are stubborn, you will be ruined. Proverbs 28:14 GNB

And he said, 'Go, and say to this people: "Hear and hear, but do not understand; see and see, but do not perceive." Make the heart of this people fat, and their ears heavy, and shut their eyes; lest they see with their eyes, and hear with their ears, and understand with their hearts, and turn and be healed.' Isaiah 6:9-10 RSV

Jesus replied, 'Moses permitted you to divorce your wives because your hearts were hard. But it was not this way from the beginning.' Matthew 19:8 NIV

And he looked around at them with anger, grieved at their hardness of heart. Mark 3:5 RSV

[Jesus to the Jews] 'You refuse to come to me that you may have life.' John 5:40 RSV

'How stubborn you are!' Stephen went on to say. 'How heathen your hearts, how deaf you are to God's message! You are just like your ancestors: you too have always resisted the Holy Spirit!' Acts 7:51 GNB

But by your hard and impenitent heart you are storing up wrath for yourself on the day of wrath when God's righteous judgment will be revealed. Romans 2:5 RSV

But their [the Israelites] minds were

hardened; for to this day, when they read the old covenant, that same veil remains unlifted, because only through Christ is it taken away. 2 Corinthians 3:14 RSV

They [the Gentiles] are darkened in their understanding, alienated from the life of God because of the ignorance that is in them, due to their hardness of heart. Ephesians 4:18 RSV

'Today, when you hear his voice do not harden your hearts as in the rebellion.' Hebrews 3:15 RSV

See also *Falling away; Rejection; Unbelief.*

Hate, hatred

Do I not hate them that hate thee, O Lord? And do I not loathe them that rise up against thee? I hate them with perfect hatred; I count them my enemies. Psalm 139:21-22 RSV

There are seven things that the Lord hates and cannot tolerate: A proud look, a lying tongue, hands that kill innocent people, a mind that thinks up wicked plans, feet that hurry off to do evil, a witness who tells one lie after another, and a man who stirs up trouble among friends. Proverbs 6:16-19 GNB

Better is a dinner of herbs where love is than a fatted ox and hatred with it. Proverbs 15:17 RSV

Hate evil, and love good, and establish justice in the gate; it may be that the Lord, the God of hosts, will be gracious to the remnant of Joseph. Amos 5:15 RSV

'Then they will deliver you up to tribulation, and put you to death; and you will be hated by all nations for my name's sake.' Matthew 24:9 RSV

For every one who does evil hates the light, and does not come to the light, lest his deeds should be exposed. John 3:20 RSV

'The world cannot hate you, but it does hate me, because I give evidence that its ways are evil.' John 7:7 JB

'If the world hates you, just remember that it has hated me first. If you belonged to the world, then the world would love you as its own. But I chose you from this world, and you do not belong to it; that is why the world hates you.' John 15:18-19 GNB

Healing

And he [Elijah] stretched himself upon the child three times, and cried unto the Lord, and said, O Lord my God, I pray thee, let this child's soul come into him again. \nd the Lord heard the voice of Elijah; and the soul of the child came into him again, and he revived. 1 Kings 17:21-22 KJV

So he [Naaman] went down and dipped himself seven times in the Jordan, according to the word of the man of God; and his flesh was restored like the flesh of a little child, and he was clean. 2 Kings 5:14 RSV

[The Lord's promise to Solomon] 'If my people who are called by my name humble themselves, and pray and seek my face, and turn from their wicked ways, then I will hear from heaven, and will forgive their sin and heal their land.' 2 Chronicles 7:14 RSV

Bless the Lord, O my soul, and forget not all his benefits: who forgiveth all thine iniquities; who healeth all thy diseases. Psalm 103:2-3 KJV

He sent forth his word, and healed them, and delivered them from destruction. Psalm 107:20 RSV

Jesus went all over Galilee, teaching in the synagogues, preaching the Good News about the Kingdom, and healing people who had all kinds of disease and sickness. Matthew 4:23 GNB

And he called to him his twelve disciples and gave them authority over unclean spirits, to cast them out, and to heal every disease and every infirmity. Matthew 10:1 RSV

Then Peter said, Silver and gold have I none; but such as I have give I thee: in the name of Jesus Christ of Nazareth rise up and walk. And he took him by the right hand, and lifted him up: and immediately his feet and ancle bones received strength. Acts 3:6-7 KJV

To another gifts of healing by the one Spirit . . . 1 Corinthians 12:9 RSV

Is any sick among you? Let him call for the elders of the church; and let them pray over him, anointing him with oil in the name of the Lord: and the prayer of faith shall save the sick, and the Lord shall raise him up; and if he have committed sins, they shall be forgiven him. Confess your faults one to another, and pray one for another, that ye may be healed. The effectual fervent prayer of a righteous man availeth much. James 5:14-16 KJV

See also *Comfort; Illness; Suffering.*

Heart

Thou shalt love the Lord thy God with

all thine heart, and with all thy soul, and with all thy might. Deuteronomy 6:5 KJV

[Samuel to Saul] 'But now your kingdom shall not continue; the Lord has sought out a man after his own heart . . . because you have not kept what the Lord commanded you.' 1 Samuel 13:14 RSV

But the Lord said unto Samuel, Look not on his countenance, or on the height of his stature; because I have refused him: for the Lord seeth not as man seeth; for man looketh on the outward appearance, but the Lord looketh on the heart. 1 Samuel 16:7 KJV

Create in me a clean heart, O God; and renew a right spirit within me. Psalm 51:10 KJV

The heart is deceitful above all things, and desperately wicked: who can know it? I the Lord search the heart. Jeremiah 17:9-10 KJV

'A new heart I will give you, and a new spirit I will put within you; and I will take out of your flesh the heart of stone and give you a heart of flesh.' Ezekiel 36:26 RSV

Blessed are the pure in heart: for they shall see God. Matthew 5:8 KJV

'For where your treasure is, there will your heart be also.' Matthew 6:21 RSV

And he said, 'What comes out of a man is what defiles a man. For from within, out of the heart of man, come evil thoughts, fornication, theft, murder, adultery, coveting, wickedness, deceit, licentiousness, envy, slander, pride, foolishness.' Mark 7:21-22 RSV

'He who believes in me, as the scripture has said, "Out of his heart shall flow rivers of living water."' Now this he said about the Spirit, which those who believed in him were to receive. John 7:38-39 RSV

But thanks be to God, that you who were once slaves of sin have become obedient from the heart to the standard of teaching to which you were committed. Romans 6:17 RSV

And he who searches the hearts of men knows what is the mind of the Spirit, because the Spirit intercedes for the saints according to the will of God. Romans 8:27 RSV

That if thou shalt confess with thy mouth the Lord Jesus, and shalt believe in thine heart that God hath raised him from the dead, thou shalt be saved. Romans 10:9 KJV

And let the peace of God rule in your hearts, to the which also ye are called in one body; and be ye thankful. Colossians 3:15 KJV

Now that by your obedience to the truth you have purified yourselves and have come to have a sincere love for your fellow-believers, love one another earnestly with all your heart. 1 Peter 1:22 GNB

By this we shall know that we are of the truth, and reassure our hearts before him whenever our hearts condemn us; for God is greater than our hearts, and he knows everything. Beloved, if our hearts do not condemn us, we have confidence before God. 1 John 3:19-21 RSV

See also *Hardness; Mind; Spirit.*

Heaven
See *Last things.*

Hell
See *Last things.*

Help
Then Samuel took a stone and set it up between Mizpah and Jeshanah, and called its name Ebenezer; for he said, 'Hitherto the Lord has helped us.' 1 Samuel 7:12 RSV

God is our refuge and strength, a very present help in trouble. Psalm 46:1 KJV

I will lift up mine eyes unto the hills, from whence cometh my help. My help cometh from the Lord, which made heaven and earth. He will not suffer thy foot to be moved: he that keepeth thee will not slumber. Behold, he that keepeth Israel shall neither slumber nor sleep. The Lord is thy keeper: the Lord is thy shade upon thy right hand. The sun shall not smite thee by day, nor the moon by night. The Lord shall preserve thee from all evil: he shall preserve thy soul. The Lord shall preserve thy going out and thy coming in from this time forth, and even for evermore. Psalm 121 KJV

But she [a Canaanite woman] came and knelt before him, saying, 'Lord, help me.' Matthew 15:25 RSV

Apollos then decided to go to Achaia, so the believers in Ephesus helped him by writing to the believers in Achaia, urging them to welcome him. When he arrived, he was a great help to those who through God's grace had become believers. Acts 18:27 GNB

'In all things I have shown you that by so toiling one must help the weak, remembering the words of the Lord Jesus, how he said, "It is more blessed to give than to receive."' Acts 20:35 RSV

Likewise the Spirit helps us in our weakness; for we do not know how to pray as we ought, but the Spirit himself intercedes for us with sighs too deep for words. Romans 8:26 RSV

And God has appointed in the church first apostles, second prophets, third teachers, then workers of miracles, then healers, helpers, administrators. 1 Corinthians 12:28 RSV

You also must help us by prayer, so that many will give thanks on our behalf for the blessing granted us in answer to many prayers. 2 Corinthians 1:11 RSV

Bear one another's burdens, and so fulfil the law of Christ. Galatians 6:2 RSV

He has said, 'I will never fail you nor forsake you.' Hence we can confidently say, 'The Lord is my helper, I will not be afraid; what can man do to me?' Hebrews 13:5-6 RSV

See also *Comfort; Kindness; Service.*

High priest
See *Priest.*

Holiness, holy
And he said, Draw not nigh hither: put off thy shoes from off thy feet, for the place whereon thou standest is holy ground. Exodus 3:5 KJV

Remember the sabbath day, to keep it holy. Exodus 20:8 KJV

'For I am the Lord your God; consecrate yourselves therefore, and be holy, for I am holy.' Leviticus 11:44 RSV

'Holy, holy, holy is the Lord of hosts; the whole earth is full of his glory.' Isaiah 6:3 RSV

But now that you have been set free from sin and have become slaves to God, the benefit you reap leads to holiness, and the result is eternal life. Romans 6:22 NIV

Since we have these promises, dear friends, let us purify ourselves from everything that contaminates body and spirit, perfecting holiness out of reverence for God. 2 Corinthians 7:1 NIV

God did not call us to live in immorality, but in holiness. 1 Thessalonians 4:7 GNB

For it was fitting that we should have such a high priest, holy, blameless, unstained, separated from sinners, exalted above the heavens. Hebrews 7:26 RSV

For they [our human fathers] disciplined us for a short time at their pleasure, but he disciplines us for our good, that we may share his holiness. Hebrews 12:10 RSV

Strive for peace with all men, and for the holiness without which no one will see the Lord. Hebrews 12:14 RSV

But you are a chosen race, a royal priesthood, a holy nation, God's own people, that you may declare the wonderful deeds of him who called you out of darkness into his marvellous light. 1 Peter 2:9 RSV

See also *Sanctification.*

Holy Spirit
And the Spirit of God moved upon the face of the waters. Genesis 1:2 KJV

'I have filled him [Bezalel] with the Spirit of God, with ability and intelligence, with knowledge and all craftsmanship.' Exodus 31:3 RSV

The spirit of the Lord came upon him [Othniel], and he became Israel's leader. Othniel went to war, and the Lord gave him victory over the king of Mesopotamia. Judges 3:10 GNB

Cast me not away from thy presence, and take not thy holy spirit from me. Psalm 51:11 KJV

And the spirit of the Lord shall rest upon him, the spirit of wisdom and understanding, the spirit of counsel and might, the spirit of knowledge and of the fear of the Lord. Isaiah 11:2 KJV

'And I will put my spirit within you, and cause you to walk in my statutes and be careful to observe my ordinances.' Ezekiel 36:27 RSV

'And it shall come to pass afterward, that I will pour out my spirit on all flesh; your sons and your daughters shall prophesy, your old men shall dream dreams, and your young men shall see visions.' Joel 2:28 RSV

This is the word of the Lord unto Zerubbabel, saying, Not by might, nor by power, but by my spirit, saith the Lord of hosts. Zechariah 4:6 KJV

[John the Baptist] 'I baptize you with water for repentance, but he who is coming after me is mightier than I, whose sandals I am not worthy to carry; he will baptize you with the Holy Spirit and with fire.' Matthew 3:11 RSV

And when Jesus was baptized, he went up immediately from the water, and behold, the heavens were opened and he saw the Spirit of God descending like a dove, and alighting on him. Matthew 3:16 RSV

'Therefore I tell you, every sin and blasphemy will be forgiven men, but the blasphemy against the Spirit will not be forgiven.' Matthew 12:31 RSV

And the angel said to her, 'The Holy Spirit will come upon you, and the power of the Most High will overshadow you; therefore the child to be born will be called holy, the Son of God.' Luke 1:35 RSV

If ye then, being evil, know how to give good gifts unto your children: how much more shall your heavenly Father give the Holy Spirit to them that ask him? Luke 11:13 KJV

Jesus answered, Verily, verily, I say unto thee, Except a man be born of water and of the Spirit, he cannot enter into the kingdom of God. That which is born of the flesh is flesh; and that which is born of the Spirit is spirit. John 3:5-6 KJV

'He who believes in me, as the scripture has said, "Out of his heart shall flow rivers of living water."' Now this he said about the Spirit, which those who believed in him were to receive; for as yet the Spirit had not been given, because Jesus was not yet glorified. John 7:38-39 RSV

And I will pray the Father, and he shall give you another Comforter, that he may abide with you for ever; even the Spirit of truth; whom the world cannot receive, because it seeth him not, neither knoweth him: but ye know him; for he dwelleth with you, and shall be in you. John 14:16-17 KJV

'But the Counsellor, the Holy Spirit, whom the Father will send in my name, he will teach you all things, and bring to your remembrance all that I have said to you.' John 14:26 RSV

'But when the Counsellor comes, whom I shall send to you from the Father, even the Spirit of truth, who proceeds from the Father, he will bear witness to me.' John 15:26 RSV

'Nevertheless I tell you the truth: it is to your advantage that I go away, for if I do not go away, the Counsellor will not come to you; but if I go, I will send him to you. And when he comes, he will convince the world concerning sin and righteousness and judgment: concerning sin, because they do not believe in me; concerning righteousness, because I go to the Father, and you will see me no more; concerning judgment, because the ruler of this world is judged . . . When the Spirit of truth comes, he will guide you into all the truth; for he will not speak on his own authority, but whatever he hears he will speak, and he will declare to you the things that are to come. He will glorify me, for he will take what is mine and declare it to you.' John 16:7-11, 13-14 RSV

'But you shall receive power when the Holy Spirit has come upon you; and you shall be my witnesses in Jerusalem and in all Judea and Samaria and to the end of the earth.' Acts 1:8 RSV

'Jesus . . . saw the Spirit of God descending like a dove, and alighting on him.'

When the day of Pentecost had come, they were all together in one place. And suddenly a sound came from heaven like the rush of a mighty wind, and it filled all the house where they were sitting. And there appeared to them tongues as of fire, distributed and resting on each one of them. And they were all filled with the Holy Spirit and began to speak in other tongues, as the Spirit gave them utterance. Acts 2:1-4 RSV

And Peter said to them, 'Repent, and be baptized every one of you in the name of Jesus Christ for the forgiveness of your sins; and you shall receive the gift of the Holy Spirit.' Acts 2:38 RSV

Then Peter, filled with the Holy Spirit, said to them, 'Rulers of the people and elders . . .' Acts 4:8 RSV

Peter said to him, 'Ananias, why did you let Satan take control of you and make you lie to the Holy Spirit by keeping part of the money you received for the property? . . . You have not lied to men—you have lied to God!' Acts 5:3-4 GNB

'How stubborn you are!' Stephen went on to say. 'How heathen your hearts, how deaf you are to God's message! You are just like your ancestors: you too have always resisted the Holy Spirit!' Acts 7:51 GNB

While they were worshipping the Lord and fasting, the Holy Spirit said, 'Set apart for me Barnabas and Saul for the work to which I have called them.' Acts 13:2 RSV

'For it has seemed good to the Holy Spirit and to us to lay upon you no greater burden than these necessary things . . .' Acts 15:28 RSV

The love of God is shed abroad in our hearts by the Holy Ghost which is given unto us. Romans 5:5 KJV

For those who live according to the flesh set their minds on the things of the flesh, but those who live according to the Spirit set their minds on the things of the Spirit. To set the mind on the flesh is death, but to set the mind on the Spirit is life and peace. Romans 8:5-6 RSV

But you are not in the flesh, you are in the Spirit, if in fact the Spirit of God dwells in you. Any one who does not have the Spirit of Christ does not belong to him . . . If the Spirit of him who raised Jesus from the dead dwells in you, he who raised Christ Jesus from the dead will give life to your mortal bodies also through his Spirit which

dwells in you . . . For if you live according to the flesh you will die, but if by the Spirit you put to death the deeds of the body you will live. For all who are led by the Spirit of God are sons of God. For you did not receive the spirit of slavery to fall back into fear, but you have received the spirit of sonship. When we cry, 'Abba! Father!' it is the Spirit himself bearing witness with our spirit that we are children of God. Romans 8:9-11, 13-16 RSV

Likewise the Spirit helps us in our weakness; for we do not know how to pray as we ought, but the Spirit himself intercedes for us with sighs too deep for words. And he who searches the hearts of men knows what is the mind of the Spirit, because the Spirit intercedes for the saints according to the will of God. Romans 8:26-27 RSV

Never flag in zeal, be aglow with the Spirit, serve the Lord. Romans 12:11 RSV

My speech and my message were not in plausible words of wisdom, but in demonstration of the Spirit and of power. 1 Corinthians 2:4 RSV

For the Spirit searches everything, even the depths of God. 1 Corinthians 2:10 RSV

To each is given the manifestation of the Spirit for the common good. 1 Corinthians 12:7 RSV

Now the Lord is the Spirit, and where the Spirit of the Lord is, there is freedom. And we all, with unveiled face, beholding the glory of the Lord, are being changed into his likeness from one degree of glory to another; for this comes from the Lord who is the Spirit. 2 Corinthians 3:17-18 RSV

But the fruit of the Spirit is love, joy, peace, patience, kindness, goodness, faithfulness, gentleness, self-control; against such there is no law. Galatians 5:22-23 RSV

And grieve not the holy Spirit of God, whereby ye are sealed unto the day of redemption. Ephesians 4:30 KJV

Be filled with the Spirit; speaking to yourselves in psalms and hymns and spiritual songs, singing and making melody in your heart to the Lord; giving thanks always for all things unto God and the Father in the name of our Lord Jesus Christ; submitting yourselves one to another in the fear of God. Ephesians 5:18-21 KJV

And take the helmet of salvation, and the sword of the Spirit, which is the word of God. Ephesians 6:17 KJV

Quench not the Spirit. 1 Thessalonians 5:19 KJV

No prophecy of scripture is a matter of one's own interpretation, because no prophecy ever came by the impulse of man, but men moved by the Holy Spirit spoke from God. 2 Peter 1:21 RSV

Homosexuality

No man is to have sexual relations with another man; God hates that. Leviticus 18:22 GNB

If a man has sexual relations with another man, they have done a disgusting thing, and both shall be put to death. They are responsible for their own death. Leviticus 20:13 GNB

Therefore God gave them over in the sinful desires of their hearts to sexual impurity for the degrading of their bodies with one another. Romans 1:24 NIV

In consequence . . . God has given them up to shameful passions. Their women have exchanged natural intercourse for unnatural, and their men in turn, giving up natural relations with women, burn with lust for one another; males behave indecently with males, and are paid in their own persons the fitting wage of such perversion. Romans 1:26-27 NEB

Do you not know that the wicked will not inherit the kingdom of God? Do not be deceived: Neither the sexually immoral nor idolaters nor adulterers nor male prostitutes nor homosexual offenders . . . will inherit the kingdom of God. 1 Corinthians 6:9-10 NIV

See also *Sex.*

Honesty

A false balance is an abomination to the Lord, but a just weight is his delight. Proverbs 11:1 RSV

'And as for that in the good soil, they are those who, hearing the word, hold it fast in an honest and good heart, and bring forth fruit with patience.' Luke 8:15 RSV

We have renounced disgraceful, underhanded ways; we refuse to practise cunning or to tamper with God's word, but by the open statement of the truth we would commend ourselves to every man's conscience in the sight of God. 2 Corinthians 4:2 RSV

Our purpose is to do what is right, not only in the sight of the Lord, but also in the sight of man. 2 Corinthians 8:21 GNB

Let the thief no longer steal, but rather let him labour, doing honest work with his hands, so that he may be able to give to those in need. Ephesians 4:28 RSV

We were not lazy when we were with you. We did not accept anyone's support without paying for it. Instead, we worked and toiled. 2 Thessalonians 3:7-8 GNB

See also *Lying; Truth.*

Hope

Why art thou cast down, O my soul? and why art thou disquieted in me? Hope thou in God: for I shall yet praise him for the help of his countenance. Psalm 42:5 KJV

Abraham believed and hoped, even when there was no reason for hoping, and so became 'the father of many nations.' Romans 4:18 GNB

We . . . rejoice in hope of the glory of God . . . hope maketh not ashamed; because the love of God is shed abroad in our hearts by the Holy Ghost which is given unto us. Romans 5:2, 5 KJV

Not only the creation, but we ourselves, who have the first fruits of the Spirit, groan inwardly as we wait for adoption as sons, the redemption of our bodies. For in this hope we were saved. Now hope that is seen is not hope. For who hopes for what he sees? But if we hope for what we do not see, we wait for it with patience. Romans 8:23-25 RSV

May the God of hope fill you with all joy and peace in believing, so that by the power of the Holy Spirit you may abound in hope. Romans 15:13 RSV

So faith, hope, love abide, these three; but the greatest of these is love. 1 Corinthians 13:13 RSV

You [Gentiles] were at that time separated from Christ, alienated from the commonwealth of Israel, and strangers to the covenants of promise, having no hope and without God in the world. Ephesians 2:12 RSV

To them God chose to make known how great among the Gentiles are the riches of the glory of this mystery, which is Christ in you, the hope of glory. Colossians 1:27 RSV

We who have fled for refuge might have strong encouragement to seize the hope set before us. We have this as a sure and steadfast anchor of the soul, a hope that enters into the inner shrine behind the curtain. Hebrews 6:18-19 RSV

Keep alert and set your hope

completely on the blessing which will be given you when Jesus Christ is revealed. 1 Peter 1:13 GNB

Hospitality

I was an hungred, and ye gave me meat: I was thirsty, and ye gave me drink: I was a stranger, and ye took me in. Matthew 25:35 KJV

She [Lydia] was baptized, and her household with her, and then she said to us, 'If you have judged me to be a believer in the Lord, I beg you to come and stay in my house.' And she insisted on our going. Acts 16:15 NEB

Contribute to the needs of the saints, practise hospitality. Romans 12:13 RSV

A bishop then must be blameless, the husband of one wife, vigilant, sober, of good behaviour, given to hospitality . . . 1 Timothy 3:2 KJV

[A widow] . . . well known for her good deeds, such as bringing up children, showing hospitality, washing the feet of the saints, helping those in trouble and devoting herself to all kinds of good deeds. 1 Timothy 5:10 NIV

Do not neglect to show hospitality to strangers, for thereby some have entertained angels unawares. Hebrews 13:2 RSV

Practise hospitality ungrudgingly to one another. 1 Peter 4:9 RSV

Humility, humble

'This is the man to whom I will look, he that is humble and contrite in spirit, and trembles at my word.' Isaiah 66:2 RSV

Blessed are the poor in spirit: for theirs is the kingdom of heaven. Matthew 5:3 KJV

Whosoever therefore shall humble himself as this little child, the same is greatest in the kingdom of heaven. Matthew 18:4 KJV

'But it shall not be so among you; but whoever would be great among you must be your servant.' Mark 10:43 RSV

Jesus, knowing that the Father had given all things into his hands, and that he had come from God and was going to God, rose from supper, laid aside his garments, and girded himself with a towel. Then he poured water into a basin, and began to wash the disciples' feet, and to wipe them with the towel with which he was girded . . . 'If I then, your Lord and Teacher, have washed your feet, you also ought to wash one another's feet.' John 13:3-5, 14 RSV

Do nothing from selfishness or conceit, but in humility count others better than yourselves . . . Have this mind among yourselves, which is yours in Christ Jesus, who, though he was in the form of God, did not count equality with God a thing to be grasped, but emptied himself, taking the form of a servant, being born in the likeness of men. And being found in human form he humbled himself and became obedient unto death, even death on a cross. Therefore God has highly exalted him and bestowed on him the name which is above every name, that at the name of Jesus every knee should bow, in heaven and on earth and under the earth, and every tongue confess that Jesus Christ is Lord, to the glory of God the Father. Philippians 2:3, 5-8 RSV

Likewise you that are younger be subject to the elders. Clothe yourselves, all of you, with humility toward one another, for 'God opposes the proud, but gives grace to the humble.' Humble yourselves therefore under the mighty hand of God, that in due time he may exalt you. 1 Peter 5:5-6 RSV

See also *Pride*.

Husband

See *Marriage*.

Hypocrisy, hypocrite

'So when you give something to a needy person, do not make a big show of it, as the hypocrites do in the houses of worship and on the streets. They do it so that people will praise them. I assure you, they have already been paid in full . . . When you pray, do not be like the hypocrites! They love to stand up and pray in the houses of worship and on the street corners, so that everyone will see them. I assure you, they have already been paid in full . . . And when you fast, do not put on a sad face as the hypocrites do. They neglect their appearance so that everyone will see that they are fasting. I assure you, they have already been paid in full.' Matthew 6:2, 5, 16 GNB

'You hypocrite, first take the log out of your own eye, and then you will see clearly to take the speck out of your brother's eye.' Matthew 7:5 RSV

[Jesus to the Pharisees and scribes] 'You hypocrites! Well did Isaiah prophesy of you, when he said: "This people honours me with their lips, but their heart is far from me; in vain do they worship me, teaching as doctrines the precepts of men."' Matthew 15:7-9 RSV

'Why do you call me, "Lord, Lord,"
and yet don't do what I tell you?' Luke
6:46 GNB

They [people in the last days] will hold to
the outward form of our religion, but
reject its real power. Keep away from
such people. 2 Timothy 3:5 GNB

See also *Pharisees; Scribes.*

Idolatry

Thou shalt have no other gods before
me. Thou shalt not make unto thee any
graven image, or any likeness of any
thing that is in heaven above, or that is
in the earth beneath, or that is in the
water under the earth: thou shalt not
bow down thyself to them, nor serve
them. Exodus 20:3-5 KJV

And he [Aaron] received the gold at
their hand, and fashioned it with a
graving tool, and made a molten calf.
Exodus 32:4 RSV

Their idols are silver and gold, made by
the hands of men. They have mouths
that cannot speak, and eyes that cannot
see; they have ears that cannot hear,
nostrils, and cannot smell; with their
hands they cannot feel, with their feet
they cannot walk, and no sound comes
from their throats. Psalm 115:4-7 NEB

Now the works of the flesh are plain . . .
idolatry. Galatians 5:19-20 RSV

For they themselves report concerning
us what a welcome we had among you,
and how you turned to God from idols,
to serve a living and true God.
1 Thessalonians 1:9 RSV

Little children, keep yourselves from
idols. 1 John 5:21 RSV

'Thou shalt not make unto thee any graven
image.'

Illness

In the thirty-ninth year of his reign Asa
was afflicted with a disease in his feet.
Though his disease was severe, even in
his illness he did not seek help from the
Lord, but only from the physicians.
2 Chronicles 16:12 NIV

So Satan went forth from the presence
of the Lord, and afflicted Job with
loathsome sores from the sole of his
foot to the crown of his head. Job 2:7
RSV

Because of your anger, I am in great
pain; my whole body is diseased
because of my sins. Psalm 38:3 GNB

He had healed many, so that all who
had diseases pressed upon him to touch
him. Mark 3:10 RSV

So the sisters sent to him, saying,
'Lord, he whom you love is ill.'
John 11:3 RSV

See also *Suffering.*

Help in

The Lord will help them when they are
sick and will restore them to health.
Psalm 41:3 GNB

Surely he hath borne our griefs, and
carried our sorrows: yet we did esteem
him stricken, smitten of God, and
afflicted. Isaiah 53:4 KJV

A leper came to him and knelt before
him, saying, 'Lord, if you will, you can
make me clean.' And he stretched out
his hand and touched him, saying, 'I
will; be clean.' And immediately his
leprosy was cleansed. Matthew 8:2-3
RSV

Is any sick among you? Let him call for
the elders of the church; and let them
pray over him, anointing him with oil in
the name of the Lord: and the prayer of
faith shall save the sick, and the Lord
shall raise him up; and if he have
committed sins, they shall be forgiven
him. Confess your faults one to
another, and pray one for another, that
ye may be healed. The effectual fervent
prayer of a righteous man availeth
much. James 5:14-16 KJV

See also *Comfort; Healing.*

Immigrants

'You shall not wrong a stranger or
oppress him, for you were strangers in
the land of Egypt.' Exodus 22:21 RSV

'Do not illtreat foreigners who are
living in your land. Treat them as you
would a fellow-Israelite, and love them
as you love yourselves.' Leviticus
19:33-34 GNB

'He executes justice for the fatherless and the widow, and loves the sojourner, giving him food and clothing. Love the sojourner therefore; for you were sojourners in the land of Egypt.' Deuteronomy 10:18-19 RSV

The Lord watches over the sojourners, he upholds the widow and the fatherless. Psalm 146:9 RSV

I was an hungred, and ye gave me meat: I was thirsty, and ye gave me drink: I was a stranger, and ye took me in. Matthew 25:35 KJV

Do not neglect to show hospitality to strangers, for thereby some have entertained angels unawares. Hebrews 13:2 RSV

Incarnation

See *Jesus Christ, Jesus, the man.*

Inheritance

Then shall the King say unto them on his right hand, Come, ye blessed of my Father, inherit the kingdom prepared for you from the foundation of the world. Matthew 25:34 KJV

'And now I commend you to God, and to the word of his grace that has power to build you up and to give you your inheritance among all the sanctified.' Acts 20:32 JB

[Children of God are] heirs, heirs of God and fellow heirs with Christ, provided we suffer with him in order that we may also be glorified with him. Romans 8:17 RSV

Do you not know that the wicked will not inherit the kingdom of God? Do not be deceived: Neither the sexually immoral nor idolaters nor adulterers nor male prostitutes nor homosexual offenders nor thieves nor the greedy nor drunkards nor slanderers nor swindlers will inherit the kingdom of God. 1 Corinthians 6:9 NIV

I tell you this, brethren: flesh and blood cannot inherit the kingdom of God, nor does the perishable inherit the imperishable. 1 Corinthians 15:50 RSV

So through God you are no longer a slave but a son, and if a son then an heir. Galatians 4:7 RSV

In whom also we have obtained an inheritance, being predestinated according to the purpose of him who worketh all things after the counsel of his own will. Ephesians 1:11 KJV

In him you also, who have heard the word of truth, the gospel of your salvation, and have believed in him,

were sealed with the promised Holy Spirit, which is the guarantee of our inheritance until we acquire possession of it, to the praise of his glory. Ephesians 1:13-14 RSV

[Paul's prayer] That you may know what is the hope to which he has called you, what are the riches of his glorious inheritance in the saints. Ephesians 1:18 RSV

So that we might be justified by his grace and become heirs in hope of eternal life. Titus 3:7 RSV

[God] hath in these last days spoken unto us by his Son, whom he hath appointed heir of all things, by whom also he made the worlds. Hebrews 1:2 KJV

By his great mercy we have been born anew . . . to an inheritance which is imperishable, undefiled, and unfading, kept in heaven for you. 1 Peter 1:3-4 RSV

[Husband and wife] Heirs together of the grace of life. 1 Peter 3:7 KJV

Injustice

'Do not spread false rumours, and do not help a guilty man by giving false evidence.' Exodus 23:1 GNB

'You shall do no injustice in judgment; you shall not be partial to the poor or defer to the great, but in righteousness shall you judge your neighbour.' Leviticus 19:15 RSV

'Do not cheat anyone by using false measures of length, weight, or quantity.' Leviticus 19:35 GNB

'Now then, let the fear of the Lord be upon you; take heed what you do, for there is no perversion of justice with the Lord our God, or partiality, or taking bribes.' 2 Chronicles 19:7 RSV

'How long will you judge unjustly and show partiality to the wicked?' Psalm 82:2 RSV

'A false balance is an abomination to the Lord, but a just weight is his delight.'

The Lord hates people who use dishonest weights and measures. Proverbs 20:10 GNB

'Woe to him who builds his house by unrighteousness, and his upper rooms by injustice; who makes his neighbour serve him for nothing, and does not give him his wages.' Jeremiah 22:13 RSV

The Lord is righteous, he does no wrong; every morning he shows forth his justice, each dawn he does not fail; but the unjust knows no shame. Zephaniah 3:5 RSV

See also *Justice; Oppression.*

Israel

And he said, Thy name shall be called no more Jacob, but Israel: for as a prince hast thou power with God and with men, and hast prevailed. Genesis 32:28 KJV

But thou, Bethlehem Ephratah, though thou be little among the thousands of Judah, yet out of thee shall he come forth unto me that is to be ruler in Israel; whose goings forth have been from of old, from everlasting. Micah 5:2 KJV

Jesus said to them, 'You can be sure that when the Son of Man sits on his glorious throne in the New Age, then you twelve followers of mine will also sit on thrones, to rule the twelve tribes of Israel.' Matthew 19:28 GNB

Pilate also wrote a title and put it on the cross; it read, 'Jesus of Nazareth, the King of the Jews.' John 19:19 RSV

For he is not a real Jew who is one outwardly, nor is true circumcision something external and physical. He is a Jew who is one inwardly, and real circumcision is a matter of the heart, spiritual and not literal. His praise is not from men but from God. Romans 2:28-29 RSV

But it is not as though the word of God had failed. For not all who are descended from Israel belong to Israel, and not all are children of Abraham because they are his descendants; but 'Through Isaac shall your descendants be named.' Romans 9:6-7 RSV

I do not want you to be ignorant of this mystery, brothers, so that you may not be conceited: Israel has experienced a hardening in part until the full number of the Gentiles has come in. And so all Israel will be saved, as it is written: 'The deliverer will come from Zion; he will turn godlessness away from Jacob.' Romans 11:25-26 NIV

Neither circumcision nor uncircumcision means anything, what counts is a new creation. Peace and mercy to all who follow this rule, even to the Israel of God. Galatians 6:15-16 NIV

For we are the true circumcision, who worship God in spirit, and glory in Christ Jesus, and put no confidence in the flesh. Philippians 3:3 RSV

See also *Gentiles.*

Jealousy

Thou shalt not bow down thyself to them [graven images], nor serve them: for I the Lord thy God am a jealous God, visiting the iniquity of the fathers upon the children unto the third and fourth generation of them that hate me. Exodus 20:5 KJV

'You shall worship no other god, for the Lord, whose name is Jealous, is a jealous God.' Exodus 34:14 RSV

Anger is cruel and destructive, but it is nothing compared to jealousy. Proverbs 27:4 GNB

'Now his elder son was in the field; and as he came and drew near to the house, he heard music and dancing . . . But he was angry and refused to go in. His father came out and entreated him, but he answered his father, "Lo, these many years I have served you, and I never disobeyed your command; yet you never gave me a kid, that I might make merry with my friends. But when this son of yours came, who has devoured your living with harlots, you killed for him the fatted calf!"' Luke 15:25, 28-30 RSV

Love is not jealous or boastful. 1 Corinthians 13:4 RSV

Now the works of the flesh are plain: . . . jealousy . . . Galatians 5:19-20 RSV

But if you have bitter jealousy and selfish ambition in your hearts, do not boast and be false to the truth . . . For where jealousy and selfish ambition exist, there will be disorder and every vile practice. James 3:14, 16 RSV

Or do you suppose it is in vain that the scripture says, 'He yearns jealously over the spirit which he has made to dwell in us'? James 4:5 RSV

See also *Envy.*

Jesus Christ
Ascension

'Was it not necessary that the Christ should suffer these things and enter into his glory?' Luke 24:26 RSV

While he blessed them, he parted from them, and was carried up into heaven. Luke 24:51 RSV

Now this he said about the Spirit, which those who believed in him were to receive; for as yet the Spirit had not been given, because Jesus was not yet glorified. John 7:39 RSV

Jesus said to her [Mary], 'Do not hold me, for I have not yet ascended to the Father; but go to my brethren and say to them, I am ascending to my Father and your Father, to my God and your God.' John 20:17 RSV

And when he had said this, as they were looking on, he was lifted up, and a cloud took him out of their sight. Acts 1:9 RSV

'Being therefore exalted at the right hand of God, and having received from the Father the promise of the Holy Spirit, he has poured out this which you see and hear.' Acts 2:33 RSV

He [God] raised him [Christ] from the dead, and set him at his own right hand in the heavenly places, far above all principality, and power, and might, and dominion, and every name that is named, not only in this world, but also in that which is to come: and hath put all things under his feet, and gave him to be the head over all things to the church, which is his body, the fulness of him that filleth all in all. Ephesians 1:20-23 KJV

Therefore God has highly exalted him and bestowed on him the name which is above every name. Philippians 2:9 RSV

Authority

He [Jesus] taught . . . as one who had authority, and not as their scribes. Matthew 7:29 RSV

'But that you may know that the Son of man has authority on earth to forgive sins'—he then said to the paralytic— 'Rise, take up your bed and go home.' Matthew 9:6 RSV

And Jesus came and said to them, 'All authority in heaven and on earth has been given to me.' Matthew 28:18 RSV

And they were all amazed and said to one another, 'What is this word? For with authority and power he commands the unclean spirits, and they come out.' Luke 4:36 RSV

'And he [God the Father] has given him authority to judge because he is the Son of Man.' John 5:27 NIV

'No-one takes it [my life] from me, but I lay it down of my own accord. I have authority to lay it down and authority to take it up again. This command I received from my Father.' John 10:18 NIV

Death

[God to the serpent] And I will put enmity between thee and the woman, and between thy seed and her seed; it shall bruise thy head, and thou shalt bruise his heel. Genesis 3:15 KJV

He is despised and rejected of men; a man of sorrows, and acquainted with grief: and we hid as it were our faces from him; he was despised, and we esteemed him not. Surely he hath borne our griefs, and carried our sorrows: yet we did esteem him stricken, smitten of God, and afflicted. But he was wounded for our transgressions, he was bruised for our iniquities: the chastisement of our peace was upon him; and with his stripes we are healed. All we like sheep have gone astray; we have turned every one to his own way; and the Lord hath laid on him the iniquity of us all. He was oppressed, and he was afflicted, yet he opened not his mouth: he is brought as a lamb to the slaughter, and as a sheep before her shearers is dumb, so he openeth not his mouth. He was taken from prison and from judgment: and who shall declare his generation? For he was cut off out of the land of the living: for the transgression of my people was he stricken. And he made his grave with the wicked, and with the rich in his death; because he had done no violence, neither was any deceit in his mouth. Isaiah 53:3-9 KJV

From that time forth began Jesus to shew unto his disciples, how that he must go unto Jerusalem, and suffer many things of the elders and chief priests and scribes, and be killed, and be raised again the third day. Matthew 16:21 KJV

'I am the good shepherd. The good shepherd lays down his life for the sheep.' John 10:11 RSV

This Jesus, delivered up according to the definite plan and foreknowledge of God, you crucified and killed by the hands of lawless men.' Acts 2:23 RSV

'You killed the author of life, but God raised him from the dead.' Acts 3:15 NIV

[Jesus] . . . was delivered for our offences, and was raised again for our justification. Romans 4:25 KJV

While we were still weak, at the right time Christ died for the ungodly. Why,

'He is brought as a lamb to the slaughter...'

one will hardly die for a righteous man—though perhaps for a good man one will dare even to die. But God shows his love for us in that while we were yet sinners Christ died for us. Romans 5:6-8 RSV

For the word of the cross is folly to those who are perishing, but to us who are being saved it is the power of God. 1 Corinthians 1:18 RSV

But we preach Christ crucified, unto the Jews a stumblingblock, and unto the Greeks foolishness; but unto them which are called, both Jews and Greeks, Christ the power of God, and the wisdom of God. 1 Corinthians 1:23-24 KJV

For I delivered to you as of first importance what I also received, that Christ died for our sins in accordance with the scriptures . . . 1 Corinthians 15:3 RSV

I have been crucified with Christ; it is no longer I who live, but Christ who lives in me; and the life I now live in the flesh I live by faith in the Son of God, who loved me and gave himself for me. Galatians 2:20 RSV

But far be it from me to glory except in the cross of our Lord Jesus Christ, by which the world has been crucified to me, and I to the world. Galatians 6:14 RSV

He disarmed the principalities and powers and made a public example of them, triumphing over them in him. Colossians 2:15 RSV

Since therefore the children share in flesh and blood, he himself likewise partook of the same nature, that through death he might destroy him who has the power of death, that is, the devil, and deliver all those who through fear of death were subject to lifelong bondage. Hebrews 2:14-15 RSV

See also *Atonement; Reconciliation.*

Eternal Son of God

'The Lord possessed me at the beginning of his work, before his deeds of old; I was appointed from eternity, from the beginning, before the world began.' Proverbs 8:22-23 NIV

In the beginning was the Word, and the Word was with God, and the Word was God. The same was in the beginning with God. John 1:1-2 KJV

Jesus said unto them, Verily, verily, I say unto you, Before Abraham was, I am. John 8:58 KJV

He is the image of the invisible God, the first-born of all creation; for in him all things were created, in heaven and on earth, visible and invisible, whether thrones or dominions or principalities or authorities—all things were created through him and for him. He is before all things, and in him all things hold together. He is the head of the body, the church; he is the beginning, the first-born from the dead, that in everything he might be pre-eminent. For in him all the fullness of God was pleased to dwell. Colossians 1:15-19 RSV

Titles and portraits of Jesus

Alpha and Omega
Revelation 1:8

Ancient of Days
Daniel 7:22

Bread of life
John 6:35

Christ
Matthew 16:16

Door
John 10:9

Emmanuel
Isaiah 7:14; Matthew 1:23

Everlasting Father
Isaiah 9:6

First-born Son
Colossians 1:18

Good Shepherd
John 10:11

Holy One of God
Mark 1:24

Jesus
Matthew 1:21

King of kings
Revelation 17:14

Lamb of God
John 1:29

Light of the world
John 8:12

Lord
Luke 1:42-44

Lord of lords
Revelation 17:14

Messiah
John 1:41

Mighty God
Isaiah 9:6

Prince of Peace
Isaiah 9:6

Resurrection and the life
John 11:25

Saviour
Titus 2:13

Second Adam
1 Corinthians 15:45

Son of God
Matthew 26:63-64

Son of man
Matthew 8:20

Vine
John 15:5

Way, the truth and the life
John 14:6

Wonderful Counsellor
Isaiah 9:6

Word
John 1:1

His Son, who he appointed heir of all things, and through whom he made the universe. The Son is the radiance of God's glory and the exact representation of his being, sustaining all things by his powerful word. After he had provided purification for sins, he sat down at the right hand of the Majesty in heaven. So he became as much superior to the angels as the name he has inherited is superior to theirs. For to which of the angels did God ever say, 'You are my Son; today I have become your Father'? Or again, 'I will be his Father, and he will be my Son'? And again, when God brings his first-born into the world, he says, 'Let all God's angels worship him.' In speaking of the angels he says, 'He makes his angels winds, his servants flames of fire.' But about the Son he says, 'Your throne, O God, will last for ever and ever, and righteousness will be the sceptre of your kingdom.' Hebrews 1:2-8 NIV

Jesus Christ is the same yesterday and today and for ever. Hebrews 13:8 RSV

I am the Alpha and the Omega,' says the Lord God, who is and who was and who is to come, the Almighty. Revelation 1:8 RSV

Holiness

'Which of you convicts me of sin?' John 8:46 RSV

For we have not a high priest who is unable to sympathize with our weaknesses, but one who in every

...ect has been tempted as we are, yet
...hout sin. Hebrews 4:15 RSV

...or it was fitting that we should have
...uch a high priest, holy, blameless,
unstained, separated from sinners,
exalted above the heavens. Hebrews
7:26 RSV

He committed no sin; no guile was
found on his lips. 1 Peter 2:22 RSV

Humility
Rejoice greatly; O Daughter of Zion!
Shout, daughter of Jerusalem! See,
your king comes to you, righteous and
having salvation, gentle and riding on a
donkey, on a colt, the foal of a donkey.
Zechariah 9:9 NIV

For ye know the grace of our Lord
Jesus Christ, that, though he was rich,
yet for your sakes he became poor, that
ye through his poverty might be rich.
2 Corinthians 8:9 KJV

Though he [Jesus] was in the form of
God, did not count equality with God a
thing to be grasped, but emptied
himself, taking the form of a servant,
being born in the likeness of men. And
being found in human form he humbled
himself and became obedient unto
death, even death on a cross.
Philippians 2:6-8 RSV ·

Jesus as king
The Lord says to my lord: 'Sit at my
right hand, till I make your enemies
your footstool.' Psalm 110:1 RSV

'Behold, the days are coming, says the
Lord, when I will raise up for David a
righteous Branch, and he shall reign as
king and deal wisely, and shall execute
justice and righteousness in the land.'
Jeremiah 23:5 RSV

'In my vision at night I looked, and
there before me was one like a son of
man, coming with the clouds of heaven.
He approached the Ancient of Days
and was led into his presence. He was
given authority, glory and sovereign
power; all peoples, nations and men of
every language worshipped him. His
dominion is an everlasting dominion
that will not pass away, and his
kingdom is one that will never be
destroyed.' Daniel 7:13-14 NIV

Rejoice greatly; O Daughter of Zion!
Shout, daughter of Jerusalem! See,
your king comes to you, righteous and
having salvation, gentle and riding on a
donkey, on a colt, the foal of a donkey.
Zechariah 9:9 NIV

Jesus answered, 'My kingship is not of
this world; if my kingship were of this

world, my servants would fight, that I
might not be handed over to the Jews;
but my kingship is not from the world.'
John 18:36 RSV

Pilate also wrote a title and put it on the
cross; it read, 'Jesus of Nazareth, the
King of the Jews.' The chief priests of
the Jews then said to Pilate, 'Do not
write, "The King of the Jews," but,
"This man said, I am King of the
Jews."' John 19:19, 21 RSV

But about the Son he says, 'Your
throne, O God, will last for ever and
ever, and righteousness will be the
sceptre of your kingdom.' Hebrews 1:8
NIV

And I heard a loud voice in heaven,
saying, 'Now the salvation and the
power and the kingdom of our God and
the authority of his Christ have come,
for the accuser of our brethren has
been thrown down, who accuses them
day and night before our God.'
Revelation 12:10 RSV

Jesus, the man
Therefore the Lord himself shall give
you a sign; behold, a virgin shall
conceive, and bear a son, and shall call
his name Immanuel. Isaiah 7:14 KJV

For unto us a child is born, unto us a
son is given: and the government shall
be upon his shoulder: and his name
shall be called Wonderful, Counsellor,
The mighty God, The everlasting
Father, The Prince of Peace. Isaiah 9:6
KJV

And she [Mary] brought forth her
firstborn son, and wrapped him in
swaddling clothes, and laid him in a
manger; because there was no room for
them in the inn. Luke 2:7 KJV

And the Word was made flesh, and
dwelt among us, (and we beheld his
glory, the glory as of the only begotten
of the Father,) full of grace and truth.
John 1:14 KJV

For God so loved the world, that he
gave his only begotten Son, that
whosoever believeth in him should not
perish, but have everlasting life. For
God sent not his Son into the world to
condemn the world; but that the world
through him might be saved. John
3:16-17 KJV

But when the time had fully come, God
sent forth his Son, born of woman,
born under the law, to redeem those
who were under the law. Galatians 4
RSV

Have this mind among yourselves
which is yours in Christ Jesus, wh...

though he was in the form of God, did not count equality with God a thing to be grasped, but emptied himself, taking the form of a servant, being born in the likeness of men. And being found in human form he humbled himself and became obedient unto death, even death on a cross. Philippians 2:5-8 RSV

For there is one God, and one mediator between God and men, the man Christ Jesus. 1 Timothy 2:5 KJV

Great indeed, we confess, is the mystery of our religion: He was manifested in the flesh, vindicated in the Spirit, seen by angels, preached among the nations, believed on in the world, taken up in glory. 1 Timothy 3:16 RSV

But we see Jesus, who was made a little lower than the angels for the suffering of death, crowned with glory and honour. Hebrews 2:9 KJV

Since therefore the children share in flesh and blood, he himself likewise partook of the same nature, that through death he might destroy him who has the power of death, that is, the devil. Hebrews 2:14 RSV

For we have not a high priest who is unable to sympathize with our weaknesses, but one who in every respect has been tempted as we are, yet without sin. Hebrews 4:15 RSV

This is how we may recognize the Spirit of God: every spirit which acknowledges that Jesus Christ has come in the flesh is from God. 1 John 4:2 NEB

Jesus, the one to be worshipped
And when they were come into the house, they saw the young child with Mary his mother, and fell down, and worshipped him: and when they had opened their treasures, they presented unto him gifts; gold, and frankincense, and myrrh. Matthew 2:11 KJV

And Simon Peter answered and said, Thou art the Christ, the Son of the living God. Matthew 16:16 KJV

When Simon Peter saw it, he fell down at Jesus' knees, saying, Depart from me; for I am a sinful man, O Lord. Luke 5:8 KJV

Thomas answered him, 'My Lord and my God!' John 20:28 RSV

'Worthy is the Lamb who was slain, to receive power and wealth and wisdom and might and honour and glory and blessing!' Revelation 5:12 RSV

Jesus as priest
there is one God, and one mediator

between God and men, the man Christ Jesus. 1 Timothy 2:5 KJV

Since then we have a great high priest who has passed through the heavens, Jesus, the Son of God, let us hold fast our confession. For we have not a high priest who is unable to sympathize with our weaknesses, but one who in every respect has been tempted as we are, yet without sin. Hebrews 4:14-15 RSV

So also Christ did not exalt himself to be made a high priest, but was appointed by him who said to him, 'Thou art my Son, today I have begotten thee'; as he says also in another place, 'Thou art a priest for ever, after the order of Melchizedek.' Hebrews 5:5-6 RSV

But he holds his priesthood permanently, because he continues for ever. Consequently he is able for all time to save those who draw near to God through him, since he always lives to make intercession for them. For it was fitting that we should have such a high priest, holy, blameless, unstained, separated from sinners, exalted above the heavens. Hebrews 7:24-26 RSV

Therefore he is the mediator of a new covenant, so that those who are called may receive the promised eternal inheritance, since a death has occurred which redeems them from the transgressions under the first covenant. Hebrews 9:15 RSV

And every priest stands daily at his service, offering repeatedly the same sacrifices, which can never take away sins. But when Christ had offered for all time a single sacrifice for sins, he sat down at the right hand of God. Hebrews 10:11-12 RSV

Jesus as prophet
'The Lord your God will raise up for you a prophet like me from among you, from your brethren—him you shall heed.' Deuteronomy 18:15 RSV

And the crowds said, 'This is the prophet Jesus from Nazareth of Galilee.' Matthew 21:11 RSV

Fear seized them all; and they glorified God, saying, 'A great prophet has arisen among us!' and 'God has visited his people!' Luke 7:16 RSV

'Concerning Jesus of Nazareth, who was a prophet mighty in deed and word before God and all the people.' Luke 24:19 RSV

Love
When he saw the crowds, he had compassion for them, because they

were harassed and helpless, like sheep without a shepherd. Matthew 9:36 RSV

Now before the feast of the Passover, when Jesus knew that his hour had come to depart out of this world to the Father, having loved his own who were in the world, he loved them to the end. John 13:1 RSV

'As the Father has loved me, so have I loved you; abide in my love.' John 15:9 RSV

For I am sure that neither death, nor life, nor angels, nor principalities, nor things present, nor things to come, nor powers, nor height, nor depth, nor anything else in all creation, will be able to separate us from the love of God in Christ Jesus our Lord. Romans 8:38-39 RSV

[Paul's prayer] That you, being rooted and grounded in love, may have power to comprehend with all the saints what is the breadth and length and height and depth, and to know the love of Christ which surpasses knowledge . . . Ephesians 3:17-19 RSV

To him who loves us and has freed us from our sins by his blood . . . Revelation 1:5 RSV

Obedience

'I delight to do thy will, O my God; thy law is within my heart.' Psalm 40:8 RSV

Again, for the second time, he went away and prayed, 'My Father, if this cannot pass unless I drink it, thy will be done.' Matthew 26:42 RSV

Jesus said to them, 'My food is to do the will of him who sent me, and to accomplish his work.' John 4:34 RSV

'And he who sent me is with me; he has not left me alone, for I always do what is pleasing to him.' John 8:29 RSV

And being found in human form he humbled himself and became obedient unto death, even death on a cross. Philippians 2:8 RSV

But even though he was God's Son, he learnt through his sufferings to be obedient. Hebrews 5:8 GNB

Resurrection

For thou dost not give me up to Sheol, or let thy godly one see the Pit. Psalm 16:10 RSV

Yet it pleased the Lord to bruise him; he hath put him to grief: when thou shalt make his soul an offering for sin, he shall see his seed, he shall prolong his days, and the pleasure of the Lord shall prosper in his hand. He shall see of the travail of his soul, and shall be satisfied: by his knowledge shall my righteous servant justify many; for he shall bear their iniquities. Therefore will I divide him a portion with the great, and he shall divide the spoil with the strong, because he hath poured out his soul unto death; and he was numbered with the transgressors; and he bare the sin of many, and made intercession for the transgressors. Isaiah 53:10-12 KJV

From that time forth began Jesus to shew unto his disciples, how that he must go unto Jerusalem, and suffer

'There was a garden in the place where Jesus had been put to death, and in it there was a new tomb where no one had ever been buried.'

Parables of Jesus

	Matthew	Mark	Luke
Lamp under a bushel	5:14-15	4:21-22	8:16, 11:33
Houses on rock and on sand	7:24-27		6:47-49
New cloth on an old garment	9:16	2:21	5:36
New wine in old wineskins	9:17	2:22	5:37-38
Sower and soils	13:3-8	4:3-8	8:5-8
Mustard seed	13:31-32	4:30-32	13:18-19
Tares	13:24-30		
Leaven (yeast)	13:33		13:20-21
Hidden treasure	13:44		
Pearl of great value	13:45-46		
Drag-net	13:47-48		
Lost sheep	18:12-13		15:4-6
Two debtors (unforgiving servant)	18:23-34		
Workers in the vineyard	20:1-16		
Two sons	21:28-31		
Wicked tenants	21:33-41	12:1-9	20:9-16
Invitation to the wedding feast; man without a wedding-garment	22:2-14		
Fig-tree as herald of summer	24:32-33	13:28-29	21:29-32
Ten 'bridesmaids'	25:1-13		
Talents (Matthew); Pounds (Luke)	25:14-30		19:12-27
Sheep and goats	25:31-36		
Seedtime to harvest		4:26-29	
Creditor and the debtors			7:41-43
Good Samaritan			10:30-37
Friend in need			11:5-8
Rich fool			12:16-21
Alert servants			12:35-40
Faithful steward			12:42-48
Fig-tree without figs			13:6-9
Places of honour at the wedding-feast			14:7-14
Great banquet and the reluctant guests			14:16-24
Counting the cost			14:28-33
Lost coin			15:8-10
The prodigal son			15:11-32
Dishonest steward			16:1-8
Rich man and Lazarus			16:19-31
The master and his servant			17:7-10
The persistent widow and the unrighteous judge			18:2-5
The Pharisee and the tax collector			18:10-14

many things of the elders and chief priests and scribes, and be killed, and be raised again the third day. Matthew 16:21 KJV

He is not here: for he is risen, as he said. Come, see the place where the Lord lay. Matthew 28:6 KJV

'This Jesus God raised up, and of that we all are witnesses.' Acts 2:32 RSV

'He has fixed a day on which he will judge the world in righteousness by a man whom he has appointed, and of this he has given assurance to all men by raising him from the dead.' Acts 17:31 RSV

[Jesus] . . . was delivered for our offences, and was raised again for our justification. Romans 4:25 KJV

By our baptism, then, we were buried with him and shared his death, in order that, just as Christ was raised from death by the glorious power of the Father, so also we might live a new life. For since we have become one with him in dying as he did, in the same way we shall be one with him by being raised to life as he was. Romans 6:4-5 GNB

Miracles of Jesus

	Matthew	Mark	Luke	John
Healing of physical and mental disorders				
Leper	8:2-3	1:40-42	5:12-13	
Centurion's servant	8:5-13		7:1-10	
Peter's mother-in-law	8:14-15	1:30-31	4:38-39	
Two Gadarenes	8:28-34	5:1-15	8:27-35	
Paralysed man	9:2-7	2:3-12	5:18-25	
Woman with a haemorrhage	9:20-22	5:25-29	8:43-48	
Two blind men	9:27-31			
Man dumb and possessed	9:32-33			
Man with a withered hand	12:10-13	3:1-5	6:6-10	
Man blind, dumb and possessed	12:22		11:14	
Canaanite woman's daughter	15:21-28	7:24-30		
Boy with epilepsy	17:14-18	9:17-29	9:38-43	
Bartimaeus, and another blind man	20:29-34	10:46-52	18:35-43	
Deaf and dumb man		7:31-37		
Man possessed, synagogue		1:23-26	4:33-35	
Blind man at Bethsaida		8:22-26		
Woman bent double			13:11-13	
Man with dropsy			14:1-4	
Ten lepers			17:11-19	
Malchus' ear			22:50-51	
Official's son at Capernaum				4:46-54
Sick man, Pool of Bethesda				5:1-9
Man born blind				9
Command over the forces of nature				
Calming of the storm	8:23-27	4:37-41	8:22-25	
Walking on the water	14:25	6:48-51		6:19-21
5,000 people fed	14:15-21	6:35-44	9:12-17	6:5-13
4,000 people fed	15:32-38	8:1-9		
Coin in the fish's mouth	17:24-27			
Fig-tree withered	21:18-22	11:12-14, 20-26		
Catch of fish			5:1-11	
Water turned into wine				2:1-11
Another catch of fish				21:1-11
Bringing the dead back to life				
Jairus' daughter	9:18-19, 23-25	5:22-24, 38-42	8:41-42, 49-56	
Widow's son at Nain			7:11-15	
Lazarus				11:1-44

For we know that Christ being raised from the dead will never die again; death no longer has dominion over him. The death he died he died to sin, once for all, but the life he lives he lives to God. So you also must consider yourselves dead to sin and alive to God in Christ Jesus. Romans 6:9-11 RSV

He was buried, . . . he was raised on the third day in accordance with the scriptures, and . . . he appeared to Cephas, then to the twelve. 1 Corinthians 15:4 RSV

Now if Christ is preached as raised from the dead, how can some of you say that there is no resurrection of the dead? But if there is no resurrection of the dead, then Christ has not been raised; if Christ has not been raised, then our preaching is in vain and your faith is in vain. We are even found to be misrepresenting God, because we testified of God that he raised Christ, whom he did not raise if it is true that the dead are not raised. For if the dead are not raised, then Christ has not been raised. If Christ has not been raised, your faith is futile and you are still in your sins. Then those also who have

fallen asleep in Christ have perished. If for this life only we have hoped in Christ, we are of all men most to be pitied. But in fact Christ has been raised from the dead, the first fruits of those who have fallen asleep. For as by a man came death, by a man has come also the resurrection of the dead.
1 Corinthians 15:12-21 RSV

If ye then be risen with Christ, seek those things which are above, where Christ sitteth on the right hand of God. Colossians 3:1 KJV

When I saw him, I fell at his feet as though dead. But he laid his right hand upon me and said, 'Do not be afraid. I am the first and the last, and I am the living one; for I was dead and now I am alive for evermore, and I hold the keys of Death and Death's domain.'
Revelation 1:17-18 NEB

Second coming
See *Last things*.

Seven words from the cross
And about the ninth hour Jesus cried with a loud voice, 'Eli, Eli, lama sabachthani?' that is, 'My God, my God, why hast thou forsaken me?'
Matthew 27:46 RSV

Then said Jesus, Father, forgive them; for they know not what they do. Luke 23:34 KJV

And Jesus said unto him, Verily I say unto thee, To day shalt thou be with me in paradise. Luke 23:43 KJV

And when Jesus had cried with a loud voice, he said, Father, into thy hands I commend my spirit: and having said thus, he gave up the ghost. Luke 23:46 KJV

When Jesus saw his mother, and the disciple whom he loved standing near, he said to his mother, 'Woman, behold, your son!' Then he said to the disciple, 'Behold, your mother!' John 19:26-27 RSV

After this Jesus, knowing that all was now finished, said (to fulfil the scripture), 'I thirst.' John 19:28 RSV

When Jesus had received the vinegar, he said, 'It is finished'; and he bowed his head and gave up his spirit. John 19:30 RSV

Joy
He [Nehemiah] said . . . 'This day is holy to our Lord; and do not be grieved, for the joy of the Lord is your strength.'
Nehemiah 8:10 RSV

Thou dost show me the path of life; in thy presence there is fullness of joy, in thy right hand are pleasures for evermore. Psalm 16:11 RSV

This is the day which the Lord has made; let us rejoice and be glad in it. Psalm 118:24 RSV

I rejoice at thy word like one who finds great spoil. Psalm 119:162 RSV

The Lord has done great things for us, and we are filled with joy. Psalm 126:3 NIV

They that sow in tears shall reap in joy. He that goeth forth and weepeth, bearing precious seed, shall doubtless come again with rejoicing, bringing his sheaves with him. Psalm 126:5-6 KJV

With joy you will draw water from the wells of salvation. Isaiah 12:3 RSV

And the ransomed of the Lord shall return, and come to Zion with singing; everlasting joy shall be upon their heads; they shall obtain joy and gladness, and sorrow and sighing shall flee away. Isaiah 35:10 RSV

Blessed are the poor in spirit: for theirs is the kingdom of heaven . . . Matthew 5:3 KJV

'As for what was sown on rocky ground, this is he who hears the word and immediately receives it with joy; yet he has no root in himself, but endures for a while, and when tribulation or persecution arises on account of the word, immediately he falls away.' Matthew 13:20-21 RSV

'Just so, I tell you, there will be more joy in heaven over one sinner who repents than over ninety-nine righteous persons who need no repentance.' Luke 15:7 RSV

'These things I have spoken to you, that my joy may be in you, and that your joy may be full.' John 15:11 RSV

'Ask and you will receive, that your joy may be complete.' John 16:24 NEB

And the disciples were filled with joy and with the Holy Spirit. Acts 13:52 RSV

Our Lord Jesus Christ: by whom also we have access by faith into this grace wherein we stand, and rejoice in hope of the glory of God. Romans 5:1-2 KJV

May the God of hope fill you with all joy and peace in believing, so that by the power of the Holy Spirit you may abound in hope. Romans 15:13 RSV

I will all the more gladly boast of my weaknesses, that the power of Christ may rest upon me. 2 Corinthians 12:9 RSV

But the fruit of the Spirit is . . . joy . . . Galatians 5:22 RSV

Rejoice in the Lord always; again I will say, Rejoice. Philippians 4:4 RSV

As for the rich in this world, charge them not to be haughty, nor to set their hopes on uncertain riches but on God who richly furnishes us with everything to enjoy. 1 Timothy 6:17 RSV

Looking unto Jesus the author and finisher of our faith; who for the joy that was set before him endured the cross, despising the shame, and is set down at the right hand of the throne of God. Hebrews 12:2 KJV

Without having seen him you love him; though you do not now see him you believe in him and rejoice with unutterable and exalted joy. 1 Peter 1:8 RSV

No greater joy can I have than this, to hear that my children follow the truth. 3 John 4 RSV

Judgement
See Last things.

Justice
'Do not take advantage of anyone or rob him. Do not hold back the wages of someone you have hired, not even for one night.' Leviticus 19:13 GNB

'Justice, and only justice, you shall follow, that you may live and inherit the land which the Lord your God gives you.' Deuteronomy 16:20 RSV

Give the king thy justice, O God, and thy righteousness to the royal son! May he judge thy people with righteousness. and thy poor with justice! Psalm 72:1-2 RSV

To do righteousness and justice is more acceptable to the Lord than sacrifice. Proverbs 21:3 RSV

Seek justice, encourage the oppressed. Defend the cause of the fatherless, plead the case of the widow. Isaiah 1:17 NIV

We all growl like bears, we moan and moan like doves; we look for justice, but there is none; for salvation, but it is far from us. Isaiah 59:11 RSV

Justice is driven away, and right cannot come near. Truth stumbles in the public square, and honesty finds no place there. Isaiah 59:14 GNB

The Lord says, 'I love justice and hate oppression and crime. I will faithfully reward my people and make an eternal covenant with them.' Isaiah 61:8 GNB

'But let justice roll down like waters, and righteousness like an ever-flowing stream.' Amos 5:24 RSV

He hath shewed thee, O man, what is good; and what doth the Lord require of thee, but to do justly, and to love mercy, and to walk humbly with thy God? Micah 6:8 KJV

Masters, treat your slaves justly and fairly, knowing that you also have a Master in heaven. Colossians 4:1 RSV

See also Injustice; Righteousness.

Justification
And he [Abraham] believed in the Lord; and he counted it to him for righteousness. Genesis 15:6 KJV

Then Job answered: 'Truly I know that it is so: But how can a man be just before God?' Job 9:1-2 RSV

Blessed is he whose transgression is forgiven, whose sin is covered. Blessed is the man to whom the Lord imputes no iniquity, and in whose spirit there is no deceit. Psalm 32:1-2 RSV

He is near that justifieth me; who will contend with me? Let us stand together: who is mine adversary? Let him come near to me. Behold, the Lord God will help me; who is he that shall condemn me? Isaiah 50:8-9 KJV

I will greatly rejoice in the Lord, my soul shall exult in my God; for he has clothed me with the garments of salvation, he has covered me with the robe of righteousness. Isaiah 61:10 RSV

'But the tax collector, standing far off, would not even lift up his eyes to heaven, but beat his breast, saying, "God, be merciful to me a sinner!" I tell you, this man went down to his house justified rather than the other; for every one who exalts himself will be humbled, but he who humbles himself will be exalted.' Luke 18:13-14 RSV

Being justified freely by his grace through the redemption that is in Christ Jesus. Romans 3:24 KJV

And to one who does not work but trusts him who justifies the ungodly, his faith is reckoned as righteousness. Romans 4:5 RSV

Therefore being justified by faith, we have peace with God through our Lord Jesus Christ. Romans 5:1 KJV

Since, therefore, we are now justified by his blood, much more shall we be saved by him from the wrath of God. Romans 5:9 RSV

For as by one man's disobedience many were made sinners, so by one man's obedience many will be made righteous. Romans 5:19 RSV

And those whom he predestined he also called; and those whom he called he also justified; and those whom he justified he also glorified . . . Who shall bring any charge against God's elect? It is God who justifies; who is to condemn? Is it Christ Jesus, who died, yes, who was raised from the dead, who is at the right hand of God, who indeed intercedes for us? Romans 8:30, 33-34 RSV

For our sake he made him to be sin who knew no sin, so that in him we might become the righteousness of God. 2 Corinthians 5:21 RSV

See also *Atonement; Faith; Righteousness.*

Kindness

'If you pour yourself out for the hungry and satisfy the desire of the afflicted, then shall your light rise in the darkness and your gloom be as the noonday.' Isaiah 58:10 RSV

When the Son of man shall come in his glory, and all the holy angels with him, then shall he sit upon the throne of his glory: and before him shall be gathered all nations: and he shall separate them one from another, as a shepherd divideth his sheep from the goats: and he shall set the sheep on his right hand, but the goats on the left. Then shall the King say unto them on his right hand, Come, ye blessed of my Father, inherit the kingdom prepared for you from the foundation of the world: for I was an hungred, and ye gave me meat: I was thirsty, and ye gave me drink: I was a stranger, and ye took me in: naked, and ye clothed me: I was sick, and ye visited me: I was in prison, and ye came unto me . . . Verily I say unto you, Inasmuch as ye have done it unto one of the least of these my brethren, ye have done it unto me. Matthew 25:35-36, 40 KJV

'A man was going down from Jerusalem to Jericho, and he fell among robbers, who stripped him and beat him, and departed, leaving him half dead . . . a Samaritan, as he journeyed, came to where he was; and when he saw him, he had compassion, and went to him and bound up his wounds, pouring on oil and wine; then he set him on his own beast and brought him to an inn, and took care of him. And the next day he took out two denarii and gave them to the innkeeper, saying, "Take care of him; and

whatever more you spend, I will repay you when I come back."' Luke 10:30, 33-35 RSV

'In all things I have shown you that by so toiling one must help the weak, remembering the words of the Lord Jesus, how he said, "It is more blessed to give than to receive."' Acts 20:35 RSV

But the fruit of the Spirit is love . . . kindness, goodness, faithfulness, gentleness, self-control . . . Galatians 5:22 RSV

Be kind to one another, tenderhearted, forgiving one another, as God in Christ forgave you. Ephesians 4:32 RSV

Let us consider how to stir up one another to love and good works. Hebrews 10:24 RSV

See also *Love; Service.*

Kingdom, kingdom of God

Blessed are the poor in spirit: for theirs is the kingdom of heaven. Matthew 5:3 KJV

Thy kingdom come. Thy will be done, in earth as it is in heaven. Matthew 6:10 BCP

But seek ye first the kingdom of God, and his righteousness; and all these things shall be added unto you. Matthew 6:33 KJV

'Not every one who says to me, "Lord, Lord," shall enter the kingdom of heaven, but he who does the will of my Father who is in heaven.' Matthew 7:21 RSV

Then shall the King say unto them on his right hand, Come, ye blessed of my Father, inherit the kingdom prepared for you from the foundation of the world. Matthew 25:34 KJV

'The time is fulfilled, and the kingdom of God is at hand; repent, and believe in the gospel.' Mark 1:15 RSV

Verily I say unto you, Whosoever shall not receive the kingdom of God as a little child, he shall not enter therein. Mark 10:15 KJV

And when he was demanded of the Pharisees, when the kingdom of God should come, he answered them and said, The kingdom of God cometh not with observation: neither shall they say, Lo here! or, lo there! for, behold, the kingdom of God is within you. Luke 17:20-21 KJV

Jesus answered and said unto him [Nicodemus], Verily, verily, I say unto thee, Except a man be born again, he annot see the kingdom of God. John 3:3 KJV

[Paul and Barnabas] Strengthening the souls of the disciples, exhorting them to continue in the faith, and saying that through many tribulations we must enter the kingdom of God. Acts 14:22 RSV

For the kingdom of God does not mean food and drink but righteousness and peace and joy in the Holy Spirit. Romans 14:17 RSV

For the kingdom of God does not consist in talk but in power. 1 Corinthians 4:20 RSV

Do you not know that the wicked will not inherit the kingdom of God? Do not be deceived. 1 Corinthians 6:9 NIV

Then the end will come; Christ will overcome all spiritual rulers, authorities, and powers, and will hand over the Kingdom to God the Father. 1 Corinthians 15:24 GNB

He [God the Father] has delivered us from the dominion of darkness and transferred us to the kingdom of his beloved Son, in whom we have redemption, the forgiveness of sins. Colossians 1:13 RSV

Therefore let us be grateful for receiving a kingdom that cannot be shaken, and thus let us offer to God acceptable worship, with reverence and awe. Hebrews 12:28 RSV

'The kingdom of the world has become the kingdom of our Lord and of his Christ, and he shall reign for ever and ever.' Revelation 11:15 RSV

Knowledge

And out of the ground made the Lord God to grow every tree that is pleasant to the sight, and good for food; the tree of life also in the midst of the garden, and the tree of knowledge of good and evil. Genesis 2:9 KJV

For I know that my redeemer liveth, and that he shall stand at the latter day upon the earth. Job 19:25 KJV

'Be still, and know that I am God. I am exalted among the nations, I am exalted in the earth!' Psalm 46:10 RSV

I am thy servant; give me understanding, that I may know thy testimonies! Psalm 119:125 RSV

O Lord, thou hast searched me and known me! Thou knowest when I sit down and when I rise up; thou discernest my thoughts from afar. Thou searchest out my path and my lying down, and art acquainted with all my ways. Even before a word is on my tongue, lo, O Lord, thou knowest it altogether. Thou dost beset me behind and before, and layest thy hand upon me. Such knowledge is too wonderful for me; it is high, I cannot attain it. Psalm 139:1-6 RSV

They shall not hurt nor destroy in all my holy mountain: for the earth shall be full of the knowledge of the Lord, as the waters cover the sea. Isaiah 11:9 KJV

'Let us know, let us press on to know the Lord; his going forth is sure as the dawn; he will come to us as the showers, as the spring rains that water the earth.' Hosea 6:3 RSV

'All things have been delivered to me by my Father; and no one knows the Son except the Father, and no one knows the Father except the Son and any one to whom the Son chooses to reveal him.' Matthew 11:27 RSV

'I am the good shepherd. As the Father knows me and I know the Father, in the same way I know my sheep and they know me. And I am willing to die for them.' John 10:14-15 GNB

'And this is eternal life, that they know thee the only true God, and Jesus Christ whom thou hast sent.' John 17:3 RSV

Knowledge . . . puffs a person up with pride; but love builds up. 1 Corinthians 8:1 GNB

And if I have prophetic powers, and understand all mysteries and all knowledge, and if I have all faith, so as to remove mountains, but have not love, I am nothing . . . For now we see in a mirror dimly, but then face to face. Now I know in part; then I shall understand fully, even as I have been fully understood. 1 Corinthians 13:2, 12 RSV

[Paul's prayer] To know the love of Christ which surpasses knowledge, that you may be filled with all the fullness of God. Ephesians 3:19 RSV

That I may know him and the power of his resurrection, and may share his sufferings, becoming like him in his death. Philippians 3:10 RSV

And so . . . we have not ceased to pray for you, asking that you may be filled with the knowledge of his will in all spiritual wisdom and understanding, to lead a life worthy of the Lord, fully pleasing to him, bearing fruit in every good work and increasing in the knowledge of God. Colossians 1:9-10 RSV

But I am not ashamed, for I know whom I have believed, and I am sure that he is able to guard until that Day what has been entrusted to me.
2 Timothy 1:12 RSV

And hereby we do know that we know him, if we keep his commandments.
1 John 2:3 KJV

See also *Discernment; Understanding; Wisdom.*

Land

'For six years you shall sow your land and gather in its yield; but the seventh year you shall let it rest and lie fallow, that the poor of your people may eat; and what they leave the wild beasts may eat.' Exodus 23:10-11 RSV

'And you shall hallow the fiftieth year, and proclaim liberty throughout the land to all its inhabitants; it shall be a jubilee for you, when each of you shall return to his property and each of you shall return to his family. A jubilee shall that fiftieth year be to you; in it you shall neither sow, nor reap what grows of itself, nor gather the grapes from the undressed vines.' Leviticus 25:10-11 RSV

Your land must not be sold on a permanent basis, because you do not own it; it belongs to God, and you are like foreigners who are allowed to make use of it. Leviticus 25:23 GNB

'He brought us into this place and gave us this land, a land flowing with milk and honey. And behold, now I bring the first of the fruit of the ground, which thou, O Lord, hast given me.'
Deuteronomy 26:9-10 RSV

'And all these blessings shall come upon you and overtake you, if you obey the voice of the Lord your God.

Blessed shall you be in the city, and blessed shall you be in the field. Blessed shall be the fruit of your body, and the fruit of your ground, and the fruit of your beasts, the increase of your cattle, and the young of your flock.' Deuteronomy 28:2-4 RSV

[The Lord's promise to Solomon] 'If my people who are called by my name humble themselves, and pray and seek my face, and turn from their wicked ways, then I will hear from heaven, and will forgive their sin and heal their land.' 2 Chronicles 7:14 RSV

The earth is the Lord's and the fullness thereof, the world and those who dwell therein. Psalm 24:1 RSV

There was not a needy person among them, for as many as were possessors of lands or houses sold them, and brought the proceeds of what was sold and laid it at the apostles' feet; and distribution was made to each as any had need. Acts 4:34-35 RSV

Last Supper

See *Communion.*

Last things

Events before second coming

'And you will hear of wars and rumours of wars; see that you are not alarmed; for this must take place, but the end is not yet.' Matthew 24:6 RSV

'Then they will deliver you up to tribulation, and put you to death; and you will be hated by all nations for my name's sake. And then many will fall away, and betray one another, and hate one another. And many false prophets will arise and lead many astray. And because wickedness is multiplied, most men's love will grow cold. But he who endures to the end will be saved. And

'For six years you shall sow your land and gather in its yield.'

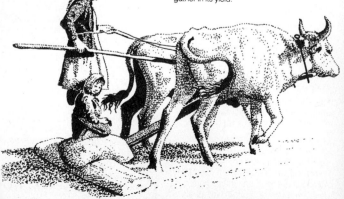

this gospel of the kingdom will be preached throughout the whole world, as a testimony to all nations; and then the end will come.' Matthew 24:9-14 RSV

'For then there will be great tribulation, such as has not been from the beginning of the world until now, no, and never will be. And if those days had not been shortened, no human being would be saved; but for the sake of the elect those days will be shortened.' Matthew 24:21-22 RSV

'Immediately after the tribulation of those days the sun will be darkened, and the moon will not give its light, and the stars will fall from heaven, and the powers of the heavens will be shaken.' Matthew 24:29 RSV

Let no one deceive you in any way; for that day [the day of the Lord] will not come, unless the rebellion comes first, and the man of lawlessness is revealed, the son of perdition, who opposes and exalts himself against every so-called god or object of worship, so that he takes his seat in the temple of God, proclaiming himself to be God. 2 Thessalonians 2:3-4 RSV

And then the lawless one will be revealed, whom the Lord Jesus will overthrow with the breath of his mouth and destroy by the splendour of his coming. 2 Thessalonians 2:8 NIV

He seized the dragon, that ancient serpent—that is, the Devil, or Satan—and chained him up for a thousand years. The angel threw him into the abyss, locked it, and sealed it, so that he could not deceive the nations any more until the thousand years were over. After that he must be let loose for a little while. Revelation 20:2-3 GNB

After the thousand years are over, Satan will be let loose from his prison, and he will go out to deceive the nations scattered over the whole world, that is, Gog and Magog. Satan will bring them all together for battle, as many as the grains of sand on the sea-shore. Revelation 20:7-8 GNB

Heaven

Whom have I in heaven but thee? And there is none upon earth that I desire beside thee. Psalm 73:25 KJV

Thus saith the Lord, The heaven is my throne, and the earth is my footstool: where is the house that ye build unto me? and where is the place of my rest? Isaiah 66:1 KJV

Our Father, which art in heaven, hallowed be thy name. Thy kingdom come. Thy will be done, in earth as it is in heaven. Matthew 6:9-10 BCP

In my Father's house are many mansions: if it were not so, I would have told you. I go to prepare a place for you. And if I go and prepare a place for you, I will come again, and receive you unto myself; that where I am, there ye may be also. John 14:2-3 KJV

'Father, I desire that they also, whom thou hast given me, may be with me where I am, to behold my glory which thou hast given me in thy love for me before the foundation of the world.' John 17:24 RSV

And suddenly a sound came from heaven like the rush of a mighty wind, and it filled all the house where they were sitting. Acts 2:2 RSV

As it is written, Eye hath not seen, nor ear heard, neither have entered into the heart of man, the things which God hath prepared for them that love him. 1 Corinthians 2:9 KJV

We, however, are citizens of heaven, and we eagerly wait for our Saviour, the Lord Jesus Christ, to come from heaven. Philippians 3:20 GNB

For Christ has entered, not into a sanctuary made with hands, a copy of the true one, but into heaven itself, now to appear in the presence of God on our behalf. Hebrews 9:24 RSV

After this I looked, and behold, a great multitude which no man could number, from every nation, from all tribes and peoples and tongues, standing before the throne and before the Lamb, clothed in white robes. Revelation 7:9 RSV

'Therefore are they before the throne of God, and serve him day and night within his temple; and he who sits upon the throne will shelter them with his presence.' Revelation 7:15 RSV

Then I saw thrones, and those who sat on them were given the power to judge. I also saw the souls of those who had been executed because they had proclaimed the truth that Jesus revealed and the word of God. Revelation 20:4 GNB

And I heard a great voice out of heaven saying, Behold, the tabernacle of God is with men, and he will dwell with them, and they shall be his people, and God himself shall be with them, and be their God. Revelation 21:3 KJV

There shall no more be anything accursed, but the throne of God and of the Lamb shall be in it, and his servants shall worship him; they shall see his face, and his name shall be on their foreheads. And night shall be no more; they need no light of lamp or sun, for the Lord God will be their light, and they shall reign for ever and ever. Revelation 22:3-5 RSV

Hell

'Enter by the narrow gate; for the gate is wide and the way is easy, that leads to destruction, and those who enter by it are many.' Matthew 7:13 RSV

But the children of the kingdom shall be cast out into outer darkness: there shall be weeping and gnashing of teeth. Matthew 8:12 KJV

'Do not be afraid of those who kill the body but cannot kill the soul; rather be afraid of God, who can destroy both body and soul in hell.' Matthew 10:28 GNB

Then shall he say also unto them on the left hand, Depart from me, ye cursed, into everlasting fire, prepared for the devil and his angels . . . And these shall go away into everlasting punishment: but the righteous into life eternal. Matthew 25:41, 46 KJV

And beside all this, between us and you [heaven and hell] there is a great gulf fixed: so that they which would pass from hence to you cannot; neither can they pass to us, that would come from thence. Luke 16:26 KJV

They will suffer the punishment of eternal destruction, separated from the presence of the Lord and from his glorious might. 2 Thessalonians 1:9 GNB

'Whoever worships the beast and its image and receives the mark on his forehead or on his hand will himself drink God's wine, the wine of his fury, which he has poured at full strength into the cup of his anger! All who do this will be tormented in fire and sulphur before the holy angels and the Lamb. The smoke of the fire that torments them goes up for ever and ever. There is no relief day or night for those who worship the beast and its image, for anyone who has the mark of its name.' Revelation 14:9-11 GNB

Then the Devil, who deceived them, was thrown into the lake of fire and sulphur, where the beast and the false prophet had already been thrown; and they will be tormented day and night for ever and ever. Revelation 20:10 GNB

And whosoever was not found written in the book of life was cast into the lake of fire. Revelation 20:15 KJV

'But as for the cowardly, the faithless, the polluted, as for murderers, fornicators, sorcerers, idolaters, and all liars, their lot shall be in the lake that burns with fire and sulphur, which is the second death.' Revelation 21:8 RSV

Judgement

'If anyone declares publicly that he belongs to me, I will do the same for him before my Father in heaven. But if anyone rejects me publicly, I will reject him before my Father in heaven.' Matthew 10:32-33 GNB

When the Son of man shall come in his glory, and all the holy angels with him, then shall he sit upon the throne of his glory: and before him shall be gathered all nations: and he shall separate them one from another, as a shepherd divideth his sheep from the goats: and he shall set the sheep on his right hand, but the goats on the left. Matthew 25:31-33 KJV

'He [God] has fixed a day on which he will judge the world in righteousness by a man whom he has appointed, and of this he has given assurance to all men by raising him from the dead.' Acts 17:31 RSV

So you should not pass judgement on anyone before the right time comes. Final judgement must wait until the Lord comes; he will bring to light the dark secrets and expose the hidden purposes of people's minds. And then everyone will receive from God the praise he deserves. 1 Corinthians 4:5 GNB

Do you not know that the saints will judge the world? And if the world is to be judged by you, are you incompetent to try trivial cases? Do you not know that we are to judge angels? How much more, matters pertaining to this life! 1 Corinthians 6:2-3 RSV

For we must all appear before the judgment seat of Christ, so that each one may receive good or evil, according to what he has done in the body. 2 Corinthians 5:10 RSV

It is appointed unto men once to die, but after this the judgment. Hebrews 9:27 KJV

And the angels that did not keep their own position but left their proper dwelling have been kept by him in eternal chains in the nether gloom until judgment of the great day. Jude 6

[They] said to the mountains and rocks, Fall on us, and hide us from the face of him that sitteth on the throne, and from the wrath of the Lamb. For the great day of his wrath is come; and who shall be able to stand? Revelation 6:16-17 KJV

And I saw a great white throne, and him that sat on it, from whose face the earth and the heaven fled away; and there was found no place for them. And I saw the dead, small and great, stand before God; and the books were opened: and another book was opened, which is the book of life: and the dead were judged out of those things which were written in the books, according to their works. And the sea gave up the dead which were in it; and death and hell delivered up the dead which were in them: and they were judged every man according to their works. And death and hell were cast into the lake of fire. This is the second death. And whosoever was not found written in the book of life was cast into the lake of fire. Revelation 20:11-15 KJV

Renewal of all things

Jesus said to them, 'You can be sure that when the Son of Man sits on his glorious throne in the New Age, then you twelve followers of mine will also sit on thrones, to rule the twelve tribes of Israel.' Matthew 19:28 GNB

[Jesus Christ] Whom the heaven must receive until the times of restitution of all things, which God hath spoken by the mouth of all his holy prophets since the world began. Acts 3:21 KJV

The creation itself will be set free from its bondage to decay and obtain the glorious liberty of the children of God. Romans 8:21 RSV

But the day of the Lord will come like a thief, and then the heavens will pass away with a loud noise, and the elements will be dissolved with fire, and the earth and the works that are upon it will be burned up. Since all these things are thus to be dissolved, what sort of persons ought you to be in lives of holiness and godliness, waiting for and hastening the coming of the day of God, because of which the heavens will be kindled and dissolved, and the elements will melt with fire! But according to his promise we wait for new heavens and a new earth in which righteousness dwells. 2 Peter 3:10-13 RSV

And I saw a new heaven and a new earth: for the first heaven and the first earth were passed away; and there was no more sea. And I John saw the holy city, new Jerusalem, coming down from God out of heaven, prepared as a bride adorned for her husband. And I heard a great voice out of heaven saying, Behold, the tabernacle of God is with men, and he will dwell with them, and they shall be his people, and God himself shall be with them, and be their God. And God shall wipe away all tears from their eyes; and there shall be no more death, neither sorrow, nor crying, neither shall there be any more pain: for the former things are passed away. And he that sat upon the throne said, Behold, I make all things new. Revelation 21:1-5 KJV

Resurrection

And they shall come out and see the dead bodies of those who have rebelled against me; their worm shall not die nor their fire be quenched, and they shall be abhorred by all mankind. Isaiah 66:24 NEB

'And many of those who sleep in the dust of the earth shall awake, some to everlasting life, and some to shame and everlasting contempt. And those who are wise shall shine like the brightness of the firmament; and those who turn many to righteousness, like the stars for ever and ever.' Daniel 12:2-3 RSV

'"I am the God of Abraham, and the God of Isaac, and the God of Jacob". He is not God of the dead, but of the living.' Matthew 22:32 RSV

'Do not be surprised at this; the time is coming when all the dead will hear his voice and come out of their graves: those who have done good will rise and live, and those who have done evil will rise and be condemned.' John 5:28-29 GNB

Martha saith unto him, I know that he shall rise again in the resurrection at the last day. Jesus said unto her, I am the resurrection, and the life: he that believeth in me, though he were dead, yet shall he live. John 11:24-25 KJV

So is it with the resurrection of the dead. What is sown is perishable, what is raised is imperishable. It is sown in dishonour, it is raised in glory. It is sown in weakness, it is raised in power. It is sown a physical body, it is raised a spiritual body. If there is a physical body, there is also a spiritual body. 1 Corinthians 15:42-44 RSV

In a moment, in the twinkling of an

eye, at the last trump: for the trumpet shall sound, and the dead shall be raised incorruptible, and we shall be changed. 1 Corinthians 15:52 KJV

The Lord Jesus Christ, who will change our lowly body to be like his glorious body, by the power which enables him even to subject all things to himself. Philippians 3:20-21 RSV

For the Lord himself shall descend from heaven with a shout, with the voice of the archangel, and with the trump of God: and the dead in Christ shall rise first. 1 Thessalonians 4:16 KJV

Then the Devil, who deceived them, was thrown into the lake of fire and sulphur, where the beast and the false prophet had already been thrown; and they will be tormented day and night for ever and ever. Revelation 20:10 GNB

Second coming of Jesus

'In my vision at night I looked, and there before me was one like a son of man, coming with the clouds of heaven. He approached the Ancient of Days and was led into his presence.' Daniel 7:13 NIV

'For as the lightning comes from the east and shines as far as the west, so will be the coming of the Son of man.' Matthew 24:27 RSV

'Immediately after the tribulation of those days the sun will be darkened, and the moon will not give its light, and the stars will fall from heaven, and the powers of the heavens will be shaken; then will appear the sign of the Son of man in heaven, and then all the tribes of the earth will mourn, and they will see the Son of man coming on the clouds of heaven with power and great glory . . . But of that day and hour no one knows, not even the angels of heaven, nor the Son, but the Father only.' Matthew 24:29-30, 36 RSV

And if I go and prepare a place for you, I will come again, and receive you unto myself; that where I am, there ye may be also. John 14:3 KJV

'Men of Galilee, why do you stand looking into heaven? This Jesus, who was taken up from you into heaven, will come in the same way as you saw him go into heaven.' Acts 1:11 RSV

For if we believe that Jesus died and rose again, even so them also which sleep in Jesus will God bring with him. For this we say unto you by the word of the Lord, that we which are alive and remain unto the coming of the Lord shall not prevent them which are asleep. For the Lord himself shall descend from heaven with a shout, with the voice of the archangel, and with the trump of God: and the dead in Christ shall rise first. Then we which are alive and remain shall be caught up together with them in the clouds, to meet the Lord in the air: and so shall we ever be with the Lord. 1 Thessalonians 4:14-17 KJV

For you yourselves know well that the day of the Lord will come like a thief in the night. 1 Thessalonians 5:2 RSV

He will do this when the Lord Jesus appears from heaven with his mighty angels . . . when he comes on that Day to receive glory from all his people and honour from all who believe. 2 Thessalonians 1:7, 10 GNB

In the same manner Christ also was offered in sacrifice once to take away the sins of many. He will appear a second time, not to deal with sin, but to save those who are waiting for him. Hebrews 9:28 GNB

Behold, he is coming with the clouds, and every eye will see him, every one who pierced him; and all tribes of the earth will wail on account of him. Even so. Amen. Revelation 1:7 RSV

State between death and resurrection

The wicked shall be turned into hell, and all the nations that forget God. Psalm 9:17 KJV

There was a certain rich man, which was clothed in purple and fine linen, and fared sumptuously every day: and there was a certain beggar named Lazarus, which was laid at his gate full of sores, and desiring to be fed with the crumbs which fell from the rich man's table: moreover the dogs came and licked his sores. And it came to pass, that the beggar died, and was carried by the angels into Abraham's bosom: the rich man also died, and was buried; and in hell he lift up his eyes, being in torments, and seeth Abraham afar off, and Lazarus in his bosom. And he cried and said, Father Abraham, have mercy on me, and send Lazarus, that he may dip the tip of his finger in water, and cool my tongue; for I am tormented in this flame . . . And beside all this, between us and you there is a great gulf fixed: so that they which would pass from hence to you cannot; neither can they pass to us, that would come from thence. Luke 16:23-24, 26 KJV

And Jesus said unto him, Verily I say unto thee, To day shalt thou be with me in paradise. Luke 23:43 KJV

And whosoever liveth and believeth in me shall never die. Believest thou this? John 11:26 KJV

We are of good courage, and we would rather be away from the body and at home with the Lord. 2 Corinthians 5:8 RSV

I am pulled in two directions. I want very much to leave this life and be with Christ, which is a far better thing. Philippians 1:23 GNB

For if we believe that Jesus died and rose again, even so them also which sleep in Jesus will God bring with him. 1 Thessalonians 4:14 KJV

To the assembly of the first-born who are enrolled in heaven, and to a judge who is God of all, and to the spirits of just men made perfect. Hebrews 12:23 RSV

Then they were each given a white robe and told to rest a little longer, until the number of their fellow servants and their brethren should be complete, who were to be killed as they themselves had been. Revelation 6:11 RSV

And I heard a voice from heaven saying, 'Write this: Blessed are the dead who die in the Lord henceforth.' 'Blessed indeed,' says the Spirit, 'that they may rest from their labours, for their deeds follow them!' Revelation 14:13 RSV

Law

The law of the Lord is perfect, converting the soul: the testimony of the Lord is sure, making wise the simple. Psalm 19:7 KJV

Open thou mine eyes, that I may behold wondrous things out of thy law. Psalm 119:18 KJV

'Do not think that I have come to do away with the Law of Moses and the teachings of the prophets. I have not come to do away with them, but to make their teachings come true.' Matthew 5:17 GNB

For the law was given through Moses; grace and truth came through Jesus Christ. John 1:17 RSV

Now we know that whatever the law says it speaks to those who are under the law, so that every mouth may be stopped, and the whole world may be held accountable to God. For no human being will be justified in his sight by works of the law since through the law comes knowledge of sin. Romans 3:19-20 RSV

Do we then make void the law through faith? God forbid: yea, we establish the law. Romans 3:31 KJV

For sin shall not have dominion over you: for ye are not under the law, but under grace. Romans 6:14 KJV

What then shall we say? That the law is sin? By no means! Yet, if it had not been for the law, I should not have known sin. I should not have known what it is to covet if the law had not said, 'You shall not covet.' Romans 7:7 RSV

So the law is holy, and the commandment is holy and just and good. Romans 7:12 RSV

For I delight in the law of God, in my inmost self, but I see in my members another law at war with the law of my mind and making me captive to the law of sin which dwells in my members. Romans 7:22-23 RSV

For the law of the Spirit of life in Christ Jesus has set me free from the law of sin and death. For God has done what the law, weakened by the flesh, could not do: sending his own Son in the likeness of sinful flesh and for sin, he condemned sin in the flesh, in order that the just requirement of the law might be fulfilled in us, who walk not according to the flesh but according to the Spirit. Romans 8:2-4 RSV

Love does no wrong to a neighbour; therefore love is the fulfilling of the law. Romans 13:10 RSV

Yet we know that a person is put right with God only through faith in Jesus Christ, never by doing what the Law requires. We, too, have believed in Christ, and not by doing what the Law requires. For no one is put right with God by doing what the Law requires. Galatians 2:16 GNB

And so the Law was in charge of us until Christ came, in order that we might then be put right with God through faith. Galatians 3:24 GNB

But when the time had fully come, God sent forth his Son, born of woman, born under the law, to redeem those who were under the law, so that we might receive adoption as sons. Galatians 4:4-5 RSV

'This is the covenant that I will make with the house of Israel after those days, says the Lord: I will put my laws into their minds, and write them on their hearts, and I will be their God, and they shall be my people.' Hebrews 8:10 RSV

For since the law has but a shadow of the good things to come instead of the true form of these realities, it can never, by the same sacrifices which are continually offered year after year, make perfect those who draw near. Hebrews 10:1 RSV

But he who looks into the perfect law, the law of liberty, and perseveres, being no hearer that forgets but a doer that acts, he shall be blessed in his doing. James 1:25 RSV

If you really fulfil the royal law, according to the scripture, 'You shall love your neighbour as yourself,' you do well. James 2:8 RSV

See also *Bible; Ten Commandments; Will of God.*

Laying on of hands

And Israel stretched out his right hand and laid it upon the head of Ephraim, who was the younger, and his left hand upon the head of Manasseh, crossing his hands, for Manasseh was the first-born. And he blessed Joseph. Genesis 48:14-15 RSV

'He [Aaron] shall put both his hands on the goat's head and confess over it all the evils, sins, and rebellions of the people of Israel, and so transfer them to the goat's head. Then the goat is to be driven off into the desert by a man appointed to do it.' Leviticus 16:21 GNB

And Joshua the son of Nun was full of the spirit of wisdom; for Moses had laid his hands upon him: and the children of Israel hearkened unto him, and did as the Lord commanded Moses. Deuteronomy 34:9 KJV

And he [Jesus] could do no mighty work there, except that he laid his hands upon a few sick people and healed them. Mark 6:5 RSV

And he took them up in his arms, put his hands upon them, and blessed them. Mark 10:16 KJV

These they set before the apostles, and they prayed and laid their hands upon them. Acts 6:6 RSV

While they were worshipping the Lord and fasting, the Holy Spirit said, 'Set apart for me Barnabas and Saul for the work to which I have called them.' Then after fasting and praying they laid their hands on them and sent them off. Acts 13:2-3 RSV

And when Paul had laid his hands upon them, the Holy Spirit came on them; and they spoke with tongues and prophesied. Acts 19:6 RSV

Do not neglect the gift you have, which was given you by prophetic utterance when the council of elders laid their hands upon you. 1 Timothy 4:14 RSV

Be in no hurry to lay hands on someone to dedicate him to the Lord's service. 1 Timothy 5:22 GNB

Let us go forward, then, to mature teaching and leave behind us the first lessons of the Christian message. We should not lay again the foundation of turning away from useless works and believing in God; of the teaching about baptisms and the laying on of hands; of the resurrection of the dead and the eternal judgement. Hebrews 6:1-2 GNB

Laziness

Go to the ant, thou sluggard; consider her ways, and be wise. Proverbs 6:6 KJV

How long wilt thou sleep, O sluggard? When wilt thou arise out of thy sleep? Proverbs 6:9 KJV

If you are lazy, you will meet difficulty everywhere, but if you are honest, you will have no trouble. Proverbs 15:19 GNB

Our brothers, we command you in the name of our Lord Jesus Christ to keep away from all brothers who are living a lazy life and who do not follow the instructions that we gave them. You yourselves know very well that you should do just what we did. We were not lazy when we were with you. We did not accept anyone's support without paying for it. Instead, we worked and toiled; we kept working day and night so as not to be an expense to any of you. 2 Thessalonians 3:6-8 GNB

While we were with you, we used to say to you, 'Whoever refuses to work is not allowed to eat.' We say this because we hear that there are some people among you who live lazy lives and who do nothing except meddle in other people's business. In the name of the Lord Jesus Christ we command these people and warn them to lead orderly lives and work to earn their own living. 2 Thessalonians 3:10-12 GNB

They [young widows] also learn to waste their time in going round from house to house; but even worse, they learn to be gossips and busybodies, talking of things they should not. 1 Timothy 5:13 GNB

We do not want you to become lazy, but to be like those who believe and are patient, and so receive what God has promised. Hebrews 6:12 GNB

See also *Work*.

Leadership

'And let them judge the people at all times; every great matter they shall bring to you, but any small matter they shall decide themselves; so it will be easier for you, and they will bear the burden with you. If you do this, and God so commands you, then you will be able to endure, and all this people also will go to their place in peace.' Exodus 18:22-23 RSV

The Lord said to Moses, 'Send men to spy out the land of Canaan, which I give to the people of Israel; from each tribe of their fathers shall you send a man, every one a leader among them.' Numbers 13:1-2 RSV

[Samuel to Saul] 'But now your kingdom shall not continue; the Lord has sought out a man after his own heart; and the Lord has appointed him to be prince over his people, because you have not kept what the Lord commanded you.' 1 Samuel 13:14 RSV

Run to and fro through the streets of Jerusalem, look and take note! Search her squares to see if you can find a man, one who does justice and seeks truth; that I may pardon her. Jeremiah 5:1 RSV

'But it shall not be so among you; but whoever would be great among you must be your servant.' Mark 10:43 RSV

If it [a man's gift] is leadership, let him govern diligently. Romans 12:8 NIV

And, apart from other things, there is the daily pressure upon me of my anxiety for all the churches. 2 Corinthians 11:28 RSV

Now we ask you, brothers, to respect those who work hard among you, who are over you in the Lord and who admonish you. Hold them in the highest regard in love because of their work. 1 Thessalonians 5:12-13 NIV

There is a popular saying: 'To aspire to leadership is an honourable ambition.' 1 Timothy 3:1 NEB

What you have heard from me before many witnesses entrust to faithful men who will be able to teach others also. 2 Timothy 2:2 RSV

You should aim not at being 'little tin gods' but as examples of Christian living in the eyes of the flock committed to your charge. 1 Peter 5:3 JBP

See also *Deacon; Elders; Service.*

Life

And the Lord God formed man of the dust of the ground, and breathed into his nostrils the breath of life; and man became a living soul . . . And out of the ground made the Lord God to grow every tree that is pleasant to the sight, and good for food; the tree of life also in the midst of the garden, and the tree of knowledge of good and evil. Genesis 2:7, 9 KJV

Honour thy father and thy mother: that thy days may be long upon the land which the Lord thy God giveth thee. Exodus 20:12 KJV

'And he humbled you and let you hunger and fed you with manna, which you did not know, nor did your fathers know; that he might make you know that man does not live by bread alone, but that man lives by everything that proceeds out of the mouth of the Lord.' Deuteronomy 8:3 RSV

'I call heaven and earth to witness against you this day, that I have set before you life and death, blessing and curse; therefore choose life, that you and your descendants may live.' Deuteronomy 30:19 RSV

For I know that my redeemer liveth, and that he shall stand at the latter day upon the earth. Job 19:25 KJV

Because thy lovingkindness is better than life, my lips shall praise thee. Psalm 63:3 KJV

With long life I will satisfy him, and show him my salvation. Psalm 91:16 RSV

For he who finds me [wisdom] finds life and obtains favour from the Lord. Proverbs 8:35 RSV

Incline your ear, and come unto me: hear, and your soul shall live; and I will make an everlasting covenant with you, even the sure mercies of David. Isaiah 55:3 KJV

And he said to me, 'Son of man, can these bones live?' And I answered, 'O Lord God, thou knowest.' Ezekiel 37:3 RSV

God says to them [the people of Israel], 'You are not my people,' but the day is coming when he will say to them, 'You are the children of the living God!' Hosea 1:10 GNB

Therefore I say unto you, Take no thought for your life, what ye shall eat, or what ye shall drink; nor yet for your body, what ye shall put on. Is not the life more than meat, and the body than raiment? Matthew 6:25 KJV

'For the gate is narrow and the way is hard, that leads to life, and those who find it are few.' Matthew 7:14 RSV

'For what will it profit a man, if he gains the whole world and forfeits his life?' Matthew 16:26 RSV

'"I am the God of Abraham, and the God of Isaac, and the God of Jacob". He is not God of the dead, but of the living.' Matthew 22:32 RSV

And these shall go away into everlasting punishment: but the righteous into life eternal. Matthew 25:46 KJV

'Truly, truly, I say to you, he who hears my word and believes him who sent me, has eternal life; he does not come into judgment, but has passed from death to life.' John 5:24 RSV

And Jesus said unto them, I am the bread of life: he that cometh to me shall never hunger; and he that believeth on me shall never thirst. John 6:35 KJV

Then Simon Peter answered him, Lord, to whom shall we go? thou hast the words of eternal life. John 6:68 KJV

'The thief comes only to steal and kill and destroy; I came that they may have life, and have it abundantly.' John 10:10 RSV

And I give unto them [my sheep] eternal life; and they shall never perish, neither shall any man pluck them out of my hand. John 10:28 KJV

Jesus said unto her, I am the resurrection, and the life: he that believeth in me, though he were dead, yet shall he live. John 11:25 KJV

Jesus saith unto him, I am the way, the truth, and the life: no man cometh unto the Father, but by me. John 14:6 KJV

'Because I live, you also will live.' John 14:19 GNB

But these are written that you may believe that Jesus is the Christ, the Son of God, and that believing you may have life in his name. John 20:31 RSV

'For "In him we live and move and have our being"; as even some of your poets have said, "For we are indeed his offspring."' Acts 17:28 RSV

For the wages of sin is death; but the gift of God is eternal life through Jesus Christ our Lord. Romans 6:23 KJV

To set the mind on the flesh is death, but to set the mind on the Spirit is life and peace. Romans 8:6 RSV

For if you live according to the flesh you will die, but if by the Spirit you put to death the deeds of the body you will live. Romans 8:13 RSV

Always carrying in the body the death of Jesus, so that the life of Jesus may also be manifested in our bodies. 2 Corinthians 4:10 RSV

I have been crucified with Christ; it is no longer I who live, but Christ who lives in me; and the life I now live in the flesh I live by faith in the Son of God, who loved me and gave himself for me. Galatians 2:20 RSV

[God] made us alive with Christ even when we were dead in transgressions— it is by grace you have been saved. Ephesians 2:5 NIV

For me to live is Christ, and to die is gain. Philippians 1:21 KJV

Holding forth the word of life. Philippians 2:16 KJV

When Christ, who is our life, shall appear, then shall ye also appear with him in glory. Colossians 3:4 KJV

We know that we have passed out of death into life, because we love the brethren. 1 John 3:14 RSV

He that hath the Son hath life; and he that hath not the Son of God hath not life. 1 John 5:12 KJV

See also *Adam; Death; Last things.*

Light

And God said, Let there be light: and there was light. Genesis 1:3 KJV

The Lord is my light and my salvation; whom shall I fear? The Lord is the strength of my life; of whom shall I be afraid? Psalm 27:1 KJV

Thy word is a lamp unto my feet, and a light unto my path. Psalm 119:105 KJV

The entrance of thy words giveth light; it giveth understanding unto the simple. Psalm 119:130 KJV

The people that walked in darkness have seen a great light: they that dwell in the land of the shadow of death, upon them hath the light shined. Isaiah 9:2 KJV

I will also give thee for a light to the Gentiles, that thou mayest be my salvation unto the end of the earth. Isaiah 49:6 KJV

Arise, shine; for thy light is come, and the glory of the Lord is risen upon thee. Isaiah 60:1 KJV

Ye are the light of the world. A city that is set on an hill cannot be hid. Neither do men light a candle, and put it under a bushel, but on a candlestick; and it giveth light unto all that are in the house. Let your light so shine before men, that they may see your good works, and glorify your Father which is in heaven. Matthew 5:14-16 KJV

In him [the Word] was life; and the life was the light of men. And the light shineth in darkness; and the darkness comprehended it not. John 1:4-5 KJV

He [John the Baptist] came for testimony, to bear witness to the light, that all might believe through him. He was not the light, but came to bear witness to the light. The true light that enlightens every man was coming into the world. John 1:7-9 RSV

And this is the judgment, that the light has come into the world, and men loved darkness rather than light, because their deeds were evil. For every one who does evil hates the light, and does not come to the light, lest his deeds should be exposed. But he who does what is true comes to the light, that it may be clearly seen that his deeds have been wrought in God. John 3:19-21 RSV

Jesus spoke to them, saying, 'I am the light of the world; he who follows me will not walk in darkness, but will have the light of life.' John 8:12 RSV

[The Lord Jesus Christ to Paul] '"I send you to open their eyes, that they may turn from darkness to light and from the power of Satan to God, that they may receive forgiveness of sins and a place among those who are sanctified by faith in me."' Acts 26:18 RSV

For it is the God who said, 'Let light shine out of darkness,' who has shone in our hearts to give the light of the knowledge of the glory of God in the face of Christ. 2 Corinthians 4:6 RSV

Be ye not unequally yoked together with unbelievers: for what fellowship hath righteousness with unrighteousness? and what communion hath light with darkness? 2 Corinthians 6:14 KJV

For once you were darkness, but now you are light in the Lord; walk as children of light (for the fruit of light is found in all that is good and right and true). Ephesians 5:8-9 RSV

But everything exposed by the light becomes visible, for it is light that makes everything visible. This is why it is said: 'Wake up, O sleeper, rise from the dead, and Christ will shine on you.' Ephesians 5:13-14 NIV

So that you may be innocent and pure as God's perfect children, who live in a world of corrupt and sinful people. You must shine among them like stars lighting up the sky. Philippians 2:15 GNB

He [God] alone is immortal; he lives in the light that no one can approach. No one has ever seen him; no one can ever see him. To him be honour and eternal dominion! Amen. 1 Timothy 6:16 GNB

But you are a chosen race, a royal priesthood, a holy nation, God's own people, that you may declare the wonderful deeds of him who called you out of darkness into his marvellous light. 1 Peter 2:9 RSV

This is the message we have heard from him and proclaim to you, that God is light and in him is no darkness at all. 1 John 1:5 RSV

If we say we have fellowship with him while we walk in darkness, we lie and do not live according to the truth; but if we walk in the light, as he is in the light, we have fellowship with one another, and the blood of Jesus his Son cleanses us from all sin. 1 John 1:7 RSV

And night shall be no more; they need no light of lamp or sun, for the Lord God will be their light, and they shall reign for ever and ever. Revelation 22:5 RSV

Loneliness

And he [Elijah] said, I have been very jealous for the Lord God of hosts: for the children of Israel have forsaken thy covenant, thrown down thine altars, and slain thy prophets with the sword; and I, even I only, am left; and they seek my life, to take it away. 1 Kings 19:10 KJV

'He has put my brethren far from me, and my acquaintances are wholly estranged from me. My kinsfolk and my close friends have failed me.' Job 19:13-14 RSV

Then he said to them, 'My soul is very sorrowful, even to death; remain here, and watch with me.' Matthew 26:38 RSV

Then all the disciples forsook him and fled. Matthew 26:56 RSV

And about the ninth hour Jesus cried with a loud voice, 'Eli, Eli, lama sabachthani?' that is, 'My God, my God, why hast thou forsaken me?' Matthew 27:46 RSV

You know that everyone in the province of Asia . . . has deserted me. 2 Timothy 1:15 GNB

See also *Comfort*.

Lord's Prayer

See *Prayer, Prayers of the Bible*.

Love

of God

'It was not because you were more in number than any other people that the Lord set his love upon you and chose you, for you were the fewest of all peoples; but it is because the Lord loves you, and is keeping the oath which he swore to your fathers, that the Lord has brought you out with a mighty hand, and redeemed you from the house of bondage, from the hand of Pharaoh king of Egypt.' Deuteronomy 7:7-8 RSV

For God so loved the world, that he gave his only begotten Son, that whosoever believeth in him should not perish, but have everlasting life. John 3:16 KJV

And hope maketh not ashamed; because the love of God is shed abroad in our hearts by the Holy Ghost which is given unto us. Romans 5:5 KJV

But God shows his love for us in that while we were yet sinners Christ died for us. Romans 5:8 RSV

Who shall separate us from the love of Christ? Shall tribulation, or distress, or persecution, or famine, or nakedness, or peril, or sword? As it is written, 'For thy sake we are being killed all the day long; we are regarded as sheep to be slaughtered.' No, in all these things we are more than conquerors through him who loved us. For I am sure that neither death, nor life, nor angels, nor principalities, nor things present, nor things to come, nor powers, nor height, nor depth, nor anything else in all creation, will be able to separate us from the love of God in Christ Jesus our Lord. Romans 8:35-39 RSV

I have been crucified with Christ; it is no longer I who live, but Christ who lives in me; and the life I now live in the flesh I live by faith in the Son of God, who loved me and gave himself for me. Galatians 2:20 RSV

But because of his great love for us, God, who is rich in mercy, made us alive with Christ. Ephesians 2:4-5 NIV

He that loveth not knoweth not God; for God is love. In this was manifested the love of God toward us, because that God sent his only begotten Son into the world, that we might live through him. Herein is love, not that we loved God, but that he loved us, and sent his Son to be the propitiation for our sins. 1 John 4:8-10 KJV

See also *Faithfulness; Grace; Mercy*.

of man for God

Thou shalt love the Lord thy God with all thine heart, and with all thy soul, and with all thy might. Deuteronomy 6:5 KJV

'And now, Israel, what does the Lord your God require of you, but to fear the Lord your God, to walk in all his ways, to love him, to serve the Lord your God with all your heart and with all your soul.' Deuteronomy 10:12 RSV

I love the Lord, because he has heard my voice and my supplications. Psalm 116:1 RSV

If ye love me, keep my commandments. John 14:15 KJV

He that hath my commandments, and keepeth them, he it is that loveth me: and he that loveth me shall be loved of my Father, and I will love him, and will manifest myself to him. John 14:21 KJV

We know that in everything God works for good with those who love him, who are called according to his purpose. Romans 8:28 RSV

As it is written, Eye hath not seen, nor ear heard, neither have entered into the heart of man, the things which God hath prepared for them that love him. 1 Corinthians 2:9 KJV

If any one has no love for the Lord, let him be accursed. Our Lord, come!
1 Corinthians 16:22 RSV

Without having seen him you love him; though you do not now see him you believe in him and rejoice with unutterable and exalted joy. 1 Peter 1:8 RSV

If any one says, 'I love God,' and hates his brother, he is a liar; for he who does not love his brother whom he has seen, cannot love God whom he has not seen. And this commandment we have from him, that he who loves God should love his brother also. 1 John 4:20-21 RSV

See also *Christian life, Longing for God; Worship.*

of man for man

Honour thy father and thy mother.
Exodus 20:12 KJV

'You shall not take vengeance or bear any grudge against the sons of your own people, but you shall love your neighbour as yourself: I am the Lord.'
Leviticus 19:18 RSV

'Treat them [foreigners] as you would a fellow-Israelite, and love them as you love yourselves.' Leviticus 19:34 GNB

But I say unto you, Love your enemies, bless them that curse you, do good to them that hate you. . . For if ye love them which love you, what reward have ye? Do not even the publicans the same? Matthew 5:44-46 KJV

'So whatever you wish that men would do to you, do so to them; for this is the law and the prophets.' Matthew 7:12 RSV

'See that you don't despise any of these little ones. Their angels in heaven, I tell you, are always in the presence of my Father in heaven.' Matthew 18:10 GNB

A new commandment I give unto you, That ye love one another; as I have loved you, that ye also love one another. By this shall all men know that ye are my disciples, if ye have love one to another. John 13:34-35 KJV

'Greater love has no man than this, that a man lay down his life for his friends.'
John 15:13 RSV

If I speak in the tongues of men and of angels, but have not love, I am a noisy gong or a clanging cymbal. And if I have prophetic powers, and understand all mysteries and all knowledge, and if I have all faith, so as to remove mountains, but have not love, I am nothing. If I give away all I have, and if I deliver my body to be burned, but have not love, I gain nothing. Love is patient and kind; love is not jealous or boastful; it is not arrogant or rude. Love does not insist on its own way; it is not irritable or resentful; it does not rejoice at wrong, but rejoices in the right. Love bears all things, believes all things, hopes all things, endures all things. So faith, hope, love abide, these three; but the greatest of these is love.
1 Corinthians 13:1-7, 13 RSV

But the fruit of the Spirit is love . . .
Galatians 5:22 RSV

Husbands, love your wives, as Christ loved the church and gave himself up for her. Ephesians 5:25 RSV

Beloved, let us love one another: for love is of God; and every one that loveth is born of God, and knoweth God . . . Beloved, if God so loved us, we ought also to love one another . . . If we love one another, God dwelleth in us, and his love is perfected in us.
1 John 4:7, 11 KJV

By this we know that we love the children of God, when we love God and obey his commandments. 1 John 5:2 RSV

See also *Kindness.*

Lying

Thou shalt not bear false witness against thy neighbour. Exodus 20:16 KJV

'God is not man, that he should lie, or a son of man, that he should repent. Has he said, and will he not do it? Or has he spoken, and will he not fulfil it?'
Numbers 23:19 RSV

Save me, Lord, from liars and deceivers. Psalm 120:2 GNB

Every one deceives his neighbour, and no one speaks the truth; they have taught their tongue to speak lies; they commit iniquity and are too weary to repent. Jeremiah 9:5 RSV

'You are of your father the devil, and your will is to do your father's desires. He was a murderer from the beginning, and has nothing to do with the truth, because there is no truth in him. When he lies, he speaks according to his own nature, for he is a liar and the father of lies.' John 8:44 RSV

Peter said to him, 'Ananias, why did you let Satan take control of you and make you lie to the Holy Spirit by keeping part of the money you received for the property? Before you sold the property, it belonged to you; and after you sold it, the money was yours. Why, then, did you decide to do such a thing? You have not lied to men—you have lied to God!' Acts 5:3-5 GNB

Do not lie to one another, seeing that you have put off the old nature with its practices. Colossians 3:9 RSV

If someone says that he knows him, but does not obey his commands, such a person is a liar and there is no truth in him. 1 John 2:4 GNB

Who is the liar? Who but he that denies that Jesus is the Christ? He is Antichrist, for he denies both the Father and the Son. 1 John 2:22 NEB

Magnificat

See *Prayer, Prayers of the Bible.*

Man

And God said, Let us make man in our image, after our likeness: and let them have dominion over the fish of the sea, and over the fowl of the air, and over the cattle, and over all the earth, and over every creeping thing that creepeth upon the earth. So God created man in his own image, in the image of God created he him; male and female created he them. Genesis 1:26-27 KJV

And unto Adam he said, Because thou hast hearkened unto the voice of thy wife, and hast eaten of the tree, of which I commanded thee, saying, Thou shalt not eat of it: cursed is the ground for thy sake; in sorrow shalt thou eat of it all the days of thy life. Genesis 3:17 KJV

The Lord saw how great man's wickedness on the earth had become, and that every inclination of the thoughts of his heart was only evil all the time. Genesis 6:5 NIV

What is man, that thou art mindful of him? and the son of man, that thou visitest him? For thou hast made him a little lower than the angels, and hast crowned him with glory and honour. Thou madest him to have dominion over the works of thy hands; thou hast put all things under his feet: all sheep and oxen, yea, and the beasts of the field; the fowl of the air, and the fish of the sea, and whatsoever passeth through the paths of the seas. Psalm 8:4-8 KJV

As for man, his days are like grass; he flourishes like a flower of the field; for the wind passes over it, and it is gone, and its place knows it no more. Psalm 103:15-16 RSV

He [Jesus] knew men so well, all of them, that he needed no evidence from others about a man, for he himself could tell what was in a man. John 2:25 NEB

As by one man sin entered into the world, and death by sin . . . so death passed upon all men, for that all have sinned. Romans 5:12 KJV

See also *Responsibility of man; Woman.*

Marriage

And the Lord God said, It is not good that the man should be alone; I will make him an help meet for him. Genesis 2:18 KJV

Therefore shall a man leave his father and his mother, and shall cleave unto his wife: and they shall be one flesh. Genesis 2:24 KJV

What therefore God hath joined together, let not man put asunder. Matthew 19:6 KJV

'For in the resurrection they neither marry nor are given in marriage, but are like angels in heaven.' Matthew 22:30 RSV

A wife is bound to her husband as long as he lives. If the husband dies, she is free to be married to whom she wishes, only in the Lord. 1 Corinthians 7:39 RSV

A bishop then must be blameless, the husband of one wife. 1 Timothy 3:2 KJV

Now the Spirit expressly says that in later times some will depart from the faith by giving heed to deceitful spirits and doctrines of demons, through the pretensions of liars whose consciences are seared, who forbid marriage and enjoin abstinence from foods which God created to be received with thanksgiving by those who believe and know the truth. 1 Timothy 4:1-3 RSV

Let marriage be held in honour among all, and let the marriage bed be undefiled; for God will judge the immoral and adulterous. Hebrews 13:4 RSV

See also *Family; Sex.*

Adultery

Thou shalt not commit adultery. Exodus 20:14 KJV

He who commits adultery has no sense; he who does it destroys himself. Proverbs 6:32 RSV

'You have heard that it was said, "Do not commit adultery." But now I tell you: anyone who looks at a woman and wants to possess her is guilty of committing adultery with her in his heart.' Matthew 5:27-28 GNB

Divorce

Has not the one God made and sustained for us the spirit of life? And what does he desire? Godly offspring. So take heed to yourselves, and let none be faithless to the wife of his youth. 'For I hate divorce, says the Lord the God of Israel . . . So take heed to yourselves and do not be faithless.' Malachi 2:15-16 RSV

'It was also said, "Anyone who divorces his wife must give her a written notice of divorce." But now I tell you: if a man divorces his wife, even though she has not been unfaithful, then he is guilty of making her commit adultery if she marries again; and the man who marries her commits adultery also.' Matthew 5:31-32 GNB

'Why then,' they asked, 'did Moses command that a man give his wife a certificate of divorce and send her away?' Jesus replied, 'Moses permitted you to divorce your wives because your hearts were hard. But it was not this way from the beginning. I tell you that anyone who divorces his wife, except for marital unfaithfulness, and marries another woman commits adultery.' Matthew 19:7-9 NIV

For married people I have a command which is not my own but the Lord's: a wife must not leave her husband; but if she does, she must remain single or else be reconciled to her husband; and a husband must not divorce his wife. 1 Corinthians 7:10-11 GNB

Maturity

See Christian life, Character of the Christian; Perfection.

Meditation

'This book of the law shall not depart out of your mouth, but you shall meditate on it day and night, that you may be careful to do according to all that is written in it; for then you shall make your way prosperous, and then you shall have good success.' Joshua 1:8 RSV

His delight is in the law of the Lord, and on his law he meditates day and night. He is like a tree planted by streams of water, that yields its fruit in its season, and its leaf does not wither. In all that he does, he prospers. Psalm 1:2-3 RSV

Be angry, but sin not; commune with your own hearts on your beds, and be silent. Psalm 4:4 RSV

Let the words of my mouth, and the meditation of my heart, be acceptable in thy sight, O Lord, my strength, and my redeemer. Psalm 19:14 KJV

Be still before the Lord and wait patiently for him; do not fret when men succeed in their ways, when they carry out their wicked schemes. Psalm 37:7 NIV

I will meditate on thy precepts, and fix my eyes on thy ways. Psalm 119:15 RSV

I remember the days gone by; I think about all that you have done, I bring to mind all your deeds. Psalm 143:5 GNB

But Mary kept all these things, and pondered them in her heart. Luke 2:19 KJV

And we all, with unveiled face, beholding the glory of the Lord, are being changed into his likeness from one degree of glory to another; for this comes from the Lord who is the Spirit. 2 Corinthians 3:18 RSV

See also Mind; Thought.

Mercy, merciful

The Lord passed before him, and proclaimed, 'The Lord, the Lord, a God merciful and gracious, slow to anger, and abounding in steadfast love and faithfulness, keeping steadfast love for thousands, forgiving iniquity and transgression and sin, but who will by no means clear the guilty, visiting the iniquity of the fathers upon the children and the children's children, to the third and the fourth generation.' Exodus 34:6-7 RSV

All the paths of the Lord are steadfast love and faithfulness, for those who keep his covenant and his testimonies. Psalm 25:10 RSV

Have mercy upon me, O God, according to thy lovingkindness: according unto the multitude of thy tender mercies blot out my transgressions. Psalm 51:1 KJV

I will not remove from him my steadfast love, or be false to my faithfulness. Psalm 89:33 RSV

O give thanks to the Lord, for he is good, for his steadfast love endures for ever. Psalm 136:1 RSV

The steadfast love of the Lord never ceases, his mercies never come to an end; they are new every morning. Lamentations 3:22-23 RSV

'O my God, incline thy ear and hear; open thy eyes and behold our desolations, and the city which is called by thy name; for we do not present our supplications before thee on the ground of our righteousness, but on the ground of thy great mercy.' Daniel 9:18 RSV

For I desire steadfast love and not sacrifice, the knowledge of God, rather than burnt offerings. Hosea 6:6 RSV

He hath shewed thee, O man, what is good; and what doth the Lord require of thee, but to do justly, and to love mercy, and to walk humbly with thy God? Micah 6:8 KJV

Blessed are the merciful: for they shall obtain mercy. Matthew 5:7 KJV

'Be merciful just as your Father is merciful.' Luke 6:36 GNB

'But the tax collector, standing far off, would not even lift up his eyes to heaven, but beat his breast, saying, "God, be merciful to me a sinner!"' Luke 18:13 RSV

I beseech you therefore, brethren, by the mercies of God, that ye present your bodies a living sacrifice, holy, acceptable unto God, which is your reasonable service. Romans 12:1 KJV

You are the people of God; he loved you and chose you for his own. So then, you must clothe yourselves with compassion, kindness, humility, gentleness, and patience. Colossians 3:12 GNB

See also *Grace*.

Mind

'Thou dost keep him in perfect peace, whose mind is stayed on thee, because he trusts in thee.' Isaiah 26:3 RSV

Jesus said unto him, Thou shalt love the Lord thy God with all thy heart, and with all thy soul, and with all thy mind. Matthew 22:37 KJV

According to his usual habit Paul went to the synagogue. There during three Sabbaths he held discussions with the people, quoting and explaining the Scriptures and proving from them that the Messiah had to suffer and rise from death . . . Some of them were convinced and joined Paul and Silas. Acts 17:2-4 GNB

For although they knew God they did not honour him as God or give thanks to him, but they became futile in their thinking and their senseless minds were darkened. Romans 1:21 RSV

For those who live according to the flesh set their minds on the things of the flesh, but those who live according to the Spirit set their minds on the things of the Spirit. To set the mind on the flesh is death, but to set the mind on the Spirit is life and peace. Romans 8:5-6 RSV

O the depth of the riches both of the wisdom and knowledge of God! how unsearchable are his judgments, and his ways past finding out! For who hath known the mind of the Lord? or who hath been his counsellor? Romans 1:33-34 KJV

And be not conformed to this world: but be ye transformed by the renewing of your mind, that ye may prove what is that good, and acceptable, and perfect, will of God. Romans 12:2 KJV

'For who has known the mind of the Lord that he may instruct him?' But we have the mind of Christ. 1 Corinthians 2:16 NIV

Have this mind among yourselves, which is yours in Christ Jesus. Philippians 2:5 RSV

And the peace of God, which passes all understanding, will keep your hearts and your minds in Christ Jesus. Philippians 4:7 RSV

Set your minds on things that are above, not on things that are on earth. Colossians 3:2 RSV

See also *Heart; Meditation; Understanding*.

Ministry

See *Service*.

Miracles

Then Moses stretched out his hand over the sea; and the Lord drove the sea back by a strong east wind all night, and made the sea dry land, and the waters were divided. Exodus 14:21 RSV

And Israel saw that great work which the Lord did upon the Egyptians; and the people feared the Lord, and believed the Lord, and his servant Moses. Exodus 14:31 KJV

[Elijah's prayer] 'Answer me, O Lord, answer me, that this people may know that thou, O Lord, art God, and that thou hast turned their hearts back.' Then the fire of the Lord fell, and consumed the burnt offering, and the wood, and the stones, and the dust, and licked up the water that was in the trench. 1 Kings 18:37-38 RSV

Praise the Lord, the God of Israel! He

alone does these wonderful things.
Psalm 72:18 GNB

'For false Christs and false prophets will arise and show great signs and wonders, so as to lead astray, if possible, even the elect.' Matthew 24:24 RSV

'For with God nothing will be impossible.' Luke 1:37 RSV

Jesus performed this first miracle in Cana in Galilee; there he revealed his glory, and his disciples believed in him. John 2:11 GNB

'Truly, truly, I say to you, he who believes in me will also do the works that I do; and greater works than these will he do, because I go to the Father.' John 14:12 RSV

'While thou stretchest out thy hand to heal, and signs and wonders are performed through the name of thy holy servant Jesus.' Acts 4:30 RSV

But Peter put them all outside and knelt down and prayed; then, turning to the body he said, 'Tabitha, rise.' And she opened her eyes, and when she saw Peter she sat up. Acts 9:40 RSV

To another the working of miracles. 1 Corinthians 12:10 RSV

The things that mark an apostle—signs, wonders and miracles—were done among you with great perseverance. 2 Corinthians 12:12 NIV

God also bore witness by signs and wonders and various miracles and by gifts of the Holy Spirit distributed according to his own will. Hebrews 2:4 RSV

See also *Jesus Christ, Miracles of Jesus.*

Money and material goods

He who loves money never has money enough, he who loves wealth never has enough profit; this, too, is vanity. Ecclesiastes 5:9 JB

'Do not lay up for yourselves treasures on earth, where moth and rust consume and where thieves break in and steal.' Matthew 6:19 RSV

'No one can serve two masters; for either he will hate the one and love the other, or he will be devoted to the one and despise the other. You cannot serve God and mammon.' Matthew 6:24 RSV

[The Pharisees] 'Tell us, then, what you think. Is it lawful to pay taxes to Caesar, or not?' But Jesus, aware of

'Do not lay up for yourselves treasures on earth.'

their malice, said, 'Why put me to the test, you hypocrites? Show me the money for the tax.' And they brought him a coin. And Jesus said to them, 'Whose likeness and inscription is this?' They said, 'Caesar's.' Then he said to them, 'Render therefore to Caesar the things that are Caesar's, and to God the things that are God's.' Matthew 22:17-21 RSV

[A church leader] must not love money. 1 Timothy 3:3 GNB

There is great gain in godliness with contentment; for we brought nothing into the world, and we cannot take anything out of the world. 1 Timothy 6:6-7 RSV

For the love of money is the root of all evil. 1 Timothy 6:10 KJV

Keep your life free from love of money, and be content with what you have; for he has said, 'I will never fail you nor forsake you.' Hebrews 13:5 RSV

See also *Giving; Rich and riches.*

Mother

See *Family.*

Murder

Cain said to Abel his brother, 'Let us go out to the field.' And when they were in the field, Cain rose up against his brother Abel, and killed him. Then the Lord said to Cain, 'Where is Abel your brother?' He said, 'I do not know; am I my brother's keeper?' And the Lord said, 'What have you done? The voice of your brother's blood is crying to me from the ground.' Genesis 4:8-10 RSV

'Whoever sheds the blood of man, by man shall his blood be shed; for God made man in his own image.' Genesis 9:6 RSV

'Do not commit murder.' Exodus 20:13 GNB

'This is the provision for the manslayer, who by fleeing there [to special cities] may save his life. If any one kills his neighbour unintentionally without having been at enmity with him in time past—as when a man goes into the forest with his neighbour to cut wood, and his hand swings the axe to cut down a tree, and the head slips from the handle and strikes his neighbour so that he dies—he may flee to one of these cities and save his life; lest the avenger of blood in hot anger pursue the manslayer and overtake him . . . and wound him mortally, though the man did not deserve to die, since he was not at enmity with his neighbour in time past.' Deuteronomy 19:4-6 RSV

'But if any man hates his neighbour, and lies in wait for him, and attacks him, and wounds him mortally so that he dies, and the man flees into one of these cities, then the elders of his city shall send and fetch him from there, and hand him over to the avenger of blood, so that he may die.' Deuteronomy 19:11-12 RSV

'You have heard that people were told in the past, "Do not commit murder; anyone who does will be brought to trial." But now I tell you: whoever is angry with his brother will be brought to trial.' Matthew 5:21-22 GNB

Any one who hates his brother is a murderer, and you know that no murderer has eternal life abiding in him. 1 John 3:15 KJV

'But as for the cowardly, the faithless, the polluted, as for murderers, fornicators, sorcerers, idolaters, and all liars, their lot shall be in the lake that burns with fire and sulphur, which is the second death.' Revelation 21:8 RSV

Name

He [Abraham] . . . pitched his tent, with Bethel on the west and Ai on the east; and there he built an altar to the Lord and called on the name of the Lord. Genesis 12:8 RSV

Then Moses said to God, 'If I come to the people of Israel and say to them, "The God of your fathers has sent me to you," and they ask me, "What is his name?" what shall I say to them?' God said to Moses, 'I am who I am.' And he said, 'Say this to the people of Israel, "I am has sent me to you."' God also said to Moses, 'Say this to the people of Israel, "The Lord, the God of your fathers, the God of Abraham, the God of Isaac, and the God of Jacob, has sent me to you": this is my name for ever,

and thus I am to be remembered throughout all generations.' Exodus 3:13-15 RSV

Thou shalt not take the name of the Lord thy God in vain; for the Lord will not hold him guiltless that taketh his name in vain. Exodus 20:7 KJV

The name of the Lord is a strong tower; the righteous man runs into it and is safe. Proverbs 18:10 RSV

Our Father, which art in heaven, hallowed be thy name. Matthew 6:9 BCP

'For where two or three are gathered in my name, there am I in the midst of them.' Matthew 18:20 RSV

'Go therefore and make disciples of all nations, baptizing them in the name of the Father and of the Son and of the Holy Spirit.' Matthew 28:19 RSV

Repentance and remission of sins should be preached in his name among all nations, beginning at Jerusalem. Luke 24:47 KJV

'Whatever you ask in my name, I will do it, that the Father may be glorified in the Son.' John 14:13 RSV

'But the Counsellor, the Holy Spirit, whom the Father will send in my name, he will teach you all things, and bring to your remembrance all that I have said to you.' John 14:26 RSV

Then Peter said, Silver and gold have I none; but such as I have give I thee: in the name of Jesus Christ of Nazareth rise up and walk. Acts 3:6 KJV

'And there is salvation in no one else, for there is no other name under heaven given among men by which we must be saved.' Acts 4:12 RSV

Fear fell upon them all; and the name of the Lord Jesus was extolled. Acts 19:17 RSV

Therefore God has highly exalted him and bestowed on him the name which is above every name, that at the name of Jesus every knee should bow, in heaven and on earth and under the earth. Philippians 2:9-10 RSV

And whatsoever ye do in word or deed, do all in the name of the Lord Jesus, giving thanks to God and the Father by him. Colossians 3:17 KJV

Neighbour

Thou shalt not bear false witness against thy neighbour. Thou shalt not covet thy neighbour's house, thou shalt not covet thy neighbour's wife, nor his manservant, nor his maidservant, nor his ox, nor his ass, nor any thing that is thy neighbour's. Exodus 20:16-17 KJV

'You shall not take vengeance or bear any grudge against the sons of your own people, but you shall love your neighbour as yourself: I am the Lord.' Leviticus 19:18 RSV

But he [a lawyer], desiring to justify himself, said to Jesus, 'And who is my neighbour?' Jesus replied, 'A man was going down from Jerusalem to Jericho, and he fell among robbers, who stripped him and beat him, and departed, leaving him half dead. Now by chance a priest was going down that road; and when he saw him he passed by on the other side. So likewise a Levite, when he came to the place and saw him, passed by on the other side. But a Samaritan, as he journeyed, came to where he was; and when he saw him, he had compassion, and went to him and bound up his wounds, pouring on oil and wine; then he set him on his own beast and brought him to an inn, and took care of him. And the next day he took out two denarii and gave them to the innkeeper, saying, "Take care of him; and whatever more you spend, I will repay you when I come back." Which of these three, do you think, proved neighbour to the man who fell among the robbers?' He said, 'The one who showed mercy on him.' And Jesus said to him, 'Go and do likewise.' Luke 10:29-37 RSV

For the whole Law is summed up in one commandment: 'Love your neighbour as you love yourself.' Galatians 5:14 GNB

See also *Love, of man for man.*

New birth

Create in me a clean heart, O God; and renew a right spirit within me. Psalm 51:10 KJV

'I will sprinkle clean water upon you, and you shall be clean from all your uncleannesses, and from all your idols I will cleanse you. A new heart I will give you, and a new spirit I will put within you; and I will take out of your flesh the heart of stone and give you a heart of flesh. And I will put my spirit within you, and cause you to walk in my statutes and be careful to observe my ordinances.' Ezekiel 36:25-27 RSV

Jesus answered and said unto him, Verily, verily, I say unto thee, Except a man be born again, he cannot see the kingdom of God. Nicodemus saith unto him, How can a man be born when he is old? Can he enter the second time into his mother's womb, and be born? Jesus answered, Verily, verily, I say unto thee, Except a man be born of water and of the Spirit, he cannot enter into the kingdom of God. That which is born of the flesh is flesh; and that which is born of the Spirit is spirit. Marvel not that I said unto thee, Ye must be born again. The wind bloweth where it listeth, and thou hearest the sound thereof, but canst not tell whence it cometh, and whither it goeth: so is every one that is born of the Spirit. John 3:3-8 KJV

Therefore, if any one is in Christ, he is a new creation; the old has passed away, behold, the new has come. 2 Corinthians 5:17 RSV

As for you, you were dead in your transgressions and sins, in which you used to live when you followed the ways of this world and of the ruler of the kingdom of the air, the spirit who is now at work in those who are disobedient. All of us also lived among them at one time, gratifying the cravings of our sinful nature and following its desires and thoughts. Like the rest, we were by nature objects of wrath. But because of his great love for us, God, who is rich in mercy, made us alive with Christ even when we were dead in transgressions—it is by grace you have been saved. Ephesians 2:1-5 NIV

[God our Saviour] He saved us, not because of deeds done by us in righteousness, but in virtue of his own mercy, by the washing of regeneration and renewal in the Holy Spirit. Titus 3:5 RSV

For through the living and eternal word of God you have been born again as the children of a parent who is immortal, not mortal. 1 Peter 1:23 GNB

Whoever is a child of God does not continue to sin, for God's very nature is in him; and because God is his Father, he cannot continue to sin. 1 John 3:9 GNB

Nunc Dimittis

See *Prayer, Prayers of the Bible.*

Obedience

'And by your descendants shall all the nations of the earth bless themselves, because you have obeyed my voice.' Genesis 22:18 RSV

'But my servant Caleb, because he has

a different spirit and has followed me fully, I will bring into the land into which he went, and his descendants shall possess it.' Numbers 14:24 RSV

'And all these blessings shall come upon you and overtake you, if you obey the voice of the Lord your God . . .' Deuteronomy 28:2 RSV

And Samuel said, 'Has the Lord as great delight in burnt offerings and sacrifices, as in obeying the voice of the Lord? Behold, to obey is better than sacrifice, and to hearken than the fat of rams.' 1 Samuel 15:22 RSV

'Not every one who says to me, "Lord, Lord," shall enter the kingdom of heaven, but he who does the will of my Father who is in heaven.' Matthew 7:21 RSV

If ye love me, keep my commandments. John 14:15 KJV

[The high priest] 'We strictly charged you not to teach in this name, yet here you have filled Jerusalem with your teaching and you intend to bring this man's blood upon us.' But Peter and the apostles answered, 'We must obey God rather than men.' Acts 5:28-29 RSV

'And we are witnesses to these things, and so is the Holy Spirit whom God has given to those who obey him.' Acts 5:32 RSV

But thanks be to God, that you who were once slaves of sin have become obedient from the heart to the standard of teaching to which you were committed. Romans 6:17 RSV

And being found in human form he humbled himself and became obedient unto death, even death on a cross. Philippians 2:8 RSV

But even though he was God's Son, he learnt through his sufferings to be obedient. Hebrews 5:8 GNB

But be ye doers of the word, and not hearers only, deceiving your own selves. James 1:22 KJV

Be obedient to God, and do not allow your lives to be shaped by those desires you had when you were still ignorant. Instead, be holy in all that you do, just as God who called you is holy. 1 Peter 1:14-15 GNB

We receive from him whatever we ask, because we keep his commandments and do what pleases him. 1 John 3:22 RSV

By this we know that we love the children of God, when we love God

and obey his commandments. 1 John 5:2 RSV

See also *Blessing; Disobedience; Submission.*

Occult

' "Do not practise divination or sorcery." ' Leviticus 19:26 NIV

'Do not go for advice to people who consult the spirits of the dead. If you do, you will be ritually unclean. I am the Lord your God.' Leviticus 19:31 GNB

'Any man or woman who consults the spirits of the dead shall be stoned to death; any person who does this is responsible for his own death.' Leviticus 20:27 GNB

Let no-one be found among you who sacrifices his son or daughter in the fire, who practises divination or sorcery, interprets omens, engages in witchcraft, or casts spells, or who is a medium or spiritist or who consults the dead. Anyone who does these things is detestable to the Lord. Deuteronomy 18:10-12 NIV

Saul died because he was unfaithful to the Lord; he did not keep the word of the Lord, and even consulted a medium for guidance and did not enquire of the Lord. So the Lord put him to death. 1 Chronicles 10:13-14 NIV

And when they say to you, 'Consult the mediums and the wizards who chirp and mutter,' should not a people consult their God? Should they consult the dead on behalf of the living? Isaiah 8:19 RSV

Let your astrologers, your star-gazers who foretell your future month by month, persist, and save you! But look, they are gone like chaff; fire burns them up; they cannot snatch themselves from the flames; this is no glowing coal to warm them, no fire for them to sit by. Isaiah 47:13-14 NEB

Now for some time a man named Simon had practised sorcery in the city and amazed all the people of Samaria. He boasted that he was someone great. Acts 8:9 NIV

A number who had practised sorcery brought their scrolls together and burned them publicly. Acts 19:19 NIV

Now the works of the flesh are plain: . . . sorcery . . . Galatians 5:19-20 RSV

Old age

'Show respect for old people and honour them. Fear me; I am the Lord.' Leviticus 19:32 GNB

'Wisdom is with the aged, and understanding in length of days.' Job 12:12 RSV

My times are in thy hand. Psalm 31:15 KJV

Do not cast me off in the time of old age; forsake me not when my strength is spent. Psalm 71:9 RSV

The days of our years are threescore years and ten; and if by reason of strength they be fourscore years, yet is their strength labour and sorrow; for it is soon cut off, and we fly away . . . So teach us to number our days, that we may apply our hearts unto wisdom. Psalm 90:10, 12 KJV

They [the righteous] are like trees planted in the house of the Lord, that flourish in the Temple of our God, that still bear fruit in old age and are always green and strong. Psalm 92:13-14 GNB

Children's children are a crown to the aged, and parents are the pride of their children. Proverbs 17:6 NIV

There was a very old prophetess, a widow named Anna, daughter of Phanuel of the tribe of Asher. She had been married for only seven years and was now eighty-four years old. She never left the Temple; day and night she worshipped God, fasting and praying. Luke 2:36-37 GNB

Here indeed we groan, and long to put on our heavenly dwelling. 2 Corinthians 5:2 RSV

For me to live is Christ, and to die is gain. Philippians 1:21 KJV

Instruct the older men to be sober, sensible, and self-controlled; to be sound in their faith, love, and endurance. In the same way instruct the older women to behave as women should who live a holy life. They must not be slanderers or slaves to wine. They must teach what is good. Titus 2:2-3 GNB

Oppression

'You shall not wrong a stranger or oppress him, for you were strangers in the land of Egypt.' Exodus 22:21 RSV

'You shall not oppress a hired servant who is poor and needy, whether he is one of your brethren or one of the sojourners who are in your land within your towns.' Deuteronomy 24:14 RSV

May the Lord be a tower of strength for the oppressed. Psalm 9:9 NEB

The Lord judges in favour of the oppressed and gives them their rights. Psalm 103:6 GNB

He who oppresses a poor man insults his Maker, but he who is kind to the needy honours him. Proverbs 14:31 RSV

My eyes are weary with looking upward. O Lord, I am oppressed; be thou my security! Isaiah 38:14 RSV

He was oppressed, and he was afflicted, yet he opened not his mouth. Isaiah 53:7 KJV

"'Do not oppress widows, orphans, foreigners who live among you, or anyone else in need. And do not plan ways of harming one another.'" Zechariah 7:10 GNB

But you have dishonoured the poor man. Is it not the rich who oppress you, is it not they who drag you into court? James 2:6 RSV

Parables

See *Jesus Christ, Parables of Jesus*.

Parent

See *Family*.

Passover

'Tell all the congregation of Israel that on the tenth day of this month they shall take every man a lamb according to their fathers' houses, a lamb for a household . . . Your lamb shall be without blemish, a male a year old; you shall take it from the sheep or from the goats; and you shall keep it until the fourteenth day of this month, when the whole assembly of the congregation of Israel shall kill their lambs in the evening. Then they shall take some of the blood, and put it on the two doorposts and the lintel of the houses in which they eat them. They shall eat the flesh that night, roasted; with unleavened bread and bitter herbs they shall eat it . . . In this manner you shall eat it: your loins girded, your sandals on your feet, and your staff in your hand; and you shall eat it in haste. It is the Lord's passover. For I will pass through the land of Egypt that night, and I will smite all the first-born in the land of Egypt, both man and beast; and on all the gods of Egypt I will execute judgments: I am the Lord. The blood shall be a sign for you, upon the houses where you are; and when I see the blood, I will pass over you, and no plague shall fall upon you to destroy you, when I smite the land of Egypt.' Exodus 12:3, 5-8, 11-13 RSV

'You shall observe this rite as an ordinance for you and for your sons for ever.' Exodus 12:24 RSV

Now his parents went to Jerusalem every year at the feast of the Passover. Luke 2:41 RSV

They went off and found everything just as Jesus had told them, and they prepared the Passover meal. Luke 22:13 GNB

You must remove the old yeast of sin so that you will be entirely pure. Then you will be like a new batch of dough without any yeast, as indeed I know you actually are. For our Passover Festival is ready, now that Christ, our Passover lamb, has been sacrificed. 1 Corinthians 5:7 GNB

See also *Communion*.

Pastor

And his gifts were that some should be apostles, some prophets, some evangelists, some pastors and teachers, to equip the saints for the work of ministry, for building up the body of Christ. Ephesians 4:11-12 RSV

For you know how, like a father with his children, we exhorted each one of you and encouraged you and charged you. 1 Thessalonians 2:11 GNB

As for you, always be steady, endure suffering, do the work of an evangelist, fulfil your ministry. 2 Timothy 4:5 RSV

See also *Elders; Shepherd; Teachers and teaching.*

Patience

Be still before the Lord and wait patiently for him; do not fret when men succeed in their ways, when they carry out their wicked schemes. Psalm 37:7 NIV

If you stay calm, you are wise, but if you have a hot temper, you only show how stupid you are. Proverbs 14:29 GNB

But they that wait upon the Lord shall renew their strength; they shall mount up with wings as eagles; they shall run, and not be weary; and they shall walk, and not faint. Isaiah 40:31 KJV

Or do you presume upon the riches of his kindness and forbearance and patience? Do you not know that God's kindness is meant to lead you to repentance? Romans 2:4 RSV

Rejoice in your hope, be patient in tribulation, be constant in prayer. Romans 12:12 RSV

Love is patient and kind . . . Love bears all things, believes all things, hopes all things, endures all things. 1 Corinthians 13:4, 7 RSV

But the fruit of the Spirit is . . . patience . . . Galatians 5:22 RSV

And we urge you, brothers, warn those who are idle, encourage the timid, help the weak, be patient with everyone. 1 Thessalonians 5:14 NIV

Be patient, therefore, brethren, until the coming of the Lord. Behold, the farmer waits for the precious fruit of the earth, being patient over it until it receives the early and the late rain. You also be patient. Establish your hearts, for the coming of the Lord is at hand. James 5:7-8 RSV

[To the church in Ephesus] '" I know your works, your toil and your patient endurance, and how you cannot bear evil men but have tested those who call themselves apostles but are not, and found them to be false."' Revelation 2:2 RSV

See also *Endurance*.

Peace

The Lord lift up his countenance upon thee, and give thee peace. Numbers 6:26 KJV

His name shall be called Wonderful, Counsellor, The mighty God, The everlasting Father, The Prince of Peace. Of the increase of his government and peace there shall be no end. Isaiah 9:6-7 KJV

'Thou dost keep him in perfect peace, whose mind is stayed on thee, because he trusts in thee.' Isaiah 26:3 RSV

'There is no peace,' says the Lord, 'for the wicked.' Isaiah 48:22 RSV

And when Jesus was baptized, he went up immediately from the water, and behold, the heavens were opened and he saw the Spirit of God descending like a dove, and alighting on him. Matthew 3:16 RSV

Blessed are the peacemakers: for they shall be called the children of God. Matthew 5:9 KJV

'Do not think that I have come to bring peace to the world. No, I did not come to bring peace, but a sword.' Matthew 10:34 GNB

And he awoke and rebuked the wind, and said to the sea, 'Peace! Be still!' And the wind ceased, and there was a great calm. Mark 4:39 RSV

'Glory to God in highest heaven, and on earth his peace for men on whom his favour rests.' Luke 2:14 NEB

[Simeon's 'Nunc Dimittis'] Lord, now lettest

thou thy servant depart in peace, according to thy word. Luke 2:29 BCP

'Whenever you go into a house, first say, "Peace be with this house." If a peace-loving man lives there, let your greeting of peace remain on him; if not, take back your greeting of peace.' Luke 10:5-6 GNB

'Peace I leave with you; my peace I give to you; not as the world gives do I give to you. Let not your hearts be troubled, neither let them be afraid.' John 14:27 RSV

These things I have spoken unto you, that in me ye might have peace. In the world ye shall have tribulation: but be of good cheer; I have overcome the world. John 16:33 KJV

Jesus came and stood among them and said to them, 'Peace be with you.' John 20:19 RSV

Therefore being justified by faith, we have peace with God through our Lord Jesus Christ. Romans 5:1 KJV

To set the mind on the flesh is death, but to set the mind on the Spirit is life and peace. Romans 8:6 RSV

If possible, so far as it depends upon you, live peaceably with all. Romans 12:18 RSV

For God is not a God of confusion but of peace. 1 Corinthians 14:33 RSV

But the fruit of the Spirit is . . . peace . . . Galatians 5:22 RSV

For he is our peace, who has made us both one, and has broken down the dividing wall of hostility. Ephesians 2:14 RSV

And your feet shod with the preparation of the gospel of peace. Ephesians 6:15 KJV

And the peace of God, which passes all understanding, will keep your hearts and your minds in Christ Jesus. Philippians 4:7 RSV

And let the peace of God rule in your hearts, to the which also ye are called in one body; and be ye thankful. Colossians 3:15 KJV

Now may the Lord of peace himself give you peace at all times in all ways. 2 Thessalonians 3:16 RSV

See also *Reconciliation*.

Pentecost

See Acts 2.

Perfection

[completeness, maturity]

[David's song of victory] 'This God—his way is perfect; the promise of the Lord proves true; he is a shield for all those who take refuge in him.' 2 Samuel 22:31 RSV

The law of the Lord is perfect, converting the soul. Psalm 19:7 KJV

Be ye therefore perfect, even as your Father which is in heaven is perfect. Matthew 5:48 KJV

Jesus said unto him [the rich young ruler], If thou wilt be perfect, go and sell that thou hast, and give to the poor, and thou shalt have treasure in heaven: and come and follow me. Matthew 19:21 KJV

And be not conformed to this world: but be ye transformed by the renewing of your mind, that ye may prove what is that good, and acceptable, and perfect, will of God. Romans 12:2 KJV

For our knowledge is imperfect and our prophecy is imperfect; but when the perfect comes, the imperfect will pass away. 1 Corinthians 13:9-10 RSV

And his gifts were that some should be apostles, some prophets, some evangelists, some pastors and teachers, to equip the saints for the work of ministry, for building up the body of Christ, until we all attain to the unity of the faith and of the knowledge of the Son of God, to mature manhood, to the measure of the stature of the fullness of Christ. Ephesians 4:11-13 RSV

Not that I have already obtained all this, or have already been made perfect, but I press on to take hold of that for which Christ Jesus took hold of me. Philippians 3:12 NIV

All of us who are spiritually mature should have this same attitude. But if some of you have a different attitude, God will make this clear to you. Philippians 3:15 GNB

Him we proclaim, warning every man and teaching every man in all wisdom, that we may present every man mature in Christ. Colossians 1:28 RSV

[The purpose of Scripture] That the man of God may be complete, equipped for every good work. 2 Timothy 3:17 RSV

But even though he was God's Son, he learnt through his sufferings to be obedient. When he was made perfect, he became the source of eternal salvation for all those who obey him. Hebrews 5:9 GNB

But solid food is for the mature, for those who have their faculties trained by practice to distinguish good from evil. Hebrews 5:14 RSV

For by a single offering he has perfected for all time those who are sanctified. Hebrews 10:14 RSV

Persecution

'Happy are those who are persecuted because they do what God requires; the Kingdom of heaven belongs to them! Happy are you when people insult you and persecute you and tell all kinds of evil lies against you because you are my followers. Be happy and glad, for a great reward is kept for you in heaven. This is how the prophets who lived before you were persecuted.' Matthew 5:10-12 GNB

But I say unto you, Love your enemies, bless them that curse you, do good to them that hate you, and pray for them which despitefully use you, and persecute you. Matthew 5:44 KJV

'He has no root in himself, but endures for a while, and when tribulation or persecution arises on account of the word, immediately he falls away.' Matthew 13:21 RSV

'But before all this they will lay their hands on you and persecute you, delivering you up to the synagogues and prisons, and you will be brought before kings and governors for my name's sake.' Luke 21:12 RSV

'Remember what I told you: "No slave is greater than his master." If they

'Now as he approached Damascus . . . he fell to the ground and heard a voice saying to him, 'Saul, Saul, why do you persecute me?' And he said, 'Who are you, Lord?' And he said, 'I am Jesus, whom you are persecuting.'

persecuted me, they will persecute you too; if they obeyed my teaching, they will obey yours too.' John 15:20 GNB

And on that day a great persecution arose against the church in Jerusalem; and they were all scattered throughout the region of Judea and Samaria, except the apostles. Acts 8:1 RSV

And he fell to the ground and heard a voice saying to him, 'Saul, Saul, why do you persecute me?' Acts 9:4 RSV

Who shall separate us from the love of Christ? Shall tribulation, or distress, or persecution, or famine, or nakedness, or peril, or sword? . . . No, in all these things we are more than conquerors through him who loved us. Romans 8:35, 37 RSV

Bless those who persecute you; bless and do not curse. Romans 12:14 NIV

Indeed all who desire to live a godly life in Christ Jesus will be persecuted. 2 Timothy 3:12 RSV

Perseverance

See Christian life, Continuing in the faith.

Pharisees

The Pharisees went out and took counsel against him, how to destroy him. Matthew 12:14 RSV

The Pharisees went off and made a plan to trap Jesus with questions. Matthew 22:15 GNB

'But woe to you, scribes and Pharisees, hypocrites! because you shut the kingdom of heaven against men; for you neither enter yourselves, nor allow those who would enter to go in.' Matthew 23:13 RSV

One day when Jesus was teaching, some Pharisees and teachers of the Law

were sitting there who had come from every town in Galilee and Judaea and from Jerusalem. Luke 5:17 GNB

And the Pharisees and their scribes murmured against his disciples, saying, 'Why do you eat and drink with tax collectors and sinners?' And Jesus answered them, 'Those who are well have no need of a physician, but those who are sick; I have not come to call the righteous, but sinners to repentance.' Luke 5:30-31 RSV

When the Pharisee saw this, he said to himself, 'If this man really were a prophet, he would know who this woman is who is touching him; he would know what kind of sinful life she lives!' Luke 7:39 GNB

The Pharisee was astonished to see that he did not first wash before dinner. And the Lord said to him, 'Now you Pharisees cleanse the outside of the cup and of the dish, but inside you are full of extortion and wickedness.' Luke 11:38-39 RSV

He also told this parable to some who trusted in themselves that they were righteous and despised others: 'Two men went up into the temple to pray, one a Pharisee and the other a tax collector. The Pharisee stood and prayed thus with himself, "God, I thank thee that I am not like other men, extortioners, unjust, adulterers, or even like this tax collector. I fast twice a week, I give tithes of all that I get."' Luke 18:9-12 RSV

Many of the Jewish authorities believed in Jesus; but because of the Pharisees they did not talk about it openly, so as not to be expelled from the synagogue. John 12:42 GNB

But when Paul perceived that one part were Sadducees and the other Pharisees, he cried out in the council, 'Brethren, I am a Pharisee, a son of Pharisees; with respect to the hope and the resurrection of the dead I am on trial.' Acts 23:6 RSV

See also *Hypocrisy; Scribes.*

Possessions

See *Money and material goods.*

Poverty

'You shall not pervert the justice due to your poor in his suit.' Exodus 23:6 RSV

'If there is among you a poor man, one of your brethren, in any of your towns within your land which the Lord your God gives you, you shall not harden your heart or shut your hand against your poor brother.' Deuteronomy 15:7 RSV

'He raises the poor from the dust, he lifts the needy from the dunghill to give them a place with princes, and to assign them a seat of honour.' 1 Samuel 2:8 JB

He who oppresses a poor man insults his Maker, but he who is kind to the needy honours him. Proverbs 14:31 RSV

He who is kind to the poor lends to the Lord, and he will repay him for his deed. Proverbs 19:17 RSV

Blessed are the poor in spirit: for theirs is the kingdom of heaven. Matthew 5:3 KJV

'For you always have the poor with you, but you will not always have me.' Matthew 26:11 RSV

And he called his disciples to him, and said to them, 'Truly, I say to you, this poor widow has put in more than all those who are contributing to the treasury. For they all contributed out of their abundance; but she out of her poverty has put in everything she had, her whole living.' Mark 12:43-44 RSV

'The Spirit of the Lord is upon me, because he has anointed me to preach good news to the poor.' Luke 4:18 RSV

'But when you give a feast, invite the poor, the maimed, the lame, the blind.' Luke 14:13 RSV

For ye know the grace of our Lord Jesus Christ, that, though he was rich, yet for your sakes he became poor, that ye through his poverty might be rich. 2 Corinthians 8:9 KJV

Has not God chosen those who are poor in the world to be rich in faith and heirs of the kingdom which he has promised to those who love him? But you have dishonoured the poor man. James 2:5-6 RSV

See also *Justice; Rich and riches.*

Power

But they that wait upon the Lord shall renew their strength: they shall mount up with wings as eagles; they shall run, and not be weary; and they shall walk, and not faint. Isaiah 40:31 KJV

For thine is the kingdom, and the power, and the glory, for ever. Amen. Matthew 6:13 KJV

But Jesus answered them, 'You are wrong, because you know neither the scriptures nor the power of God.' Matthew 22:29 RSV

'Then will appear the sign of the Son of man in heaven, and then all the tribes of the earth will mourn, and they will see the Son of man coming on the clouds of heaven with power and great glory.' Matthew 24:30 RSV

And Jesus, perceiving in himself that power had gone forth from him, immediately turned about in the crowd, and said, 'Who touched my garments?' Mark 5:30 RSV

And Jesus returned in the power of the Spirit into Galilee. Luke 4:14 KJV

'But you shall receive power when the Holy Spirit has come upon you; and you shall be my witnesses in Jerusalem and in all Judea and Samaria and to the end of the earth.' Acts 1:8 RSV

And with great power the apostles gave their testimony to the resurrection of the Lord Jesus, and great grace was upon them all. Acts 4:33 RSV

For I am not ashamed of the gospel of Christ: for it is the power of God unto salvation to every one that believeth; to the Jew first, and also to the Greek. Romans 1:16 KJV

May the God of hope fill you with all joy and peace in believing, so that by the power of the Holy Spirit you may abound in hope. Romans 15:13 RSV

But we preach Christ crucified, unto the Jews a stumblingblock, and unto the Greeks foolishness; but unto them which are called, both Jews and Greeks, Christ the power of God, and the wisdom of God. 1 Corinthians 1:23-24 KJV

But we have this treasure in earthen vessels, that the excellency of the power may be of God, and not of us. 2 Corinthians 4:7 KJV

He said to me, 'My grace is sufficient for you, for my power is made perfect in weakness.' I will all the more gladly boast of my weaknesses, that the power of Christ may rest upon me. 2 Corinthians 12:9 RSV

How very great is his power at work in us who believe. This power working in us is the same as the mighty strength which he used when he raised Christ from death and seated him at his right side in the heavenly world. Ephesians 1:19-20 GNB

Finally, my brethren, be strong in the Lord, and in the power of his might. Put on the whole armour of God, that ye may be able to stand against the wiles of the devil. Ephesians 6:10-11 KJV

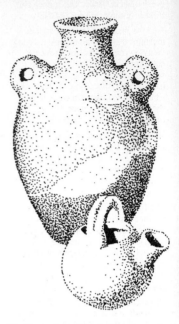

'We have this treasure in earthen vessels. . .'

That I may know him and the power of his resurrection, and may share his sufferings, becoming like him in his death. Philippians 3:10 RSV

I can do all things in him who strengthens me. Philippians 4:13 RSV

For our gospel came to you not only in word, but also in power and in the Holy Spirit and with full conviction. 1 Thessalonians 1:5 RSV

They [people in the last days] will hold to the outward form of our religion, but reject its real power. Keep away from such people. 2 Timothy 3:5 GNB

You, who by God's power are guarded through faith for a salvation ready to be revealed in the last time. 1 Peter 1:4-5 RSV

See also Authority.

Praise

I will bless the Lord at all times; his praise shall continually be in my mouth . . . O magnify the Lord with me, and let us exalt his name together! Psalm 34:1,3 RSV

Whoso offereth praise glorifieth me: and to him that ordereth his conversation aright will I shew the salvation of God. Psalm 50:23 KJV

Make a joyful noise unto the Lord, all ye lands. Serve the Lord with gladness: come before his presence with singing.

Know ye that the Lord he is God: it is he that hath made us, and not we ourselves; we are his people, and the sheep of his pasture. Enter into his gates with thanksgiving, and into his courts with praise: be thankful unto him, and bless his name. Psalm 100:1-4 KJV

The people whom I formed for myself that they might declare my praise. Isaiah 43:21 RSV

He hath sent me . . . to appoint unto them that mourn in Zion, to give unto them beauty for ashes, the oil of joy for mourning, the garment of praise for the spirit of heaviness; that they might be called trees of righteousness, the planting of the Lord, that he might be glorified. Isaiah 61:1, 3 KJV

Day after day they met as a group in the Temple, and they had their meals together in their homes, eating with glad and humble hearts, praising God, and enjoying the good will of all the people. And every day the Lord added to their group those who were being saved. Acts 2:46-47 GNB

Speaking to yourselves in psalms and hymns and spiritual songs, singing and making melody in your heart to the Lord. Ephesians 5:19 KJV

Let us, then, always offer praise to God as our sacrifice through Jesus, which is the offering presented by lips that confess him as Lord. Hebrews 13:15 GNB

'Worthy is the Lamb who was slain, to receive power and wealth and wisdom and might and honour and glory and blessing!' Revelation 5:12 RSV

See also *Prayer; Worship.*

Prayer

Answers to prayer

This poor man cried, and the Lord heard him, and saved him out of all his troubles. Psalm 34:6 RSV

And when he had entered the house, his disciples asked him privately, 'Why could we not cast it out?' And he said to them, 'This kind cannot be driven out by anything but prayer.' Mark 9:28-29 RSV

You also must help us by prayer, so that many will give thanks on our behalf for the blessing granted us in answer to many prayers. 2 Corinthians 1:11 RSV

Three times I besought the Lord about this, that it should leave me; but he said to me, 'My grace is sufficient for you,

for my power is made perfect in weakness.' 2 Corinthians 12:8-9 RSV

Now unto him that is able to do exceeding abundantly above all that we ask or think, according to the power that worketh in us, unto him be glory in the church by Christ Jesus throughout all ages, world without end. Amen. Ephesians 3:20-21 KJV

Have no anxiety about anything, but in everything by prayer and supplication with thanksgiving let your requests be made known to God. And the peace of God, which passes all understanding, will keep your hearts and your minds in Christ Jesus. Philippians 4:6-7 RSV

Let us then with confidence draw near to the throne of grace, that we may receive mercy and find grace to help in time of need. Hebrews 4:16 RSV

You ask and do not receive, because you ask wrongly, to spend it on your passions. James 4:3 RSV

The effectual fervent prayer of a righteous man availeth much. James 5:16 KJV

Encouragements to pray

[David's thanksgiving] Seek the Lord and his strength, seek his face continually. 1 Chronicles 16:11 KJV

The Lord watches over the righteous and listens to their cries. Psalm 34:15 GNB

Trust in God at all times, my people. Tell him all your troubles, for he is our refuge. Psalm 62:8 GNB

'Before they call I will answer, while they are yet speaking I will hear.' Isaiah 65:24 RSV

'But when you pray, go to your room, close the door, and pray to your Father, who is unseen. And your Father, who sees what you do in private, will reward you.' Matthew 6:6 GNB

And he told them a parable, to the effect that they ought always to pray and not lose heart. Luke 18:1 RSV

Pray without ceasing. 1 Thessalonians 5:17 KJV

Behold, I stand at the door, and knock: if any man hear my voice, and open the door, I will come in to him, and will sup with him, and he with me. Revelation 3:20 KJV

How to pray

'When you pray, do not use a lot of meaningless words, as the pagans do, who think that God will hear them because their prayers are long. Do not be like them. Your Father already knows what you need before you ask him. This, then, is how you should pray . . .' Matthew 6:7-9 GNB

Our Father, which art in heaven, hallowed be thy name. Thy kingdom come. Thy will be done, in earth as it is in heaven. Give us this day our daily bread. And forgive us our trespasses, as we forgive them that trespass against us. And lead us not into temptation; but deliver us from evil. Matthew 6:9-13 BCP

For thine is the kingdom, and the power, and the glory, for ever. Amen. Matthew 6:13 KJV

'Watch and pray that you may not enter into temptation; the spirit indeed is willing, but the flesh is weak.' Matthew 26:41 RSV

Likewise the Spirit helps us in our weakness; for we do not know how to pray as we ought, but the Spirit himself intercedes for us with sighs too deep for words. Romans 8:26 RSV

Praying always with all prayer and supplication in the Spirit, and watching thereunto with all perseverance and supplication for all saints; and for me, that utterance may be given unto me, that I may open my mouth boldly, to make known the mystery of the gospel. Ephesians 6:18-19 KJV

I exhort, therefore, that, first of all, supplications, prayers, intercessions, and giving of thanks, be made for all men; for kings, and for all that are in authority; that we may lead a quiet and peaceable life in all godliness and honesty. 1 Timothy 2:1-2 KJV

Prayers of the Bible

Abraham's prayer for Sodom, Genesis 18:22-33
Issac's blessing, Genesis 27
Jacob's desperate prayer at Penuel, Genesis 32
Jacob blesses his sons, Genesis 48-49
Moses' song of thanksgiving for deliverance from Egypt, Exodus 15
Moses' plea for Israel when they had worshipped the golden calf, Exodus 32; Deuteronomy 9
Moses asks to see God's glory, Exodus 33
Aaron's blessing, Numbers 6
Moses' song: God and his people, Deuteronomy 32
Moses blesses the people of Israel, Deuteronomy 33
Deborah's song of thanksgiving for victory, Judges 5
Gideon's prayer for signs, Judges 6
Hannah's prayer for a son, 1 Samuel 1; **her thanksgiving,** 1 Samuel 2
Samuel's prayer for the nation, 1 Samuel 7
David's prayer following God's promise of a lasting succession, 2 Samuel 7; 1 Chronicles 17
David's song of thanksgiving for deliverance, 2 Samuel 22; Psalm 18
Solomon's prayer for wisdom, 1 Kings 3; 2 Chronicles 1
Solomon's prayer at the dedication of the temple, 1 Kings 8; 2 Chronicles 6
Elijah's prayer on Mt Carmel, 1 Kings 18
Elijah and the 'still, small voice', 1 Kings 19
Hezekiah's prayer at the time of

Sennacherib's siege, 2 Kings 19; Isaiah 37
Thanksgiving as the ark is brought to Jerusalem, 1 Chronicles 16
David's prayer for Solomon, 1 Chronicles 29
Ezra's confession of the nation's sin, Ezra 9
Nehemiah's prayer for his people, Nehemiah 1
The public confession led by Ezra, Nehemiah 9
Job seeks the reason for his suffering, Job 10
Job pleads his case, Job 13-14
Job's confession, Job 42

The Psalms include an enormous number of prayers: some are listed here, under themes:
Evening prayer, 4
Morning prayer, 5
The shepherd psalm, 23
Praise and worship, 24; 67; 92; 95-98; 100; 113; 145; 148; 150
Guidance, 25
Trust, 37; 62
Deliverance, 40; 116
Longing for God, 27; 42; 63; 84
Forgiveness, 51; 130
Thanksgiving, 65; 111; 136
Help in trouble, 69; 86; 88; 102; 140; 143
God's constant love and care, 89; 103; 107; 146
God's majesty and glory, 8; 29; 93; 104
God's knowledge and presence, 139
God's word, 19; 119
God's protection, 46; 91; 125

If any of you lacks wisdom, let him ask God, who gives to all men generously and without reproaching, and it will be given him. But let him ask in faith, with no doubting, for he who doubts is like a wave of the sea that is driven and tossed by the wind. James 1:5-6 RSV

Promises in prayer

[The Lord's promise to Solomon] 'If my people who are called by my name humble themselves, and pray and seek my face, and turn from their wicked ways, then I will hear from heaven, and will forgive their sin and heal their land.' 2 Chronicles 7:14 RSV

Take delight in the Lord, and he will give you the desires of your heart. Psalm 37:4 RSV

If I had cherished iniquity in my heart, the Lord would not have listened. Psalm 66:18 RSV

'Ask, and it will be given you; seek, and you will find; knock, and it will be opened to you. For every one who asks receives, and he who seeks finds, and to him who knocks it will be opened.' Matthew 7:7-8 RSV

'Again I say to you, if two of you agree on earth about anything they ask, it will be done for them by my Father in heaven. For where two or three are gathered in my name, there am I in the midst of them.' Matthew 18:19-20 RSV

'Whatever you ask in prayer, you will receive, if you have faith.' Matthew 21:22 RSV

'Whatever you ask in my name, I will do it, that the Father may be glorified in the Son.' John 14:13 RSV

'If you abide in me, and my words abide in you, ask whatever you will, and it shall be done for you.' John 15:7 RSV

'When that day comes you will ask nothing of me. In very truth I tell you, if you ask the Father for anything in my name, he will give it you. So far you have asked nothing in my name. Ask and you will receive, that your joy may be complete.' John 16:23-24 NEB

We receive from him whatever we ask, because we keep his commandments and do what pleases him. 1 John 3:22 RSV

And this is the confidence which we have in him, that if we ask anything according to his will he hears us. 1 John 5:14 RSV

See also *Praise; Worship.*

Preaching

How beautiful upon the mountains are the feet of him that bringeth good tidings, that publisheth peace; that bringeth good tidings of good, that publisheth salvation; that saith unto Zion, Thy God reigneth! Isaiah 52:7 KJV

The Spirit of the Lord God is upon me; because the Lord hath anointed me to preach good tidings unto the meek . . . Isaiah 61:1 KJV

Repentance and remission of sins should be preached in his name among all nations, beginning at Jerusalem. Luke 24:47 KJV

[Paul] 'For I did not shrink from declaring to you the whole counsel of God.' Acts 20:27 RSV

But how are men to call upon him in whom they have not believed? And how are they to believe in him of whom they have never heard? And how are they to hear without a preacher? And how can men preach unless they are sent? As it is written, 'How beautiful are the feet of those who preach good news!' Romans 10:14-15 RSV

For after that in the wisdom of God the world by wisdom knew not God, it pleased God by the foolishness of preaching to save them that believe . . . But we preach Christ crucified, unto the Jews a stumblingblock, and unto the Greeks foolishness; but unto them which are called, both Jews and Greeks, Christ the power of God, and the wisdom of God. 1 Corinthians 1:21, 23 KJV

For necessity is laid upon me. Woe to me if I do not preach the gospel! 1 Corinthians 9:16 RSV

Our gospel came to you not only in word, but also in power and in the Holy Spirit and with full conviction 1 Thessalonians 1:5 RSV

Till I come, attend to the public reading of scripture, to preaching, to teaching. 1 Timothy 4:13 RSV

Let the elders who rule well be considered worthy of double honour, especially those who labour in preaching and teaching. 1 Timothy 5:17 RSV

Do your best to present yourself to God as one approved, a workman who has no need to be ashamed, rightly handling the word of truth. 2 Timothy 2:15 RSV

Preach the word, be urgent in season and out of season, convince, rebuke, and exhort, be unfailing in patience and in teaching. 2 Timothy 4:2 RSV

See also *Teachers and teaching.*

Pride

'Beware lest you say in your heart, "My power and the might of my hand have gotten me this wealth."' Deuteronomy 8:17 RSV

Pride goes before destruction, and a haughty spirit before a fall. Proverbs 16:18 RSV

'Whoever exalts himself will be humbled, and whoever humbles himself will be exalted.' Matthew 23:12 RSV

And he said, 'What comes out of a man is what defiles a man. For from within, out of the heart of man, come evil thoughts . . . pride . . .' Mark 7:21-22 RSV

He hath shewed strength with his arm, he hath scattered the proud in the imaginations of their hearts. Luke 1:51 BCP

For by the grace given to me I bid every one among you not to think of himself more highly than he ought to think, but to think with sober judgment, each according to the measure of faith which God has assigned him. Romans 12:3 RSV

Do not be proud, but be willing to associate with people of low position. Do not be conceited. Romans 12:16 NIV

Therefore, as it is written, 'Let him who boasts, boast of the Lord.'
1 Corinthians 1:31 RSV

Therefore let any one who thinks that he stands take heed lest he fall.
1 Corinthians 10:12 RSV

Love is not jealous or boastful.
1 Corinthians 13:4 RSV

And to keep me from being too elated by the abundance of revelations, a thorn was given me in the flesh, a messenger of Satan, to harass me, to keep me from being too elated.
2 Corinthians 12:7 RSV

See also *Humility; Self-righteousness.*

Priest

'And you shall be to me a kingdom of priests and a holy nation.' Exodus 19:6 RSV

'Then bring near to you Aaron your brother, and his sons with him, from among the people of Israel, to serve me as priests.' Exodus 28:1 RSV

'Whenever cattle or sheep are sacrificed, the priests are to be given the shoulder, the jaw, and the stomach.' Deuteronomy 18:3 GNB

'And the priests the sons of Levi shall come forward, for the Lord your God has chosen them to minister to him and to bless in the name of the Lord, and by their word every dispute and every assault shall be settled.' Deuteronomy 21:5 RSV

'They shall teach Jacob thy ordinances, and Israel thy law; they shall put incense before thee, and whole burnt offering upon thy altar.' Deuteronomy 33:10 RSV

And they led Jesus to the high priest; and all the chief priests and the elders and the scribes were assembled. Mark 14:53 RSV

So Judas went off and spoke with the chief priests and the officers of the temple guard about how he could betray Jesus to them. Luke 22:4 GNB

And the word of God increased; and the number of the disciples multiplied greatly in Jerusalem, and a great many of the priests were obedient to the faith. Acts 6:7 RSV

For every high priest chosen from among men is appointed to act on behalf of men in relation to God, to offer gifts and sacrifices for sins. He can deal gently with the ignorant and wayward, since he himself is beset with weakness. Because of this he is bound to offer sacrifice for his own sins as well as for those of the people. And one does not take the honour upon himself, but he is called by God, just as Aaron was. Hebrews 5:1-4 RSV

For every high priest is appointed to offer gifts and sacrifices; hence it is necessary for this priest also to have something to offer. Hebrews 8:3 RSV

And every priest stands daily at his service, offering repeatedly the same sacrifices, which can never take away sins. But when Christ had offered for all time a single sacrifice for sins, he sat down at the right hand of God. Hebrews 10:11-12 RSV

Like living stones be yourselves built into a spiritual house, to be a holy priesthood, to offer spiritual sacrifices acceptable to God through Jesus Christ ... you are a chosen race, a royal priesthood, a holy nation, God's own people. 1 Peter 2:5, 9 RSV

See also *Jesus Christ, Jesus as priest.*

Prodigal son

See *Jesus Christ, Parables of Jesus.*

Promise

And, behold, I send the promise of my Father upon you: but tarry ye in the city of Jerusalem, until ye be endued with power from on high. Luke 24:49 KJV

It is not the natural children who are God's children, but it is the children of the promise who are regarded as Abraham's offspring. Romans 9:8 NIV

For all the promises of God find their Yes in him [Jesus Christ]. 2 Corinthians 1:20 RSV

In him you also, who have heard the word of truth, the gospel of your salvation, and have believed in him, were sealed with the promised Holy Spirit. Ephesians 1:13 RSV

Remember that you were at that time separated from Christ, alienated from the commonwealth of Israel, and strangers to the covenants of promise, having no hope and without God in the world. Ephesians 2:12 RSV

Christ has obtained a ministry which is as much more excellent than the old as the covenant he mediates is better, since it is enacted on better promises. Hebrews 8:6 RSV

Let us hold fast the confession of our hope without wavering, for he who promised is faithful. Hebrews 10:23 RSV

Blessed is the man who endures trial, for when he has stood the test he will receive the crown of life which God has promised to those who love him. James 1:12 RSV

Through these he has given us his very great and precious promises, so that through them you may participate in the divine nature and escape the corruption in the world caused by evil desires. 2 Peter 1:4 NIV

The Lord is not slow about his promise as some count slowness, but is forbearing toward you, not wishing that any should perish, but that all should reach repentance . . . But according to his promise we wait for new heavens and a new earth in which righteousness dwells. 2 Peter 3:9, 13 RSV

Prophets and prophecy

'When a prophet speaks in the name of the Lord, if the word does not come to pass or come true, that is a word which the Lord has not spoken; the prophet has spoken it presumptuously, you need not be afraid of him.' Deuteronomy 18:22 RSV

'From the day that your fathers came out of the land of Egypt to this day, I have persistently sent all my servants the prophets to them, day after day; yet they did not listen to me, or incline their ear, but stiffened their neck.' Jeremiah 7:25-26 RSV

Many will say to me in that day, Lord, Lord, have we not prophesied in thy name? And in thy name have cast out devils? And in thy name done many wonderful works? And then will I profess unto them, I never knew you: depart from me, ye that work iniquity. Matthew 7:22-23 KJV

'For false Christs and false prophets will arise and show great signs and wonders, so as to lead astray, if possible, even the elect.' Matthew 24:24 RSV

'"On my menservants and my maidservants in those days I will pour out my Spirit; and they shall prophesy."' Acts 2:18 RSV

Now in these days prophets came down from Jerusalem to Antioch. And one of them named Agabus stood up and foretold by the Spirit that there would be a great famine over all the world; and this took place in the days of Claudius. Acts 11:27-28 RSV

And God has appointed in the church first apostles, second prophets . . . 1 Corinthians 12:28 RSV

Love never ends; as for prophecies, they will pass away. 1 Corinthians 13:8 RSV

Make love your aim, and earnestly desire the spiritual gifts, especially that you may prophesy. 1 Corinthians 14:1 RSV

For you can all prophesy in turn, so that everybody will learn something and everybody will be encouraged. Prophets can always control their prophetic spirits. 1 Corinthians 14:31-32 JB

[The household of God] Built upon the foundation of the apostles and prophets, Christ Jesus himself being the cornerstone. Ephesians 2:20 RSV

Despise not prophesyings. Prove all things; hold fast that which is good. 1 Thessalonians 5:20-21 KJV

No prophecy ever came by the impulse of man, but men moved by the Holy Spirit spoke from God. 2 Peter 1:21 RSV

Propitiation

Yet it pleased the Lord to bruise him; he hath put him to grief: when thou shalt make his soul an offering for sin, he shall see his seed, he shall prolong his days, and the pleasure of the Lord shall prosper in his hand. Isaiah 53:10 KJV

'But the tax collector, standing far off, would not even lift up his eyes to heaven, but beat his breast, saying, "God, be merciful to me a sinner!"' Luke 18:13 RSV

[Christ Jesus] Whom God hath set forth to be a propitiation through faith in his blood, to declare his righteousness for the remission of sins that are past, through the forbearance of God. Romans 3:25 KJV

But by becoming a curse for us Christ has redeemed us from the curse that the Law brings; for the scripture says, 'Anyone who is hanged on a tree is under God's curse.' Galatians 3:13 GNB

For this reason he had to be made like his brothers in every way, in order that he might become a merciful and faithful high priest in service to God, and that he might make atonement for the sins of the people. Hebrews 2:17 NIV

And over it the cherubims of glory shadowing the mercy seat; of which we cannot now speak particularly. Hebrews 9:5 KJV

And he is the propitiation for our sins: and not for ours only, but also for the sins of the whole world. 1 John 2:2 KJV

Herein is love, not that we loved God, but that he loved us, and sent his Son to be the propitiation for our sins. 1 John 4:10 KJV

See also *Anger, of God; Atonement; Reconciliation.*

Providence

'While the earth remains, seedtime and harvest, cold and heat, summer and winter, day and night, shall not cease.' Genesis 8:22 RSV

So Abraham called the name of that place The Lord will provide; as it is said to this day, 'On the mount of the Lord it shall be provided.' Genesis 22:14 RSV

For all things come of thee, and of thine own have we given thee. 1 Chronicles 29:14 KJV

And Ezra said: 'Thou art the Lord, thou alone; thou hast made heaven, the heaven of heavens, with all their host, the earth and all that is on it, the seas and all that is in them; and thou preservest all of them; and the host of heaven worships thee.' Nehemiah 9:6 RSV

Whatever the Lord pleases he does, in heaven and on earth, in the seas and all deeps. He it is who makes the clouds rise at the end of the earth, who makes lightnings for the rain and brings forth the wind from his storehouses. Psalm 135:6-7 RSV

The plans of the mind belong to man, but the answer of the tongue is from the Lord. Proverbs 16:1 RSV

The lot is cast into the lap, but the decision is wholly from the Lord. Proverbs 16:33 RSV

'For only a penny you can buy two sparrows, yet not one sparrow falls to the ground without your Father's consent. As for you, even the hairs of your head have all been counted. So do not be afraid; you are worth much more than many sparrows!' Matthew 10:29-31 GNB

'"In him we live and move and have our being."' Acts 17:28 RSV

[God] who worketh all things after the counsel of his own will. Ephesians 1:11 KJV

[Christ] He is before all things, and in him all things hold together. Colossians 1:17 RSV

[God] Upholding all things by the word of his power. Hebrews 1:3 KJV

See also *Sovereignty of God.*

Punishment

'Whoever hits a man and kills him is to be put to death.' Exodus 2:12 GNB

Be sure your sin will find you out. Numbers 32:23 KJV

'If I say to the wicked, O wicked man, you shall surely die, and you do not speak to warn the wicked to turn from his way, that wicked man shall die in his iniquity, but his blood I will require at your hand.' Ezekiel 33:8 RSV

And these shall go away into everlasting punishment: but the righteous into life eternal. Matthew 25:46 KJV

He who believes in him is not condemned; he who does not believe is condemned already, because he has not believed in the name of the only Son of God. John 3:18 RSV

For those who are factious and do not

obey the truth, but obey wickedness, there will be wrath and fury. There will be tribulation and distress for every human being who does evil, the Jew first and also the Greek. Romans 2:8-9 RSV

For the wages of sin is death; but the gift of God is eternal life through Jesus Christ our Lord. Romans 6:23 KJV

He [the man in authority] is God's servant working for your own good. But if you do evil, then be afraid of him, because his power to punish is real. Romans 13:4 GNB

They [those who do not obey the Good News about the Lord Jesus] will suffer the punishment of eternal destruction, separated from the presence of the Lord and from his glorious might. 2 Thessalonians 1:9 GNB

What, then, of the person who despises the Son of God? who treats as a cheap thing the blood of God's covenant which purified him from sin? who insults the Spirit of grace? Just think how much worse is the punishment he will deserve! Hebrews 10:29 GNB

See also *Anger, of God; Discipline; Last things, Hell.*

Purity, pure

The statutes of the Lord are right, rejoicing the heart: the commandment of the Lord is pure, enlightening the eyes. Psalm 19:8 KJV

Thou who art of purer eyes than to behold evil and canst not look on wrong . . . Habakkuk 1:13 RSV

Blessed are the pure in heart: for they shall see God. Matthew 5:8 KJV

Take no part in the sins of others; keep yourself pure. 1 Timothy 5:22 GNB

To the pure, all things are pure, but to the corrupt and unbelieving nothing is pure; their very minds and consciences are corrupted. Titus 1:15 RSV

But the wisdom from above is first pure . . . James 3:17 RSV

Draw near to God and he will draw near to you. Cleanse your hands, you sinners, and purify your hearts, you men of double mind. James 4:8 RSV

Now that by your obedience to the truth you have purified yourselves and have come to have a sincere love for your fellow-believers, love one another earnestly with all your heart. 1 Peter 1:22 GNB

Race

[ethnic]
So God created man in his own image, in the image of God created he him; male and female created he them. And God blessed them, and God said unto them, Be fruitful, and multiply, and replenish the earth, and subdue it. Genesis 1:27-28 KJV

And Peter opened his mouth and said: 'Truly I perceive that God shows no partiality, but in every nation any one who fears him and does what is right is acceptable to him.' Acts 10:34-35 RSV

'And he made from one every nation of men to live on all the face of the earth, having determined allotted periods and the boundaries of their habitation.' Acts 17:26 RSV

There is neither Jew nor Greek, there is neither bond nor free, there is neither male nor female: for ye are all one in Christ Jesus. Galatians 3:28 KJV

After this I looked, and behold, a great multitude which no man could number, from every nation, from all tribes and peoples and tongues, standing before the throne and before the Lamb.' Revelation 7:9 RSV

See also *Immigrants.*

Reconciliation

He shall judge between the nations, and shall decide for many peoples; and they shall beat their swords into ploughshares, and their spears into pruning hooks; nation shall not lift up sword against nation, neither shall they learn war any more. Isaiah 2:4 RSV

'If you are bringing your offering to the altar and there remember that your brother has something against you, leave your offering there before the altar, go and be reconciled with your brother first, and then come back and present your offering.' Matthew 5:23-24 JB

For if while we were enemies we were reconciled to God by the death of his Son, much more, now that we are reconciled, shall we be saved by his life. Not only so, but we also rejoice in God through our Lord Jesus Christ, through whom we have now received our reconciliation. Romans 5:10-11 RSV

All this is from God, who through Christ reconciled us to himself and gave us the ministry of reconciliation; that is, in Christ God was reconciling the world to himself, not counting their trespasses against them, and entrusting to us the message of reconciliation. So we are ambassadors for Christ, God making his appeal through us. We beseech you on behalf of Christ, be reconciled to God. 2 Corinthians 5:18-20 RSV

[Christ] might reconcile us both [Jew and Gentile] to God in one body through the cross, thereby bringing the hostility to an end. Ephesians 2:16 RSV

Through him [Christ] to reconcile to himself all things, whether on earth or in heaven, making peace by the blood of his cross. Colossians 1:20 RSV

But now, by means of the physical death of his Son, God has made you his friends, in order to bring you, holy, pure, and faultless, into his presence. Colossians 1:22 GNB

See also *Atonement; Peace; Propitiation.*

Redemption

'Say therefore to the people of Israel, "I am the Lord, and I will bring you out from under the burdens of the Egyptians, and I will deliver you from their bondage, and I will redeem you with an outstretched arm and with great acts of judgment." ' Exodus 6:6 RSV

For I know that my redeemer liveth, and that he shall stand at the latter day upon the earth. Job 19:25 KJV

And the ransomed of the Lord shall return, and come to Zion with singing; everlasting joy shall be upon their heads; they shall obtain joy and gladness, and sorrow and sighing shall flee away. Isaiah 35:10 RSV

But now thus saith the Lord that created thee, O Jacob, and he that formed thee, O Israel, Fear not: for I have redeemed thee, I have called thee by thy name; thou art mine. Isaiah 43:1 KJV

'For the Son of man also came not to be served but to serve, and to give his life as a ransom for many.' Mark 10:45 RSV

Being justified freely by his grace through the redemption that is in Christ Jesus. Romans 3:24 KJV

Not only the creation, but we ourselves, who have the first fruits of the Spirit, groan inwardly as we wait for adoption as sons, the redemption of our bodies. Romans 8:23 RSV

He is the source of your life in Christ Jesus, whom God made our wisdom, our righteousness and sanctification and redemption. 1 Corinthians 1:30 RSV

You were bought with a price. So glorify God in your body. 1 Corinthians 6:20 RSV

But by becoming a curse for us Christ has redeemed us from the curse that the Law brings; for the scripture says, 'Anyone who is hanged on a tree is under God's curse.' Galatians 3:13 GNB

But when the time had fully come, God sent forth his Son, born of woman, born under the law, to redeem those who were under the law, so that we might receive adoption as sons. Galatians 4:4-5 RSV

In him we have redemption through his blood, the forgiveness of our trespasses, according to the riches of his grace. Ephesians 1:7 RSV

[God's beloved Son] In whom we have redemption, the forgiveness of sins. Colossians 1:14 RSV

Christ Jesus, who gave himself as a ransom for all. 1 Timothy 2:5-6 RSV

[Jesus Christ] who gave himself for us to redeem us from all iniquity and to purify for himself a people of his own who are zealous for good deeds. Titus 2:14 RSV

He entered once for all into the Holy Place, taking not the blood of goats and calves but his own blood, thus securing an eternal redemption. Hebrews 9:12 RSV

You know that you were ransomed from the futile ways inherited from your fathers, not with perishable things such as silver or gold, but with the precious blood of Christ, like that of a lamb without blemish or spot. 1 Peter 1:18-19 RSV

Regeneration

See *New birth.*

Rejection

'For rebellion is as the sin of divination, and stubbornness is as iniquity and idolatry. Because you have rejected the word of the Lord, he has also rejected you from being king.' 1 Samuel 15:23 RSV

The stone which the builders rejected has become the head of the corner. Psalm 118:22 RSV

The Lord God hath opened mine ear, and I was not rebellious, neither turned away back. I gave my back to the smiters, and my cheeks to them that plucked off the hair: I hid not my face from shame and spitting. Isaiah 50:5-6 KJV

He is despised and rejected of men; a man of sorrows, and acquainted with grief: and we hid as it were our faces from him; he was despised, and we esteemed him not. Isaiah 53:3 KJV

'But this people has a stubborn and rebellious heart; they have turned aside and gone away.' Jeremiah 5:23 RSV

'And if any one will not receive you or listen to your words, shake off the dust from your feet as you leave that house or town.' Matthew 10:14 RSV

And he said to them, 'You have a fine way of rejecting the commandment of God, in order to keep your tradition!' Mark 7:9 RSV

He came unto his own, and his own received him not. John 1:11 KJV

'He who rejects me and does not receive my sayings has a judge; the word that I have spoken will be his judge on the last day.' John 12:48 RSV

Come to him, to that living stone, rejected by men but in God's sight chosen and precious. 1 Peter 2:4 RSV

See also *Hardness; Unbelief.*

Repentance

[The Lord's promise to Solomon] 'If my people who are called by my name humble themselves, and pray and seek my face, and turn from their wicked ways, then I will hear from heaven, and will forgive their sin and heal their land.' 2 Chronicles 7:14 RSV

Let the wicked forsake his way, and the unrighteous man his thoughts: and let him return unto the Lord, and he will have mercy upon him; and to our God, for he will abundantly pardon. Isaiah 55:7 KJV

'Therefore, O house of Israel, I will judge you, each one according to his ways, declares the Sovereign Lord. Repent! Turn away from all your offences; then sin will not be your downfall.' Ezekiel 18:30 NIV

'Yet even now,' says the Lord, 'return to me with all your heart, with fasting, with weeping, and with mourning; and rend your hearts and not your garments.' Return to the Lord, your God, for he is gracious and merciful, slow to anger, and abounding in steadfast love, and repents of evil. Joel 2:12-13 RSV

'Bear fruit that befits repentance.' Matthew 3:8 RSV

'The time is fulfilled, and the kingdom of God is at hand; repent, and believe in the gospel.' Mark 1:15 RSV

'I have not come to call the righteous, but sinners to repentance.' Luke 5:32 RSV

'Unless you repent you will all likewise perish.' Luke 13:3 RSV

'Just so, I tell you, there will be more joy in heaven over one sinner who repents than over ninety-nine righteous persons who need no repentance.' Luke 15:7 RSV

And when he [the prodigal son] came to himself, he said, How many hired servants of my father's have bread enough and to spare, and I perish with hunger! I will arise and go to my father, and will say unto him, Father, I have sinned against heaven, and before thee. Luke 15:17-18 KJV

Repentance and remission of sins should be preached in his name among all nations, beginning at Jerusalem. Luke 24:47 KJV

Repent ye therefore, and be converted, that your sins may be blotted out, when the times of refreshing shall come from the presence of the Lord. Acts 3:19 KJV

And they glorified God, saying, 'Then to the Gentiles also God has granted repentance unto life.' Acts 11:18 RSV

'The times of ignorance God overlooked, but now he commands all men everywhere to repent . . . Acts 17:30 RSV

'Testifying both to Jews and to Greeks of repentance to God and of faith in our Lord Jesus Christ.' Acts 20:21 RSV

Or do you presume upon the riches of his kindness and forbearance and patience? Do you not know that God's kindness is meant to lead you to repentance? Romans 2:4 RSV

For godly grief produces a repentance that leads to salvation and brings no regret, but worldly grief produces death. 2 Corinthians 7:10 RSV

The Lord is not slow about his promise as some count slowness, but is forbearing toward you, not wishing that any should perish, but that all should reach repentance. 2 Peter 3:9 RSV

'"Remember then from what you have fallen, repent and do the works you did at first. If not, I will come to you and remove your lampstand from its place,

unless you repent.'' ' Revelation 2:5
RSV

See also *Conversion; Faith; Grief.*

Responsibility of man

Let us hear the conclusion of the whole
matter: Fear God, and keep his
commandments: for this is the whole
duty of man. Ecclesiastes 12:13 KJV

He hath shewed thee, O man, what is
good; and what doth the Lord require
of thee, but to do justly, and to love
mercy, and to walk humbly with thy
God? Micah 6:8 KJV

Jesus said unto him, Thou shalt love
the Lord thy God with all thy heart,
and with all thy soul, and with all thy
mind. This is the first and great
commandment. And the second is like
unto it, Thou shalt love thy neighbour
as thyself. Matthew 22:37-39 KJV

'For truly in this city there were
gathered together against thy holy
servant Jesus, whom thou didst anoint,
both Herod and Pontius Pilate, with
the Gentiles and the peoples of Israel,
to do whatever thy hand and thy plan
had predestined to take place.' Acts
4:27-28 RSV

And when the Gentiles heard this, they
were glad and glorified the word of
God; and as many as were ordained to
eternal life believed. Acts 13:48 RSV

None of us lives to himself, and none of
us dies to himself. If we live, we live to
the Lord, and if we die, we die to the
Lord; so then, whether we live or
whether we die, we are the Lord's.
Romans 14:7-8 RSV

So, whether you eat or drink, or
whatever you do, do all to the glory of
God. 1 Corinthians 10:31 RSV

Work out your own salvation with fear
and trembling; for God is at work in
you, both to will and to work for his
good pleasure. Philippians 2:12-13 RSV

Therefore, brethren, be the more
zealous to confirm your call and
election, for if you do this you will
never fall. 2 Peter 1:10 RSV

See also *Service; Sovereignty of God.*

Rest

For thus said the Lord God, the Holy
One of Israel, 'In returning and rest
you shall be saved; in quietness and in
trust shall be your strength.' Isaiah
30:15 RSV

'Come to me, all who labour and are
heavy-laden, and I will give you rest.
Take my yoke upon you, and learn

from me; for I am gentle and lowly in
heart, and you will find rest for your
souls. For my yoke is easy, and my
burden is light.' Matthew 11:28-29 RSV

And he said to them, 'Come away by
yourselves to a lonely place, and rest a
while.' For many were coming and
going, and they had no leisure even to
eat. Mark 6:31 RSV

Therefore, while the promise of
entering his rest remains, let us fear lest
any of you be judged to have failed to
reach it . . . For we who have believed
enter that rest, as he has said, 'As I
swore in my wrath, "They shall never
enter my rest,"' although his works
were finished from the foundation of
the world. For he has somewhere
spoken of the seventh day in this way,
'And God rested on the seventh day
from all his works.' And again in this
place he said, 'They shall never enter
my rest.' Since therefore it remains for
some to enter it, and those who
formerly received the good news failed
to enter because of disobedience, again
he sets a certain day, 'Today,' saying
through David so long afterward, in the
words already quoted, 'Today, when
you hear his voice, do not harden your
hearts.' For if Joshua had given them
rest, God would not speak later of
another day. So then, there remains a
sabbath rest for the people of God; for
whoever enters God's rest also ceases
from his labours as God did from his.
Let us therefore strive to enter that
rest, that no one fall by the same sort of
disobedience. Hebrews 4:1, 3-11 RSV

See also *Sabbath.*

Resurrection

See *Jesus Christ; Last things.*

Retaliation

'You shall not take vengeance or bear
any grudge against the sons of your
own people, but you shall love your
neighbour as yourself: I am the Lord.'
Leviticus 19:18 RSV

'Vengeance is mine, and recompense,
for the time when their foot shall slip;
for the day of their calamity is at hand,
and their doom comes swiftly.'
Deuteronomy 32:35 RSV

Do not think to repay evil for evil, wait
for the Lord to deliver you. Proverbs
20:22 NEB

'You have heard that it was said, "An
eye for an eye and a tooth for a tooth."
But I say to you, Do not resist one who
is evil. But if any one strikes you on the
right cheek, turn to him the other also;

and if any one would sue you and take your coat, let him have your cloak as well; and if any one forces you to go one mile, go with him two miles. Give to him who begs from you, and do not refuse him who would borrow from you.' Matthew 5:38-42 RSV

Beloved, never avenge yourselves, but leave it to the wrath of God; for it is written, 'Vengeance is mine, I will repay, says the Lord.' No, 'if your enemy is hungry, feed him; if he is thirsty, give him drink; for by so doing you will heap burning coals upon his head.' Do not be overcome by evil, but overcome evil with good. Romans 12:19-21 RSV

Revelation

The heavens declare the glory of God; and the firmament sheweth his handywork. Day unto day uttereth speech, and night unto night sheweth knowledge. Psalm 19:1-2 KJV

For my thoughts are not your thoughts, neither are your ways my ways, saith the Lord. For as the heavens are higher than the earth, so are my ways higher than your ways, and my thoughts than your thoughts. For as the rain cometh down, and the snow from heaven, and returneth not thither, but watereth the earth, and maketh it bring forth and bud, that it may give seed to the sower, and bread to the eater: so shall my word be that goeth forth out of my mouth: it shall not return unto me void, but it shall accomplish that which I please, and it shall prosper in the thing whereto I sent it. Isaiah 55:8-11 KJV

'All things have been delivered to me by my Father; and no one knows the Son except the Father, and no one knows the Father except the Son and any one to whom the Son chooses to reveal him.' Matthew 11:27 RSV

And Simon Peter answered and said, Thou art the Christ, the Son of the living God. And Jesus answered and said unto him, Blessed art thou, Simon Bar-jona: for flesh and blood hath not revealed it unto thee, but my Father which is in heaven. Matthew 16:16-17 KJV

'He did not leave himself without witness, for he did good and gave you from heaven rains and fruitful seasons, satisfying your hearts with food and gladness.' Acts 14:17 RSV

For what can be known about God is plain to them, because God has shown it to them. Ever since the creation of the world his invisible nature, namely, his eternal power and deity, has been clearly perceived in the things that have been made. So they are without excuse. Romans 1:19-20 RSV

As it is written, Eye hath not seen, nor ear heard, neither have entered into the heart of man, the things which God hath prepared for them that love him. But God hath revealed them unto us by his Spirit. 1 Corinthians 2:9-10 KJV

Let me tell you, my brothers, that the gospel I preach is not of human origin. I did not receive it from any man, nor did anyone teach it to me. It was Jesus Christ himself who revealed it to me. Galatians 1:11-12 GNB

All scripture is inspired by God and profitable for teaching, for reproof, for correction . . . 2 Timothy 3:16 RSV

God, who at sundry times and in divers manners spake in time past unto the fathers by the prophets, hath in these last days spoken unto us by his Son, whom he hath appointed heir of all things, by whom also he made the worlds . . . Hebrews 1:1-2 KJV

See also *Bible; Will of God.*

Reverence

'That you may fear the Lord your God, you and your son and your son's son, by keeping all his statutes and his commandments, which I command you, all the days of your life.' Deuteronomy 6:2 RSV

The fear of the Lord is clean, enduring for ever: the judgments of the Lord are true and righteous altogether. Psalm 19:9 KJV

For as the heaven is high above the earth, so great is his mercy toward them that fear him. Psalm 103:11 KJV

The fear of the Lord is the beginning of wisdom: a good understanding have all they that do his commandments: his praise endureth for ever. Psalm 111:10 KJV

To honour the Lord is to hate evil; I hate pride and arrogance, evil ways and false words. Proverbs 8:13 GNB

Let us hear the conclusion of the whole matter: Fear God, and keep his commandments: for this is the whole duty of man. Ecclesiastes 1:12-13 KJV

And the spirit of the Lord shall rest upon him, the spirit of wisdom and understanding, the spirit of counsel and might, the spirit of knowledge and of the fear of the Lord. Isaiah 11:2 KJV

And they were filled with awe, and said to one another, 'Who then is this, that even wind and sea obey him?' Mark 4:41 RSV

And so it was that the church throughout Judaea, Galilee, and Samaria had a time of peace. Through the help of the Holy Spirit it was strengthened and grew in numbers, as it lived in reverence for the Lord. Acts 9:31 GNB

There is no fear of God before their eyes. Romans 3:18 KJV

Therefore, knowing the fear of the Lord, we persuade men; but what we are is known to God, and I hope it is known also to your conscience. 2 Corinthians 5:11 RSV

Since we have these promises, dear friends, let us purify ourselves from everything that contaminates body and spirit, perfecting holiness out of reverence for God. 2 Corinthians 7:1 NIV

Work out your own salvation with fear and trembling; for God is at work in you, both to will and to work for his good pleasure. Philippians 2:12 RSV

Therefore let us be grateful for receiving a kingdom that cannot be shaken, and thus let us offer to God acceptable worship, with reverence and awe. Hebrews 12:28 RSV

But in your hearts reverence Christ as Lord. Always be prepared to make a defence to any one who calls you to account for the hope that is in you, yet do it with gentleness and reverence. 1 Peter 3:15 RSV

See also *Worship*.

Revival

[The Lord's promise to Solomon] 'If my people who are called by my name humble themselves, and pray and seek my face, and turn from their wicked ways, then I will hear from heaven, and will forgive their sin and heal their land.' 2 Chronicles 7:14 RSV

Wilt thou not revive us again: that thy people may rejoice in thee? Psalm 85:6 KJV

Oh, that you would rend the heavens and come down, that the mountains would tremble before you! As when fire sets twigs ablaze and causes water to boil, come down to make your name known to your enemies and cause the nations to quake before you! Isaiah 64:1-2 NIV

And he said to me, 'Son of man, can these bones live?' And I answered, 'O Lord God, thou knowest.' Again he said to me, 'Prophesy to these bones, and say to them, O dry bones, hear the word of the Lord. Thus says the Lord God to these bones: Behold, I will cause breath to enter you, and you shall live.' Ezekiel 37:3-5 RSV

'And it shall come to pass afterward, that I will pour out my spirit on all flesh; your sons and your daughters shall prophesy, your old men shall dream dreams, and your young men shall see visions . . .' Joel 2:28 RSV

O Lord, revive thy work in the midst of the years, in the midst of the years make known; in wrath remember mercy. Habakkuk 3:2 KJV

Repent ye therefore, and be converted, that your sins may be blotted out, when the times of refreshing shall come from the presence of the Lord. Acts 3:19 KJV

And when they had prayed, the place in which they were gathered together was shaken; and they were all filled with the Holy Spirit and spoke the word of God with boldness. Acts 4:31 RSV

And the word of God increased; and the number of the disciples multiplied greatly in Jerusalem, and a great many of the priests were obedient to the faith. Acts 6:7 RSV

Reward

After these things the word of the Lord came unto Abram in a vision, saying, Fear not, Abram: I am thy shield, and thy exceeding great reward. Genesis 15:1 KJV

Moreover by them [the judgements of the Lord] is thy servant warned: and in keeping of them there is great reward. Psalm 19:11 KJV

'Happy are you when people insult you and persecute you and tell all kinds of evil lies against you because you are my followers. Be happy and glad, for a great reward is kept for you in heaven.' Matthew 5:11-12 GNB

Then Peter spoke up. 'Look,' he said, 'we have left everything and followed you. What will we have?' Jesus said to them, 'You can be sure that when the Son of Man sits on his glorious throne in the New Age, then you twelve followers of mine will also sit on thrones, to rule the twelve tribes of Israel. And everyone who has left houses or brothers or sisters or father or mother or children or fields for my sake, will receive a hundred times more and will be given eternal life.' Matthew 19:27-29 GNB

And these shall go away into everlasting punishment: but the righteous into life eternal. Matthew 25:46 KJV

'Love your enemies and do good to them; lend and expect nothing back. You will then have a great reward, and you will be sons of the Most High God. For he is good to the ungrateful and the wicked.' Luke 6:35 GNB

Each man's work will become manifest; for the Day will disclose it, because it will be revealed with fire, and the fire will test what sort of work each one has done. If the work which any man has built on the foundation survives, he will receive a reward. 1 Corinthians 3:13-14 RSV

The scripture says, 'You shall not muzzle an ox when it is treading out the grain,' and 'The labourer deserves his wages.' 1 Timothy 5:18 RSV

But without faith it is impossible to please him: for he that cometh to God must believe that he is, and that he is a rewarder of them that diligently seek him. Hebrews 11:6 KJV

See also *Last things, Heaven; Obedience.*

Rich and riches

'Beware lest you say in your heart, "My power and the might of my hand have gotten me this wealth." You shall remember the Lord your God, for it is he who gives you power to get wealth; that he may confirm his covenant which he swore to your fathers, as at this day.' Deuteronomy 8:17-18 RSV

For I was envious of the arrogant, when I saw the prosperity of the wicked. Psalm 73:3 RSV

Woe to them that are at ease in Zion, and trust in the mountain of Samaria. Amos 6:1 KJV

He hath filled the hungry with good things, and the rich he hath sent empty away. Luke 1:53 BCP

There was a certain rich man, which was clothed in purple and fine linen, and fared sumptuously every day: and there was a certain beggar named Lazarus, which was laid at his gate full of sores, and desiring to be fed with the crumbs which fell from the rich man's table: moreover the dogs came and licked his sores. And it came to pass, that the beggar died, and was carried by the angels into Abraham's bosom: the rich man also died, and was buried; and in hell he lift up his eyes, being in torments, and seeth Abraham afar off, and Lazarus in his bosom. And he cried and said, Father Abraham, have mercy on me, and send Lazarus, that he may dip the tip of his finger in water, and cool my tongue; for I am tormented in this flame. But Abraham said, Son, remember that thou in thy lifetime receivedst thy good things, and likewise Lazarus evil things: but now he is comforted, and thou art tormented. And beside all this, between us and you there is a great gulf fixed: so that they which would pass from hence to you cannot; neither can they pass to us, that would come from thence. Then he said, I pray thee therefore, father, that thou wouldest send him to my father's house: for I have five brethren; that he may testify unto them, lest they also come into this place of torment. Luke 16:19-28 KJV

On hearing this Jesus said [to the rich young ruler], 'There is still one thing lacking: sell everything you have and distribute to the poor, and you will have riches in heaven; and come, follow me.' At these words his heart sank; for he was a very rich man. When Jesus saw it he said, 'How hard it is for the wealthy to enter the kingdom of God! It is easier for a camel to go through the eye of a needle than for a rich man to enter the kingdom of God.' Luke 18:22-25 NEB

The unsearchable riches of Christ. Ephesians 3:8 KJV

As for the rich in this world, charge them not to be haughty, nor to set their hopes on uncertain riches but on God who richly furnishes us with everything to enjoy. 1 Timothy 6:17 RSV

Come now, you rich, weep and howl for the miseries that are coming upon you. Your riches have rotted and your garments are moth-eaten. Your gold and silver have rusted, and their rust will be evidence against you and will eat your flesh like fire. You have laid up treasure for the last days. Behold, the wages of the labourers who mowed your fields, which you kept back by fraud, cry out; and the cries of the harvesters have reached the ears of the Lord of hosts. You have lived on the earth in luxury and in pleasure; you have fattened your hearts in a day of slaughter. James 5:1-5 RSV

But if any one has the world's goods and sees his brother in need, yet closes his heart against him, how does God's love abide in him? 1 John 3:17 RSV

See also *Desire, wrong; Money and material goods; Poverty.*

Righteousness

Noah was a righteous man, blameless among the people of his time, and he walked with God. Genesis 6:9 NIV

And he [Abraham] believed in the Lord; and he counted it to him for righteousness. Genesis 15:6 KJV

Righteousness exalteth a nation: but sin is a reproach to any people. Proverbs 14:34 KJV

The effect of righteousness will be peace, and the result of righteousness, quietness and trust for ever. Isaiah 32:17 RSV

All our righteousnesses are as filthy rags; and we all do fade as a leaf; and our iniquities, like the wind, have taken us away. Isaiah 64:6 KJV

'Let justice roll down like waters, and righteousness like an ever-flowing stream.' Amos 5:24 RSV

Blessed are they that mourn: for they shall be comforted. Blessed are the meek; for they shall inherit the earth. Blessed are they which do hunger and thirst after righteousness: for they shall be filled. Matthew 5:6 KJV

'For I tell you, unless your righteousness exceeds that of the scribes and Pharisees, you will never enter the kingdom of heaven.' Matthew 5:20 RSV

But seek ye first the kingdom of God, and his righteousness; and all these things shall be added unto you. Matthew 6:33 KJV

'He has fixed a day on which he will judge the world in righteousness by a man whom he has appointed, and of this he has given assurance to all men by raising him from the dead.' Acts 17:31 RSV

For therein [in the gospel] is the righteousness of God revealed from faith to faith: as it is written, The just shall live by faith. Romans 1:17 KJV

As it is written, There is none righteous, no, not one. Romans 3:10 KJV

But now the righteousness of God without the law is manifested, being witnessed by the law and the prophets; even the righteousness of God which is by faith of Jesus Christ unto all and upon all them that believe: for there is no difference: for all have sinned, and come short of the glory of God; being justified freely by his grace through the redemption that is in Christ Jesus: whom God hath set forth to be a propitiation through faith in his blood, to declare his righteousness for the remission of sins that are past, through the forbearance of God; to declare, I say, at this time his righteousness: that he might be just, and the justifier of him which believeth in Jesus. Romans 3:21-26 KJV

If, because of one man's trespass, death reigned through that one man, much more will those who receive the abundance of grace and the free gift of

righteousness reign in life through the one man Jesus Christ. Then as one man's trespass led to condemnation for all men, so one man's act of righteousness leads to acquittal and life for all men. For as by one man's disobedience many were made sinners, so by one man's obedience many will be made righteous. Law came in, to increase the trespass; but where sin increased, grace abounded all the more, so that, as sin reigned in death, grace also might reign through righteousness to eternal life through Jesus Christ our Lord. Romans 5:17-21 RSV

He is the source of your life in Christ Jesus, whom God made our wisdom, our righteousness and sanctification and redemption; therefore, as it is written, 'Let him who boasts, boast of the Lord.' 1 Corinthians 1:30 RSV

For our sake he made him to be sin who knew no sin, so that in him we might become the righteousness of God. 2 Corinthians 5:21 RSV

Stand therefore, having your loins girt about with truth, and having on the breastplate of righteousness . . . Ephesians 6:14 KJV

In order that I may gain Christ and be found in him, not having a righteousness of my own, based on law, but that which is through faith in Christ, the righteousness from God that depends on faith. Philippians 3:8-9 RSV

And the harvest of righteousness is sown in peace by those who make peace. James 3:18 RSV

For Christ also died for sins once for all, the righteous for the unrighteous, that he might bring us to God, being put to death in the flesh but made alive in the spirit. 1 Peter 3:18 RSV

See also *Justification*.

Ritual

And Samuel said, 'Has the Lord as great delight in burnt offerings and sacrifices, as in obeying the voice of the Lord? Behold, to obey is better than sacrifice, and to hearken than the fat of rams.' 1 Samuel 15:22 RSV

And the Lord said: 'Because this people draw near with their mouth and honour me with their lips, while their hearts are far from me, and their fear of me is a commandment of men learned by rote.' Isaiah 29:13 RSV

'Even though you offer me your burnt offerings and cereal offerings, I will not accept them, and the peace offerings of your fatted beasts I will not look upon . . . But let justice roll down like waters, and righteousness like an ever-flowing stream.' Amos 5:22, 24 RSV

'"What a weariness this is," you say, and you sniff at me, says the Lord of hosts. You bring what has been taken by violence or is lame or sick, and this you bring as your offering! Shall I accept that from your hand? says the Lord.' Malachi 1:13 RSV

'Woe to you, scribes and Pharisees, hypocrites! for you cleanse the outside of the cup and of the plate, but inside they are full of extortion and rapacity. You blind Pharisee! first cleanse the inside of the cup and of the plate, that the outside also may be clean. Woe to you, scribes and Pharisees, hypocrites! for you are like whitewashed tombs, which outwardly appear beautiful, but within they are full of dead men's bones and all uncleanness. So you also outwardly appear righteous to men, but within you are full of hypocrisy and iniquity.' Matthew 23:25-28 RSV

He is a Jew who is one inwardly, and real circumcision is a matter of the heart, spiritual and not literal. Romans 2:29 RSV

They [people in the last days] will hold to the outward form of our religion, but reject its real power. Keep away from such people. 2 Timothy 3:5 GNB

Sabbath

Remember the sabbath day, to keep it holy. Six days shalt thou labour, and do all thy work: but the seventh day is the sabbath of the Lord thy God: in it thou shalt not do any work, thou, nor thy son, nor thy daughter, thy manservant, nor thy maidservant, nor thy cattle, nor thy stranger that is within thy gates: for in six days the Lord made heaven and earth, the sea, and all that in them is, and rested the seventh day: wherefore the Lord blessed the sabbath day, and hallowed it. Exodus 20:8-11 KJV

At that time I saw people in Judah pressing juice from grapes on the Sabbath. Others were loading corn, wine, grapes, figs, and other things on their donkeys and taking them into Jerusalem; I warned them not to sell anything on the Sabbath. Some men from the city of Tyre were living in Jerusalem, and they brought fish and all kinds of goods into the city to sell to our people on the Sabbath. I reprimanded the Jewish leaders and said, 'Look at the evil you're doing!

...'re making the Sabbath unholy. ...is is exactly why God punished your ...ncestors when he brought destruction ...n this city. And yet you insist on bringing more of God's anger down on Israel by profaning the Sabbath.' Nehemiah 13:15-18 GNB

The Lord says, 'If you treat the Sabbath as sacred and do not pursue your own interests on that day; if you value my holy day and honour it by not travelling, working, or talking idly on that day, then you will find the joy that comes from serving me. I will make you honoured all over the world, and you will enjoy the land I gave to your ancestor, Jacob.' Isaiah 58:13-14 GNB

Jesus answered, 'What if one of you has a sheep and it falls into a deep hole on the Sabbath? Will he not take hold of it and lift it out? And a man is worth much more than a sheep! So then, our Law does allow us to help someone on the Sabbath.' Matthew 12:11-12 GNB

'The sabbath was made for man, not man for the sabbath; so the Son of man is lord even of the sabbath.' Mark 2:27-28 RSV

On the first day of the week we met to break bread. Paul was due to leave the next day, and he preached a sermon that went on till the middle of the night. Acts 20:7 JB

On the first day of every week, each of you is to put something aside and store it up, as he may prosper, so that contributions need not be made when I come. 1 Corinthians 16:2 RSV

Sacrifice

Then [after the flood] Noah built an altar to the Lord, and took of every clean animal and of every clean bird, and offered burnt offerings on the altar. Genesis 8:20 RSV

'Your lamb shall be without blemish, a male a year old; you shall take it from the sheep or from the goats; and you shall keep it until the fourteenth day of this month, when the whole assembly of the congregation of Israel shall kill their lambs in the evening. Then they shall take some of the blood, and put it on the two doorposts and the lintel of the houses in which they eat them.' Exodus 12:5-7 RSV

And he shall put his hand upon the head of the burnt offering; and it shall be accepted for him to make atonement for him. Leviticus 1:4 KJV

And Samuel said, 'Has the Lord as great delight in burnt offerings and sacrifices, as in obeying the voice of the Lord? Behold, to obey is better than sacrifice, and to hearken than the fat of rams.' 1 Samuel 15:22 RSV

For thou desirest not sacrifice; else would I give it: thou delightest not in burnt offering. The sacrifices of God are a broken spirit: a broken and a contrite heart, O God, thou wilt not despise. Psalm 51:16-17 KJV

'I hate, I despise your feasts, and I take no delight in your solemn assemblies. Even though you offer me your burnt offerings and cereal offerings, I will not accept them, and the peace offerings of your fatted beasts I will not look upon. Take away from me the noise of your songs; to the melody of your harps I will not listen. But let justice roll down like waters, and righteousness like an ever-flowing stream.' Amos 5:21-24 RSV

'Go and learn what this means, "I desire mercy, and not sacrifice." For I came not to call the righteous, but sinners.' Matthew 9:13 RSV

I beseech you therefore, brethren, by the mercies of God, that ye present your bodies a living sacrifice, holy, acceptable unto God, which is your reasonable service. Romans 12:1 KJV

And every priest stands daily at his service, offering repeatedly the same sacrifices, which can never take away sins. But when Christ had offered for all time a single sacrifice for sins, he sat down at the right hand of God. Hebrews 10:11-12 RSV

Let us, then, always offer praise to God as our sacrifice through Jesus, which is the offering presented by lips that confess him as Lord. Do not forget to do good and to help one another, because these are the sacrifices that please God. Hebrews 13:15-16 GNB

See also *Blood; Passover.*

Sadness

See *Grief.*

Salvation and Saviour

The Lord is my light and my salvation; whom shall I fear? The Lord is the strength of my life; of whom shall I be afraid? Psalm 27:1 KJV

'And it shall come to pass that all who call upon the name of the Lord shall be delivered; for in Mount Zion and in Jerusalem there shall be those who escape, as the Lord has said, and among the survivors shall be those whom the Lord calls.' Joel 2:32 RSV

[An angel of the Lord to Joseph] 'You shall call his name Jesus, for he will save his people from their sins.' Matthew 1:21 RSV

'Who, then, can be saved?' they [the disciples] asked. Jesus looked straight at them and answered, 'This is impossible for man, but for God everything is possible.' Matthew 19:25-26 GNB

'But he who endures to the end will be saved.' Matthew 24:13 RSV

For unto you is born this day in the city of David a Saviour, which is Christ the Lord. Luke 2:11 KJV

Someone said to him, 'Sir, will there be only a few saved?' He said to them, 'Try your best to enter by the narrow door, because, I tell you, many will try to enter and will not succeed.' Luke 13:23-24 JB

For the Son of man is come to seek and to save that which was lost. Luke 19:10 KJV

For God sent not his Son into the world to condemn the world; but that the world through him might be saved. John 3:17 KJV

'And there is salvation in no one else, for there is no other name under heaven given among men by which we must be saved.' Acts 4:12 RSV

'Men, what must I do to be saved?' And they said, 'Believe in the Lord Jesus, and you will be saved, you and your household.' Acts 16:30-31 RSV

For the word of the cross is folly to those who are perishing, but to us who are being saved it is the power of God. 1 Corinthians 1:18 RSV

For he says, 'At the acceptable time I have listened to you, and helped you on the day of salvation.' Behold, now is the acceptable time; behold, now is the day of salvation. 2 Corinthians 6:2 RSV

For by grace are ye saved through faith; and that not of yourselves: it is the gift of God. Ephesians 2:8 KJV

Work out your own salvation with fear and trembling; for God is at work in you, both to will and to work for his good pleasure. Philippians 2:12-13 RSV

God our Saviour, who desires all men to be saved and to come to the knowledge of the truth. 1 Timothy 2:3-4 RSV

From childhood you have been acquainted with the sacred writings which are able to instruct you for salvation through faith in Christ Jesus. Timothy 3:15 RSV

How shall we escape if we neglect so a great salvation? Hebrews 2:3 RSV

[We] who by God's power are guarded through faith for a salvation ready to be revealed in the last time. 1 Peter 1:5 RSV

And we have seen and do testify that the Father sent the Son to be the Saviour of the world. 1 John 4:14 KJV

'Salvation belongs to our God who sits upon the throne, and to the Lamb!' Revelation 7:10 RSV

See also *Atonement; Christian life, Coming to faith; Sin.*

Sanctification

Sanctify them through thy truth: thy word is truth. John 17:17 KJV

For just as you once yielded your members to impurity and to greater and greater iniquity, so now yield your members to righteousness for sanctification. Romans 6:19 RSV

For I delight in the law of God, in my inmost self, but I see in my members another law at war with the law of my mind and making me captive to the law of sin which dwells in my members. Romans 7:22-23 RSV

I beseech you therefore, brethren, by the mercies of God, that ye present your bodies a living sacrifice, holy, acceptable unto God, which is your reasonable service. And be not conformed to this world: but be ye transformed by the renewing of your mind, that ye may prove what is that good, and acceptable, and perfect, will of God. Romans 12:1-2 KJV

He is the source of your life in Christ Jesus, whom God made our wisdom, our righteousness and sanctification and redemption. 1 Corinthians 1:30 RSV

For this is the will of God, your sanctification: that you abstain from unchastity. 1 Thessalonians 4:3 RSV

And the very God of peace sanctify you wholly; and I pray God your whole spirit and soul and body be preserved blameless unto the coming of our Lord Jesus Christ. 1 Thessalonians 5:23 KJV

Elect according to the foreknowledge of God the Father, through sanctification of the Spirit, unto obedience and sprinkling of the blood of Jesus Christ. 1 Peter 1:2 KJV

See also *Christian life, Character of the Christian; Holiness.*

Satan

See *Devil*.

Scribes

And all the people gathered as one man into the square before the Water Gate; and they told Ezra the scribe to bring the book of the law of Moses which the Lord had given to Israel. Nehemiah 8:1 RSV

'For I tell you, unless your righteousness exceeds that of the scribes and Pharisees, you will never enter the kingdom of heaven.' Matthew 5:20 RSV

He [Jesus] taught . . . as one who had authority, and not as their scribes. Matthew 7:29 RSV

And a scribe came up and said to him, 'Teacher, I will follow you wherever you go.' Matthew 8:19 RSV

But when the chief priests and the scribes saw the wonderful things that he did, and the children crying out in the temple, 'Hosanna to the Son of David!' they were indignant. Matthew 21:15 RSV

'The scribes and the Pharisees sit on Moses' seat; so practise and observe whatever they tell you, but not what they do; for they preach, but do not practise. They bind heavy burdens, hard to bear, and lay them on men's shoulders; but they themselves will not move them with their finger. They do all their deeds to be seen by men; for they make their phylacteries broad and their fringes long, and they love the place of honour at feasts and the best seats in the synagogues, and salutations in the market places, and being called rabbi by men.' Matthew 23:2-7 RSV

And immediately, while he was still speaking, Judas came, one of the twelve, and with him a crowd with swords and clubs, from the chief priests and the scribes and the elders. Mark 14:43 RSV

See also *Hypocrisy; Pharisees*.

Second coming

See *Last things*.

Self-denial

And a poor widow came, and put in two copper coins, which make a penny. And he called his disciples to him, and said to them, 'Truly, I say to you, this poor widow has put in more than all those who are contributing to the treasury. For they all contributed out of their abundance; but she out of her poverty has put in everything she had, her whole living.' Mark 12:42-44 RSV

And he said to all, 'If any man would come after me, let him deny himself and take up his cross daily and follow me. For whoever would save his life will lose it; and whoever loses his life for my sake, he will save it.' Luke 9:23-24 RSV

He must increase, but I must decrease. John 3:30 KJV

'Whoever loves his own life will lose it; whoever hates his own life in this world will keep it for life eternal.' John 12:25 GNB

But the fruit of the Spirit is . . . faithfulness, gentleness, self-control . . . Galatians 5:22 23 RSV

See also *Disciples; Service*.

Self-examination

When I think of thy ways, I turn my feet to thy testimonies. Psalm 119:59 RSV

Now these are the words of the Lord of Hosts: Consider your way of life. Haggai 1:5 NEB

Let a man examine himself, and so eat of the bread and drink of the cup. For any one who eats and drinks without discerning the body eats and drinks judgment upon himself. That is why many of you are weak and ill, and some have died. 1 Corinthians 11:28-29 RSV

Examine yourselves to make sure you are in the faith; test yourselves. Do you acknowledge that Jesus Christ is really in you? If not, you have failed the test. 2 Corinthians 13:5 JB

If someone thinks he is somebody when really he is nobody, he is only deceiving himself. Each one should judge his own conduct. If it is good, then he can be proud of what he himself has done, without having to compare it with what someone else has done. Galatians 6:3-4 GNB

See also *Examination*.

Self-righteousness

'After the Lord your God has driven them out for you, do not say to yourselves that he brought you in to possess this land because you deserved it. No, the Lord is going to drive these people out for you because they are wicked.' Deuteronomy 9:4 GNB

All the ways of a man are pure in his own eyes, but the Lord weighs the spirit. Proverbs 16:2 RSV

'Beware of practising your piety before

men in order to be seen by them; for then you will have no reward from your Father who is in heaven.' Matthew 6:1 RSV

'So you also outwardly appear righteous to men, but within you are full of hypocrisy and iniquity.' Matthew 23:28 RSV

He also told this parable to some who trusted in themselves that they were righteous and despised others: 'Two men went up into the temple to pray, one a Pharisee and the other a tax collector. The Pharisee stood and prayed thus with himself, "God, I thank thee that I am not like other men, extortioners, unjust, adulterers, or even like this tax collector. I fast twice a week, I give tithes of all that I get." But the tax collector, standing far off, would not even lift up his eyes to heaven, but beat his breast, saying, "God, be merciful to me a sinner!" I tell you, this man went down to his house justified rather than the other; for every one who exalts himself will be humbled, but he who humbles himself will be exalted.' Luke 18:9-14 RSV

See also *Hypocrisy; Pride; Righteousness.*

Sermon on the Mount

See Matthew 5–7.

Service

[God to Moses] He said, 'But I will be with you; and this shall be the sign for you, that I have sent you: when you have brought forth the people out of Egypt, you shall serve God upon this mountain.' Exodus 3:12 RSV

It is written, Thou shalt worship the Lord thy God, and him only shalt thou serve. Matthew 4:10 KJV

'A disciple is not above his teacher, nor a servant above his master.' Matthew 10:24 RSV

'Whoever would be great among you must be your servant, and whoever would be first among you must be slave of all. For the Son of man also came not to be served but to serve, and to give his life as a ransom for many.' Mark 10:43-45 RSV

'Whoever wants to serve me must follow me, so that my servant will be with me where I am. And my Father will honour anyone who serves me.' John 12:26 GNB

When he had washed their feet, and taken his garments, and resumed his place, he said to them, 'Do you know what I have done to you? You call me Teacher and Lord; and you are right, for so I am. If I then, your Lord and Teacher, have washed your feet, you also ought to wash one another's feet.' John 13:12-14 RSV

If it [a man's gift] is serving, let him serve. Romans 12:7 NIV

So then, as we have opportunity, let us do good to all men, and especially to those who are of the household of faith. Galatians 6:10 RSV

Whatever your task, work heartily, as serving the Lord and not men. Colossians 3:23 RSV

Whoever renders service, as one who renders it by the strength which God supplies; in order that in everything God may be glorified through Jesus Christ. 1 Peter 4:11 RSV

See also *Help; Kindness.*

Sex

Gift of

So God created man in his own image, in the image of God created he him; male and female created he them. And God blessed them, and God said unto them, Be fruitful, and multiply, and replenish the earth, and subdue it. Genesis 1:27-28 KJV

Therefore shall a man leave his father and his mother, and shall cleave unto his wife: and they shall be one flesh. And they were both naked, the man and his wife, and were not ashamed. Genesis 2:24-25 KJV

A man should fulfil his duty as a husband, and a woman should fulfil her duty as a wife, and each should satisfy the other's needs. A wife is not the master of her own body, but her husband is; in the same way a husband is not the master of his own body, but his wife is. Do not deny yourselves to each other, unless you first agree to do so for a while in order to spend your time in prayer; but then resume normal marital relations. In this way you will be kept from giving in to Satan's temptation because of your lack of self-control. 1 Corinthians 7:3-5 GNB

See also *Marriage.*

Misuse of

Now Joseph was handsome and good-looking. And after a time his master's wife cast her eyes upon Joseph, and said, 'Lie with me.' But he refused and said to his master's wife, '... how then can I do this great wickedness, and sin

...inst God?' Genesis 39:6-9 RSV

...o you not know that the wicked will ...ot inherit the kingdom of God? Do not be deceived: Neither the sexually immoral nor idolaters nor adulterers nor male prostitutes nor homosexual offenders ... will inherit the kingdom of God. 1 Corinthians 6:9-10 NIV

You know that your bodies are parts of the body of Christ. Shall I take a part of Christ's body and make it part of the body of a prostitute? Impossible! Or perhaps you don't know that the man who joins his body to a prostitute becomes physically one with her? The scripture says quite plainly, 'The two will become one body.' But he who joins himself to the Lord becomes spiritually one with him. Avoid immorality. Any other sin a man commits does not affect his body; but the man who is guilty of sexual immorality sins against his own body. Don't you know that your body is the temple of the Holy Spirit, who lives in you and who was given to you by God? You do not belong to yourselves but to God. 1 Corinthians 6:15-19 GNB

Now the works of the flesh are plain: immorality, impurity, licentiousness ... Galatians 5:19 RSV

Since you are God's people, it is not right that any matters of sexual immorality or indecency or greed should even be mentioned among you. Ephesians 5:3 GNB

See also *Homosexuality.*

Shame, ashamed

And they were both naked, the man and his wife, and were not ashamed ... And he [Adam] said, I heard thy voice in the garden, and I was afraid, because I was naked; and I hid myself. Genesis 2:25, 3:10 KJV

Look to him, and be radiant; so your faces shall never be ashamed. Psalm 34:5 RSV

'For whoever is ashamed of me and of my words in this adulterous and sinful generation, of him will the Son of man also be ashamed, when he comes in the glory of his Father with the holy angels.' Mark 8:38 RSV

For I am not ashamed of the gospel of Christ: for it is the power of God unto salvation to every one that believeth; to the Jew first, and also to the Greek. Romans 1:16 KJV

But I am not ashamed, for I know whom I have believed, and I am sure that he is able to guard until that Day

what has been entrusted to me. 2 Timothy 1:12 RSV

Instead, it was a better country they longed for, the heavenly country. And so God is not ashamed for them to call him their God, because he has prepared a city for them. Hebrews 11:16 GNB

Looking unto Jesus the author and finisher of our faith; who for the joy that was set before him endured the cross, despising the shame, and is set down at the right hand of the throne of God. Hebrews 12:2 KJV

However, if you suffer because you are a Christian, don't be ashamed of it, but thank God that you bear Christ's name. 1 Peter 4:16 GNB

And now, little children, abide in him, so that when he appears we may have confidence and not shrink from him in shame at his coming. 1 John 2:28 RSV

Shepherd

The Lord is my shepherd; I shall not want. Psalm 23:1 KJV

He shall feed his flock like a shepherd: he shall gather the lambs with his arm, and carry them in his bosom, and shall gently lead those that are with young. Isaiah 40:11 KJV

'My people have been lost sheep; their shepherds have led them astray and caused them to roam on the mountains. They wandered over mountain and hill and forgot their own resting place.' Jeremiah 50:6 NIV

The word of the Lord came to me: 'Son of man, prophesy against the shepherds of Israel, prophesy, and say to them, even to the shepherds, Thus says the Lord God: Ho, shepherds of Israel who have been feeding yourselves! Should not shepherds feed the sheep?' Ezekiel 34:1-2 RSV

'And I will set up over them one shepherd, my servant David, and he shall feed them: he shall feed them and be their shepherd.' Ezekiel 34:23 RSV

Then Jesus said to them, 'You will all fall away because of me this night; for it is written, "I will strike the shepherd, and the sheep of the flock will be scattered." ' Matthew 26:31 RSV

And the shepherds returned, glorifying and praising God for all they had heard and seen, as it had been told them. Luke 2:20 RSV

'I am the good shepherd. The good shepherd lays down his life for the sheep.' John 10:11 RSV

Now the God of peace, that brought again from the dead our Lord Jesus, that great shepherd of the sheep, through the blood of the everlasting covenant . . . Hebrews 13:20 KJV

For you were straying like sheep, but have now returned to the Shepherd and Guardian of your souls. 1 Peter 2:25 RSV

And when the chief Shepherd is manifested you will obtain the unfading crown of glory. 1 Peter 5:4 RSV

Sin

Be sure your sin will find you out. Numbers 32:23 KJV

Against thee, thee only, have I sinned, and done this evil in thy sight: that thou mightest be justified when thou speakest, and be clear when thou judgest. Behold, I was shapen in iniquity; and in sin did my mother conceive me. Psalm 51:4-5 KJV

'Come now, let us reason together,' says the Lord. 'Though your sins are like scarlet, they shall be as white as snow; though they are red as crimson, they shall be like wool.' Isaiah 1:18 NIV

All we like sheep have gone astray; we have turned every one to his own way; and the Lord hath laid on him the iniquity of us all. Isaiah 53:6 KJV

Your iniquities have made a separation between you and your God, and your sins have hid his face from you so that he does not hear. Isaiah 59:2 RSV

Thou who art of purer eyes than to behold evil and canst not look on wrong . . . Habakkuk 1:13 RSV

[An angel of the Lord to Joseph] 'You shall call his name Jesus, for he will save his people from their sins.' Matthew 1:21 RSV

The next day he [John the Baptist] saw Jesus coming toward him, and said, 'Behold, the Lamb of God, who takes away the sin of the world!' John 1:29 RSV

Jesus answered them, 'Truly, truly, I say to you, every one who commits sin is a slave to sin.' John 8:34 RSV

For all have sinned, and come short of the glory of God. Romans 3:23 KJV

As by one man sin entered into the world, and death by sin . . . so death passed upon all men, for that all have sinned. Romans 5:12 KJV

What shall we say then? Shall we continue in sin, that grace may abound? God forbid. How shall we, that are dead to sin, live any longer therein? Romans 6:1-2 KJV

For the wages of sin is death; but the gift of God is eternal life through Jesus Christ our Lord. Romans 6:23 KJV

For our sake he made him to be sin who knew no sin, so that in him we might become the righteousness of God. 2 Corinthians 5:21 RSV

As for you, you were dead in your transgressions and sins, in which you used to live when you followed the ways of this world and of the ruler of the kingdom of the air, the spirit who is now at work in those who are disobedient. All of us also lived among them at one time, gratifying the cravings of our sinful nature and following its desires and thoughts. Like the rest, we were by nature objects of wrath. Ephesians 2:1-3 NIV

This is a faithful saying, and worthy of all acceptation, that Christ Jesus came into the world to save sinners; of whom I am chief. 1 Timothy 1:15 KJV

Indeed, under the law almost everything is purified with blood, and without the shedding of blood there is no forgiveness of sins. Hebrews 9:22 RSV

He himself bore our sins in his body on the tree, that we might die to sin and live to righteousness. 1 Peter 2:24 RSV

If we walk in the light, as he is in the light, we have fellowship with one another, and the blood of Jesus his Son cleanses us from all sin. If we say we have no sin, we deceive ourselves, and the truth is not in us. If we confess our sins, he is faithful and just and will forgive our sins and cleanse us from all unrighteousness. 1 John 1:7-9 RSV

Every one who commits sin is guilty of lawlessness; sin is lawlessness. You know that he appeared to take away sins, and in him there is no sin. 1 John 3:4-5 RSV

Whoever is a child of God does not continue to sin, for God's very nature is in him; and because God is his Father, he cannot continue to sin. 1 John 3:9 GNB

See also *Forgiveness; Repentance; Salvation and Saviour.*

Son of God

See *Jesus Christ.*

Sorrow

See *Grief.*

Soul

He restoreth my soul: he leadeth me in the paths of righteousness for his name's sake. Psalm 23.3 KJV

My soul thirsteth for God, for the living God: when shall I come and appear before God? . . . Why art thou cast down, O my soul? and why art thou disquieted in me? Hope thou in God: for I shall yet praise him for the help of his countenance. O my God, my soul is cast down within me: therefore will I remember thee from the land of Jordan. Psalm 42:2, 5-6 KJV

Bless the Lord, O my soul: and all that is within me, bless his holy name. Bless the Lord, O my soul, and forget not all his benefits. Psalm 103:1-2 KJV

[The Lord] 'Behold, all souls are mine; the soul of the father as well as the soul of the son is mine: the soul that sins shall die.' Ezekiel 18:4 RSV

'Do not be afraid of those who kill the body but cannot kill the soul; rather be afraid of God, who can destroy both body and soul in hell.' Matthew 10:28 GNB

'Take my yoke upon you, and learn from me; for I am gentle and lowly in heart, and you will find rest for your souls.' Matthew 11:29 RSV

Then he said to them, 'My soul is very sorrowful, even to death; remain here, and watch with me.' Matthew 26:38 RSV

[Mary's 'Magnificat'] My soul doth magnify the Lord . . . Luke 1:46 BCP

See also *Heart; Spirit.*

Sovereignty of God

Know therefore this day, and consider it in thine heart, that the Lord he is God in heaven above, and upon the earth beneath: there is none else. Deuteronomy 4:39 KJV

And the Lord said to Satan, 'Behold, all that he has is in your power; only upon himself do not put forth your hand.' Job 1:12 RSV

Many are the plans in the mind of a man, but it is the purpose of the Lord that will be established. Proverbs 19:21 RSV

'For the Son of man goes as it has been determined; but woe to that man by whom he is betrayed!' Luke 22:22 RSV

The wind bloweth where it listeth, and thou hearest the sound thereof, but canst not tell whence it cometh, and whither it goeth: so is every one that is born of the Spirit. John 3:8 KJV

All that the Father giveth me shall come to me; and him that cometh to me I will in no wise cast out. John 6:37 KJV

'This Jesus, delivered up according to the definite plan and foreknowledge of God, you crucified and killed by the hands of lawless men.' Acts 2:23 RSV

We know that in everything God works for good with those who love him, who are called according to his purpose. Romans 8:28 RSV

All these [gifts] are inspired by one and the same Spirit, who apportions to each one individually as he wills. 1 Corinthians 12:11 RSV

[God] who worketh all things after the counsel of his own will. Ephesians 1:11 KJV

Work out your own salvation with fear and trembling; for God is at work in you, both to will and to work for his good pleasure. Philippians 2:12-13 RSV

See also *Election; Providence; Responsibility of man.*

Speech

Set a guard over my mouth, O Lord, keep watch over the door of my lips! Psalm 141:3 RSV

A word fitly spoken is like apples of gold in pictures of silver. Proverbs 25:11 KJV

'You can be sure that on Judgement

Day everyone will have to give account of every useless word he has ever spoken.' Matthew 12:36 GNB

Rather, speaking the truth in love, we are to grow up in every way into him who is the head, into Christ. Ephesians 4:15 RSV

Let no evil talk come out of your mouths, but only such as is good for edifying, as fits the occasion, that it may impart grace to those who hear. Ephesians 4:29 RSV

Let your speech always be gracious, seasoned with salt, so that you may know how you ought to answer every one. Colossians 4:6 RSV

And the tongue is like a fire. It is a world of wrong, occupying its place in our bodies and spreading evil through our whole being. It sets on fire the entire course of our existence with the fire that comes to it from hell itself . . . But no one has ever been able to tame the tongue. It is evil and uncontrollable, full of deadly poison. We use it to give thanks to our Lord and Father and also to curse our fellow-man, who is created in the likeness of God. Words of thanksgiving and cursing pour out from the same mouth. My brothers, this should not happen! James 3:6, 8-10 GNB

'He that would love life and see good days, let him keep his tongue from evil and his lips from speaking guile.' 1 Peter 3:10 RSV

Always be prepared to make a defence to any one who calls you to account for the hope that is in you, yet do it with gentleness and reverence. 1 Peter 3:15 RSV

Spirit

When they had crossed, Elijah said to Elisha, 'Ask what I shall do for you, before I am taken from you.' And Elisha said, 'I pray you, let me inherit a double share of your spirit.' 2 Kings 2:9 RSV

Create in me a clean heart, O God; and renew a right spirit within me. Psalm 51:10 KJV

All the ways of a man are pure in his own eyes, but the Lord weighs the spirit. Proverbs 16:2 RSV

Blessed are the poor in spirit: for theirs is the kingdom of heaven. Matthew 5:3 KJV

'Watch and pray that you may not enter into temptation; the spirit indeed is willing, but the flesh is weak.' Matthew 26:41 RSV

And Jesus cried again with a loud voice and yielded up his spirit. Matthew 27:50 RSV

'But the hour is coming, and now is, when the true worshippers will worship the Father in spirit and truth, for such the Father seeks to worship him. God is spirit, and those who worship him must worship in spirit and truth.' John 4:23-24 RSV

For you did not receive the spirit of slavery to fall back into fear, but you have received the spirit of sonship. When we cry, 'Abba! Father!' it is the Spirit himself bearing witness with our spirit that we are children of God. Romans 8:15-16 RSV

For what person knows a man's thoughts except the spirit of the man which is in him? So also no one comprehends the thoughts of God except the Spirit of God. 1 Corinthians 2:11 RSV

The spiritual man makes judgments about all things, but he himself is not subject to any man's judgment. 1 Corinthians 2:15 NIV

For if I pray in a tongue, my spirit prays but my mind is unfruitful. What am I to do? I will pray with the spirit and I will pray with the mind also; I will sing with the spirit and I will sing with the mind also. 1 Corinthians 14:14-15 RSV

See also *Heart; Holy Spirit; Soul.*

State, *responsibility to*

He said to them, 'Render therefore to Caesar the things that are Caesar's, and to God the things that are God's.' Matthew 22:21 RSV

[The high priest] 'We strictly charged you not to teach in this name, yet here you have filled Jerusalem with your teaching and you intend to bring this man's blood upon us.' But Peter and the apostles answered, 'We must obey God rather than men.' Acts 5:28-29 RSV

Everyone must obey the state authorities, because no authority exists without God's permission, and the existing authorities have been put there by God. Whoever opposes the existing authority opposes what God has ordered; and anyone who does so will bring judgement on himself. For rulers are not to be feared by those who do good, but by those who do evil. Would you like to be unafraid of the man in authority? Then do what is good, and he will praise you, because he is God's servant working for your own good. But if you do evil, then be afraid of him, because his power to punish is real. He is God's servant and carries out God's punishment on those who do evil. For this reason you must obey the authorities—not just because of God's punishment, but also as a matter of conscience. That is also why you pay taxes, because the authorities are working for God when they fulfil their duties. Pay, then, what you owe them; pay them your personal and property taxes, and show respect and honour for them all. Romans 13:1-7 GNB

[An encouragement to pray] for kings, and for all that are in authority; that we may lead a quiet and peaceable life in all godliness and honesty. 1 Timothy 2:2 KJV

Live as free men, yet without using your freedom as a pretext for evil; but live as servants of God. Honour all men. Love the brotherhood. Fear God. Honour the emperor. 1 Peter 2:16-17 RSV

Stealing

Thou shalt not steal. Exodus 20:15 KJV

'If a man steals an ox or a sheep, and kills it or sells it, he shall pay five oxen for an ox, and four sheep for a sheep. He shall make restitution; if he has nothing, then he shall be sold for his theft.' Exodus 22:1 RSV

And [Jesus] said unto them, It is written, My house shall be called the house of prayer; but ye have made it a den of thieves. Matthew 21:13 KJV

'For from within, out of the heart of man, come evil thoughts . . . theft . . . Mark 7:21 RSV

He [Judas] said this, not because he cared about the poor, but because he was a thief. He carried the money bag and would help himself from it. John 12:6 GNB

Neither . . . thieves nor the greedy nor . . . swindlers will inherit the kingdom of God. 1 Corinthians 6:9-10 NIV

Let the thief no longer steal, but rather let him labour, doing honest work with his hands, so that he may be able to give to those in need. Ephesians 4:28 RSV

Bid slaves to be submissive to their masters and to give satisfaction in every respect; they are not to be refractory, nor to pilfer. Titus 2:9-10 RSV

But let none of you suffer as a murderer, or a thief, or a wrongdoer, or a mischief-maker. 1 Peter 4:15 RSV

Stewardship

'For it will be as when a man going on a journey called his servants and entrusted to them his property; to one he gave five talents, to another two, to another one, to each according to his ability. . . Matthew 25:14-15 RSV

He also said to the disciples, 'There was a rich man who had a steward, and charges were brought to him that this man was wasting his goods. And he called him and said to him, "What is this that I hear about you? Turn in the account of your stewardship, for you can no longer be steward." And the steward said to himself, "What shall I do, since my master is taking the stewardship away from me?"' Luke 16:1-3 RSV

This is how one should regard us, as servants of Christ and stewards of the mysteries of God. Moreover it is required of stewards that they be found trustworthy. 1 Corinthians 4:1-2 RSV

For if I preach the gospel, that gives me no ground for boasting. For necessity is laid upon me. Woe to me if I do not preach the gospel! For if I do this of my own will, I have a reward; but if not of my own will, I am entrusted with a commission. 1 Corinthians 9:16-17 RSV

Assuming that you have heard of the stewardship of God's grace that was given to me for you. Ephesians 3:2 RSV

But I am not ashamed, for I know whom I have believed, and I am sure that he is able to guard until that Day what has been entrusted to me . . . guard the truth that has been entrusted to you by the Holy Spirit who dwells within us. 2 Timothy 1:12, 14 RSV

As each has received a gift, employ it for one another, as good stewards of God's varied grace. 1 Peter 4:10 RSV

See also *Giving; Time.*

Strength

See *Power.*

Submission

Everyone must obey the state authorities, because no authority exists without God's permission, and the existing authorities have been put there by God. Romans 13:1 GNB

Be subject to one another out of reverence for Christ. Wives, be subject to your husbands, as to the Lord . . . As the church is subject to Christ, so let wives also be subject in everything to their husbands. Ephesians 5:21-22, 24 RSV

Children, obey your parents in the Lord, for this is right. 'Honour your father and mother' (this is the first commandment with a promise). Ephesians 6:1 RSV

Slaves, obey your human masters with fear and trembling; and do it with a sincere heart, as though you were serving Christ. Ephesians 6:5 GNB

Obey your leaders and submit to them; for they are keeping watch over your souls, as men who will have to give account. Let them do this joyfully, and not sadly, for that would be of no advantage to you. Hebrews 13:17 RSV

Submit yourselves therefore to God. Resist the devil and he will flee from you. James 4:7 RSV

See also Obedience.

Suffering

Yet man is born unto trouble, as the sparks fly upward. Job 5:7 KJV

'He has no root in himself, but endures for a while, and when tribulation or persecution arises on account of the word, immediately he falls away.' Matthew 13:21 RSV

'Then they will deliver you up to tribulation, and put you to death; and you will be hated by all nations for my name's sake.' Matthew 24:9 RSV

'For then there will be great tribulation, such as has not been from the beginning of the world until now, no, and never will be.' Matthew 24:21 RSV

'Was it not necessary that the Christ should suffer these things and enter into his glory?' Luke 24:26 RSV

[Paul and Barnabas] Strengthening the souls of the disciples, exhorting them to continue in the faith, and saying that through many tribulations we must enter the kingdom of God. Acts 14:22 RSV

There will be tribulation and distress for every human being who does evil, the Jew first and also the Greek. Romans 2:9 RSV

I consider that the sufferings of this present time are not worth comparing with the glory that is to be revealed to us. For the creation waits with eager longing for the revealing of the sons of God; for the creation was subjected to futility, not of its own will but by the will of him who subjected it in hope; because the creation itself will be set free from its bondage to decay and obtain the glorious liberty of the children of God. Romans 8:18-21 RSV

If one member suffers, all suffer together; if one member is honoured, all rejoice together. 1 Corinthians 12:26 RSV

We are afflicted in every way, but not crushed; perplexed, but not driven to despair; persecuted, but not forsaken; struck down, but not destroyed . . . 2 Corinthians 4:8-9 RSV

Now I rejoice in my sufferings for your sake, and in my flesh I complete what is lacking in Christ's afflictions for the sake of his body, that is, the church. Colossians 1:24 RSV

Resist him[the devil], firm in your faith, knowing that the same experience of suffering is required of your brotherhood throughout the world. 1 Peter 5:9 RSV

Purposes of

'He delivers the afflicted by their affliction, and opens their ear by adversity.' Job 36:15 RSV

It is good for me that I was afflicted, that I might learn thy statutes. Psalm 119:71 RSV

As Jesus was walking along, he saw a man who had been born blind. His disciples asked him, 'Teacher, whose sin caused him to be born blind? Was it his own or his parents' sin?' Jesus answered, 'His blindess has nothing to do with his sins or his parents' sins. He is blind so that God's power might be seen at work in him.' John 9:1-3 GNB

We glory in tribulations also: knowing that tribulation worketh patience. Romans 5:3 KJV

[God] comforts us in all our troubles, so that we can comfort those in any trouble with the comfort we ourselves have received from God. 2 Corinthians 1:4 NIV

And to keep me from being too elated by the abundance of revelations, a thorn was given me in the flesh, a messenger of Satan, to harass me, to keep me from being too elated. 2 Corinthians 12:7 RSV

For they [our human fathers] disciplined us for a short time at their pleasure, but he disciplines us for our good, that we may share his holiness. Hebrews 12:10 RSV

In this you rejoice, though now for a little while you may have to suffer various trials, so that the genuineness of your faith, more precious than gold which though perishable is tested by fire, may redound to praise and glory and honour at the revelation of Jesus Christ. 1 Peter 1:6-7 RSV

See also *Comfort.*

Sunday

See *Sabbath.*

Swearing

See *Blasphemy.*

Talents

See *Gift.*

Teachers and teaching

'You shall teach them [the words the Lord commands] diligently to your children, and shall talk of them when you sit in your house, and when you walk by the way, and when you lie down, and when you rise.' Deuteronomy 6:7 RSV

Teach me, O Lord, the way of thy statutes; and I will keep it to the end. Psalm 119:33 RSV

'Go therefore and make disciples of all nations . . . teaching them to observe all that I have commanded you . . .' Matthew 28:19-20 RSV

Jesus answered, 'What I teach is not my own teaching, but it comes from God, who sent me.' John 7:16 GNB

'But the Counsellor, the Holy Spirit, whom the Father will send in my name, he will teach you all things, and bring to your remembrance all that I have said to you.' John 14:26 RSV

And they continued stedfastly in the apostles' doctrine and fellowship, and in breaking of bread, and in prayers. Acts 2:42 KJV

'How I did not shrink from declaring to you anything that was profitable, and teaching you in public and from house to house . . .' Acts 20:20 RSV

Now you are the body of Christ and individually members of it. And God has appointed in the church first apostles, second prophets, third teachers . . . 1 Corinthians 12:28 RSV

Let the word of Christ dwell in you richly in all wisdom; teaching and admonishing one another in psalms and hymns and spiritual songs, singing with grace in your hearts to the Lord. Colossians 3:16 KJV

From childhood you have been acquainted with the sacred writings which are able to instruct you for salvation through faith in Christ Jesus. All scripture is inspired by God and profitable for teaching, for reproof, for correction, and for training in righteousness . . . 2 Timothy 3:15-16 RSV

See also *Family; Pastor; Preaching.*

Teachers, *false*

'A prophet or an interpreter of dreams may promise a miracle or a wonder, in order to lead you to worship and serve gods that you have not worshipped before. Even if what he promises comes true, do not pay any attention to him. The Lord your God is using him to test you, to see if you love the Lord with all your heart.' Deuteronomy 13:1-3 GNB

'Beware of false prophets, who come to you in sheep's clothing but inwardly are ravenous wolves. You will know them by their fruits.' Matthew 7:15-16 RSV

"'In vain do they worship me, teaching as doctrines the precepts of men.'" Matthew 15:9 RSV

And Jesus answered them, 'Take heed that no one leads you astray. For many will come in my name, saying, "I am the Christ," and they will lead many astray.' Matthew 24:4-5 RSV

I appeal to you, brethren, to take note of those who create dissensions and difficulties, in opposition to the doctrine which you have been taught; avoid them. Romans 16:17 RSV

I am astonished that you are so quickly deserting him who called you in the grace of Christ and turning to a different gospel—not that there is another gospel, but there are some who trouble you and want to pervert the gospel of Christ. But even if we, or an angel from heaven, should preach to you a gospel contrary to that which we preached to you, let him be accursed. Galatians 1:6-8 RSV

Now the Spirit expressly says that in later times some will depart from the faith by giving heed to deceitful spirits and doctrines of demons. 1 Timothy 4:1 RSV

They profess to know God, but they deny him by their deeds; they are detestable, disobedient, unfit for any good deed. Titus 1:16 RSV

But false prophets also arose among the people, just as there will be false teachers among you, who will secretly bring in destructive heresies, even denying the Master who bought them, bringing upon themselves swift destruction. 2 Peter 2:1 RSV

Beloved, do not believe every spirit, but test the spirits to see whether they are of God; for many false prophets have gone out into the world. By this you know the Spirit of God: every spirit which confesses that Jesus Christ has come in the flesh is of God. 1 John 4:1-2 RSV

Beloved, being very eager to write to you of our common salvation, I found it necessary to write appealing to you to contend for the faith which was once for all delivered to the saints. For admission has been secretly gained by some who long ago were designated for this condemnation, ungodly persons who pervert the grace of our God into licentiousness and deny our only Master and Lord, Jesus Christ. Jude 3-4 RSV

Temperance

Let us then pursue what makes for peace and for mutual upbuilding . . . it is right not to eat meat or drink wine or do anything that makes your brother stumble. Romans 14:19, 21 RSV

But the fruit of the Spirit is . . . self-control . . . Galatians 5:22-23 RSV

For those who sleep sleep at night, and those who get drunk are drunk at night. But, since we belong to the day, let us be sober. 1 Thessalonians 5:7-8 RSV

Deacons likewise must be serious, not double-tongued, not addicted to much wine . . . The women likewise must be . . . temperate, faithful in all things. 1 Timothy 3:8, 11 RSV

Drink no longer water, but use a little wine for thy stomach's sake and thine often infirmities. 1 Timothy 5:23 KJV

See also *Drunkenness*.

Temptation

'And you shall remember all the way which the Lord your God has led you these forty years in the wilderness, that he might humble you, testing you to know what was in your heart, whether you would keep his commandments, or not.' Deuteronomy 8:2 RSV

And the Lord said to Satan, 'Behold, all that he has is in your power; only upon himself do not put forth your hand.' Job 1:12 RSV

Can a man take fire in his bosom, and his clothes not be burned? Proverbs 6:27 KJV

Then Jesus was led up by the Spirit into the wilderness to be tempted by the devil. Matthew 4:1 RSV

And lead us not into temptation; but deliver us from evil. Matthew 6:13 BCP

'Watch and pray that you may not enter into temptation; the spirit indeed is willing, but the flesh is weak.' Matthew 26:41 RSV

And he said to his disciples, 'Temptations to sin are sure to come; but woe to him by whom they come!' Luke 17:1 RSV

But I am afraid that as the serpent deceived Eve by his cunning, your thoughts will be led astray from a sincere and pure devotion to Christ. 2 Corinthians 11:3 RSV

Brethren, if a man is overtaken in any trespass, you who are spiritual should restore him in a spirit of gentleness. Look to yourself, lest you too be tempted. Galatians 6:1 RSV

It was faith that made Abraham offer his son Isaac as a sacrifice when God put Abraham to the test. Abraham was the one to whom God had made the promise, yet he was ready to offer his only son as a sacrifice. Hebrews 11:17 GNB

Let no one say when he is tempted, 'I am tempted by God'; for God cannot be tempted with evil and he himself tempts no one; but each person is tempted when he is lured and enticed by his own desire. James 1:13-14 RSV

Help in

Keep back thy servant also from presumptuous sins; let them not have dominion over me: then shall I be upright, and I shall be innocent from the great transgression. Psalm 19:13 KJV

Set a guard over my mouth, O Lord, keep watch over the door of my lips! Psalm 141:3 RSV

Never set your foot on the path of the wicked, do not walk the way that the evil go. Proverbs 4:14 JB

And the Lord said, Simon, Simon, behold, Satan hath desired to have you, that he may sift you as wheat: but I have prayed for thee, that thy faith fail not: and when thou art converted, strengthen thy brethren. Luke 22:31-32 KJV

How shall we, that are dead to sin, live any longer therein? Romans 6:2 KJV

No temptation has overtaken you that is not common to man. God is faithful, and he will not let you be tempted beyond your strength; but with the temptation will also provide the way of escape, that you may be able to endure it. 1 Corinthians 10:13 RSV

Put on the whole armour of God, that ye may be able to stand against the wiles of the devil. Ephesians 6:11 KJV

Because he himself suffered when he was tempted, he is able to help those who are being tempted. Hebrews 2:18 NIV

For we have not a high priest who is unable to sympathize with our weaknesses, but one who in every respect has been tempted as we are, yet without sin. Hebrews 4:15 RSV

Count it all joy, my brethren, when you meet various trials, for you know that the testing of your faith produces steadfastness. James 1:2-3 RSV

In this you rejoice, though now for a little while you may have to suffer various trials, so that the genuineness of your faith, more precious than gold which though perishable is tested by fire, may redound to praise and glory and honour at the revelation of Jesus Christ. 1 Peter 1:6-7 RSV

Beloved, do not be surprised at the fiery ordeal which comes upon you to prove you, as though something strange were happening to you. But rejoice in so far as you share Christ's sufferings, that you may also rejoice and be glad when his glory is revealed. 1 Peter 4:12-13 RSV

Be sober, be watchful. Your adversary the devil prowls around like a roaring lion, seeking some one to devour. Resist him, firm in your faith, knowing that the same experience of suffering is required of your brotherhood throughout the world. 1 Peter 5:8-9 RSV

See also *Victory.*

Ten Commandments

See Exodus 20; Deuteronomy 5.

Tests of faith

See *Temptation.*

Thanksgiving

'Offer to God a sacrifice of thanksgiving, and pay your vows to the Most High.' Psalm 50:14 RSV

O give thanks to the Lord, for he is good, for his steadfast love endures for ever. Psalm 136:1 RSV

He fell on his face at Jesus' feet, giving him thanks. Now he was a Samaritan. Then said Jesus, 'Were not ten

cleansed? Where are the nine? Was no one found to return and give praise to God except this foreigner?' Luke 17:16-18 RSV

But thanks be to God, who gives us the victory through our Lord Jesus Christ. 1 Corinthians 15:57 RSV

Thanks be to God for his inexpressible gift! 2 Corinthians 9:15 RSV

I do not cease to give thanks for you, remembering you in my prayers . . . Ephesians 1:16 RSV

Nor is it fitting for you to use language which is obscene, profane, or vulgar. Rather you should give thanks to God. Ephesians 5:4 GNB

Speaking to yourselves in psalms and hymns and spiritual songs, singing and making melody in your heart to the Lord; giving thanks always for all things unto God and the Father in the name of our Lord Jesus Christ. Ephesians 5:19-20 KJV

Have no anxiety about anything, but in everything by prayer and supplication with thanksgiving let your requests be made known to God. Philippians 4:6 RSV

In every thing give thanks: for this is the will of God in Christ Jesus concerning you. 1 Thessalonians 5:18 KJV

See also *Joy; Praise; Worship.*

Thought

We have thought on thy steadfast love, O God, in the midst of thy temple. Psalm 48:9 RSV

How precious to me are thy thoughts, O God! How vast is the sum of them! If I would count them, they are more than the sand. When I awake, I am still with thee. Psalm 139:17-18 RSV

Search me, O God, and know my heart: try me, and know my thoughts. And see if there be any wicked way in me, and lead me in the way everlasting. Psalm 139:23-24 KJV

For my thoughts are not your thoughts, neither are your ways my ways, saith the Lord. For as the heavens are higher than the earth, so are my ways higher than your ways, and my thoughts than your thoughts. Isaiah 55:8-9 KJV

What think ye of Christ? whose son is he? Matthew 22:42 KJV

For what person knows a man's thoughts except the spirit of the man which is in him? So also no one comprehends the thoughts of God except the Spirit of God. 1 Corinthians 2:11 RSV

Brethren, do not be children in your thinking; be babes in evil, but in thinking be mature. 1 Corinthians 14:20 RSV

We destroy arguments and every proud obstacle to the knowledge of God, and take every thought captive to obey Christ. 2 Corinthians 10:5 RSV

Finally, brethren, whatsoever things are true, whatsoever things are honest, whatsoever things are just, whatsoever things are pure, whatsoever things are lovely, whatsoever things are of good report; if there be any virtue, and if there be any praise, think on these things. Philippians 4:8 KJV

See also *Meditation; Mind.*

Time

And God said, Let there be lights in the firmament of the heaven to divide the day from the night; and let them be for signs, and for seasons, and for days, and years. Genesis 1:14 KJV

Remember the sabbath day, to keep it holy. Exodus 20:8 KJV

For everything there is a season, and a time for every matter under heaven: a time to be born, and a time to die. Ecclesiastes 3:1-2 RSV

'The time is fulfilled, and the kingdom of God is at hand; repent, and believe in the gospel.' Mark 1:15 RSV

Jesus said to them, 'My time has not yet come, but your time is always here.' John 7:6 RSV

Jesus answered, 'Are there not twelve hours in the day? If any one walks in the day, he does not stumble, because he sees the light of this world.' John 11:9 RSV

He said to them, 'It is not for you to know times or seasons which the Father has fixed by his own authority.' Acts 1:7 RSV

[Jesus Christ] Whom the heaven must receive until the times of restitution of all things, which God hath spoken by the mouth of all his holy prophets since the world began. Acts 3:21 KJV

For he says, 'At the acceptable time I have listened to you, and helped you on the day of salvation.' Behold, now is the acceptable time; behold, now is the day of salvation. 2 Corinthians 6:2 RSV

But when the time had fully come, God sent forth his Son, born of woman, born under the law, to redeem those who were under the law. Galatians 4:4 RSV

Making the most of the time, because the days are evil. Ephesians 5:16 RSV

Conduct yourselves wisely toward outsiders, making the most of the time. Colossians 4:5 RSV

But do not ignore this one fact, beloved, that with the Lord one day is as a thousand years, and a thousand years as one day. 2 Peter 3:8 RSV

See also *Old age; Youth.*

Tiredness

Of making many books there is no end; and much study is a weariness of the flesh. Ecclesiastes 12:12 KJV

Hast thou not known? hast thou not heard, that the everlasting God, the Lord, the Creator of the ends of the earth, fainteth not, neither is weary? There is no searching of his understanding. He giveth power to the faint; and to them that have no might he increaseth strength. Even the youths shall faint and be weary, and the young men shall utterly fall: But they that wait upon the Lord shall renew their strength; they shall mount up with wings as eagles; they shall run, and not be weary; and they shall walk, and not faint. Isaiah 40:28-31 KJV

The Lord God hath given me the tongue of the learned, that I should know how to speak a word in season to him that is weary: he wakeneth morning by morning, he wakeneth mine ear to hear as the learned. Isaiah 50:4 KJV

'Come to me, all who labour and are heavy-laden, and I will give you rest.' Matthew 11:28 RSV

'They that wait upon the Lord shall renew their strength; they shall mount up with wings as eagles.'

Jesus, tired out by the journey, sat down by the well. John 4:6 GNB

So we do not lose heart. Though our outer nature is wasting away, our inner nature is being renewed every day. 2 Corinthians 4:16 RSV

And let us not grow weary in well-doing, for in due season we shall reap, if we do not lose heart. Galatians 6:9 RSV

Think of him [Jesus] who submitted to such opposition from sinners: that will help you not to lose heart and grow faint. Hebrews 12:3 NEB

See also *Power.*

Tithing

See *Giving.*

Tongues, *gift of*

Speaking in tongues

And they were all filled with the Holy Spirit and began to speak in other tongues, as the Spirit gave them utterance. Acts 2:4 RSV

And when Paul had laid his hands upon them, the Holy Spirit came on them; and they spoke with tongues and prophesied. Acts 19:6 RSV

Now you are the body of Christ and individually members of it. And God has appointed in the church first apostles, second prophets, third teachers, then workers of miracles, then . . . speakers in various kinds of tongues . . . Do all speak with tongues? . . . But earnestly desire the higher gifts. 1 Corinthians 12:28, 30 RSV

If I speak in the tongues of men and of angels, but have not love, I am a noisy gong or a clanging cymbal . . . as for tongues, they will cease. 1 Corinthians 13:1, 8 RSV

For one who speaks in a tongue speaks not to men but to God; for no one understands him, but he utters mysteries in the Spirit . . . He who speaks in a tongue edifies himself, but he who prophesies edifies the church. 1 Corinthians 14:2, 4 RSV

He who speaks in a tongue should pray for the power to interpret. For if I pray in a tongue, my spirit prays but my mind is unfruitful. 1 Corinthians 14:13-14 RSV

I thank God that I speak in tongues more than all of you. But in the church I would rather speak five intelligible words to instruct others than ten thousand words in a tongue. 1 Corinthians 14:18-19 NIV

We read in the Law: 'I will speak to this nation through men of strange tongues, and by the lips of foreigners; and even so they will not heed me, says the Lord.' Clearly then these 'strange tongues' are not intended as a sign for believers, but for unbelievers, whereas prophecy is designed not for unbelievers but for those who hold the faith. 1 Corinthians 14:21-22 NEB

Interpretation

To another various kinds of tongues, to another the interpretation of tongues. 1 Corinthians 12:10 RSV

He who prophesies is greater than one who speaks in tongues, unless some one interprets, so that the church may be edified. 1 Corinthians 14:5 RSV

If anyone speaks in a tongue, two—or at the most three—should speak, one at a time, and someone must interpret. If there is no interpreter, the speaker should keep quiet in the church and speak to himself and God. 1 Corinthians 14:27-28 NIV

Transfiguration

See Matthew 17:1-8.

Trinity

Hear, O Israel: The Lord our God is one Lord . . . Deuteronomy 6:4 KJV

And when Jesus was baptized, he went up immediately from the water, and behold, the heavens were opened and he saw the Spirit of God descending like a dove, and alighting on him; and lo, a voice from heaven, saying, 'This is my beloved Son, with whom I am well pleased.' Matthew 3:16-17 RSV

'Go therefore and make disciples of all nations, baptizing them in the name of the Father and of the Son and of the Holy Spirit . . .' Matthew 28:19 RSV

Now there are varieties of gifts, but the same Spirit; and there are varieties of service, but the same Lord; and there are varieties of working, but it is the same God who inspires them all in every one. 1 Corinthians 12:4-6 RSV

The grace of the Lord Jesus Christ, the love of God, and the fellowship of the Holy Spirit be with you all. 2 Corinthians 13:13 GNB

There is one body and one Spirit, just as you were called to the one hope that belongs to your call, one Lord, one faith, one baptism, one God and Father of us all, who is above all and through all and in all. Ephesians 4:4-6 RSV

Elect according to the foreknowledge

of God the Father, through sanctification of the Spirit, unto obedience and sprinkling of the blood of Jesus Christ: Grace unto you, and peace, be multiplied. 1 Peter 1:2 KJV

Trust

See *Faith*.

Truth

'But you, Lord, are the true God, you are the living God and the eternal king.' Jeremiah 10:10 GNB

And the Word was made flesh, and dwelt among us . . . John 1:14 KJV

But he who does what is true comes to the light, that it may be clearly seen that his deeds have been wrought in God. John 3:21 RSV

Jesus then said to the Jews who had believed in him, 'If you continue in my word, you are truly my disciples, and you will know the truth, and the truth will make you free.' John 8:31-32 RSV

Jesus saith unto him, I am the way, the truth, and the life: no man cometh unto the Father, but by me. John 14:6 KJV

'When the Spirit of truth comes, he will guide you into all the truth; for he will not speak on his own authority, but whatever he hears he will speak, and he will declare to you the things that are to come.' John 16:13 RSV

Sanctify them through thy truth: thy word is truth. John 17:17 KJV

Pilate said to him, 'What is truth?' John 18:38 RSV

Rather, speaking the truth in love, we are to grow up in every way into him who is the head, into Christ. Ephesians 4:15 RSV

Stand therefore, having your loins girt about with truth . . . Ephesians 6:14 KJV

The household of God, which is the church of the living God, the pillar and bulwark of the truth. 1 Timothy 3:15 RSV

Do your best to present yourself to God as one approved, a workman who has no need to be ashamed, rightly handling the word of truth. 2 Timothy 2:15 RSV

Unbelief

They [the children of Israel] spoke against God, saying, 'Can God spread a table in the wilderness?' . . . In spite of all this they still sinned; despite his wonders they did not believe. Psalm 78:19, 32 RSV

And he did not do many mighty works there, because of their unbelief. Matthew 13:58 RSV

'O unbelieving and perverse generation,' Jesus replied, 'how long shall I stay with you? How long shall I put up with you?' Matthew 17:17 NIV

He was amazed at their lack of faith. Mark 6:6 JB

And Jesus said to him, '. . . All things are possible to him who believes.' Immediately the father of the child cried out and said, 'I believe; help my unbelief!' Mark 9:23-24 RSV

Afterwards he appeared to the eleven themselves as they sat at table; and he upbraided them for their unbelief and hardness of heart, because they had not believed those who saw him after he had risen. Mark 16:14 RSV

'The ones along the path are those who have heard; then the devil comes and takes away the word from their hearts, that they may not believe and be saved.' Luke 8:12 RSV

He [the Holy Spirit] will convince the world . . . concerning sin, because they do not believe in me.' John 16:8-9 RSV

But he [Thomas] said to them, 'Unless I see in his hands the print of the nails, and place my finger in the mark of the nails, and place my hand in his side, I will not believe.' . . . Then he said to Thomas, 'Put your finger here, and see my hands; and put out your hand, and place it in my side; do not be faithless, but believing.' John 20:25, 27 RSV

See to it, brothers, that none of you has a sinful, unbelieving heart that turns away from the living God. Hebrews 3:12 NIV

See also *Doubt; Faith; Hardness*.

Unbeliever

He who believes in him is not condemned; he who does not believe is condemned already, because he has not believed in the name of the only Son of God. And this is the judgment, that the light has come into the world, and men loved darkness rather than light, because their deeds were evil. John 3:18-19 RSV

'I told you that you would die in your sins, for you will die in your sins unless you believe that I am he.' John 8:24 RSV

For although they knew God they did not honour him as God or give thanks to him, but they became futile in their thinking and their senseless minds were darkened. Romans 1:21 RSV

The man without the Spirit does not accept the things that come from the Spirit of God, for they are foolishness to him and he cannot understand them, because they are spiritually discerned. 1 Corinthians 2:14 NIV

In their case the god of this world has blinded the minds of the unbelievers, to keep them from seeing the light of the gospel of the glory of Christ, who is the likeness of God. 2 Corinthians 4:4 RSV

Be ye not unequally yoked together with unbelievers: for what fellowship hath righteousness with unrighteousness? and what communion hath light with darkness? 2 Corinthians 6:14 KJV

As for you, you were dead in your transgressions and sins, in which you used to live when you followed the ways of this world and of the ruler of the kingdom of the air, the spirit who is now at work in those who are disobedient. All of us also lived among them at one time, gratifying the cravings of our sinful nature and following its desires and thoughts. Like the rest, we were by nature objects of wrath. Ephesians 2:1-3 NIV

Remember that you were at that time separated from Christ, alienated from the commonwealth of Israel, and strangers to the covenants of promise, having no hope and without God in the world. Ephesians 2:12 RSV

He that hath the Son hath life; and he that hath not the Son of God hath not life. 1 John 5:12 KJV

See also *Godless; Sin.*

Understanding

Be not like a horse or a mule, without understanding, which must be curbed with bit and bridle. Psalm 32:9 RSV

Beg for knowledge; plead for insight. Look for it as hard as you would for silver or some hidden treasure. If you do, you will know what it means to fear the Lord and you will succeed in learning about God. It is the Lord who gives wisdom; from him come knowledge and understanding. Proverbs 2:3-6 GNB

Trust in the Lord with all thine heart; and lean not unto thine own understanding. Proverbs 3:5 KJV

'The fear of the Lord is the beginning of wisdom, and knowledge of the Holy One is understanding.' Proverbs 9:10 NIV

The Lord says, 'My people are stupid; they don't know me. They are like foolish children; they have no understanding. They are experts at doing what is evil, but failures at doing what is good.' Jeremiah 4:22 GNB

'When any one hears the word of the kingdom and does not understand it, the evil one comes and snatches away what is sown in his heart ... As for what was sown on good soil, this is he who hears the word and understands it; he indeed bears fruit, and yields, in one case a hundredfold, in another sixty, and in another thirty.' Matthew 13:19, 23 RSV

So Philip ran to him, and heard him reading Isaiah the prophet, and asked, 'Do you understand what you are reading?' And he said, 'How can I, unless some one guides me?' And he invited Philip to come up and sit with him. Acts 8:30-31 RSV

Therefore do not be foolish, but understand what the will of the Lord is. Ephesians 5:17 RSV

And the peace of God, which passes all understanding, will keep your hearts and your minds in Christ Jesus. Philippians 4:7 RSV

By faith we understand that the world was created by the word of God, so that what is seen was made out of things which do not appear. Hebrews 11:3 RSV

See also *Knowledge; Thought; Wisdom.*

Unity

Behold, how good and how pleasant it is for brethren to dwell together in unity! Psalm 133:1 KJV

And though a man might prevail against one who is alone, two will withstand him. A threefold cord is not quickly broken. Ecclesiastes 4:12 RSV

Can two walk together, except they be agreed? Amos 3:3 KJV

'Again I say to you, if two of you agree on earth about anything they ask, it will be done for them by my Father in heaven. For where two or three are gathered in my name, there am I in the midst of them.' Matthew 18:19-20 RSV

[Jesus' prayer] 'That they may all be one; even as thou, Father, art in me, and I in thee, that they also may be in us, so that the world may believe that thou hast sent me.' John 17:21 RSV

Now the company of those who believed were of one heart and soul, and no one said that any of the things which he possessed was his own, but they had everything in common. Acts 4:32 RSV

Eager to maintain the unity of the Spirit in the bond of peace. There is one body and one Spirit, just as you were called to the one hope that belongs to your call, one Lord, one faith, one baptism, one God and Father of us all, who is above all and through all and in all. Ephesians 4:3-6 RSV

Complete my joy by being of the same mind, having the same love, being in full accord and of one mind. Philippians 2:2 RSV

Vengeance

See *Retaliation*.

Victory

Fear not, for I am with you, be not dismayed, for I am your God; I will strengthen you, I will help you, I will uphold you with my victorious right hand. Isaiah 41:10 RSV

These things I have spoken unto you, that in me ye might have peace. In the world ye shall have tribulation: but be of good cheer; I have overcome the world. John 16:33 KJV

What then shall we say to this? If God is for us, who is against us? . . . in all these things we are more than conquerors through him who loved us. Romans 8:31, 37 RSV

The God of peace will soon crush Satan under your feet. Romans 16:20 RSV

But thanks be to God, who gives us the victory through our Lord Jesus Christ. 1 Corinthians 15:57 RSV

For the weapons of our warfare are not worldly but have divine power to destroy strongholds. 2 Corinthians 10:4 RSV

He said to me, 'My grace is sufficient for you, for my power is made perfect in weakness.' I will all the more gladly boast of my weaknesses, that the power of Christ may rest upon me. 2 Corinthians 12:9 RSV

He disarmed the principalities and powers and made a public example of them, triumphing over them in him. Colossians 2:15 RSV

He who is in you is greater than he who is in the world. 1 John 4:4 RSV

For whatever is born of God overcomes the world; and this is the victory that overcomes the world, our faith. 1 John 5:4 RSV

'And they have conquered him by the blood of the Lamb and by the word of their testimony, for they loved not their lives even unto death.' Revelation 12:11 RSV

See also *Endurance*.

Vow

Then Jacob made a vow to the Lord: 'If you will be with me and protect me on the journey I am making and give me food and clothing, and if I return safely to my father's home, then you will be my God. This memorial stone which I have set up will be the place where you are worshipped, and I will give you a tenth of everything you give me.' Genesis 28:20-22 GNB

'When you make a vow to the Lord your God, you shall not be slack to pay it; for the Lord your God will surely require it of you, and it would be a sin in you. But if you refrain from vowing, it shall be no sin in you. You shall be careful to perform what has passed your lips, for you have voluntarily vowed to the Lord your God what you have promised with your mouth.' Deuteronomy 23:21-23 RSV

From thee comes my praise in the great congregation; my vows I will pay before those who fear him. Psalm 22:25 RSV

'Offer to God a sacrifice of thanksgiving, and pay your vows to the Most High.' Psalm 50:14 RSV

It is dangerous to dedicate a gift rashly or to make a vow and have second thoughts. Proverbs 20:25 NEB

Keep your feasts, O Judah, fulfil your vows, for never again shall the wicked come against you, he is utterly cut off. Nahum 1:15 RSV

See also *Blasphemy*.

War

The Lord is a man of war. Exodus 15:3 KJV

'When you go forth to war against your enemies, and see horses and chariots and an army larger than your own, you shall not be afraid of them; for the Lord your God is with you, who brought you out of the land of Egypt.' Deuteronomy 20:1 RSV

[Jehoshaphat's prayer] 'O our God, wilt thou not execute judgment upon them? For we are powerless against this great multitude that is coming against us. We do not know what to do, but our eyes are upon thee.' 2 Chronicles 20:12 RSV

Though an host should encamp against me, my heart shall not fear: though war

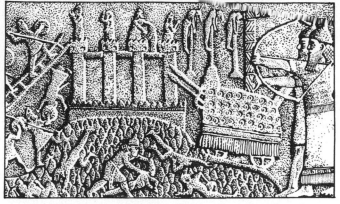

'I sent Assyria to attack a godless nation, people who have made me angry.'

should rise against me, in this will I be confident. One thing have I desired of the Lord, that will I seek after; that I may dwell in the house of the Lord all the days of my life. Psalm 27:3-4 KJV

A king is not saved by his great army; a warrior is not delivered by his great strength. Psalm 33:16 RSV

The Lord said, 'Assyria! I use Assyria like a club to punish those with whom I am angry. I sent Assyria to attack a godless nation, people who have made me angry.' Isaiah 10:5-6 GNB

'And you will hear of wars and rumours of wars; see that you are not alarmed; for this must take place, but the end is not yet. For nation will rise against nation, and kingdom against kingdom, and there will be famines and earthquakes in various places.' Matthew 24:6-7 RSV

Who shall separate us from the love of Christ? Shall tribulation, or distress, or persecution, or famine, or nakedness, or peril, or sword? As it is written, 'For thy sake we are being killed all the day long; we are regarded as sheep to be slaughtered.' No, in all these things we are more than conquerors through him who loved us. Romans 8:35-37 RSV

[The man in authority] is God's servant working for your own good. But if you do evil, then be afraid of him, because his power to punish is real. He is God's servant and carries out God's punishment on those who do evil. Romans 13:4 GNB

What causes wars, and what causes fightings among you? Is it not your passions that are at war in your members? James 4:1 RSV

For 'Spiritual warfare' see also *Christian life, Continuing in the faith; Endurance.*

Water

They shall not hurt nor destroy in all my holy mountain: for the earth shall be full of the knowledge of the Lord, as the waters cover the sea. Isaiah 11:9 KJV

With joy you will draw water from the wells of salvation. Isaiah 12:13 RSV

Ho, every one that thirsteth, come ye to the waters, and he that hath no money; come ye, buy, and eat. Isaiah 55:1 KJV

The Lord, the fountain of living waters. Jeremiah 17:13 KJV

'I will sprinkle clean water upon you, and you shall be clean from all your uncleannesses, and from all your idols I will cleanse you.' Ezekiel 36:25 RSV

[John the Baptist] 'I baptize you with water for repentance, but he who is coming after me is mightier than I, whose sandals I am not worthy to carry; he will baptize you with the Holy Spirit and with fire.' Matthew 3:11 RSV

Jesus answered, Verily, verily, I say unto thee, Except a man be born of water and of the Spirit, he cannot enter into the kingdom of God. John 3:5 KJV

'Whoever drinks of the water that I shall give him will never thirst; the water that I shall give him will become in him a spring of water welling up to eternal life.' John 4:14 RSV

And Jesus said unto them, I am the bread of life: he that cometh to me shall never hunger; and he that believeth on me shall never thirst. John 6:35 KJV

On the last day of the feast, the great day, Jesus stood up and proclaimed, 'If any one thirst, let him come to me and drink. He who believes in me, as the scripture has said, "Out of his heart shall flow rivers of living water."' Now this he said about the Spirit, which those who believed in him were to receive; for as yet the Spirit had not been given, because Jesus was not yet glorified. John 7:37-39 RSV

Christ loved the church and gave himself up for her, that he might sanctify her, having cleansed her by the washing of water with the word. Ephesians 5:25-26 RSV

He [God] saved us, not because of deeds done by us in righteousness, but in virtue of his own mercy, by the washing of regeneration and renewal in the Holy Spirit. Titus 3:5 RSV

Let us draw near with a true heart in full assurance of faith, with our hearts sprinkled clean from an evil conscience and our bodies washed with pure water. Hebrews 10:22 RSV

Way

[David's song of victory] 'This God—his way is perfect; the promise of the Lord proves true; he is a shield for all those who take refuge in him.' 2 Samuel 22:31 RSV

For the Lord knows the way of the righteous, but the way of the wicked will perish. Psalm 1:6 RSV

Good and upright is the Lord; therefore he instructs sinners in the way. He leads the humble in what is right, and teaches the humble his way. Psalm 25:8-9 RSV

There is a way which seemeth right unto a man, but the end thereof are the ways of death. Proverbs 14:12 KJV

And though the Lord give you the bread of adversity, and the water of affliction, yet shall not thy teachers be removed into a corner any more, but thine eyes shall see thy teachers: and thine ears shall hear a word behind thee, saying, This is the way, walk ye in it, when ye turn to the right hand, and when ye turn to the left. Isaiah 30:20-21 KJV

Why sayest thou, O Jacob, and speakest, O Israel, My way is hid from the Lord, and my judgment is passed over from my God? Hast thou not known? hast thou not heard, that the everlasting God, the Lord, the Creator of the ends of the earth, fainteth not, neither is weary? Isaiah 40:27-28 KJV

'Say to them, As I live, says the Lord God, I have no pleasure in the death of the wicked, but that the wicked turn from his way and live; turn back, turn

back from your evil ways; for why will you die, O house of Israel?' . . . 'Yet your people say, "The way of the Lord is not just"; when it is their own way that is not just.' Ezekiel 33:11, 17 RSV

'Enter by the narrow gate; for the gate is wide and the way is easy, that leads to destruction, and those who enter by it are many. For the gate is narrow and the way is hard, that leads to life, and those who find it are few.' Matthew 7:13-14 RSV

Jesus saith unto him, I am the way, the truth, and the life: no man cometh unto the Father, but by me. John 14:6 KJV

[Paul] 'I do admit this to you: I worship the God of our ancestors by following that Way which they [the Jews] say is false.' Acts 24:14 GNB

Therefore, brethren, since we have confidence to enter the sanctuary by the blood of Jesus, by the new and living way which he opened for us through the curtain, that is, through his flesh . . . Hebrews 10:19-20 RSV

See also *Guidance.*

Weakness

Strengthen the weak hands, and make firm the feeble knees. Isaiah 35:3 RSV

'When my soul fainted within me, I remembered the Lord; and my prayer came to thee, into thy holy temple.' Jonah 2:7 RSV

'Watch and pray that you may not enter into temptation; the spirit indeed is willing, but the flesh is weak.' Matthew 26:41 RSV

'In all things I have shown you that by so toiling one must help the weak, remembering the words of the Lord Jesus, how he said, "It is more blessed to give than to receive."' Acts 20:35 RSV

Welcome the person who is weak in faith, but do not argue with him about his personal opinions. Romans 14:1 GNB

We who are strong ought to bear with the failings of the weak, and not to please ourselves. Romans 15:1 RSV

But God hath chosen the foolish things of the world to confound the wise; and God hath chosen the weak things of the world to confound the things which are mighty. 1 Corinthians 1:27 KJV

Be careful, however, not to let your freedom of action make those who are weak in the faith fall into sin. 1 Corinthians 8:9 GNB

To the weak I became weak, that I might win the weak. I have become all things to all men, that I might by all means save some. 1 Corinthians 9:22 RSV

It is sown in dishonour, it is raised in glory. It is sown in weakness, it is raised in power. 1 Corinthians 15:43 RSV

But he said to me, 'My grace is sufficient for you, for my power is made perfect in weakness.' I will all the more gladly boast of my weaknesses, that the power of Christ may rest upon me. 2 Corinthians 12:9 RSV

For he was crucified in weakness, but lives by the power of God. For we are weak in him, but in dealing with you we shall live with him by the power of God. 2 Corinthians 13:4 RSV

See also *Power*.

Widows

'He executes justice for the fatherless and the widow, and loves the sojourner, giving him food and clothing.' Deuteronomy 10:18 RSV

'The Levite, because he has no portion or inheritance with you, and the . . . widow, who are within your towns, shall come and eat and be filled; that the Lord your God may bless you in all the work of your hands that you do.' Deuteronomy 14:29 RSV

The Lord watches over the sojourners, he upholds the widow and the fatherless; but the way of the wicked he brings to ruin. Psalm 146:9 RSV

Seek justice, encourage the oppressed. Defend the cause of the fatherless, plead the case of the widow. Isaiah 1:17 NIV

And he sat down opposite the treasury, and watched the multitude putting money into the treasury. Many rich people put in large sums. And a poor widow came, and put in two copper coins, which make a penny. And he called his disciples to him, and said to them, 'Truly, I say to you, this poor widow has put in more than all those who are contributing to the treasury. For they all contributed out of their abundance; but she out of her poverty has put in everything she had, her whole living.' Mark 12:41-44 RSV

There was a very old prophetess, a widow named Anna, daughter of Phanuel of the tribe of Asher. She had been married for only seven years and was now eighty-four years old. She never left the Temple; day and night she worshipped God, fasting and praying. Luke 2:36-37 GNB

Now in these days when the disciples were increasing in number, the Hellenists murmured against the Hebrews because their widows were neglected in the daily distribution. Acts 6:1 RSV

A wife is bound to her husband as long as he lives. If the husband dies, she is free to be married to whom she wishes, only in the Lord. 1 Corinthians 7:39 RSV

A widow who is all alone, with no one to take care of her, has placed her hope in God and continues to pray and ask him for his help night and day. 1 Timothy 5:5 GNB

[A widow] . . . well known for her good deeds, such as bringing up children, showing hospitality, washing the feet of the saints, helping those in trouble and devoting herself to all kinds of good deeds. 1 Timothy 5:10 NIV

They [young widows] also learn to waste their time in going round from house to house; but even worse, they learn to be gossips and busybodies, talking of things they should not. So I would prefer that the younger widows get married, have children, and take care of their homes, so as to give our enemies no chance of speaking evil of us. 1 Timothy 5:13-14 GNB

Religion that is pure and undefiled before God and the Father is this: to visit orphans and widows in their affliction, and to keep oneself unstained from the world. James 1:27 RSV

Wife

See *Marriage*.

Will of God

'I delight to do thy will, O my God; thy law is within my heart.' Psalm 40:8 RSV

Yet it pleased the Lord to bruise him; he hath put him to grief: when thou shalt make his soul an offering for sin, he shall see his seed, he shall prolong his days, and the pleasure of the Lord shall prosper in his hand. Isaiah 53:10 KJV

Jesus said to them, 'My food is to do the will of him who sent me, and to accomplish his work.' John 4:34 RSV

And be not conformed to this world: but be ye transformed by the renewing of your mind, that ye may prove what is that good, and acceptable, and perfect, will of God. Romans 12:2 KJV

He made known to us the mystery of his will according to his good pleasure, which he purposed in Christ, to be put into effect when the times will have reached their fulfilment—to bring all things in heaven and on earth together under one head, even Christ. Ephesians 1:9-10 NIV

Therefore do not be foolish, but understand what the will of the Lord is. Ephesians 5:17 RSV

For this is the will of God, your sanctification: that you abstain from unchastity. 1 Thessalonians 4:3 RSV

Rejoice evermore. Pray without ceasing. In every thing give thanks: for this is the will of God in Christ Jesus concerning you. 1 Thessalonians 5:16-18 KJV

And the world passeth away, and the lust thereof: but he that doeth the will of God abideth for ever. 1 John 2:17 KJV

And this is his commandment, that we should believe in the name of his Son Jesus Christ and love one another, just as he has commanded us. 1 John 3:23 RSV

See also *Accepting the will of God; Guidance.*

Wisdom

And God gave Solomon wisdom and understanding beyond measure, and largeness of mind like the sand on the seashore, so that Solomon's wisdom surpassed the wisdom of all the people of the east, and all the wisdom of Egypt. 1 Kings 4:29-30 RSV

The fear of the Lord is the beginning of wisdom: a good understanding have all they that do his commandments. Psalm 111:10 KJV

Happy is the man who finds wisdom, and the man who gets understanding . . . She [wisdom] is more precious than jewels, and nothing you desire can compare with her. Long life is in her right hand; in her left hand are riches and honour. Her ways are ways of pleasantness, and all her paths are peace. She is a tree of life to those who lay hold of her. Proverbs 3:13, 15-18 RSV

And the spirit of the Lord shall rest upon him, the spirit of wisdom and understanding, the spirit of counsel and might, the spirit of knowledge and of the fear of the Lord. Isaiah 11:2 KJV

'Every one then who hears these words of mine and does them will be like a wise man who built his house upon the rock.' Matthew 7:24 RSV

'Behold, I send you out as sheep in the midst of wolves; so be wise as serpents and innocent as doves.' Matthew 10:16 RSV

'The Son of man came eating and drinking, and they say, "Behold, a glutton and a drunkard, a friend of tax collectors and sinners!" Yet wisdom is justified by her deeds.' Matthew 11:19 RSV

And Jesus increased in wisdom and in stature, and in favour with God and man. Luke 2:52 RSV

And the lord commended the unjust steward, because he had done wisely: for the children of this world are in their generation wiser than the children of light. Luke 16:8 KJV

'Therefore, brethren, pick out from among you seven men of good repute, full of the Spirit and of wisdom, whom we may appoint to this duty.' Acts 6:3 RSV

O the depth of the riches both of the wisdom and knowledge of God! how unsearchable are his judgments, and his ways past finding out! Romans 11:33 KJV

For after that in the wisdom of God the world by wisdom knew not God, it pleased God by the foolishness of preaching to save them that believe. 1 Corinthians 1:21 KJV

He is the source of your life in Christ Jesus, whom God made our wisdom . . . 1 Corinthians 1:30 RSV

Yet I do proclaim a message of wisdom to those who are spiritually mature. But it is not the wisdom that belongs to this world or to the powers that rule this world—powers that are losing their power. The wisdom I proclaim is God's secret wisdom, which is hidden from mankind, but which he had already chosen for our glory even before the world was made. 1 Corinthians 2:6-7 GNB

To one is given through the Spirit the utterance of wisdom . . . 1 Corinthians 12:8 RSV

[Paul's prayer] That the God of our Lord Jesus Christ, the Father of glory, may give you a spirit of wisdom and of revelation in the knowledge of him . Ephesians 1:17 RSV

[Christ] in whom are hid all the treasures

of wisdom and knowledge. Colossians 2:3 RSV

If any of you lacks wisdom, let him ask God, who gives to all men generously and without reproaching, and it will be given him. James 1:5 RSV

But the wisdom from above is first pure, then peaceable, gentle, open to reason, full of mercy and good fruits, without uncertainty or insincerity. James 3:17 RSV

See also *Fool; Knowledge; Understanding.*

Witness

And I heard the voice of the Lord saying, 'Whom shall I send, and who will go for us?' Then I said, 'Here I am! Send me.' Isaiah 6:8 RSV

[Jesus to Simon, Peter and Andrew] And he said to them, 'Follow me, and I will make you fishers of men.' Matthew 4:19 RSV

Then he said to his disciples, 'The harvest is plentiful, but the labourers are few; pray therefore the Lord of the harvest to send out labourers into his harvest.' Matthew 9:37-38 RSV

'Go therefore and make disciples of all nations, baptizing them in the name of the Father and of the Son and of the Holy Spirit, teaching them to observe all that I have commanded you; and lo, I am with you always, to the close of the age.' Matthew 28:19-20 RSV

And [Jesus] said unto them, Thus it is written, and thus it behoved Christ to suffer, and to rise from the dead the third day: and that repentance and remission of sins should be preached in his name among all nations, beginning at Jerusalem. And ye are witnesses of these things. Luke 24:46-48 KJV

'But when the Counsellor comes, whom I shall send to you from the Father, even the Spirit of truth, who proceeds from the Father, he will bear witness to me; and you also are witnesses, because you have been with me from the beginning.' John 15:26-27 RSV

'But you shall receive power when the Holy Spirit has come upon you; and you shall be my witnesses in Jerusalem and in all Judea and Samaria and to the end of the earth.' Acts 1:8 RSV

[Peter and John] 'We cannot but speak of what we have seen and heard.' Acts 4:20 RSV

So we are ambassadors for Christ, God making his appeal through us. We beseech you on behalf of Christ, be reconciled to God. 2 Corinthians 5:20 RSV

[Paul asks for prayer] That utterance may be given unto me, that I may open my mouth boldly, to make known the mystery of the gospel. Ephesians 6:19 KJV

See also *Evangelists; Preaching.*

Woman

And the Lord God said, It is not good that the man should be alone; I will make him an help meet for him . . . And the Lord God caused a deep sleep to fall upon Adam, and he slept: and he took one of his ribs, and closed up the flesh instead thereof. And the rib, which the Lord God had taken from man, made he a woman, and brought her unto the man. And Adam said, This is now bone of my bones, and flesh of my flesh: she shall be called Woman, because she was taken out of Man. Genesis 2:18, 21-23 KJV

Unto the woman he said, I will greatly multiply thy sorrow and thy conception; in sorrow thou shalt bring forth children; and thy desire shall be to thy husband, and he shall rule over thee. Genesis 3:16 KJV

And Adam called his wife's name Eve; because she was the mother of all living. Genesis 3:20 KJV

There were also many women there, looking on from afar, who had followed Jesus from Galilee, ministering to him. Matthew 27:55 RSV

Now when he rose early on the first day of the week, he appeared first to Mary Magdalene, from whom he had cast out seven demons. Mark 16:9 RSV

She [Elizabeth] exclaimed with a loud cry, 'Blessed are you among women, and blessed is the fruit of your womb!' Luke 1:42 RSV

Many of the Samaritans in that town believed in Jesus because the woman had said, 'He told me everything I have ever done.' John 4:39 GNB

But I want you to understand that the head of every man is Christ, the head of a woman is her husband, and the head of Christ is God. 1 Corinthians 11:3 RSV

For man was not made from woman, but woman from man. 1 Corinthians 11:8 RSV

As in all the churches of the saints, the women should keep silence in the churches. For they are not permitted to speak, but should be subordinate, as even the law says. 1 Corinthians 14:33-34 RSV

There is neither Jew nor Greek, there is neither bond nor free, there is neither male nor female: for ye are all one in Christ Jesus. Galatians 3:28 KJV

Let a woman learn in silence with all submissiveness. I permit no woman to teach or to have authority over men; she is to keep silent . . . the woman was deceived and became a transgressor. Yet woman will be saved through bearing children, if she continues in faith and love and holiness, with modesty. 1 Timothy 2:11-12, 14-15 RSV

See also *Man.*

Word of God

See *Bible; Jesus Christ.*

Work

And the Lord God took the man, and put him into the garden of Eden to dress it and to keep it. Genesis 2:15 KJV

In the sweat of thy face shalt thou eat bread, till thou return unto the ground. Genesis 3:19 KJV

Six days shalt thou labour, and do all thy work: but the seventh day is the sabbath of the Lord thy God: in it thou shalt not do any work. Exodus 20:9-10 KJV

Man goes forth to his work and to his labour until the evening. Psalm 104:23 RSV

Except the Lord build the house, they labour in vain that build it: except the Lord keep the city, the watchman waketh but in vain. Psalm 127:1 KJV

Commit your work to the Lord, and your plans will be established. Proverbs 16:3 RSV

Whatsoever thy hand findeth to do, do it with thy might; for there is no work, nor device, nor knowledge, nor wisdom, in the grave, whither thou goest. Ecclesiastes 9:10 KJV

'For the kingdom of heaven is like a householder who went out early in the morning to hire labourers for his vineyard.' Matthew 20:1 RSV

The labourer is worthy of his hire. Luke 10:7 KJV

Slaves, obey your human masters with

fear and trembling; and do it with a sincere heart, as though you were serving Christ. Do this not only when they are watching you, because you want to gain their approval; but with all your heart do what God wants, as slaves of Christ. Do your work as slaves cheerfully, as though you served the Lord, and not merely men. Remember that the Lord will reward everyone, whether slave or free, for the good work he does. Masters, behave in the same way towards your slaves and stop using threats. Remember that you and your slaves belong to the same Master in heaven, who judges everyone by the same standard. Ephesians 6:5-9 GNB

And whatsoever ye do in word or deed, do all in the name of the Lord Jesus, giving thanks to God and the Father by him. Colossians 3:17 KJV

If any one does not provide for his relatives, and especially for his own family, he has disowned the faith and is worse than an unbeliever. 1 Timothy 5:8 RSV

The scripture says, 'You shall not muzzle an ox when it is treading out the grain,' and 'The labourer deserves his wages.' 1 Timothy 5:18 RSV

See also *Laziness*.

Works, *good*

Let your light so shine before men, that they may see your good works, and glorify your Father which is in heaven. Matthew 5:16 KJV

'Why do you call me, "Lord, Lord," and yet don't do what I tell you?' Luke 6:46 GNB

Then they said to him, 'What must we do, to be doing the works of God?' Jesus answered them, 'This is the work of God, that you believe in him whom he has sent.' John 6:28-29 RSV

'I turned first to the inhabitants of Damascus, and then to Jerusalem and all the country of Judaea, and to the Gentiles, and sounded the call to repent and turn to God, and to prove their repentance by deeds.' Acts 26:20 NEB

Therefore, my beloved brethren, be steadfast, immovable, always abounding in the work of the Lord, knowing that in the Lord your labour is not in vain. 1 Corinthians 15:58 RSV

For by grace are ye saved through faith; and that not of yourselves: it is the gift of God: not of works, lest any man should boast. For we are his workmanship, created in Christ Jesus unto good works, which God hath before ordained that we should walk in them. Ephesians 2:8-10 KJV

[The purpose of scripture] That the man of God may be complete, equipped for every good work. 2 Timothy 3:17 RSV

Let us consider how to stir up one another to love and good works. Hebrews 10:24 RSV

But be ye doers of the word, and not hearers only, deceiving your own selves. James 1:22 KJV

What does it profit, my brethren, if a man says he has faith but has not works? Can his faith save him? . . . Faith by itself, if it has no works, is dead. But some one will say, 'You have faith and I have works.' Show me your faith apart from your works, and I by my works will show you my faith. James 2:14, 17-18 RSV

You see that faith was active along with his works, and faith was completed by works, and the scripture was fulfilled which says, 'Abraham believed God, and it was reckoned to him as righteousness'; and he was called the friend of God. James 2:22 RSV

You see that a man is justified by works and not by faith alone. James 2:24 RSV

For as the body apart from the spirit is dead, so faith apart from works is dead. James 2:24, 26 RSV

See also *Service*.

World

Created universe

The earth is the Lord's and the fullness thereof, the world and those who dwell therein. Psalm 24:1 RSV

'The God who made the world and everything in it, being Lord of heaven and earth, does not live in shrines made by man.' Acts 17:24 RSV

[The Son] He is the one through whom God created the universe. Hebrews 1:2 GNB

See also *Creation*.

Man

For God so loved the world, that he gave his only begotten Son, that whosoever believeth in him should not perish, but have everlasting life. For God sent not his Son into the world to condemn the world; but that the world through him might be saved. John 3:16-17 KJV

Man rebelling against God

'If the world hates you, just remember that it has hated me first. If you belonged to the world, then the world would love you as its own. But I chose you from this world, and you do not belong to it; that is why the world hates you.' John 15:18-19 GNB

'And now I am no more in the world, but they are in the world, and I am coming to thee. Holy Father, keep them in thy name which thou hast given me, that they may be one, even as we are one.' John 17:11 RSV

They are not of the world, even as I am not of the world. John 17:16 KJV

Love not the world, neither the things that are in the world. If any man love the world, the love of the Father is not in him. For all that is in the world, the lust of the flesh, and the lust of the eyes, and the pride of life, is not of the Father, but is of the world. And the world passeth away, and the lust thereof: but he that doeth the will of God abideth for ever. 1 John 2:15-17 KJV

Worry

See *Comfort, when anxious.*

Worship

Thou shalt have no other gods before me. Thou shalt not make unto thee any graven image, or any likeness of any thing that is in heaven above, or that is in the earth beneath, or that is in the water under the earth. Exodus 20:3-4 KJV

Give unto the Lord the glory due unto his name: bring an offering, and come before him: worship the Lord in the beauty of holiness. 1 Chronicles 16:29 KJV

O come, let us worship, and fall down, and kneel before the Lord our Maker. Psalm 95:6 BCP

And when they were come into the house, they saw the young child with Mary his mother, and fell down, and worshipped him: and when they had opened their treasures, they presented unto him gifts; gold, and frankincense, and myrrh. Matthew 2:11 KJV

It is written, Thou shalt worship the Lord thy God, and him only shalt thou serve. Matthew 4:10 KJV

'But the hour is coming, and now is, when the true worshippers will worship the Father in spirit and truth, for such the Father seeks to worship him. God is spirit, and those who worship him must worship in spirit and truth.' John 4:23-24 RSV

Day after day they met as a group in the Temple, and they had their meals together in their homes, eating with glad and humble hearts, praising God, and enjoying the good will of all the people. And every day the Lord added to their group those who were being saved. Acts 2:46-47 GNB

'It is good to praise the Lord and make music to your name, O Most High.'

At the name of Jesus every knee should bow, in heaven and on earth and under the earth. Philippians 2:10 RSV

Lead a life worthy of the Lord, fully pleasing to him, bearing fruit in every good work and increasing in the knowledge of God. Colossians 1:10 RSV

Let the word of Christ dwell in you richly in all wisdom; teaching and admonishing one another in psalms and hymns and spiritual songs, singing with grace in your hearts to the Lord. And whatsoever ye do in word or deed, do all in the name of the Lord Jesus, giving thanks to God and the Father by him. Colossians 3:16-17 KJV

Thou art worthy, O Lord, to receive glory and honour and power: for thou hast created all things, and for thy pleasure they are and were created. Revelation 4:11 KJV

See also *Praise; Reverence; Service.*

Youth

Honour thy father and thy mother: that thy days may be long upon the land which the Lord thy God giveth thee. Exodus 20.12 KJV

Would you like to enjoy life? Do you want long life and happiness? Then hold back from speaking evil and from telling lies. Turn away from evil and do good; strive for peace with all your heart. Psalm 34:12-14 GNB

How can a young man keep his way pure? By guarding it according to thy word. Psalm 119:9 RSV

A foolish son brings grief to his father and bitter regrets to his mother. Proverbs 17:25 GNB

Remember now thy Creator in the days of thy youth, while the evil days come not, nor the years draw nigh, when thou shalt say, I have no pleasure in them. Ecclesiastes 12:1 KJV

Even the youths shall faint and be weary, and the young men shall utterly fall: But they that wait upon the Lord shall renew their strength. Isaiah 40:30-31 KJV

It is good for a man that he bear the yoke in his youth. Lamentations 3:27 RSV

Jesus said unto him [the rich young ruler], If thou wilt be perfect, go and sell that thou hast, and give to the poor, and thou shalt have treasure in heaven: and come and follow me. Matthew 19:21-22 KJV

And he said, A certain man had two sons: and the younger of them said to his father, Father, give me the portion of goods that falleth to me. And he divided unto them his living. And not many days after the younger son gathered all together, and took his journey into a far country, and there wasted his substance with riotous living. And when he had spent all, there arose a mighty famine in that land; and he began to be in want. And he went and joined himself to a citizen of that country; and he sent him into his fields to feed swine. And he would fain have filled his belly with the husks that the swine did eat: and no man gave unto him. And when he came to himself, he said, How many hired servants of my father's have bread enough and to spare, and I perish with hunger! I will arise and go to my father, and will say unto him, Father, I have sinned against heaven, and before thee, and am no more worthy to be called thy son: make me as one of thy hired servants. And he arose, and came to his father. But when he was yet a great way off, his father saw him, and had compassion, and ran, and fell on his neck, and kissed him. And the son said unto him, Father, I have sinned against heaven, and in thy sight, and am no more worthy to be called thy son. But the father said to his servants, Bring forth the best robe, and put it on him; and put a ring on his hand, and shoes on his feet: and bring hither the fatted calf, and kill it; and let us eat, and be merry: for this my son was dead, and is alive again; he was lost, and is found. And they began to be merry. Luke 15:11-24 KJV

Let no one despise your youth, but set the believers an example in speech and conduct, in love, in faith, in purity. 1 Timothy 4:12 RSV

Avoid the passions of youth, and strive for righteousness, faith, love, and peace, together with those who with a pure heart call out to the Lord for help. 2 Timothy 2:22 GNB

I write to you, young men, because you are strong, and the word of God abides in you, and you have overcome the evil one. 1 John 2:14 RSV

See also *Family.*

Zeal

For zeal for thy house has consumed me, and the insults of those who insult thee have fallen on me. Psalm 69:9 RSV

For I can testify about them [the Israelites] that they are zealous for God, but their zeal is not based on knowledge. Since they did not know the righteousness that comes from God and sought to establish their own, they did not submit to God's righteousness. Romans 10:2-3 NIV

Never flag in zeal, be aglow with the Spirit, serve the Lord. Romans 12:11 RSV

For necessity is laid upon me. Woe to me if I do not preach the gospel! 1 Corinthians 9:16 RSV

Therefore, my beloved brethren, be steadfast, immovable, always abounding in the work of the Lord, knowing that in the Lord your labour is not in vain. 1 Corinthians 15:58 RSV

And let us not grow weary in well-doing, for in due season we shall reap, if we do not lose heart. So then, as we have opportunity, let us do good to all men, and especially to those who are of the household of faith. Galatians 6:9 RSV

As to zeal a persecutor of the church, as to righteousness under the law blameless. But whatever gain I had, I counted as loss for the sake of Christ. Philippians 3:6-7 RSV

I press on toward the goal for the prize of the upward call of God in Christ Jesus. Philippians 3:14 RSV

[Jesus Christ] who gave himself for us to redeem us from all iniquity and to purify for himself a people of his own who are zealous for good deeds. Titus 2:14 RSV

Now that by your obedience to the truth you have purified yourselves and have come to have a sincere love for your fellow-believers, love one another earnestly with all your heart. 1 Peter 1:22 GNB

Beloved, being very eager to write to you of our common salvation, I found it necessary to write appealing to you to contend for the faith which was once for all delivered to the saints. Jude 3 RSV

'"Those whom I love, I reprove and chasten; so be zealous and repent."' Revelation 3:19 RSV

PART
2

BOOK 1

Psalm 1

Blessed is the man
  who walks not in the counsel of the wicked,
nor stands in the way of sinners,
  nor sits in the seat of scoffers;
2 but his delight is in the law of the LORD,
  and on his law he meditates day and night.
3 He is like a tree
  planted by streams of water,
that yields its fruit in its season,
  and its leaf does not wither.
In all that he does, he prospers.

4 The wicked are not so,
  but are like chaff which the wind drives away.
5 Therefore the wicked will not stand in the judgment,
  nor sinners in the congregation of the righteous;
6 for the LORD knows the way of the righteous,
  but the way of the wicked will perish.

Psalm 2

Why do the nations conspire,
  and the peoples plot in vain?
2 The kings of the earth set themselves,
  and the rulers take counsel together,
  against the LORD and his anointed, saying,
3 "Let us burst their bonds asunder, and cast their cords from us."

4 He who sits in the heavens laughs;
  the LORD has them in derision.
5 Then he will speak to them in his wrath,
  and terrify them in his fury, saying,
6 "I have set my king
  on Zion, my holy hill."

7 I will tell of the decree of the LORD:
He said to me, "You are my son,
  today I have begotten you.
8 Ask of me, and I will make the nations your heritage,
  and the ends of the earth your possession.
9 You shall break them with a rod of iron,
  and dash them in pieces like a potter's vessel."

10 Now therefore, O kings, be wise;
  be warned, O rulers of the earth.
11 Serve the LORD with fear,
  with trembling 12 kiss his feet,[a]
lest he be angry, and you perish in the way;
  for his wrath is quickly kindled.

Blessed are all who take refuge in him.

[a] Cn: The Hebrew of 11b and 12a is uncertain

Psalm 3

A Psalm of David, when he fled from Absalom his son.

O LORD, how many are my foes!
  Many are rising against me;
2 many are saying of me,
  there is no help for him in God. *Selah*

3 But thou, O LORD, art a shield about me,
  my glory, and the lifter of my head.
4 I cry aloud to the LORD,
  and he answers me from his holy hill. *Selah*

5 I lie down and sleep;
  I wake again, for the LORD sustains me.
6 I am not afraid of ten thousands of people
  who have set themselves against me round about.

7 Arise, O LORD!
  Deliver me, O my God!
For thou dost smite all my enemies on the cheek,
  thou dost break the teeth of the wicked.

8 Deliverance belongs to the LORD;
  thy blessing be upon thy people! *Selah*

Psalm 4

To the choirmaster: with stringed instruments. A Psalm of David.

Answer me when I call, O God of my right!
  Thou hast given me room when I was in distress.
  Be gracious to me, and hear my prayer.

2 O men, how long shall my honor suffer shame?
  How long will you love vain words, and seek after lies? *Selah*
3 But know that the LORD has set apart the godly for himself;
  the LORD hears when I call to him.

4 Be angry, but sin not;
  commune with your own hearts on your beds,
    and be silent. *Selah*
5 Offer right sacrifices,
  and put your trust in the LORD.

6 There are many who say, "O that we might see some good!
  Lift up the light of thy countenance upon us, O LORD!"
7 Thou hast put more joy in my heart
  than they have when their grain and wine abound.

8 In peace I will both lie down and sleep;
  for thou alone, O LORD, makest me dwell in safety.

Psalm 5

To the choirmaster: for the flutes. A Psalm of David.

Give ear to my words, O LORD;
  give heed to my groaning.
2 Hearken to the sound of my cry,
  my King and my God,
  for to thee do I pray.
3 O LORD, in the morning thou dost hear my voice;
  in the morning I prepare a sacrifice for thee, and watch.

4 For thou art not a God who delights in wickedness;
  evil may not sojourn with thee.
5 The boastful may not stand before thy eyes;
  thou hatest all evildoers.
6 Thou destroyest those who speak lies;
  the LORD abhors bloodthirsty and deceitful men.

7 But I through the abundance of thy steadfast love
  will enter thy house,
I will worship toward thy holy temple
  in the fear of thee.
8 Lead me, O LORD, in thy righteousness
  because of my enemies;
  make thy way straight before me.

9 For there is no truth in their mouth;
  their heart is destruction,
their throat is an open sepulchre,
  they flatter with their tongue.
10 Make them bear their guilt, O God;
  let them fall by their own counsels;
because of their many transgressions cast them out,
  for they have rebelled against thee.

11 But let all who take refuge in thee rejoice,
  let them ever sing for joy;
and do thou defend them,
  that those who love thy name may exult in thee.
12 For thou dost bless the righteous, O LORD;
  thou dost cover him with favor as with a shield.

Psalm 6

To the choirmaster: with stringed instruments; according to The Sheminith. A Psalm of David.

O LORD, rebuke me not in thy anger,
  nor chasten me in thy wrath.
2 Be gracious to me, O LORD, for I am languishing;
  O LORD, heal me, for my bones are troubled.
3 My soul also is sorely troubled.
  But thou, O LORD—how long?

4 Turn, O LORD, save my life;
  deliver me for the sake of thy steadfast love.
5 For in death there is no remembrance of thee;
  in Sheol who can give thee praise?

6 I am weary with my moaning;
  every night I flood my bed with tears;

I drench my couch with my weeping.
7 My eye wastes away because of grief,
it grows weak because of all my foes.

8 Depart from me, all you workers of evil;
for the LORD has heard the sound of my weeping.
9 The LORD has heard my supplication;
the LORD accepts my prayer.
10 All my enemies shall be ashamed and sorely troubled;
they shall turn back, and be put to shame in a moment.

Psalm 7

A Shiggaion of David, which he sang to the LORD concerning Cush a Benjaminite.

O LORD my God, in thee do I take refuge;
save me from all my pursuers, and deliver me,
2 lest like a lion they rend me,
dragging me away, with none to rescue.

3 O LORD my God, if I have done this,
if there is wrong in my hands,
4 if I have requited my friend with evil
or plundered my enemy without cause,
5 let the enemy pursue me and overtake me,
and let him trample my life to the ground,
and lay my soul in the dust. *Selah*

6 Arise, O LORD, in thy anger,
lift thyself up against the fury of my enemies;
awake, O my God;*b* thou hast appointed a judgment.
7 Let the assembly of the peoples be gathered about thee;
and over it take thy seat*c* on high.

b Or for me

c Cn: Heb return

8 The LORD judges the peoples;
judge me, O LORD, according to my righteousness
and according to the integrity that is in me.

9 O let the evil of the wicked come to an end,
but establish thou the righteous,
thou who triest the minds and hearts,
thou righteous God.
10 My shield is with God,
who saves the upright in heart.
11 God is a righteous judge,
and a God who has indignation every day.

d Heb he

12 If a man *d* does not repent, God*d* will whet his sword;
he has bent and strung his bow;
13 he has prepared his deadly weapons,
making his arrows fiery shafts.
14 Behold, the wicked man conceives evil,
and is pregnant with mischief,
and brings forth lies.
15 He makes a pit, digging it out,
and falls into the hole which he has made.
16 His mischief returns upon his own head,
and on his own pate his violence descends.

17 I will give to the LORD the thanks due to his righteousness,
and I will sing praise to the name of the LORD, the Most High.

Psalm 8

To the choirmaster: according to The Gittith. A Psalm of David.

O LORD, our Lord,
how majestic is thy name in all the earth!

Thou whose glory above the heavens is chanted
2   by the mouth of babes and infants,
thou hast founded a bulwark because of thy foes,
to still the enemy and the avenger.

3 When I look at thy heavens, the work of thy fingers,
the moon and the stars which thou hast established;
4 what is man that thou art mindful of him,
and the son of man that thou dost care for him?
5 Yet thou has made him little less than God,
and dost crown him with glory and honor.
6 Thou hast given him dominion over the works of thy hands;
thou hast put all things under his feet,
7 all sheep and oxen.

and also the beasts of the field,
8 the birds of the air, and the fish of the sea,
  whatever passes along the paths of the sea.

9 O LORD, our Lord,
  how majestic is thy name in all the earth!

Psalm 9

To the choirmaster: according to Muth-labben. A Psalm of David.

I will give thanks to the LORD with my whole heart;
I will tell of all thy wonderful deeds.
2 I will be glad and exult in thee,
  I will sing praise to thy name, O Most High.

3 When my enemies turned back,
  they stumbled and perished before thee.
4 For thou hast maintained my just cause;
  thou hast sat on the throne giving righteous judgment.
5 Thou hast rebuked the nations, thou hast destroyed the wicked;
  thou hast blotted out their name for ever and ever.
6 The enemy have vanished in everlasting ruins;
  their cities thou hast rooted out;
  the very memory of them has perished.

7 But the LORD sits enthroned for ever,
  he has established his throne for judgment;
8 and he judges the world with righteousness,
  he judges the peoples with equity.

9 The LORD is a stronghold for the oppressed,
  a stronghold in times of trouble.
10 And those who know thy name put their trust in thee,
  for thou, O LORD, hast not forsaken those who seek thee.

11 Sing praises to the LORD, who dwells in Zion!
  Tell among the peoples his deeds!
12 For he who avenges blood is mindful of them;
  he does not forget the cry of the afflicted.

13 Be gracious to me, O LORD!
  Behold what I suffer from those who hate me,
  O thou who liftest me up from the gates of death,
14 that I may recount all thy praises,
  that in the gates of the daughter of Zion
  I may rejoice in thy deliverance.

15 The nations have sunk in the pit which they made;
  in the net which they hid has their own foot been caught.
16 The LORD has made himself known, he has executed judgment;
  the wicked are snared in the work of their own hands.
    Higgaion. Selah

17 The wicked shall depart to Sheol,
  all the nations that forget God.

18 For the needy shall not always be forgotten,
  and the hope of the poor shall not perish for ever.
19 Arise, O LORD! Let not man prevail;
  let the nations be judged before thee!
20 Put them in fear, O LORD!
  Let the nations know that they are but men! *Selah*

Psalm 10

Why dost thou stand afar off, O LORD?
  Why dost thou hide thyself in times of trouble?
2 In arrogance the wicked hotly pursue the poor;
  let them be caught in the schemes which they have devised.

3 For the wicked boasts of the desires of his heart,
  and the man greedy for gain curses and renounces the LORD.
4 In the pride of his countenance the wicked does not seek him;
  all his thoughts are, "There is no God."

5 His ways prosper at all times;
  thy judgments are on high, out of his sight;
  as for all his foes, he puffs at them.
6 He thinks in his heart, "I shall not be moved;
  throughout all generations I shall not meet adversity."

7 His mouth is filled with cursing and deceit and oppression;

under his tongue are mischief and iniquity.
8 He sits in ambush in the villages;
  in hiding places he murders the innocent.

His eyes stealthily watch for the hapless,
9   he lurks in secret like a lion in his covert;
he lurks that he may seize the poor,
  he seizes the poor when he draws him into his net.

10 The hapless is crushed, sinks down,
   and falls by his might.
11 He thinks in his heart, "God has forgotten,
   he has hidden his face, he will never see it."

12 Arise, O LORD; O God, lift up thy hand;
   forget not the afflicted.
13 Why does the wicked renounce God,
   and say in his heart, "Thou wilt not call to account"?

14 Thou dost see; yea, thou dost note trouble and vexation,
   that thou mayst take it into thy hands;
the hapless commits himself to thee;
   thou hast been the helper of the fatherless.

15 Break thou the arm of the wicked and evildoer;
   seek out his wickedness till thou find none.
16 The LORD is king for ever and ever;
   the nations shall perish from his land.

17 O LORD, thou wilt hear the desire of the meek;
   thou wilt strengthen their heart, thou wilt incline thy ear
18 to do justice to the fatherless and the oppressed,
   so that man who is of the earth may strike terror no more.

Psalm 11

To the
choirmaster.
Of David.

e Gk Syr Jerome
Tg: Heb *flee to
your mountain, O
bird*

In the LORD I take refuge; how can you say to me,
  "Flee like a bird to the mountains;*e*
2 for lo, the wicked bend the bow,
  they have fitted their arrow to the string,
  to shoot in the dark at the upright in heart;
3 if the foundations are destroyed,
  what can the righteous do"?

4 The LORD is in his holy temple,
  the LORD's throne is in heaven;
  his eyes behold, his eyelids test, the children of men.
5 The LORD tests the righteous and the wicked,
  and his soul hates him that loves violence.
6 On the wicked he will rain coals of fire and brimstone;
  a scorching wind shall be the portion of their cup.
7 For the LORD is righteous, he loves righteous deeds;
  the upright shall behold his face.

Psalm 12

To the
choirmaster:
according to
The Sheminith.
A Psalm of
David.

Help, LORD; for there is no longer any that is godly;
  for the faithful have vanished from among the sons of men.
2 Every one utters lies to his neighbor;
  with flattering lips and a double heart they speak.

3 May the LORD cut off all flattering lips,
  the tongue that makes great boasts,
4 those who say, "With our tongue we will prevail,
  our lips are with us; who is our master?"

5 "Because the poor are despoiled, because the needy groan,
  I will now arise," says the LORD;
  "I will place him in the safety for which he longs."
6 The promises of the LORD are promises that are pure,
  silver refined in a furnace on the ground,
  purified seven times.

7 Do thou, O LORD, protect us,
  guard us ever from this generation.
8 On every side the wicked prowl,
  as vileness is exalted among the sons of men.

Psalm 13

To the choirmaster. A Psalm of David.

f Syr: Heb *hold counsels*

How long, O Lord? Wilt thou forget me for ever?
  How long wilt thou hide thy face from me?
2 How long must I bear pain*f* in my soul,
  and have sorrow in my heart all the day?
How long shall my enemy be exalted over me?

3 Consider and answer me, O Lord my God;
  lighten my eyes, lest I sleep the sleep of death;
4 lest my enemy say, "I have prevailed over him";
  lest my foes rejoice because I am shaken.

5 But I have trusted in thy steadfast love;
  my heart shall rejoice in thy salvation.
6 I will sing to the Lord,
  because he has dealt bountifully with me.

Psalm 14

To the choirmaster. Of David.

The fool says in his heart, "There is no God."
  They are corrupt, they do abominable deeds,
    there is none that does good.
2 The Lord looks down from heaven upon the children of men,
  to see if there are any that act wisely,
    that seek after God.

3 They have all gone astray, they are all alike corrupt;
  there is none that does good,
    no, not one.

4 Have they no knowledge, all the evildoers
  who eat up my people as they eat bread,
    and do not call upon the Lord?
5 There they shall be in great terror,
  for God is with the generation of the righteous.
6 You would confound the plans of the poor,
  but the Lord is his refuge.

7 O that deliverance for Israel would come out of Zion!
  When the Lord restores the fortunes of his people,
    Jacob shall rejoice, Israel shall be glad.

Psalm 15

A Psalm of David.

O Lord, who shall sojourn in thy tent?
  Who shall dwell on thy holy hill?

2 He who walks blamelessly, and does what is right,
  and speaks truth from his heart;
3 who does not slander with his tongue,
  and does no evil to his friend,
    nor takes up a reproach against his neighbor;
4 in whose eyes a reprobate is despised,
  but who honors those who fear the Lord;

who swears to his own hurt and does not change;
5 who does not put out his money at interest,
  and does not take a bribe against the innocent.

He who does these things shall never be moved.

Psalm 16

A Miktam of David.

g Jerome Tg: The meaning of the Hebrew is uncertain
h Cn: The meaning of the Hebrew is uncertain

Preserve me, O God, for in thee I take refuge.
2   I say to the Lord, "Thou art my Lord;
  I have no good apart from thee."*g*

3 As for the saints in the land, they are the noble,
  in whom is all my delight.

4 Those who choose another god multiply their sorrows; *h*
  their libations of blood I will not pour out
    or take their names upon my lips.

5 The Lord is my chosen portion and my cup;
  thou holdest my lot.
6 The lines have fallen for me in pleasant places;
  yea, I have a goodly heritage.

7 I bless the Lord who gives me counsel;
  in the night also my heart instructs me.
8 I keep the Lord always before me;
  because he is at my right hand, I shall not be moved.

9 Therefore my heart is glad, and my soul rejoices;
   my body also dwells secure.
10 For thou dost not give me up to Sheol,
   or let thy godly one see the Pit.
11 Thou dost show me the path of life;
   in thy presence there is fulness of joy,
   in thy right hand are pleasures for evermore.

Psalm 17

A Prayer of
David.

Hear a just cause, O LORD; attend to my cry!
   Give ear to my prayer from lips free of deceit!
2 From thee let my vindication come!
   Let thy eyes see the right!
3 If thou triest my heart, if thou visitest me by night,
   if thou testest me, thou wilt find no wickedness in me;
   my mouth does not transgress.
4 With regard to the works of men, by the word of thy lips
   I have avoided the ways of the violent.
5 My steps have held fast to thy paths,
   my feet have not slipped.
6 I call upon thee, for thou wilt answer me, O God;
   incline thy ear to me, hear my words.
7 Wondrously show thy steadfast love,
   O savior of those who seek refuge
   from their adversaries at thy right hand.
8 Keep me as the apple of the eye;
   hide me in the shadow of thy wings,
9 from the wicked who despoil me,
   my deadly enemies who surround me.
10 They close their hearts to pity;
   with their mouths they speak arrogantly.
11 They track me down; now they surround me;
   they set their eyes to cast me to the ground.
12 They are like a lion eager to tear,
   as a young lion lurking in ambush.
13 Arise, O LORD! confront them, overthrow them!
   Deliver my life from the wicked by thy sword,
14 from men by thy hand, O LORD,
   from men whose portion in life is of the world.
May their belly be filled with what thou hast stored up for them;
   may their children have more than enough;
   may they leave something over to their babes.
15 As for me, I shall behold thy face in righteousness;
   when I awake, I shall be satisfied with beholding thy form.

Psalm 18

To the
choirmaster.
A Psalm of
David the
servant of the
LORD, who
addressed the
words of this
song to the LORD
on the day
when the LORD
delivered him
from the hand
of all his
enemies, and
from the hand
of Saul. He
said:

I love thee, O LORD, my strength.
2 The LORD is my rock, and my fortress, and my deliverer,
   my God, my rock, in whom I take refuge,
   my shield, and the horn of my salvation, my stronghold.
3 I call upon the LORD, who is worthy to be praised,
   and I am saved from my enemies.
4 The cords of death encompassed me,
   the torrents of perdition assailed me;
5 the cords of Sheol entangled me,
   the snares of death confronted me.
6 In my distress I called upon the LORD;
   to my God I cried for help.
From his temple he heard my voice,
   and my cry to him reached his ears.
7 Then the earth reeled and rocked;
   the foundations also of the mountains trembled
   and quaked, because he was angry.
8 Smoke went up from his nostrils,
   and devouring fire from his mouth;
   glowing coals flamed forth from him.
9 He bowed the heavens, and came down;

thick darkness was under his feet.
10 He rode on a cherub, and flew;
   he came swiftly upon the wings of the wind.
11 He made darkness his covering around him,
   his canopy thick clouds dark with water.
12 Out of the brightness before him
   there broke through his clouds
   hailstones and coals of fire.
13 The LORD also thundered in the heavens,
   and the Most High uttered his voice,
   hailstones and coals of fire.
14 And he sent out his arrows, and scattered them;
   he flashed forth lightnings, and routed them.
15 Then the channels of the sea were seen,
   and the foundations of the world were laid bare,
at thy rebuke, O LORD,
   at the blast of the breath of thy nostrils.

16 He reached from on high, he took me,
   he drew me out of many waters.
17 He delivered me from my strong enemy,
   and from those who hated me;
   for they were too mighty for me.
18 They came upon me in the day of my calamity;
   but the LORD was my stay.
19 He brought me forth into a broad place;
   he delivered me, because he delighted in me.

20 The LORD rewarded me according to my righteousness;
   according to the cleanness of my hands he recompensed me.
21 For I have kept the ways of the LORD,
   and have not wickedly departed from my God.
22 For all his ordinances were before me,
   and his statutes I did not put away from me.
23 I was blameless before him,
   and I kept myself from guilt.
24 Therefore the LORD has recompensed me according to my
      righteousness,
   according to the cleanness of my hands in his sight.

25 With the loyal thou dost show thyself loyal;
   with the blameless man thou dost show thyself blameless;
26 with the pure thou dost show thyself pure;
   and with the crooked thou dost show thyself perverse.
27 For thou dost deliver a humble people;
   but the haughty eyes thou dost bring down.
28 Yea, thou dost light my lamp;
   the LORD my God lightens my darkness.
29 Yea, by thee I can crush a troop;
   and by my God I can leap over a wall.
30 This God—his way is perfect;
   the promise of the LORD proves true;
   he is a shield for all those who take refuge in him.

31 For who is God, but the LORD?
   And who is a rock, except our God?—
32 the God who girded me with strength,
   and made my way safe.
33 He made my feet like hinds' feet,
   and set me secure on the heights.
34 He trains my hands for war,
   so that my arms can bend a bow of bronze.
35 Thou hast given me the shield of thy salvation,
   and thy right hand supported me,
Or gentleness   and thy help*f* made me great.
36 Thou didst give a wide place for my steps under me,
   and my feet did not slip.
37 I pursued my enemies and overtook them;
   and did not turn back till they were consumed.
38 I thrust them through, so that they were not able to rise;
   they fell under my feet.

39 For thou didst gird me with strength for the battle;
  thou didst make my assailants sink under me.
40 Thou didst make my enemies turn their backs to me,
  and those who hated me I destroyed.
41 They cried for help, but there was none to save,
  they cried to the LORD, but he did not answer them.
42 I beat them fine as dust before the wind;
  I cast them out like the mire of the streets.

j Gk Tg: Heb
people

43 Thou didst deliver me from strife with the peoples;*j*
  thou didst make me the head of the nations;
  people whom I had not known served me.
44 As soon as they heard of me they obeyed me;
  foreigners came cringing to me.
45 Foreigners lost heart,
  and came trembling out of their fastnesses.

46 The LORD lives; and blessed be my rock,
  and exalted be the God of my salvation,
47 the God who gave me vengeance
  and subdued peoples under me;
48 who delivered me from my enemies;
  yea, thou didst exalt me above my adversaries;
  thou didst deliver me from men of violence.

49 For this I will extol thee, O LORD, among the nations,
  and sing praises to thy name.
50 Great triumphs he gives to his king,
  and shows steadfast love to his anointed,
  to David and his descendants for ever.

Psalm 19

To the
choirmaster.
A Psalm of
David.

k Gk Jerome
Compare Syr:
Heb *line*

The heavens are telling the glory of God;
  and the firmament proclaims his handiwork.
2 Day to day pours forth speech,
  and night to night declares knowledge.
3 There is no speech, nor are there words;
  their voice is not heard;
4 yet their voice*k* goes out through all the earth,
  and their words to the end of the world.

 In them he has set a tent for the sun,
5 which comes forth like a bridegroom leaving his chamber,
  and like a strong man runs its course with joy.
6 Its rising is from the end of the heavens,
  and its circuit to the end of them;
  and there is nothing hid from its heat.

7 The law of the LORD is perfect,
  reviving the soul;
the testimony of the LORD is sure,
  making wise the simple;
8 the precepts of the LORD are right,
  rejoicing the heart;
the commandment of the LORD is pure,
  enlightening the eyes;
9 the fear of the LORD is clean,
  enduring for ever;
the ordinances of the LORD are true,
  and righteous altogether.
10 More to be desired are they than gold,
  even much fine gold;
sweeter also than honey
  and drippings of the honeycomb.

11 Moreover by them is thy servant warned;
  in keeping them there is great reward.
12 But who can discern his errors?
  Clear thou me from hidden faults.
13 Keep back thy servant also from presumptuous sins;
  let them not have dominion over me!
Then I shall be blameless,
  and innocent of great transgression.

14 Let the words of my mouth and the meditation of my heart
   be acceptable in thy sight,
O LORD, my rock and my redeemer.

Psalm 20

To the
choirmaster.
A Psalm of
David.

The LORD answer you in the day of trouble!
   The name of the God of Jacob protect you!
2 May he send you help from the sanctuary,
   and give you support from Zion!
3 May he remember all your offerings,
   and regard with favor your burnt sacrifices! *Selah*
4 May he grant you your heart's desire,
   and fulfil all your plans!
5 May we shout for joy over your victory,
   and in the name of our God set up our banners!
May the LORD fulfil all your petitions!
6 Now I know that the LORD will help his anointed;
   he will answer him from his holy heaven
   with mighty victories by his right hand.
7 Some boast of chariots, and some of horses;
   but we boast of the name of the LORD our God.
8 They will collapse and fall;
   but we shall rise and stand upright.
9 Give victory to the king, O LORD;
   answer us when we call.[1]

*[1] Gk: Heb give
victory, O LORD, let
the King answer
us when we call*

Psalm 21

To the
choirmaster.
A Psalm of
David.

In thy strength the king rejoices, O LORD;
   and in thy help how greatly he exults!
2 Thou hast given him his heart's desire,
   and hast not withheld the request of his lips. *Selah*
3 For thou dost meet him with goodly blessings;
   thou dost set a crown of fine gold upon his head.
4 He asked life of thee; thou gavest it to him,
   length of days for ever and ever.
5 His glory is great through thy help;
   splendor and majesty thou dost bestow upon him.
6 Yea, thou dost make him most blessed for ever;
   thou dost make him glad with the joy of thy presence.
7 For the king trusts in the LORD;
   and through the steadfast love of the Most High he shall not be
      moved.
8 Your hand will find out all your enemies;
   your right hand will find out those who hate you.
9 You will make them as a blazing oven
   when you appear.
The LORD will swallow them up in his wrath;
   and fire will consume them.
10 You will destroy their offspring from the earth,
   and their children from among the sons of men.
11 If they plan evil against you,
   if they devise mischief, they will not succeed.
12 For you will put them to flight;
   you will aim at their faces with your bows.
13 Be exalted, O LORD, in thy strength!
   We will sing and praise thy power.

Psalm 22

To the
choirmaster:
according to
The Hind of the
Dawn. A Psalm
of David.

My God, my God, why hast thou forsaken me?
   Why art thou so far from helping me, from the words of my
      groaning?
2 O my God, I cry by day, but thou dost not answer;
   and by night, but find no rest.
3 Yet thou art holy,
   enthroned on the praises of Israel.
4 In thee our fathers trusted;
   they trusted, and thou didst deliver them.
5 To thee they cried, and were saved;
   in thee they trusted, and were not disappointed.

6 But I am a worm, and no man;
    scorned by men, and despised by the people.
7 All who see me mock at me,
    they make mouths at me, they wag their heads;
8 "He committed his cause to the LORD; let him deliver him,
    let him rescue him, for he delights in him!"

9 Yet thou art he who took me from the womb;
    thou didst keep me safe upon my mother's breasts.
10 Upon thee was I cast from my birth,
    and since my mother bore me thou hast been my God.
11 Be not far from me,
    for trouble is near
    and there is none to help.
12 Many bulls encompass me,
    strong bulls of Bashan surround me;
13 they open wide their mouths at me,
    like a ravening and roaring lion.

14 I am poured out like water,
    and all my bones are out of joint;
my heart is like wax,
    it is melted within my breast;
15 my strength is dried up like a potsherd,
    and my tongue cleaves to my jaws;
    thou dost lay me in the dust of death.

16 Yea, dogs are round about me;
    a company of evildoers encircle me;
    they have pierced*m* my hands and feet—

m Gk Syr Jerome: Heb *like a lion*

17 I can count all my bones—
    they stare and gloat over me;
18 they divide my garments among them,
    and for my raiment they cast lots.

19 But thou, O LORD, be not far off!
    O thou my help, hasten to my aid!
20 Deliver my soul from the sword,
    my life*n* from the power of the dog!

n Heb *my only one*

21 Save me from the mouth of the lion,
    my afflicted soul*o* from the horns of the wild oxen!

o Gk Syr: Heb *thou hast answered me*

22 I will tell of thy name to my brethren;
    in the midst of the congregation I will praise thee:
23 You who fear the LORD, praise him!
    all you sons of Jacob, glorify him,
    and stand in awe of him, all you sons of Israel!
24 For he has not despised or abhorred
    the affliction of the afflicted;
and he has not hid his face from him,
    but has heard, when he cried to him.

25 From thee comes my praise in the great congregation;
    my vows I will pay before those who fear him.

p Or *poor*

26 The afflicted*p* shall eat and be satisfied;
    those who seek him shall praise the LORD!
    May your hearts live for ever!

27 All the ends of the earth shall remember
    and turn to the LORD;

q Gk Syr Jerome: Heb *thee*

and all the families of the nations shall worship before him.*q*
28 For dominion belongs to the LORD,
    and he rules over the nations.

r Cn: Heb *they have eaten and*

29 Yea, to him*r* shall all the proud of the earth bow down;
    before him shall bow all who go down to the dust,
    and he who cannot keep himself alive.
30 Posterity shall serve him;
    men shall tell of the Lord to the coming generation,
31 and proclaim his deliverance to a people yet unborn,
    that he has wrought it.

Psalm 23

A Psalm of David.

The LORD is my shepherd, I shall not want;
2 he makes me lie down in green pastures.
He leads me beside still waters;[s]
3 he restores my soul.[t]
He leads me in paths of righteousness[u]
for his name's sake.

4 Even though I walk through the valley of the shadow of death,[v]
I fear no evil;
for thou art with me;
thy rod and thy staff,
they comfort me.

5 Thou preparest a table before me
in the presence of my enemies;
thou anointest my head with oil,
my cup overflows.
6 Surely[w] goodness and mercy[x] shall follow me
all the days of my life;
and I shall dwell in the house of the LORD
for ever.[y]

[s]Heb *the waters of rest*
[t]Or *life*
[u]Or *right paths*
[v]Or *the valley of deep darkness*
[w]Or *only*
[x]Or *kindness*
[y]Or *as long as I live*

Psalm 24

A Psalm of David.

The earth is the LORD's and the fulness thereof,
the world and those who dwell therein;
2 for he has founded it upon the seas,
and established it upon the rivers.

3 Who shall ascend the hill of the LORD?
And who shall stand in his holy place?
4 He who has clean hands and a pure heart,
who does not lift up his soul to what is false,
and does not swear deceitfully.
5 He will receive blessing from the LORD,
and vindication from the God of his salvation.
6 Such is the generation of those who seek him,
who seek the face of the God of Jacob.[z] *Selah*
7 Lift up your heads, O gates!
and be lifted up, O ancient doors!
that the King of glory may come in.
8 Who is the King of glory?
The LORD, strong and mighty,
the LORD, mighty in battle!
9 Lift up your heads, O gates!
and be lifted up,[a] O ancient doors!
that the King of glory may come in.
10 Who is this King of glory?
the LORD of hosts,
he is the King of glory! *Selah*

[z]Gk Syr: Heb *thy face, O Jacob*
[a]Gk Syr Jerome Tg Compare verse 7: Heb *lift up*

Psalm 25

A Psalm of David.

To thee, O LORD, I lift up my soul.
2 O my God, in thee I trust,
let me not be put to shame;
let not my enemies exult over me.
3 Yea, let none that wait for thee be put to shame;
let them be ashamed who are wantonly treacherous.

4 Make me to know thy ways, O LORD;
teach me thy paths.
5 Lead me in thy truth, and teach me,
for thou art the God of my salvation;
for thee I wait all the day long.

6 Be mindful of thy mercy, O LORD, and of thy steadfast love,
for they have been from of old.
7 Remember not the sins of my youth, or my transgressions;
according to thy steadfast love remember me,
for thy goodness' sake, O LORD!
8 Good and upright is the LORD;
therefore he instructs sinners in the way.
9 He leads the humble in what is right,
and teaches the humble his way.
10 All the paths of the LORD are steadfast love and faithfulness,
for those who keep his covenant and his testimonies.

11 For thy name's sake, O LORD,
    pardon my guilt, for it is great.
12 Who is the man that fears the LORD?
    Him will he instruct in the way that he should choose.
13 He himself shall abide in prosperity,
    and his children shall possess the land.
14 The friendship of the LORD is for those who fear him,
    and he makes known to them his covenant.
15 My eyes are ever toward the LORD,
    for he will pluck my feet out of the net.

16 Turn thou to me, and be gracious to me;
    for I am lonely and afflicted.
17 Relieve the troubles of my heart,
    and bring me*b* out of my distresses.

b Or The troubles of my heart are enlarged; bring me

18 Consider my affliction and my trouble,
    and forgive all my sins.
19 Consider how many are my foes,
    and with what violent hatred they hate me.
20 Oh guard my life, and deliver me;
    let me not be put to shame, for I take refuge in thee.
21 May integrity and uprightness preserve me,
    for I wait for thee.

22 Redeem Israel, O God,
    out of all his troubles.

Psalm 26

A Psalm of David.

Vindicate me, O LORD, for I have walked in my integrity,
    and I have trusted in the LORD without wavering.
2 Prove me, O LORD, and try me;
    test my heart and my mind.
3 For thy steadfast love is before my eyes,
    and I walk in faithfulness to thee.*c*

c Or in thy faithfulness

4 I do not sit with false men,
    nor do I consort with dissemblers;
5 I hate the company of evildoers,
    and I will not sit with the wicked.
6 I wash my hands in innocence,
    and go about thy altar, O LORD,
7 singing aloud a song of thanksgiving,
    and telling all thy wondrous deeds.
8 O LORD, I love the habitation of thy house,
    and the place where thy glory dwells.
9 Sweep me not away with sinners,
    nor my life with bloodthirsty men,
10 men in whose hands are evil devices,
    and whose right hands are full of bribes.
11 But as for me, I walk in my integrity;
    redeem me, and be gracious to me.
12 My foot stands on level ground;
    in the great congregation I will bless the LORD.

Psalm 27

A Psalm of David.

The LORD is my light and my salvation;
    whom shall I fear?
The LORD is the stronghold*d* of my life;
    of whom shall I be afraid?
2 When evildoers assail me,
    uttering slanders against me,*e*
my adversaries and foes,
    they shall stumble and fall.

d Or refuge
e Heb to eat up my flesh

3 Though a host encamp against me,
    my heart shall not fear;
though war arise against me,
    yet I will be confident.
4 One thing have I asked of the LORD,
    that will I seek after;
that I may dwell in the house of the LORD
    all the days of my life,

to behold the beauty of the LORD,
and to inquire in his temple.

5 For he will hide me in his shelter
in the day of trouble;
he will conceal me under the cover of his tent,
he will set me high upon a rock.

6 And now my head shall be lifted
up above my enemies round about me;
and I will offer in his tent
sacrifices with shouts of joy;
I will sing and make melody to the LORD.

7 Hear, O LORD, when I cry aloud,
be gracious to me and answer me!
8 Thou hast said, "Seek ye my face."
My heart says to thee,
"Thy face, LORD, do I seek."
9   Hide not thy face from me.

Turn not thy servant away in anger,
thou who hast been my help.
Cast me not off, forsake me not,
O God of my salvation!
10 For my father and my mother have forsaken me,
but the LORD will take me up.

11 Teach me thy way, O LORD;
and lead me on a level path
because of my enemies.
12 Give me not up to the will of my adversaries;
for false witnesses have risen against me,
and they breathe out violence.

13 I believe that I shall see the goodness of the LORD
in the land of the living!
14 Wait for the LORD;
be strong, and let your heart take courage;
yea, wait for the LORD!

Psalm 28

A Psalm of
David.

ᶠHeb *thy
innermost
sanctuary*

To thee, O LORD, I call;
my rock, be not deaf to me,
lest, if thou be silent to me,
I become like those who go down to the Pit.
2 Hear the voice of my supplication,
as I cry to thee for help,
as I lift up my hands
toward thy most holy sanctuary.ᶠ

3 Take me not off with the wicked,
with those who are workers of evil,
who speak peace with their neighbors,
while mischief is in their hearts.
4 Requite them according to their work,
and according to the evil of their deeds;
requite them according to the work of their hands;
render them their due reward.
5 Because they do not regard the works of the LORD,
or the work of his hands,
he will break them down and build them up no more.

6 Blessed be the LORD!
for he has heard the voice of my supplications.
7 The LORD is my strength and my shield;
in him my heart trusts;
so I am helped, and my heart exults,
and with my song I give thanks to him.

8 The LORD is the strength of his people,
he is the saving refuge of his anointed.
9 O save thy people, and bless thy heritage;
be thou their shepherd, and carry them for ever.

Psalm 29

A Psalm of David.

g Heb *sons of gods*

h Or *makes the hinds to calve*

Ascribe to the LORD, O heavenly beings,*g*
  ascribe to the LORD glory and strength.
2 Ascribe to the LORD the glory of his name;
  worship the LORD in holy array.

3 The voice of the LORD is upon the waters;
  the God of glory thunders,
  the LORD, upon many waters.
4 The voice of the LORD is powerful,
  the voice of the LORD is full of majesty.
5 The voice of the LORD breaks the cedars,
  the LORD breaks the cedars of Lebanon.
6 He makes Lebanon to skip like a calf,
  and Sir'ion like a young wild ox.

7 The voice of the LORD flashes forth flames of fire.
8 The voice of the LORD shakes the wilderness,
  the LORD shakes the wilderness of Kadesh.
9 The voice of the LORD makes the oaks to whirl, *h*
  and strips the forests bare;
  and in his temple all cry, "Glory!"

10 The LORD sits enthroned over the flood;
  the LORD sits enthroned as king for ever.
11 May the LORD give strength to his people!
  May the LORD bless his people with peace!

Psalm 30

A Psalm of David. A Song at the dedication of the Temple.

i Or *that I should not go down to the Pit*

j Heb *that glory*

I will extol thee, O LORD, for thou hast drawn me up,
  and hast not let my foes rejoice over me.
2 O LORD my God, I cried to thee for help,
  and thou hast healed me.
3 O LORD, thou hast brought up my soul from Sheol,
  restored me to life from among those gone down to the Pit.*i*
4 Sing praises to the LORD, O you his saints,
  and give thanks to his holy name.
5 For his anger is but for a moment,
  and his favor is for a lifetime.
Weeping may tarry for the night,
  but joy comes with the morning.

6 As for me, I said in my prosperity,
  "I shall never be moved."
7 By thy favor, O LORD,
  thou hadst established me as a strong mountain;
thou didst hide thy face,
  I was dismayed.

8 To thee, O LORD, I cried;
  and to the LORD I made supplication:
9 "What profit is there in my death,
  if I go down to the Pit?
Will the dust praise thee?
  Will it tell of thy faithfulness?
10 Hear, O LORD, and be gracious to me!
  O LORD, be thou my helper!"

11 Thou hast turned for me my mourning into dancing;
  thou hast loosed my sackcloth
  and girded me with gladness,
12 that my soul*j* may praise thee and not be silent.
  O LORD my God, I will give thanks to thee for ever.

Psalm 31

To the choirmaster. A Psalm of David.

In thee, O LORD, do I seek refuge;
  let me never be put to shame;
  in thy righteousness deliver me!
2 Incline thy ear to me,
  rescue me speedily!
Be thou a rock of refuge for me,
  a strong fortress to save me!

3 Yea, thou art my rock and my fortress;
  for thy name's sake lead me and guide me,
4 take me out of the net which is hidden for me,

for thou art my refuge.
5 Into thy hand I commit my spirit;
thou hast redeemed me, O LORD, faithful God.

*With one Heb
Ms Gk Syr
Jerome: Heb
I hate

6 Thou hatest[k] those who pay regard to vain idols;
but I trust in the LORD.
7 I will rejoice and be glad for thy steadfast love,
because thou hast seen my affliction,
thou hast taken heed of my adversities,
8 and hast not delivered me into the hand of the enemy;
thou hast set my feet in a broad place.

9 Be gracious to me, O LORD, for I am in distress;
my eye is wasted from grief,
my soul and my body also.
10 For my life is spent with sorrow
and my years with sighing;

*Gk Syr: Heb
iniquity*

my strength fails because of my misery,[l]
and my bones waste away.

*Cn: Heb
exceedingly*

11 I am the scorn of all my adversaries,
a horror[m] to my neighbors,
an object of dread to my acquaintances;
those who see me in the street flee from me.
12 I have passed out of mind like one who is dead;
I have become like a broken vessel.

13 Yea, I hear the whispering of many—
terror on every side!—
as they scheme together against me,
as they plot to take my life.

14 But I trust in thee, O LORD,
I say, "Thou art my God."
15 My times are in thy hand;
deliver me from the hand of my enemies and persecutors!
16 Let thy face shine on thy servant;
save me in thy steadfast love!
17 Let me not be put to shame, O LORD,
for I call on thee;
let the wicked be put to shame,
let them go dumbfounded to Sheol.
18 Let the lying lips be dumb,
which speak insolently against the righteous
in pride and contempt.

19 O how abundant is thy goodness,
which thou hast laid up for those who fear thee,
and wrought for those who take refuge in thee,
in the sight of the sons of men!
20 In the covert of thy presence thou hidest them
from the plots of men;
thou holdest them safe under thy shelter
from the strife of tongues.

21 Blessed be the LORD,
for he has wondrously shown his steadfast love to me
when I was beset as in a besieged city.
22 I had said in my alarm,

*Another reading
is cut off*

"I am driven far[n] from thy sight."
But thou didst hear my supplications,
when I cried to thee for help.

23 Love the LORD, all you his saints!
The LORD preserves the faithful,
but abundantly requires him who acts haughtily.
24 Be strong, and let your heart take courage,
all you who wait for the LORD!

Psalm 32

A Psalm of
David. A Maskil.

Blessed is he whose transgression is forgiven,
whose sin is covered.
2 Blessed is the man to whom the LORD imputes no iniquity,
and in whose spirit there is no deceit.
3 When I declared not my sin, my body wasted away
through my groaning all day long.

4 For day and night thy hand was heavy upon me;
    my strength was dried up[o] as by the heat of summer. *Selah*

o Heb obscure

5 I acknowledged my sin to thee,
    and I did not hide my iniquity;
I said, "I will confess my transgressions to the LORD";
    then thou didst forgive the guilt of my sin. *Selah*

6 Therefore let every one who is godly
    offer prayer to thee;

p Cn: Heb *at a time of finding only*

at a time of distress,[p] in the rush of great waters,
    they shall not reach him.
7 Thou art a hiding place for me,
    thou preservest me from trouble;

q Cn: Heb *shouts of deliverance*

thou dost encompass me with deliverance.[q] *Selah*

8 I will instruct you and teach you the way you should go;
    I will counsel you with my eye upon you.
9 Be not like a horse or a mule, without understanding,
    which must be curbed with bit and bridle,
    else it will not keep with you.

10 Many are the pangs of the wicked;
    but steadfast love surrounds him who trusts in the LORD.
11 Be glad in the LORD, and rejoice, O righteous,
    and shout for joy, all you upright in heart!

Psalm 33

Rejoice in the LORD, O you righteous!
    Praise befits the upright.
2 Praise the LORD with the lyre,
    make melody to him with the harp of ten strings!
3 Sing to him a new song,
    play skilfully on the strings, with loud shouts.

4 For the word of the LORD is upright,
    and all his work is done in faithfulness.
5 He loves righteousness and justice;
    the earth is full of the steadfast love of the LORD.

6 By the word of the LORD the heavens were made,
    and all their host by the breath of his mouth.
7 He gathered the waters of the sea as in a bottle;
    he put the deeps in storehouses.

8 Let all the earth fear the LORD,
    let all the inhabitants of the world stand in awe of him!
9 For he spoke, and it came to be;
    he commanded, and it stood forth.

10 The LORD brings the counsel of the nations to nought;
    he frustrates the plans of the peoples,
11 The counsel of the LORD stands for ever,
    the thoughts of his heart to all generations.
12 Blessed is the nation whose God is the LORD,
    the people whom he has chosen as his heritage!

13 The LORD looks down from heaven,
    he sees all the sons of men;
14 from where he sits enthroned he looks forth
    on all the inhabitants of the earth,
15 he who fashions the hearts of them all,
    and observes all their deeds.

16 A king is not saved by his great army;
    a warrior is not delivered by his great strength.
17 The war horse is a vain hope for victory,
    and by its great might it cannot save.

18 Behold, the eye of the LORD is on those who fear him,
    on those who hope in his steadfast love,
19 that he may deliver their soul from death,
    and keep them alive in famine.

20 Our soul waits for the LORD;
    he is our help and shield.
21 Yea, our heart is glad in him,
    because we trust in his holy name.
22 Let thy steadfast love, O LORD, be upon us,
    even as we hope in thee.

Psalm 34

A Psalm of David, when he feigned madness before Abimelech, so that he drove him out, and he went away.

ʳGk Syr Jerome: Heb *their*

I will bless the LORD at all times;
  his praise shall continually be in my mouth.
2 My soul makes its boast in the LORD;
  let the afflicted hear and be glad.
3 O magnify the LORD with me,
  and let us exalt his name together!
4 I sought the LORD, and he answered me,
  and delivered me from all my fears.
5 Look to him, and be radiant;
  so yourʳ faces shall never be ashamed.
6 This poor man cried, and the LORD heard him,
  and saved him out of all his troubles.
7 The angel of the LORD encamps
  around those who fear him, and delivers them.
8 O taste and see that the LORD is good!
  Happy is the man who takes refuge in him!
9 O fear the LORD, you his saints,
  for those who fear him have no want!
10 The young lions suffer want and hunger;
  but those who seek the LORD lack no good thing.

11 Come, O sons, listen to me,
  I will teach you the fear of the LORD.
12 What man is there who desires life,
  and covets many days, that he may enjoy good?
13 Keep your tongue from evil,
  and your lips from speaking deceit.
14 Depart from evil, and do good;
  seek peace, and pursue it.

15 The eyes of the LORD are toward the righteous,
  and his ears toward their cry.
16 The face of the LORD is against evildoers,
  to cut off the remembrance of them from the earth.
17 When the righteous cry for help, the LORD hears,
  and delivers them out of all their troubles.
18 The LORD is near to the broken-hearted,
  and saves the crushed in spirit.
19 Many are the afflictions of the righteous;
  but the LORD delivers him out of them all.
20 He keeps all his bones;
  not one of them is broken.
21 Evil shall slay the wicked;
  and those who hate the righteous will be condemned.
22 The LORD redeems the life of his servants;
  none of those who take refuge in him will be condemned.

Psalm 35

A Psalm of David.

Contend, O LORD, with those who contend with me;
  fight against those who fight against me!
2 Take hold of shield and buckler,
  and rise for my help!
3 Draw the spear and javelin
  against my pursuers!
Say to my soul,
  "I am your deliverance!"

4 Let them be put to shame and dishonor
  who seek after my life!
Let them be turned back and confounded
  who devise evil against me!
5 Let them be like chaff before the wind,
  with the angel of the LORD driving them on!
6 Let their way be dark and slippery,
  with the angel of the LORD pursuing them!

7 For without cause they hid their net for me;
  without cause they dug a pitˢ for my life.
8 Let ruin come upon them unawares!
And let the net which they hid ensnare them;
  let them fall therein to ruin!

9 Then my soul shall rejoice in the LORD,
  exulting in his deliverance.

ˢThe word *pit* is transposed from the preceding line

10 All my bones shall say,
    "O LORD, who is like thee,
thou who deliverest the weak
    from him who is too strong for him,
    the weak and needy from him who despoils him?"
11 Malicious witnesses rise up;
    they ask me of things that I know not.
12 They requite me evil for good;
    my soul is forlorn.
13 But I, when they were sick—
    I wore sackcloth,
    I afflicted myself with fasting.

¹Or My prayer turned back

I prayed with head bowed¹ on my bosom,
14 as though I grieved for my friend or my brother;
I went about as one who laments his mother,
    bowed down and in mourning.

15 But at my stumbling they gathered in glee,
    they gathered together against me;
cripples whom I knew not
    slandered me without ceasing;

ᵘCn Compare Gk: Heb like the profanest of mockers of a cake

16 they impiously mocked more and more,ᵘ
    gnashing at me with their teeth.

17 How long, O LORD, wilt thou look on?
    Rescue me from their ravages,
    my life from the lions!
18 Then I will thank thee in the great congregation;
    in the mighty throng I will praise thee.

19 Let not those rejoice over me
    who are wrongfully my foes,
and let not those wink the eye
    who hate me without cause.
20 For they do not speak peace,
    but against those who are quiet in the land
    they conceive words of deceit.
21 They open wide their mouths against me;
    they say, "Aha, Aha!
    our eyes have seen it!"

22 Thou hast seen, O LORD; be not silent!
    O Lord, be not far from me!
23 Bestir thyself, and awake for my right,
    for my cause, my God and my Lord!
24 Vindicate me, O LORD, my God, according to thy
    righteousness;
    and let them not rejoice over me!
25 Let them not say to themselves,
    "Aha, we have our heart's desire!"
Let them not say, "We have swallowed him up."

26 Let them be put to shame and confusion altogether
    who rejoice at my calamity!
Let them be clothed with shame and dishonor
    who magnify themselves against me!

27 Let those who desire my vindication
    shout for joy and be glad,
    and say evermore,
"Great is the LORD,
    who delights in the welfare of his servant!"
28 Then my tongue shall tell of thy righteousness
    and of thy praise all the day long.

Psalm 36

To the choirmaster. A Psalm of

Transgression speaks to the wicked
    deep in his heart;
there is no fear of God
    before his eyes.
2 For he flatters himself in his own eyes
    that his iniquity cannot be found out and hated.
3 The words of his mouth are mischief and deceit;

David, the
servant of the
LORD.

he has ceased to act wisely and do good.

4 He plots mischief while on his bed;
   he sets himself in a way that is not good;
   he spurns not evil.

5 Thy steadfast love, O LORD, extends to the heavens,
   thy faithfulness to the clouds.
6 Thy righteousness is like the mountains of God,
   thy judgments are like the great deep;
   man and beast thou savest, O LORD.

7 How precious is thy steadfast love, O God!
   The children of men take refuge in the shadow of thy wings.
8 They feast on the abundance of thy house,
   and thou givest them drink from the river of thy delights.
9 For with thee is the fountain of life;
   in thy light do we see light.

10 O continue thy steadfast love to those who know thee,
   and thy salvation to the upright of heart!
11 Let not the foot of arrogance come upon me,
   nor the hand of the wicked drive me away.
12 There the evildoers lie prostrate,
   they are thrust down, unable to rise.

Psalm 37

A Psalm of
David.

Fret not yourself because of the wicked,
be not envious of wrongdoers!
2 For they will soon fade like the grass,
   and wither like the green herb.

3 Trust in the LORD, and do good;
   so you will dwell in the land, and enjoy security.
4 Take delight in the LORD,
   and he will give you the desires of your heart.

5 Commit your way to the LORD;
   trust in him, and he will act.
6 He will bring forth your vindication as the light,
   and your right as the noonday.

7 Be still before the LORD, and wait patiently for him;
   fret not yourself over him who prospers in his way,
   over the man who carries out evil devices!

8 Refrain from anger, and forsake wrath!
   Fret not yourself; it tends only to evil.
9 For the wicked shall be cut off;
   but those who wait for the LORD shall possess the land.
10 Yet a little while, and the wicked will be no more;
   though you look well at his place, he will not be there.
11 But the meek shall possess the land,
   and delight themselves in abundant prosperity.

12 The wicked plots against the righteous,
   and gnashes his teeth at him;
13 but the LORD laughs at the wicked,
   for he sees that his day is coming.

14 The wicked draw the sword and bend their bows,
   to bring down the poor and needy,
   to slay those who walk uprightly;
15 their sword shall enter their own heart,
   and their bows shall be broken.

16 Better is a little that the righteous has
   than the abundance of many wicked.
17 For the arms of the wicked shall be broken;
   but the LORD upholds the righteous.

18 The LORD knows the days of the blameless,
   and their heritage will abide for ever;
19 they are not put to shame in evil times,
   in the days of famine they have abundance.

20 But the wicked perish;
   the enemies of the LORD are like the glory of the pastures,
   they vanish—like smoke they vanish away.

21 The wicked borrows, and cannot pay back,
    but the righteous is generous and gives;
22 for those blessed by the Lord shall possess the land,
    but those cursed by him shall be cut off.

23 The steps of a man are from the Lord,
    and he establishes him in whose way he delights;
24 though he fall, he shall not be cast headlong,
    for the Lord is the stay of his hand.

25 I have been young, and now am old;
    yet I have not seen the righteous forsaken
    or his children begging bread.
26 He is ever giving liberally and lending,
    and his children become a blessing.

27 Depart from evil, and do good;
    so shall you abide for ever.
28 For the Lord loves justice;
    he will not forsake his saints.

    The righteous shall be preserved for ever,
    but the children of the wicked shall be cut off.
29 The righteous shall possess the land,
    and dwell upon it for ever.

30 the mouth of the righteous utters wisdom,
    and his tongue speaks justice.
31 The law of his God is in his heart;
    his steps do not slip.

32 The wicked watches the righteous,
    and seeks to slay him.
33 The Lord will not abandon him to his power,
    or let him be condemned when he is brought to trial.

34 Wait for the Lord, and keep to his way,
    and he will exalt you to possess the land;
    you will look on the destruction of the wicked.

35 I have seen a wicked man overbearing,
    and towering like a cedar of Lebanon.[v]
36 Again I[w] passed by, and, lo, he was no more;
    though I sought him, he could not be found.

v Gk : Heb
obscure
w Gk Syr Jerome:
Heb *he*

37 Mark the blameless man, and behold the upright,
    for there is posterity for the man of peace.
38 But transgressors shall be altogether destroyed;
    the posterity of the wicked shall be cut off.

39 The salvation of the righteous is from the Lord;
    he is their refuge in the time of trouble.
40 The Lord helps them and delivers them;
    he delivers them from the wicked, and saves them,
    because they take refuge in him.

Psalm 38

A Psalm of
David, for the
memorial
offering.

O Lord, rebuke me not in thy anger,
    nor chasten me in thy wrath!
2 For thy arrows have sunk into me,
    and thy hand has come down on me.

3 There is no soundness in my flesh
    because of thy indignation;
there is no health in my bones
    because of my sin.
4 For my iniquities have gone over my head;
    they weigh like a burden too heavy for me.

5 My wounds grow foul and fester
    because of my foolishness,
6 I am utterly bowed down and prostrate;
    all the day I go about mourning.

7 For my loins are filled with burning,
    and there is no soundness in my flesh.
8 I am utterly spent and crushed;
    I groan because of the tumult of my heart.

9 Lord, all my longing is known to thee,
    my sighing is not hidden from thee.

10 My heart throbs, my strength fails me;
    and the light of my eyes—it also has gone from me.

11 My friends and companions stand aloof from my plague,
    and my kinsmen stand afar off.

12 Those who seek my life lay their snares,
    those who seek my hurt speak of ruin,
    and meditate treachery all the day long.

13 But I am like a deaf man, I do not hear,
    like a dumb man who does not open his mouth.
14 Yea, I am like a man who does not hear,
    and in whose mouth are no rebukes.

15 But for thee, O Lord, do I wait;
    it is thou, O Lord my God, who wilt answer.
16 For I pray, "Only let them not rejoice over me,
    who boast against me when my foot slips!"

17 For I am ready to fall,
    and my pain is ever with me,
18 I confess my iniquity,
    I am sorry for my sin.

*Cn: Heb *living* 19 Those who are my foes without cause* are mighty.
    and many are those who hate me wrongfully.
20 Those who render me evil for good
    are my adversaries because I follow after good.

21 Do not forsake me, O Lord!
    O my God, be not far from me!
22 Make haste to help me,
    O Lord, my salvation!

Psalm 39

To the
choirmaster:
to Jeduthun.
A Psalm of
David.

I said, "I will guard my ways,
    that I may not sin with my tongue;
    I will bridle[y] my mouth,
    so long as the wicked are in my presence."
2 I was dumb and silent,
    I held my peace to no avail;
my distress grew worse,
3   my heart became hot within me.
As I mused, the fire burned;
    then I spoke with my tongue:

[y] Heb *muzzle*

4 "Lord, let me know my end,
    and what is the measure of my days;
    let me know how fleeting my life is!
5 Behold, thou hast made my days a few handbreadths,
    and my lifetime is as nothing in thy sight.
Surely every man stands as a mere breath! *Selah*
6   Surely man goes about as a shadow!
Surely for nought are they in turmoil;
    man heaps up, and knows not who will gather!

7 "And now, Lord, for what do I wait?
    My hope is in thee.
8 Deliver me from all my transgressions.
    Make me not the scorn of the fool!
9 I am dumb, I do not open my mouth;
    for it is thou who hast done it.
10 Remove thy stroke from me;
    I am spent by the blows[z] of thy hand.

[z] Heb *hostility*

11 When thou dost chasten man
    with rebukes for sin,
thou dost consume like a moth what is dear to him;
    surely every man is a mere breath! *Selah*

12 "Hear my prayer, O Lord,
    and give ear to my cry;
    hold not thy peace at my tears!
for I am thy passing guest,
    a sojourner, like all my fathers.
13 Look away from me, that I may know gladness,
    before I depart and be no more!"

Psalm 40

To the
choirmaster.
A Psalm of
David.

*a*Cn: Heb *pit of
tumult*

*b*Heb *ears thou
hast dug for me*

I waited patiently for the LORD;
　　he inclined to me and heard my cry.
2 He drew me up from the desolate pit,*a*
　　out of the miry bog,
and set my feet upon a rock,
　　making my steps secure.
3 He put a new song in my mouth,
　　a song of praise to our God.
Many will see and fear,
　　and put their trust in the LORD.

4 Blessed is the man
　　who makes the LORD his trust,
who does not turn to the proud,
　　to those who go astray after false gods!
5 Thou hast multiplied, O LORD my God,
　　thy wondrous deeds and thy thoughts toward us;
　　none can compare with thee!
Were I to proclaim and tell of them,
　　they would be more than can be numbered.

6 Sacrifice and offering thou dost not desire;
　　but thou hast given me an open ear.*b*
Burnt offering and sin offering
　　thou hast not required.
7 Then I said, "Lo, I come;
　　in the roll of the book it is written of me;
8 I delight to do thy will, O my God;
　　thy law is within my heart."
9 I have told the glad news of deliverance
　　in the great congregation;
lo, I have not restrained my lips,
　　as thou knowest, O LORD.
10 I have not hid thy saving help within my heart,
　　I have spoken of thy faithfulness and thy salvation;
I have not concealed thy steadfast love and thy faithfulness
　　from the great congregation.

11 Do not thou, O LORD, withhold
　　thy mercy from me,
let thy steadfast love and thy faithfulness
　　ever preserve me!
12 For evils have encompassed me
　　without number;
my iniquities have overtaken me,
　　till I cannot see;
they are more than the hairs of my head;
　　my heart fails me.

13 Be pleased, O LORD, to deliver me!
　　O LORD, make haste to help me!
14 Let them be put to shame and confusion altogether
　　who seek to snatch away my life;
let them be turned back and brought to dishonor
　　who desire my hurt!
15 Let them be appalled because of their shame
　　who say to me, "Aha, Aha!"

16 But may all who seek thee
　　rejoice and be glad in thee;
may those who love thy salvation
　　say continually, "Great is the LORD!"
17 As for me, I am poor and needy;
　　but the Lord takes thought for me.
Thou art my help and my deliverer;
　　do not tarry, O my God!

Psalm 41

To the
choirmaster.

Blessed is he who considers the poor!*c*
　　The LORD delivers him in the day of trouble;
2 the LORD protects him and keeps him alive;
　　he is called blessed in the land;
　　thou dost not give him up to the will of his enemies.
3 The LORD sustains him on his sick-bed;

A Psalm of
David.

c Or *weak*
d Heb *thou
changest all his
bed*

in his illness thou healest all his infirmities.*d*

4 As for me, I said, "O Lord, be gracious to me;
    heal me, for I have sinned against thee!"
5 My enemies say of me in malice;
    "When will he die, and his name perish?"
6 And when one comes to see me, he utters empty words,
    while his heart gathers mischief;
    when he goes out, he tells it abroad.
7 All who hate me whisper together about me;
    they imagine the worst for me.
8 They say, "A deadly thing has fastened upon him;
    he will not rise again from where he lies."
9 Even my bosom friend in whom I trusted,
    who ate of my bread, has lifted his heel against me.
10 But do thou, O Lord, be gracious to me,
    and raise me up, that I may requite them!

11 By this I know that thou art pleased with me,
    in that my enemy has not triumphed over me.
12 But thou hast upheld me because of my integrity,
    and set me in thy presence for ever.

13 Blessed be the Lord, the God of Israel,
    from everlasting to everlasting!
    Amen and Amen.

BOOK II

Psalm 42

To the
choirmaster.
A Maskil of the
Sons of Korah.

As a hart longs for flowing streams,
so longs my soul
    for thee, O God.
2 My soul thirsts for God,
    for the living God.
When shall I come and behold
    the face of God?
3 My tears have been my food
    day and night,
while men say to me continually,
    "Where is your God?"

4 These things I remember,
    as I pour out my soul:
how I went with the throng,
    and led them in procession to the house of God,
with glad shouts and songs of thanksgiving,
    a multitude keeping festival.
5 Why are you cast down, O my soul,
    and why are you disquieted within me?
Hope in God; for I shall again praise him,
    my help 6 and my God.

My soul is cast down within me,
    therefore I remember thee
from the land of Jordan and of Hermon,
    from Mount Mizar.
7 Deep calls to deep
    at the thunder of thy cataracts;
all thy waves and thy billows
    have gone over me.
8 By day the Lord commands his steadfast love;
    and at night his song is with me,
    a prayer to the God of my life.

9 I say to God, my rock:
    "Why hast thou forgotten me?
Why go I mourning
    because of the oppression of the enemy?"
10 As with a deadly wound in my body,
    my adversaries taunt me,
while they say to me continually,
    "Where is your God?"

11 Why are you cast down, O my soul,
and why are you disquieted within me?
Hope in God; for I shall again praise him,
my help and my God.

Psalm 43

Vindicate me, O God, and defend my cause
against an ungodly people;
from deceitful and unjust men
deliver me!
2 For thou art the God in whom I take refuge;
why hast thou cast me off?
Why go I mourning
because of the oppression of the enemy?

3 Oh send out thy light and thy truth;
let them lead me,
let them bring me to thy holy hill
and to thy dwelling!
4 Then I will go to the altar of God,
to God my exceeding joy;
and I will praise thee with the lyre,
O God, my God.

5 Why are you cast down, O my soul,
and why are you disquieted within me?
Hope in God; for I shall again praise him,
my help and my God.

Psalm 44

To the
choirmaster.
A Maskil of the
Sons of Korah.

We have heard with our ears, O God,
our fathers have told us,
what deeds thou didst perform in their days,
in the days of old:
2 thou with thy own hand didst drive out the nations,
but them thou didst plant;
thou didst afflict the peoples,
but them thou didst set free;
3 for not by their own sword did they win the land,
nor did their own arm give them victory;
but thy right hand, and thy arm,
and the light of thy countenance;
for thou didst delight in them.

e Gk Syr: Heb
*Thou art my King,
O God; ordain*

4 Thou art my King and my God,
who ordainest*e* victories for Jacob.
5 Through thee we push down our foes;
through thy name we tread down our assailants.
6 For not in my bow do I trust,
nor can my sword save me.
7 But thou hast saved us from our foes,
and hast put to confusion those who hate us.
8 In God we have boasted continually,
and we will give thanks to thy name for ever. *Selah*

9 Yet thou hast cast us off and abased us,
and hast not gone out with our armies.
10 Thou hast made us turn back from the foe;
and our enemies have gotten spoil.
11 Thou hast made us like sheep for slaughter,
and hast scattered us among the nations.
12 Thou hast sold thy people for a trifle,
demanding no high price for them.

13 Thou hast made us the taunt of our neighbors,
the derision and scorn of those about us.
14 Thou hast made us a byword among the nations,
a laughingstock*f* among the peoples.

f Heb *a shaking of
the head*

15 All day long my disgrace is before me,
and shame has covered my face,
16 at the words of the taunters and revilers,
at the sight of the enemy and the avenger.

17 All this has come upon us,
though we have not forgotten thee,

or been false to thy covenant.
18 Our heart has not turned back,
    nor have our steps departed from thy way,
19 that thou shouldst have broken us in the place of jackals,
    and covered us with deep darkness.

20 If we had forgotten the name of our God,
    or spread forth our hands to a strange god,
21 would not God discover this?
    For he knows the secrets of the heart.
22 Nay, for thy sake we are slain all the day long,
    and accounted as sheep for the slaughter.
23 Rouse thyself! Why sleepest thou, O Lord?
    Awake! Do not cast us off for ever!
24 Why dost thou hide thy face?
    Why dost thou forget our affliction and oppression?
25 For our soul is bowed down to the dust;
    our body cleaves to the ground.
26 Rise up, come to our help!
    Deliver us for the sake of thy steadfast love!

Psalm 45

To the choirmaster: according to Lilies. A Maskil of the Sons of Korah; a love song.

My heart overflows with a goodly theme;
    I address my verses to the king;
    my tongue is like the pen of a ready scribe.

2 You are the fairest of the sons of men;
    grace is poured upon your lips;
    therefore God has blessed you for ever.
3 Gird your sword upon your thigh, O mighty one,
    in your glory and majesty!

4 In your majesty ride forth victoriously
    for the cause of the truth and to defend[g] the right;
    let your right hand teach you dread deeds!

[g] Cn: Heb *and the meekness of*

5 Your arrows are sharp
    in the heart of the king's enemies;
    the peoples fall under you.

[h] Or *Your throne is a throne of God*, or *Thy throne, O God*

6 Your divine throne[h] endures for ever and ever.
    Your royal scepter is a scepter of equity;
7   you love righteousness and hate wickedness.
Therefore God, your God, has anointed you
    with the oil of gladness above your fellows;
8   your robes are all fragrant with myrrh and aloes and cassia.
From ivory palaces stringed instruments make you glad;
9   daughters of kings are among your ladies of honor;
    at your right hand stands the queen in gold of Ophir.

10 Hear, O daughter, consider, and incline your ear;
    forget your people and your father's house;
11   and the king will desire your beauty.
Since he is your lord, bow to him;

[i] Heb *daughter*

12   the people[i] of Tyre will sue your favor with gifts,
    the richest of the people 13 with all kinds of wealth.

[j] Or *people. All glorious is the princess within, gold embroidery is her clothing*
[k] Heb *those brought to you*

The princess is decked in her chamber with gold-woven robes;[j]
14   in many-colored robes she is led to the king,
    with her virgin companions, her escort,[k] in her train.
15 With joy and gladness they are led along
    as they enter the palace of the king.

16 Instead of your fathers shall be your sons;
    you will make them princes in all the earth.
17 I will cause your name to be celebrated in all generations;
    therefore the peoples will praise you for ever and ever.

Psalm 46

To the choirmaster. A Psalm of the Sons of Korah.

God is our refuge and strength,
    a very present[l] help in trouble.
2 Therefore we will not fear though the earth should change,
    though the mountains shake in the heart of the sea;
3 though its waters roar and foam,
    though the mountains tremble with its tumult. *Selah*
4 There is a river whose streams make glad the city of God,
    the holy habitation of the Most High.

According to Alamoth. A Song.

*Or well proved

m Or fortress

5 God is in the midst of her, she shall not be moved;
    God will help her right early.
6 The nations rage, the kingdoms totter;
    he utters his voice, the earth melts.
7 The Lord of hosts is with us;
    the God of Jacob is our refuge.*m* Selah

8 Come, behold the works of the Lord,
    how he has wrought desolations in the earth.
9 He makes wars cease to the end of the earth;
    he breaks the bow, and shatters the spear,
    he burns the chariots with fire!
10 "Be still, and know that I am God.
    I am exalted among the nations,
    I am exalted in the earth!"
11 The Lord of hosts is with us;
    the God of Jacob is our refuge.*m* Selah

Psalm 47

To the choirmaster. A Psalm of the Sons of Korah.

n Heb Maskil

Clap your hands, all peoples!
    Shout to God with loud songs of joy!
2 For the Lord, the Most High, is terrible,
    a great king over all the earth.
3 He subdued peoples under us,
    and nations under our feet.
4 He chose our heritage for us,
    the pride of Jacob whom he loves. *Selah*

5 God has gone up with a shout,
    the Lord with the sound of a trumpet.
6 Sing praises to God, sing praises!
    Sing praises to our King, sing praises!
7 For God is the king of all the earth;
    sing praises with a psalm!*n*

8 God reigns over the nations;
    God sits on his holy throne.
9 The princes of the peoples gather
    as the people of the God of Abraham.
For the shields of the earth belong to God;
    he is highly exalted!

Psalm 48

A Song. A Psalm of the Sons of Korah.

Great is the Lord and greatly to be praised
    in the city of our God!
His holy mountain, 2 beautiful in elevation,
    is the joy of all the earth,
Mount Zion, in the far north,
    the city of the great King.
3 Within her citadels God
    has shown himself a sure defense.

4 For lo, the kings assembled,
    they came on together.
5 As soon as they saw it, they were astounded,
    they were in panic, they took to flight;
6 trembling took hold of them there,
    anguish as of a woman in travail.
7 By the east wind thou didst shatter
    the ships of Tarshish.
8 As we have heard, so have we seen
    in the city of the Lord of hosts,
in the city of our God,
    which God establishes for ever. *Selah*

9 We have thought on thy steadfast love, O God,
    in the midst of thy temple.
10 As thy name, O God,
    so thy praise reaches to the ends of the earth.
Thy right hand is filled with victory;
11   let Mount Zion be glad!
Let the daughters of Judah rejoice
    because of thy judgments!

12 Walk about Zion, go round about her,
 number her towers,
13 consider well her ramparts,
 go through her citadels;
that you may tell the next generation
14   that this is God,
our God for ever and ever.
 He will be our guide for ever.

Psalm 49

To the
choirmaster.
A Psalm of the
Sons of Korah.

Hear this, all peoples!
Give ear, all inhabitants of the world,
2 both low and high;
 rich and poor together!

3 My mouth shall speak wisdom;
 the meditation of my heart shall be understanding.
4 I will incline my ear to a proverb;
 I will solve my riddle to the music of the lyre.

5 Why should I fear in times of trouble,
 when the iniquity of my persecutors surrounds me,
6 men who trust in their wealth
 and boast of the abundance of their riches?

o Another reading
is *no man can
ransom his
brother*
p Gk. Heb *their*

7 Truly no man can ransom himself,*o*
 or give to God the price of his life,
8 for the ransom of his*p* life is costly,
 and can never suffice,
9 that he should continue to live on for ever,
 and never see the Pit.

10 Yea, he shall see that even the wise die,
 the fool and the stupid alike must perish
 and leave their wealth to others.

q Gk Syr
Compare Tg: Heb
*their inward
(thought)*

11 Their graves*q* are their homes for ever,
 their dwelling places to all generations,
 though they named lands their own.
12 Man cannot abide in his pomp,
 he is like the beasts that perish.

r Tg: Heb *after
them*

13 This is the fate of those who have foolish confidence,
 the end of those*r* who are pleased with their portion. *Selah*

14 Like sheep they are appointed for Sheol;
 Death shall be their shepherd;

s Cn: Heb *the
upright shall have
dominion over
them in the
morning*
t Heb uncertain

straight to the grave they descend,*s*
 and their form shall waste away;
 Sheol shall be their home.*t*
15 But God will ransom my soul from the power of Sheol,
 for he will receive me. *Selah*

u Or *wealth*

16 Be not afraid when one becomes rich,
 when the glory*u* of his house increases.
17 For when he dies he will carry nothing away;
 his glory*u* will not go down after him.
18 Though, while he lives, he counts himself happy,
 and though a man gets praise when he does well for himself,
19 he will go to the generation of his fathers,
 who will never more see the light.
20 Man cannot abide in his pomp,
 he is like the beasts that perish.

Psalm 50

A Psalm of
Asaph.

The Mighty One, God the LORD,
 speaks and summons the earth
 from the rising of the sun to its setting.
2 Out of Zion, the perfection of beauty,
 God shines forth.

3 Our God comes, he does not keep silence,
 before him is a devouring fire,
 round about him a mighty tempest.
4 He calls to the heavens above
 and to the earth, that he may judge his people:
5 "Gather to me my faithful ones,

who made a covenant with me by sacrifice!"
6 The heavens declare his righteousness,
for God himself is judge! *Selah*

7 "Hear, O my people, and I will speak,
O Israel, I will testify against you.
I am God, your God.
8 I do not reprove you for your sacrifices;
your burnt offerings are continually before me.
9 I will accept no bull from your house,
nor he-goat from your folds.
10 For every beast of the forest is mine,
the cattle on a thousand hills.

v Gk Syr Tg: Heb mountains

11 I know all the birds of the air,[v]
and all that moves in the field is mine.

12 "If I were hungry, I would not tell you;
for the world and all that is in it is mine.
13 Do I eat the flesh of bulls,
or drink the blood of goats?

w Or make thanksgiving your sacrifice to God

14 Offer to God a sacrifice of thanksgiving,[w]
and pay your vows to the Most High;
15 and call upon me in the day of trouble;
I will deliver you, and you shall glorify me."

16 But to the wicked God says:
"What right have you to recite my statutes,
or take my covenant on your lips?
17 For you hate discipline,
and you cast my words behind you.
18 If you see a thief, you are a friend of his;
and you keep company with adulterers.

19 "You give your mouth free rein for evil,
and your tongue frames deceit.
20 You sit and speak against your brother;
you slander your own mother's son.
21 These things you have done and I have been silent;
you thought that I was one like yourself.
But now I rebuke you, and lay the charge before you.

22 "Mark this, then, you who forget God,
lest I rend, and there be none to deliver!
23 He who brings thanksgiving as his sacrifice honors me;
to him who orders his way aright
I will show the salvation of God!"

Psalm 51

To the choirmaster. A Psalm of David, when Nathan the prophet came to him, after he had gone in to Bathsheba.

Have mercy on me, O God,
according to thy steadfast love;
according to thy abundant mercy blot out my transgressions.
2 Wash me thoroughly from my iniquity,
and cleanse me from my sin!

3 For I know my transgressions,
and my sin is ever before me.
4 Against thee, thee only, have I sinned,
and done that which is evil in thy sight,
so that thou art justified in thy sentence
and blameless in thy judgment.
5 Behold, I was brought forth in iniquity,
and in sin did my mother conceive me.
6 Behold, thou desirest truth in the inward being;
therefore teach me wisdom in my secret heart.
7 Purge me with hyssop, and I shall be clean;
wash me, and I shall be whiter than snow.

x Syr: Heb Make to hear

8 Fill[x] me with joy and gladness;
let the bones which thou hast broken rejoice.
9 Hide thy face from my sins,
and blot out all my iniquities.

y Or steadfast

10 Create in me a clean heart, O God,
and put a new and right[y] spirit within me.
11 Cast me not away from thy presence,

and take not thy holy Spirit from me.
12 Restore to me the joy of thy salvation,
and uphold me with a willing spirit.

13 Then I will teach transgressors thy ways,
and sinners will return to thee.

²Or death 14 Deliver me from bloodguiltiness,² O God,
thou God of my salvation,
and my tongue will sing aloud of thy deliverance.
15 O Lord, open thou my lips,
and my mouth shall show forth thy praise.
16 For thou hast no delight in sacrifice;
were I to give a burnt offering, thou wouldst not be pleased.

ᵃOr My sacrifice, 17 The sacrifice acceptable to Godᵃ is a broken spirit;
O God a broken and contrite heart, O God, thou wilt not despise.

18 Do good to Zion in thy good pleasure;
rebuild the walls of Jerusalem;
19 then wilt thou delight in right sacrifices,
in burnt offerings and whole burnt offerings;
then bulls will be offered on thy altar.

Psalm 52

To the
choirmaster.
A Maskil of
David, when
Doeg, the
Edomite, came
and told Saul,
"David has
come to the
house of
Ahimelech."

ᵇCn Compare
Syr: Heb the
kindness of God
ᶜSyr Tg: Heb his
destruction

ᵈCn: Heb wait for

Why do you boast, O mighty man,
of mischief done against the godly?ᵇ
All the day 2 you are plotting destruction.
Your tongue is like a sharp razor,
you worker of treachery.
3 You love evil more than good,
and lying more than speaking the truth. *Selah*
4 You love all words that devour,
O deceitful tongue.

5 But God will break you down for ever;
he will snatch and tear you from your tent;
he will uproot you from the land of the living. *Selah*
6 The righteous shall see, and fear,
and shall laugh at him, saying,

7 "See the man who would not make God his refuge,
but trusted in the abundance of his riches,
and sought refuge in his wealth!"ᶜ
8 But I am like a green olive tree
in the house of God.
I trust in the steadfast love of God
for ever and ever.
I will thank thee for ever,
because thou hast done it.
I will proclaimᵈ thy name, for it is good,
in the presence of the godly.

Psalm 53

To the
choirmaster:
according to
Mahalath.
A Maskil of
David.

ᵉCn Compare Gk
Syr: Heb him who
encamps against
you
ᶠGk: Heb you will
put to shame

The fool says in his heart,
"There is no God."
They are corrupt, doing abominable iniquity;
there is none that does good.

2 God looks down from heaven
upon the sons of men
to see if there are any that are wise,
that seek after God.

3 They have all fallen away;
they are all alike depraved;
there is none that does good,
no, not one.

4 Have those who work evil no understanding,
who eat up my people as they eat bread,
and do not call upon God?

5 There they are, in great terror,
in terror such as has not been!
For God will scatter the bones of the ungodly;ᵉ
they will be put to shame,ᶠ for God has rejected them.

6 O that deliverance for Israel would come from Zion!
When God restores the fortunes of his people,
Jacob will rejoice and Israel be glad.

Psalm 54

To the choirmaster: with stringed instruments. A Maskil of David, when the Ziphites went and told Saul, "David is in hiding among us."

g Another reading is *strangers*
h Gk Syr Jerome: Heb *of* or *with those who uphold*

Save me, O God, by thy name,
and vindicate me by thy might.
2 Hear my prayer, O God;
give ear to the words of my mouth.
3 For insolent men*g* have risen against me,
ruthless men seek my life;
they do not set God before them. *Selah*
4 Behold, God is my helper;
the Lord is the upholder*h* of my life.
5 He will requite my enemies with evil;
in thy faithfulness put an end to them.
6 With a freewill offering I will sacrifice to thee;
I will give thanks to thy name, O LORD, for it is good.
7 For thou hast delivered me from every trouble,
and my eye has looked in triumph on my enemies.

Psalm 55

To the choirmaster: with stringed instruments. A Maskil of David.

i Cn Compare Gk: Heb *they cause to totter*

j Tg: Heb lacks *their plans*

k Or *desolations*

l Cn: Heb *evils are in their habitation, in their midst*

Give ear to my prayer, O God;
and hide not thyself from my supplication!
2 Attend to me, and answer me;
I am overcome by my trouble.
I am distraught 3 by the noise of the enemy,
because of the oppression of the wicked.
For they bring*i* trouble upon me,
and in anger they cherish enmity against me.
4 My heart is in anguish within me,
the terrors of death have fallen upon me.
5 Fear and trembling come upon me,
and horror overwhelms me.
6 And I say, "O that I had wings like a dove!
I would fly away and be at rest;
7 yea, I would wander afar,
I would lodge in the wilderness, *Selah*
8 I would haste to find me a shelter
from the raging wind and tempest."
9 Destroy their plans,*j* O Lord, confuse their tongues;
for I see violence and strife in the city.
10 Day and night they go around it on its walls;
and mischief and trouble are within it,
11   ruin is in its midst;
oppression and fraud
do not depart from its market place.
12 It is not an enemy who taunts me—
then I could bear it;
it is not an adversary who deals insolently with me—
then I could hide from him.
13 But it is you, my equal,
my companion, my familiar friend.
14 We used to hold sweet converse together;
within God's house we walked in fellowship.
15 Let death*k* come upon them;
let them go down to Sheol alive;
let them go away in terror into their graves.*l*
16 But I call upon God;
and the LORD will save me.
17 Evening and morning and at noon
I utter my complaint and moan,
and he will hear my voice.
18 He will deliver my soul in safety
from the battle that I wage,
for many are arrayed against me.

19 God will give ear, and humble them,
    he who is enthroned from of old;

m Or *do not change*

because they keep no law,*m*
    and do not fear God. *Selah*

20 My companion stretched out his hand against his friends,
    he violated his covenant.
21 His speech was smoother than butter,
    yet war was in his heart;
his words were softer than oil, yet they were drawn swords.

n Or *what he has given you*

22 Cast your burden*n* on the LORD,
    and he will sustain you;
he will never permit
    the righteous to be moved.

23 But thou, O God, wilt cast them down
    into the lowest pit;
men of blood and treachery
    shall not live out half their days.
But I will trust in thee.

Psalm 56

To the choirmaster: according to The Dove on Far-off Terebinths. A Miktam of David, when the Philistines seized him in Gath.

Be gracious to me, O God, for men trample upon me;
    all day long foemen oppress me;
2 my enemies trample upon me all day long,
    for many fight against me proudly
3 When I am afraid,
    I put my trust in thee.
4 In God, whose word I praise,
    in God I trust without a fear.
    What can flesh do to me?
5 All day long they seek to injure my cause;
    all their thoughts are against me for evil.
6 They band themselves together, they lurk,
    they watch my steps.
As they have waited for my life,
7   so recompense*o* them for their crime,
    in wrath cast down the peoples, O God!

o Cn: Heb *deliver*

8 Thou hast kept count of my tossings;
    put thou my tears in thy bottle!
    Are they not in thy book?
9 Then my enemies will be turned back
    in the day when I call.

p Or *because*

    This I know, that*p* God is for me.
10 In God, whose word I praise,
    in the LORD, whose word I praise,
11 in God I trust without a fear.
    What can man do to me?

12 My vows to thee I must perform, O God;
    I will render thank offerings to thee.
13 For thou hast delivered my soul from death,
    yea, my feet from falling,
that I may walk before God
    in the light of life.

Psalm 57

To the choirmaster: according to Do Not Destroy. A Miktam of David, when he fled from Saul, in the cave.

Be merciful to me, O God, be merciful to me,
    for in thee my soul takes refuge;
in the shadow of thy wings I will take refuge,
    till the storms of destruction pass by.
2 I cry to God Most High,
    to God who fulfils his purpose for me.
3 He will send from heaven and save me,
    he will put to shame those who trample upon me. *Selah*
God will send forth his steadfast love and his faithfulness!
4 I lie in the midst of lions
    that greedily devour*q* the sons of men;
their teeth are spears and arrows,
    their tongues sharp swords.

q Cn: Heb *are aflame*

5 Be exalted, O God, above the heavens!
    Let thy glory be over all the earth!

6 They set a net for my steps;
  my soul was bowed down.
They dug a pit in my way,
  but they have fallen into it themselves. *Selah*

7 My heart is steadfast, O God,
  my heart is steadfast!
I will sing and make melody!
8   Awake, my soul!
Awake, O harp and lyre!
  I will awake the dawn!
9 I will give thanks to thee, O Lord, among the peoples;
  I will sing praises to thee among the nations.
10 For thy steadfast love is great to the heavens,
  thy faithfulness to the clouds.
11 Be exalted, O God, above the heavens!
  Let thy glory be over all the earth!

Psalm 58

To the
choirmaster:
according to Do
Not Destroy.
A Miktam of
David.

s Or *mighty lords*

t Cn: Heb
uncertain

Do you indeed decree what is right, you gods?*s*
  Do you judge the sons of men uprightly?
2 Nay, in your hearts you devise wrongs;
  your hands deal out violence on earth.

3 The wicked go astray from the womb,
  they err from their birth, speaking lies.
4 They have venom like the venom of a serpent,
  like the deaf adder that stops its ear,
5 so that it does not hear the voice of charmers
  or of the cunning enchanter.

6 O God, break the teeth in their mouths;
  tear out the fangs of the young lions, O LORD!
7 Let them vanish like water that runs away;
  like grass let them be trodden down and wither.*t*
8 Let them be like the snail which dissolves into slime,
  like the untimely birth that never sees the sun.
9 Sooner than your pots can feel the heat of thorns,
  whether green or ablaze, may he sweep them away!

10 The righteous will rejoice when he sees the vengeance;
  he will bathe his feet in the blood of the wicked.
11 Men will say, "Surely there is a reward for the righteous;
  surely there is a God who judges on earth."

Psalm 59

To the
choirmaster:
according to Do
Not Destroy.
A Miktam of
David, when
Saul sent men to
watch his house
in order to kill
him.

u Cn: Heb *swords*
in

v Syr: Heb *I will*
watch for thee

Deliver me from my enemies, O my God,
  protect me from those who rise up against me,
2 deliver me from those who work evil,
  and save me from bloodthirsty men.

3 For, lo, they lie in wait for my life;
  fierce men band themselves against me.
For no transgression or sin of mine, O LORD,
4   for no fault of mine, they run and make ready.

Rouse thyself, come to my help, and see!
5   Thou, LORD God of hosts, art God of Israel.
Awake to punish all the nations;
  spare none of those who treacherously plot evil. *Selah*

6 Each evening they come back,
  howling like dogs
  and prowling about the city.
7 There they are, bellowing with their mouths,
  and snarling with*u* their lips—
  for 'Who,' they think, "will hear us?"

8 But thou, O LORD, dost laugh at them;
  thou dost hold all the nations in derision.
9 O my Strength, I will sing praises to thee;*v*
  for thou, O God, art my fortress.
10 My God in his steadfast love will meet me;
  my God will let me look in triumph on my enemies.

11 Slay them not, lest my people forget;
  make them totter by thy power,

and bring them down,
O Lord, our shield!
12 For the sin of their mouths, the words of their lips,
let them be trapped in their pride.
For the cursing and lies which they utter,
13   consume them in wrath,
consume them till they are no more,
that men may know that God rules over Jacob
to the ends of the earth. *Selah*

14 Each evening they come back,
howling like dogs
and prowling about the city.
15 They roam about for food,
and growl if they do not get their fill.

16 But I will sing of thy might;
I will sing aloud of thy steadfast love in the morning.
For thou hast been to me a fortress
and a refuge in the day of my distress.
17 O my Strength, I will sing praises to thee,
for thou, O God, art my fortress,
the God who shows me steadfast love.

Psalm 60

To the
choirmaster:
according to
Shushan Eduth.
A Miktam of
David; for
instruction;
when he strove
with Aram-
naharaim and
with Aram-
zobah, and
when Joab on
his return killed
twelve thousand
of Edom in the
Valley of Salt.

w Gk Syr Jerome:
Heb *truth*
x Or *by his
holiness*

O God, thou hast rejected us, broken our defenses;
thou hast been angry; oh, restore us.
2 Thou hast made the land to quake, thou hast rent it open;
repair its breaches, for it totters.
3 Thou hast made thy people suffer hard things;
thou hast given us wine to drink that made us reel.
4 Thou hast set up a banner for those who fear thee,
to rally to it from the bow.*w* *Selah*
5 That thy beloved may be delivered,
give victory by thy right hand and answer us!
6 God has spoken in his sanctuary:*x*
"With exultation I will divide up Shechem
and portion out the Vale of Succoth.
7 Gilead is mine; Manas'seh is mine;
E'phraim is my helmet;
Judah is my scepter.
8 Moab is my washbasin;
upon Edom I cast my shoe;
over Philistia I shout in triumph."
9 Who will bring me to the fortified city?
Who will lead me to Edom?
10 Hast thou not rejected us, O God?
Thou dost not go forth, O God, with our armies.
11 O grant us help against the foe,
for vain is the help of man!
12 With God we shall do valiantly;
it is he who will tread down our foes.

Psalm 61

To the
choirmaster:
with stringed
instruments.
A Psalm of
David.

Hear my cry, O God, listen to my prayer;
2 from the end of the earth I call to thee,
when my heart is faint.
Lead thou me
to the rock that is higher than I;
3 for thou art my refuge,
a strong tower against the enemy.
4 Let me dwell in thy tent for ever!
Oh to be safe under the shelter of thy wings! *Selah*
5 For thou, O God, hast heard my vows,
thou hast given me the heritage of those who fear thy name.
6 Prolong the life of the king;
may his years endure to all generations!
7 May he be enthroned for ever before God;
bid steadfast love and faithfulness watch over him!
8 So will I ever sing praises to thy name,
as I pay my vows day after day.

Psalm 62

To the choirmaster: according to Jeduthun. A Psalm of David.

For God alone my soul waits in silence;
    from him comes my salvation.
2 He only is my rock and my salvation,
    my fortress; I shall not be greatly moved.

3 How long will you set upon a man
    to shatter him, all of you,
    like a leaning wall, a tottering fence?
4 They only plan to thrust him down from his eminence.
    They take pleasure in falsehood.
They bless with their mouths,
    but inwardly they curse. *Selah*

5 For God alone my soul waits in silence,
    for my hope is from him.
6 He only is my rock and my salvation,
    my fortress; I shall not be shaken.
7 On God rests my deliverance and my honor;
    my mighty rock, my refuge is God.

8 Trust in him at all times, O people;
    pour out your heart before him;
    God is a refuge for us. *Selah*
9 Men of low estate are but a breath,
    men of high estate are a delusion;
in the balances they go up;
    they are together lighter than a breath.
10 Put no confidence in extortion,
    set no vain hopes on robbery;
    if riches increase, set not your heart on them.

11 Once God has spoken;
    twice have I heard this:
that power belongs to God;
12   and that to thee, O Lord, belongs steadfast love.
For thou dost requite a man
    according to his work.

Psalm 63

A Psalm of David, when he was in the Wilderness of Judah.

O God, thou art my God, I seek thee,
    my soul thirsts for thee;
my flesh faints for thee,
    as in a dry and weary land where no water is.
2 So I have looked upon thee in the sanctuary,
    beholding thy power and glory.
3 Because thy steadfast love is better than life,
    my lips will praise thee.
4 So I will bless thee as long as I live;
    I will lift up my hands and call on thy name.

5 My soul is feasted as with marrow and fat,
    and my mouth praises thee with joyful lips,
6 when I think of thee upon my bed,
    and meditate on thee in the watches of the night;
7 for thou hast been my help,
    and in the shadow of thy wings I sing for joy.
8 My soul clings to thee;
    thy right hand upholds me.

9 But those who seek to destroy my life
    shall go down into the depths of the earth;
10 they shall be given over to the power of the sword,
    they shall be prey for jackals.
11 But the king shall rejoice in God;
    all who swear by him shall glory;
    for the mouths of liars will be stopped.

Psalm 64

To the choirmaster. A Psalm of David.

Hear my voice, O God, in my complaint;
    preserve my life from dread of the enemy,
2 hide me from the secret plots of the wicked,
    from the scheming of evildoers,
3 who whet their tongues like swords,
    who aim bitter words like arrows,
4 shooting from ambush at the blameless,

shooting at him suddenly and without fear.
5 They hold fast to their evil purpose;
    they talk of laying snares secretly,
thinking, "Who can see us?"[y]
6   Who can search out our crimes?[z]
We have thought out a cunningly conceived plot."
    For the inward mind and heart of a man are deep!

7 But God will shoot his arrow at them;
    they will be wounded suddenly.
8 Because of their tongue he will bring them to ruin;[a]
    all who see them will wag their heads.
9 Then all men will fear;
    they will tell what God has wrought,
    and ponder what he has done.

10 Let the righteous rejoice in the LORD,
    and take refuge in him!
Let all the upright in heart glory!

[y] Syr: Heb *them*
[z] Cn: Heb *they search out crimes*

[a] Cn: Heb *They will bring him to ruin, their tongue being against them*

Psalm 65

To the choirmaster. A Psalm of David. A Song.

[b] Gk: Heb *me*

Praise is due to thee, O God, in Zion;
and to thee shall vows be performed,
2   O thou who hearest prayer!
To thee shall all flesh come
3   on account of sins.
When our transgressions prevail over us,[b]
    thou dost forgive them.
4 Blessed is he whom thou dost choose and bring near,
    to dwell in thy courts!
We shall be satisfied with the goodness of thy house,
    thy holy temple!

5 By dread deeds thou dost answer us with deliverance,
    O God of our salvation,
who art the hope of all the ends of the earth,
    and of the farthest seas;
6 who by thy strength hast established the mountains,
    being girded with might;
7 who dost still the roaring of the seas,
    the roaring of their waves,
    the tumult of the peoples;
8 so that those who dwell at earth's farthest bounds
    are afraid at thy signs;
thou makest the outgoings of the morning and the evening
    to shout for joy.

9 Thou visitest the earth and waterest it,
    thou greatly enrichest it;
the river of God is full of water;
    thou providest their grain,
    for so thou hast prepared it.
10 Thou waterest its furrows abundantly,
    settling its ridges,
softening it with showers,
    and blessing its growth.
11 Thou crownest the year with thy bounty;
    the tracks of thy chariot drip with fatness.
12 The pastures of the wilderness drip,
    the hills gird themselves with joy,
13 the meadows clothe themselves with flocks,
    the valleys deck themselves with grain,
    they shout and sing together for joy.

Psalm 66

To the choirmaster. A Song. A Psalm.

Make a joyful noise to God, all the earth;
2   sing the glory of his name;
    give to him glorious praise!
3 Say to God, "How terrible are thy deeds!
    So great is thy power that thy enemies cringe before thee.
4 All the earth worships thee;
    they sing praises to thee,
    sing praises to thy name." *Selah*

5 Come and see what God has done:
    he is terrible in his deeds among men.
6 He turned the sea into dry land;
    men passed through the river on foot.
There did we rejoice in him,
7   who rules by his might for ever,
whose eyes keep watch on the nations—
    let not the rebellious exalt themselves. *Selah*

8 Bless our God, O peoples,
    let the sound of his praise be heard,
9 who has kept us among the living,
    and has not let our feet slip.
10 For thou, O God, hast tested us;
    thou hast tried us as silver is tried.
11 Thou didst bring us into the net;
    thou didst lay affliction on our loins;
12 thou didst let men ride over our heads;
    we went through fire and through water;

c Cn Compare Gk Syr Jerome Tg: Heb *saturation*

yet thou hast brought us forth to a spacious place.*c*

13 I will come into thy house with burnt offerings;
    I will pay thee my vows,
14 that which my lips uttered
    and my mouth promised when I was in trouble.
15 I will offer to thee burnt offerings of fatlings,
    with the smoke of the sacrifice of rams;
I will make an offering of bulls and goats. *Selah*

16 Come and hear, all you who fear God,
    and I will tell what he has done for me.
17 I cried aloud to him,
    and he was extolled with my tongue.
18 If I had cherished iniquity in my heart,
    the Lord would not have listened.
19 But truly God has listened;
    he has given heed to the voice of my prayer.

20 Blessed be God,
    because he has not rejected my prayer
    or removed his steadfast love from me!

Psalm 67

To the choirmaster: with stringed instruments. A Psalm. A Song.

May God be gracious to us and bless us
    and make his face to shine upon us, *Selah*
2 that thy way may be known upon earth,
    thy saving power among all nations.
3 Let the peoples praise thee, O God;
    let all the peoples praise thee!

4 Let the nations be glad and sing for joy,
    for thou dost judge the peoples with equity
    and guide the nations upon earth. *Selah*
5 Let the peoples praise thee, O God;
    let all the peoples praise thee!

6 The earth has yielded its increase;
    God, our God, has blessed us.
7 God has blessed us;
    let all the ends of the earth fear him!

Psalm 68

To the choirmaster. A Psalm of David. A Song.

d Or *cast up a highway for him who rides through the deserts*

Let God arise, let his enemies be scattered;
    let those who hate him flee before him!
2 As smoke is driven away, so drive them away;
    as wax melts before fire,
    let the wicked perish before God!
3 But let the righteous be joyful;
    let them exult before God;
    let them be jubilant with joy!

4 Sing to God, sing praises to his name;
    lift up a song to him who rides upon the clouds;*d*
    his name is the LORD, exult before him!
5 Father of the fatherless and protector of widows
    is God in his holy habitation.

6 God gives the desolate a home to dwell in;
    he leads out the prisoners to prosperity;
    but the rebellious dwell in a parched land.

7 O God, when thou didst go forth before thy people,
    when thou didst march through the wilderness, *Selah*
8 the earth quaked, the heavens poured down rain,
    at the presence of God;
yon Sinai quaked at the presence of God,
    the God of Israel.

9 Rain in abundance, O God, thou didst shed abroad;
    thou didst restore thy heritage as it languished;
10 thy flock found a dwelling in it;
    in thy goodness, O God, thou didst provide for the needy.

11 The Lord gives the command;
    great is the host of those who bore the tidings:
12   "The kings of the armies, they flee, they flee!"
The women at home divide the spoil,
13   though they stay among the sheepfolds—
the wings of a dove covered with silver,
    its pinions with green gold.
14 When the Almighty scattered kings there,
    snow fell on Zalmon.

15 O mighty mountain, mountain of Bashan;
    O many-peaked mountain, mountain of Bashan!
16 Why look you with envy, O many-peaked mountain,
    at the mount which God desired for his abode,
    yea, where the Lord will dwell for ever?

17 With mighty chariotry, twice ten thousand,
    thousands upon thousands,

[e] Cn: Heb *The Lord among them Sinai in the holy place*

    the Lord came from Sinai into the holy place.*[e]*
18 Thou didst ascend the high mount,
    leading captives in thy train,
    and receiving gifts among men,
even among the rebellious, that the Lord God may dwell there.

19 Blessed be the Lord,
    who daily bears us up;
    God is our salvation. *Selah*
20 Our God is a God of salvation;
    and to God, the Lord, belongs escape from death.

21 But God will shatter the heads of his enemies,
    the hairy crown of him who walks in his guilty ways.
22 The Lord said,
    "I will bring them back from Bashan,
    I will bring them back from the depths of the sea,

[f] Gk Syr Tg: Heb *shatter*

23 that you may bathe*[f]* your feet in blood,
    that the tongues of your dogs may have their portion
      from the foe."

[g] Or *have been seen*

24 Thy solemn processions are seen,*[g]* O God,
    the processions of my God, my King, into the sanctuary—
25 the singers in front, the minstrels last,
    between them maidens playing timbrels:
26 "Bless God in the great congregation,
    the Lord, O you who are of Israel's fountain!"
27 There is Benjamin, the least of them, in the lead,
    the princes of Judah in their throng,
    the princes of Zeb'ulun, the princes of Naph'tali.

28 Summon thy might, O God;
    show thy strength, O God, thou who hast wrought for us.
29 Because of thy temple at Jerusalem
    kings bear gifts to thee.
30 Rebuke the beasts that dwell among the reeds,
    the herd of bulls with the calves of the peoples.

[h] Cn: Heb *trampling*
[i] *The Hebrew of verse 30 is obscure*

Trample*[h]* under foot those who lust after tribute;
    scatter the peoples who delight in war.*[i]*
31 Let bronze be brought from Egypt;
    let Ethiopia hasten to stretch out her hands to God.

32 Sing to God, O kingdoms of the earth;
   sing praises to the Lord, *Selah*
33 to him who rides in the heavens, the ancient heavens;
   lo, he sends forth his voice, his mighty voice.
34 Ascribe power to God,
   whose majesty is over Israel,
   and his power is in the skies.

ʲ Gk: Heb from thy   35 Terrible is God in his*ʲ* sanctuary,
   the God of Israel,
   he gives power and strength to his people.

Blessed be God!

Psalm 69

To the
choirmaster:
according to
Lilies. A Psalm
of David.

Save me, O God!
For the waters have come up to my neck.
2 I sink in deep mire,
   where there is no foothold;
I have come into deep waters,
   and the flood sweeps over me.
3 I am weary with my crying;
   my throat is parched.
My eyes grow dim
   with waiting for my God.

4 More in number than the hairs of my head
   are those who hate me without cause;
mighty are those who would destroy me,
   those who attack me with lies.
What I did not steal
   must I now restore?
5 O God, thou knowest my folly;
   the wrongs I have done are not hidden from thee.

6 Let not those who hope in thee be put to shame through me,
   O Lord GOD of hosts;
let not those who seek thee be brought to dishonor through me,
   O God of Israel.
7 For it is for thy sake that I have borne reproach,
   that shame has covered my face.
8 I have become a stranger to my brethren,
   an alien to my mother's sons.

9 For zeal for thy house has consumed me,
   and the insults of those who insult thee have fallen on me.

ᵏ Gk Syr: Heb I
wept with fasting
my soul *or* I made
my soul mourn
with fasting

10 When I humbled*ᵏ* my soul with fasting,
   it became my reproach.
11 When I made sackcloth my clothing,
   I became a byword to them.
12 I am the talk of those who sit in the gate,
   and the drunkards make songs about me.

13 But as for me, my prayer is to thee, O LORD.
   At an acceptable time, O God,
   in the abundance of thy steadfast love answer me.
With thy faithful help 14 rescue me
   from sinking in the mire;
let me be delivered from my enemies
   and from the deep waters.
15 Let not the flood sweep over me,
   or the deep swallow me up,
   or the pit close its mouth over me.

16 Answer me, O LORD, for thy steadfast love is good;
   according to thy abundant mercy, turn to me.
17 Hide not thy face from thy servant;
   for I am in distress, make haste to answer me.
18 Draw near to me, redeem me,
   set me free because of my enemies!

19 Thou knowest my reproach,
   and my shame and my dishonor;
   my foes are all known to thee.
20 Insults have broken my heart,
   so that I am in despair.

I looked for pity, but there was none;
   and for comforters, but I found none.
21 They gave me poison for food,
   and for my thirst they gave me vinegar to drink.
22 Let their own table before them become a snare;
   let their sacrificial feasts[l] be a trap.
23 Let their eyes be darkened, so that they cannot see;
   and make their loins tremble continually.
24 Pour out thy indignation upon them,
   and let thy burning anger overtake them.
25 May their camp be a desolation,
   let no one dwell in their tents.
26 For they persecute him whom thou hast smitten,
   and him[m] whom thou hast wounded, they afflict still more.[n]
27 Add to them punishment upon punishment;
   may they have no acquittal from thee.
28 Let them be blotted out of the book of the living;
   let them not be enrolled among the righteous.

29 But I am afflicted and in pain;
   let thy salvation, O God, set me on high!

30 I will praise the name of God with a song;
   I will magnify him with thanksgiving.
31 This will please the LORD more than an ox
   or a bull with horns and hoofs.
32 Let the oppressed see it and be glad;
   you who seek God, let your hearts revive.
33 For the LORD hears the needy,
   and does not despise his own that are in bonds.

34 Let heaven and earth praise him,
   the seas and everything that moves therein.
35 For God will save Zion
   and rebuild the cities of Judah;
and his servants shall dwell[o] there and possess it;
36   the children of his servants shall inherit it,
   and those who love his name shall dwell in it.

Psalm 70

Be pleased, O God, to deliver me!
   O LORD, make haste to help me!
2 Let them be put to shame and confusion
   who seek my life!
Let them be turned back and brought to dishonor
   who desire my hurt!
3 Let them be appalled because of their shame
   who say, "Aha, Aha!"

4 May all who seek thee
   rejoice and be glad in thee!
May those who love thy salvation
   say evermore, "God is great!"
5 But I am poor and needy;
   hasten to me, O God!
Thou art my help and my deliverer;
   O LORD, do not tarry!

Psalm 71

In thee, O LORD, do I take refuge;
   let me never be put to shame!
2 In thy righteousness deliver me and rescue me;
   incline thy ear to me, and save me!
3 Be thou to me a rock of refuge,
   a strong fortress,[p] to save me,
   for thou art my rock and my fortress.

4 Rescue me, O my God, from the hand of the wicked,
   from the grasp of the unjust and cruel man.
5 For thou, O Lord, art my hope,
   my trust, O LORD, from my youth.
6 Upon thee I have leaned from my birth;
   thou art he who took me from my mother's womb.
My praise is continually of thee.

[l] Tg: Heb for security

[m] One Ms Tg Compare Syr: Heb those

[n] Gk Syr: Heb recount the pain of

[o] Syr: Heb and they shall dwell

Psalm 70

To the choirmaster. A Psalm of David, for the memorial offering.

Psalm 71

[p] Gk Compare 31.3: Heb to come continually thou hast commanded

7 I have been as a portent to many;
  but thou art my strong refuge.
8 My mouth is filled with thy praise,
  and with thy glory all the day.
9 Do not cast me off in the time of old age;
  forsake me not when my strength is spent.
10 For my enemies speak concerning me
  those who watch for my life consult together,
11 and say, "God has forsaken him;
  pursue and seize him,
  for there is none to deliver him."

12 O God, be not far from me;
  O my God, make haste to help me!
13 May my accusers be put to shame and consumed;
  with scorn and disgrace may they be covered
  who seek my hurt.
14 But I will hope continually,
  and will praise thee yet more and more.
15 My mouth will tell of thy righteous acts,
  of thy deeds of salvation all the day,
  for their number is past my knowledge.
16 With the mighty deeds of the Lord GOD I will come,
  I will praise thy righteousness, thine alone.

17 O God, from my youth thou hast taught me,
  and I still proclaim thy wondrous deeds.
18 So even to old age and gray hairs,
  O God, do not forsake me,
till I proclaim thy might
  to all the generations to come.*q*

q Gk Compare
Syr: Heb *to a
generation, to all
that come*

Thy power 19 and thy righteousness, O God,
  reach the high heavens.

Thou who hast done great things,
  O God, who is like thee?
20 Thou who hast made me see many sore troubles
  wilt revive me again;
from the depths of the earth
  thou wilt bring me up again.
21 Thou wilt increase my honor,
  and comfort me again.

22 I will also praise thee with the harp
  for thy faithfulness, O my God;
I will sing praises to thee with the lyre,
  O Holy One of Israel.
23 My lips will shout for joy,
  when I sing praises to thee;
  my soul also, which thou hast rescued.
24 And my tongue will talk of thy righteous help
  all the day long,
for they have been put to shame and disgraced
  who sought to do me hurt.

Psalm 72

A Psalm to
Solomon.

Give the king thy justice, O God,
  and thy righteousness to the royal son!
2 May he judge thy people with righteousness,
  and thy poor with justice!
3 Let the mountains bear prosperity for the people,
  and the hills, in righteousness!
4 May he defend the cause of the poor of the people,
  give deliverance to the needy,
  and crush the oppressor!

r Gk: Heb *may
they fear thee*

5 May he live*r* while the sun endures,
  and as long as the moon, throughout all generations!
6 May he be like rain that falls on the mown grass,
  like showers that water the earth!
7 In his days may righteousness flourish,
  and peace abound, till the moon be no more!

8 May he have dominion from sea to sea,
  and from the River to the ends of the earth!
9 May his foes[s] bow down before him,
  and his enemies lick the dust!
10 May the kings of Tarshish and of the isles
  render him tribute,
may the kings of Sheba and Seba bring gifts!
11 May all kings fall down before him,
  all nations serve him!

12 For he delivers the needy when he calls,
  the poor and him who has no helper.
13 He has pity on the weak and the needy,
  and saves the lives of the needy.
14 From oppression and violence he redeems their life;
  and precious is their blood in his sight.

15 Long may he live,
  may gold of Sheba be given to him!
May prayer be made for him continually,
  and blessings invoked for him all the day!

16 May there be abundance of grain in the land;
  on the tops of the mountains may it wave;
  may its fruit be like Lebanon;
and may men blossom forth from the cities
  like the grass of the field!
17 May his name endure for ever,
  his fame continue as long as the sun!
May men bless themselves by him,
  all nations call him blessed!

18 Blessed be the LORD, the God of Israel,
  who alone does wondrous things.
19 Blessed be his glorious name for ever;
  may his glory fill the whole earth! Amen and Amen!

20 The prayers of David, the son of Jesse, are ended.

BOOK III

Psalm 73

A Psalm of Asaph.

Truly God is good to the upright,
  to those who are pure in heart.[t]
2 But as for me, my feet had almost stumbled,
  my steps had well nigh slipped.
3 For I was envious of the arrogant,
  when I saw the prosperity of the wicked.

4 For they have no pangs;
  their bodies are sound and sleek.
5 They are not in trouble as other men are;
  they are not stricken like other men.
6 Therefore pride is their necklace;
  violence covers them as a garment.
7 Their eyes swell out with fatness,
  their hearts overflow with follies.
8 They scoff and speak with malice;
  loftily they threaten oppression.
9 They set their mouths against the heavens,
  and their tongue struts through the earth.

10 Therefore the people turn and praise them;[u]
  and find no fault in them.[v]
11 And they say, "How can God know?
  Is there knowledge in the Most High?"
12 Behold, these are the wicked;
  always at ease, they increase in riches.
13 All in vain have I kept my heart clean
  and washed my hands in innocence.
14 For all the day long I have been stricken,
  and chastened every morning.

15 If I had said, "I will speak thus,"
  I would have been untrue to the generation of thy children.

[s] Cn: Heb *those who dwell in the wilderness*

[t] Or *Truly God is good to Israel, to those who are pure in heart*

[u] Cn: Heb *his people return hither*
[v] Cn: Heb *abundant waters are drained by them*

16 But when I thought how to understand this,
   it seemed to me a wearisome task,
17 until I went into the sanctuary of God;
   then I perceived their end.
18 Truly thou dost set them in slippery places;
   thou dost make them fall to ruin.
19 How they are destroyed in a moment,
   swept away utterly by terrors!

*Cn: Heb *Lord*

20 They are*ʷ* like a dream when one awakes,
   on awaking you despise their phantoms.
21 When my soul was embittered,
   when I was pricked in heart,
22 I was stupid and ignorant,
   I was like a beast toward thee.
23 Nevertheless I am continually with thee;
   thou dost hold my right hand.
24 Thou dost guide me with thy counsel,

*Or *honor*

   and afterward thou wilt receive me to glory.*ˣ*
25 Whom have I in heaven but thee?
   And there is nothing upon earth that I desire besides thee.
26 My flesh and my heart may fail,

*Heb *rock*

   but God is the strength*ʸ* of my heart and my portion for ever.
27 For lo, those who are far from thee shall perish;
   thou dost put an end to those who are false to thee.
28 But for me it is good to be near God;
   I have made the Lord God my refuge,
   that I may tell of all thy works.

Psalm 74

A Maskil of
Asaph.

O God, why dost thou cast us off for ever?
   Why does thy anger smoke against the sheep of thy pasture?
2 Remember thy congregation, which thou hast gotten of old,
   which thou hast redeemed to be the tribe of thy heritage!
   Remember Mount Zion, where thou hast dwelt.
3 Direct thy steps to the perpetual ruins;
   the enemy has destroyed everything in the sanctuary!

4 Thy foes have roared in the midst of thy holy place;
   they set up their own signs for signs.
5 At the upper entrance they hacked

*Cn Compare Gk
Syr: Heb
uncertain

   the wooden trellis with axes.*ᶻ*
6 And then all its carved wood
   they broke down with hatchets and hammers.
7 They set thy sanctuary on fire;
   to the ground they desecrated the dwelling place of thy name.
8 They said to themselves, "We will utterly subdue them";
   they burned all the meeting places of God in the land.

9 We do not see our signs;
   there is no longer any prophet,
   and there is none among us who knows how long.
10 How long, O God, is the foe to scoff?
   Is the enemy to revile thy name for ever?
11 Why dost thou hold back thy hand,

*Cn: Heb
consume thy right
hand from

   why dost thou keep thy right hand in*ᵃ* thy bosom?
12 Yet God my King is from of old,
   working salvation in the midst of the earth.
13 Thou didst divide the sea by thy might;
   thou didst break the heads of the dragons on the waters.
14 Thou didst crush the heads of Leviathan,

*Heb *food for the
people

   thou didst give him as food*ᵇ* for the creatures of the wilderness.
15 Thou didst cleave open springs and brooks;
   thou didst dry up ever-flowing streams.
16 Thine is the day, thine also the night;
   thou hast established the luminaries and the sun.
17 Thou hast fixed all the bounds of the earth;
   thou hast made summer and winter.
18 Remember this, O Lord, how the enemy scoffs,
   and an impious people reviles thy name.
19 Do not deliver the soul of thy dove to the wild beasts;
   do not forget the life of thy poor for ever.

*c*Gk Syr: Heb *the* 20 Have regard for thy*c* covenant;
 for the dark places of the land are full of the habitations of
  violence.
21 Let not the downtrodden be put to shame;
 let the poor and needy praise thy name.
22 Arise, O God, plead thy cause;
 remember how the impious scoff at thee all the day!
23 Do not forget the clamor of thy foes,
 the uproar of thy adversaries which goes up continually!

Psalm 75

To the
choirmaster:
according to Do
Not Destroy.
A Psalm of
Asaph. A Song.

We give thanks to thee, O God; we give thanks;
 we call on thy name and recount*d* thy wondrous deeds.
2 At the set time which I appoint
 I will judge with equity.
3 When the earth totters, and all its inhabitants,
 it is I who keep steady its pillars. *Selah*
4 I say to the boastful, "Do not boast,"
 and to the wicked, "Do not lift up your horn;
5 do not lift up your horn on high,
 or speak with insolent neck."

*d*Syr Compare
Gk: Heb *and near
is thy name. They
recount*

6 For not from the east or from the west
 and not from the wilderness comes lifting up;
7 but it is God who executes judgment,
 putting down one and lifting up another.
8 For in the hand of the LORD there is a cup,
 with foaming wine, well mixed;
and he will pour a draught from it,
 and all the wicked of the earth
 shall drain it down to the dregs.

*e*Gk: Heb *declare* 9 But I will rejoice*e* for ever,
 I will sing praises to the God of Jacob.
*f*Heb *I* 10 All the horns of the wicked he*f* will cut off,
 but the horns of the righteous shall be exalted.

Psalm 76

To the
choirmaster:
with stringed
instruments.
A Psalm of
Asaph. A Song.

In Judah God is known, his name is great in Israel.
2 His abode has been established in Salem,
 his dwelling place in Zion.
3 There he broke the flashing arrows,
 the shield, the sword, and the weapons of war. *Selah*
4 Glorious art thou, more majestic
 than the everlasting mountains.*g*
5 The stouthearted were stripped of their spoil;
 they sank into sleep;
all the men of war
 were unable to use their hands.

*g*Gk: Heb *the
mountains of prey*

6 At thy rebuke, O God of Jacob,
 both rider and horse lay stunned.
7 But thou, terrible art thou!
 Who can stand before thee
 when once thy anger is roused?
8 From the heavens thou didst utter judgment;
 the earth feared and was still,
9 when God arose to establish judgment
 to save all the oppressed of the earth. *Selah*
10 Surely the wrath of men shall praise thee;
 the residue of wrath thou wilt gird upon thee.
11 Make your vows to the LORD your God, and perform them;
 let all around him bring gifts
 to him who is to be feared,
12 who cuts off the spirit of princes,
 who is terrible to the kings of the earth.

Psalm 77

I cry aloud to God,
 aloud to God, that he may hear me.
2 In the day of my trouble I seek the Lord;
 in the night my hand is stretched out without wearying;
 my soul refuses to be comforted.

To the
choirmaster:
according to
Jeduthun.
A Psalm of
Asaph.

3 I think of God, and I moan;
 I meditate, and my spirit faints. *Selah*
4 Thou dost hold my eyelids from closing;
 I am so troubled that I cannot speak.
5 I consider the days of old,
 I remember the years long ago.

h Gk Syr: Heb *my music*
i Syr Jerome: Heb *my spirit searches*

6 I commune[h] with my heart in the night;
 I meditate and search my spirit:[i]
7 "Will the Lord spurn for ever,
 and never again be favorable?
8 Has his steadfast love for ever ceased?
 Are his promises at an end for all time?
9 Has God forgotten to be gracious?
 Has he in anger shut up his compassion?" *Selah*
10 And I say, "It is my grief
 that the right hand of the Most High has changed."

11 I will call to mind the deeds of the LORD;
 yea, I will remember thy wonders of old.
12 I will meditate on all thy work,
 and muse on thy mighty deeds.
13 Thy way, O God, is holy.
 What god is great like our God?
14 Thou art the God who workest wonders,
 who hast manifested thy might among the peoples.
15 Thou didst with thy arm redeem thy people,
 the sons of Jacob and Joseph. *Selah*

16 When the waters saw thee, O God,
 when the waters saw thee, they were afraid,
 yea, the deep trembled.
17 The clouds poured out water;
 the skies gave forth thunder;
 thy arrows flashed on every side.
18 The crash of thy thunder was in the whirlwind;
 thy lightnings lighted up the world;
 the earth trembled and shook.
19 Thy way was through the sea,
 thy path through the great waters;
 yet thy footprints were unseen.
20 Thou didst lead thy people like a flock
 by the hand of Moses and Aaron.

Psalm 78

A Maskil of
Asaph.

Give ear, O my people, to my teaching;
 incline your ears to the words of my mouth!
2 I will open my mouth in a parable;
 I will utter dark sayings from of old,
3 things that we have heard and known,
 that our fathers have told us.
4 We will not hide them from their children,
 but tell to the coming generation
the glorious deeds of the LORD, and his might,
 and the wonders which he has wrought.

5 He established a testimony in Jacob,
 and appointed a law in Israel,
which he commanded our fathers to teach to their children;
6 that the next generation might know them,
 the children yet unborn,
and arise and tell them to their children,
7   so that they should set their hope in God,
and not forget the works of God,
 but keep his commandments;
8 and that they should not be like their fathers,
 a stubborn and rebellious generation,
a generation whose heart was not steadfast,
 whose spirit was not faithful to God.

j Heb *armed with shooting*

9 The E'phraimites, armed with[j] the bow,
 turned back on the day of battle.
10 They did not keep God's covenant,
 but refused to walk according to his law.

11 They forgot what he had done,
  and the miracles that he had shown them.
12 In the sight of their fathers he wrought marvels
  in the land of Egypt, in the fields of Zo'an.
13 He divided the sea and let them pass through it,
  and made the waters stand like a heap.
14 In the daytime he led them with a cloud,
  and all the night with a fiery light.
15 He cleft rocks in the wilderness,
  and gave them drink abundantly as from the deep.
16 He made streams come out of the rock,
  and caused waters to flow down like rivers.

17 Yet they sinned still more against him,
  rebelling against the Most High in the desert.
18 They tested God in their heart
  by demanding the food they craved.
19 They spoke against God, saying,
  "Can God spread a table in the wilderness?
20 He smote the rock so that water gushed out
  and streams overflowed.
Can he also give bread,
  or provide meat for his people?"

21 Therefore, when the LORD heard, he was full of wrath;
  a fire was kindled against Jacob,
  his anger mounted against Israel;
22 because they had no faith in God,
  and did not trust his saving power.
23 Yet he commanded the skies above,
  and opened the doors of heaven;
24 and he rained down upon them manna to eat,
  and gave them the grain of heaven.
25 Man ate of the bread of the angels;
  he sent them food in abundance.
26 He caused the east wind to blow in the heavens,
  and by his power he led out the south wind;
27 he rained flesh upon them like dust,
  winged birds like the sand of the seas;
28 he let them fall in the midst of their camp,
  all around their habitations.
29 And they ate and were well filled,
  for he gave them what they craved.
30 But before they had sated their craving,
  while the food was still in their mouths,
31 the anger of God rose against them
  and he slew the strongest of them,
  and laid low the picked men of Israel.

32 In spite of all this they still sinned;
  despite his wonders they did not believe.
33 So he made their days vanish like a breath.
  and their years in terror.
34 When he slew them, they sought for him;
  they repented and sought God earnestly.
35 They remembered that God was their rock,
  the Most High God their redeemer.
36 But they flattered him with their mouths;
  they lied to him with their tongues.
37 Their heart was not steadfast toward him;
  they were not true to his covenant.
38 Yet he, being compassionate,
  forgave their iniquity,
  and did not destroy them;
he restrained his anger often,
  and did not stir up all his wrath.
39 He remembered that they were but flesh,
  a wind that passes and comes not again.
40 How often they rebelled against him in the wilderness
  and grieved him in the desert!
41 They tested him again and again,

and provoked the Holy One of Israel.
42 They did not keep in mind his power,
   or the day when he redeemed them from the foe;
43 when he wrought his signs in Egypt,
   and his miracles in the fields of Zo'an.
44 He turned their rivers to blood
   so that they could not drink of their streams.
45 He sent among them swarms of flies, which devoured them,
   and frogs, which destroyed them.
46 He gave their crops to the caterpillar,
   and the fruit of their labor to the locust.
47 He destroyed their vines with hail,
   and their sycamores with frost.
48 He gave over their cattle to the hail,
   and their flocks to thunderbolts.
49 He let loose on them his fierce anger,
   wrath, indignation, and distress,
   a company of destroying angels.
50 He made a path for his anger;
   he did not spare them from death,
   but gave their lives over to the plague.
51 He smote all the first-born in Egypt,
   the first issue of their strength in the tents of Ham.

52 Then he led forth his people like sheep,
   and guided them in the wilderness like a flock.
53 He led them in safety, so that they were not afraid;
   but the sea overwhelmed their enemies.
54 And he brought them to his holy land,
   to the mountain which his right hand had won.
55 He drove out nations before them;
   he apportioned them for a possession
   and settled the tribes of Israel in their tents.

56 Yet they tested and rebelled against the Most High God,
   and did not observe his testimonies,
57 but turned away and acted treacherously like their fathers;
   they twisted like a deceitful bow.
58 For they provoked him to anger with their high places;
   they moved him to jealousy with their graven images.
59 When God heard, he was full of wrath,
   and he utterly rejected Israel.
60 He forsook his dwelling at Shiloh,
   the tent where he dwelt among men,
61 and delivered his power to captivity,
   his glory to the hand of the foe.
62 He gave his people over to the sword,
   and vented his wrath on his heritage.
63 Fire devoured their young men,
   and their maidens had no marriage song.
64 Their priests fell by the sword,
   and their widows made no lamentation.
65 Then the Lord awoke as from sleep,
   like a strong man shouting because of wine.
66 And he put his adversaries to rout;
   he put them to everlasting shame.

67 He rejected the tent of Joseph,
   he did not choose the tribe of E'phraim;
68 but he chose the tribe of Judah,
   Mount Zion, which he loves.
69 He built his sanctuary like the high heavens,
   like the earth, which he has founded for ever.
70 He chose David his servant,
   and took him from the sheepfolds;
71 from tending the ewes that had young he brought him
   to be the shepherd of Jacob his people,
   of Israel his inheritance.
72 With upright heart he tended them,
   and guided them with skilful hand.

Psalm 79

A Psalm of Asaph.

O God, the heathen have come into thy inheritance;
  they have defiled thy holy temple;
  they have laid Jerusalem in ruins.
2 They have given the bodies of thy servants
  to the birds of the air for food,
  the flesh of thy saints to the beasts of the earth.
3 They have poured out their blood like water
  round about Jerusalem,
  and there was none to bury them.
4 We have become a taunt to our neighbors,
  mocked and derided by those round about us.

5 How long, O LORD? Wilt thou be angry for ever?
  Will thy jealous wrath burn like fire?
6 Pour out thy anger on the nations that do not know thee,
and on the kingdoms
  that do not call on thy name!
7 For they have devoured Jacob,
  and laid waste his habitation.

8 Do not remember against us the iniquities of our forefathers;
  let thy compassion come speedily to meet us,
  for we are brought very low.
9 Help us, O God of our salvation,
  for the glory of thy name;
deliver us, and forgive our sins,
  for thy name's sake!
10 Why should the nations say,
  "Where is their God?"
Let the avenging of the outpoured blood of thy servants
  be known among the nations before our eyes!

11 Let the groans of the prisoners come before thee;
  according to thy great power preserve those doomed to die!
12 Return sevenfold into the bosom of our neighbors
  the taunts with which they have taunted thee, O Lord!
13 Then we thy people, the flock of thy pasture,
  will give thanks to thee for ever;
  from generation to generation we will recount thy praise.

Psalm 80

To the choirmaster: according to Lilies. A Testimony of Asaph. A Psalm.

Give ear, O Shepherd of Israel,
  thou who leadest Joseph like a flock!
Thou who art enthroned upon the cherubim, shine forth
2   before E'phraim and Benjamin and Manas'seh!
Stir up thy might,
  and come to save us!

3 Restore us, O God;
  let thy face shine, that we may be saved!

4 O LORD God of hosts,
  how long wilt thou be angry with thy people's prayers?
5 Thou hast fed them with the bread of tears,
  and given them tears to drink in full measure.

*Syr: Heb *strife*

6 Thou dost make us the scorn[k] of our neighbors;
  and our enemies laugh among themselves.

7 Restore us, O God of hosts;
  let thy face shine, that we may be saved!

8 Thou didst bring a vine out of Egypt;
  thou didst drive out the nations and plant it.
9 Thou didst clear the ground for it;
  it took deep root and filled the land.
10 The mountains were covered with its shade,
  the mighty cedars with its branches;
11 it sent out its branches to the sea,
  and its shoots to the River.
12 Why then hast thou broken down its walls,
  so that all who pass along the way pluck its fruit?
13 The boar from the forest ravages it,
  and all that move in the field feed on it.

14 Turn again, O God of hosts!
  Look down from heaven, and see;

have regard for this vine,

l Heb *planted and upon the son whom thou hast reared for thyself*

15   the stock which thy right hand planted.*l*
16 They have burned it with fire, they have cut it down;
  may they perish at the rebuke of thy countenance!
17 But let thy hand be upon the man of thy right hand,
  the son of man whom thou hast made strong for thyself!
18 Then we will never turn back from thee;
  give us life, and we will call on thy name!
19 Restore us, O LORD God of hosts!
  let thy face shine, that we may be saved!

Psalm 81

To the choirmaster: according to The Gittith. A Psalm of Asaph.

Sing aloud to God our strength;
  shout for joy to the God of Jacob!
2 Raise a song, sound the timbrel,
  the sweet lyre with the harp.
3 Blow the trumpet at the new moon,
  at the full moon, on our feast day.
4 For it is a statute for Israel,
  an ordinance of the God of Jacob.
5 He made it a decree in Joseph,
  when he went out over*m* the land of Egypt.

m Or *against*
n Heb *his*

I hear a voice I had not known:
6 "I relieved your*n* shoulder of the burden;
  your*n* hands were freed from the basket.
7 In distress you called, and I delivered you;
  I answered you in the secret place of thunder;
  I tested you at the waters of Mer'ibah. *Selah*
8 Hear, O my people, while I admonish you!
  O Israel, if you would but listen to me!
9 There shall be no strange god among you;
  you shall not bow down to a foreign god.
10 I am the LORD your God,
  who brought you up out of the land of Egypt.
  Open your mouth wide, and I will fill it.

11 "But my people did not listen to my voice;
  Israel would have none of me.
12 So I gave them over to their stubborn hearts,
  to follow their own counsels.
13 O that my people would listen to me,
  that Israel would walk in my ways!
14 I would soon subdue their enemies,
  and turn my hand against their foes.

o Cn Compare verse 16b: Heb *he would feed him*

15 Those who hate the LORD would cringe toward him,
  and their fate would last for ever.
16 I would feed you*o* with the finest of the wheat,
  and with honey from the rock I would satisfy you."

Psalm 82

A Psalm of Asaph.

God has taken his place in the divine council;
  in the midst of the gods he holds judgment:
2 "How long will you judge unjustly
  and show partiality to the wicked? *Selah*
3 Give justice to the weak and the fatherless;
  maintain the right of the afflicted and the destitute.
4 Rescue the weak and the needy;
  deliver them from the hand of the wicked."
5 They have neither knowledge nor understanding,
  they walk about in darkness;
  all the foundations of the earth are shaken.

6 I say, "You are gods,
  sons of the Most High, all of you;
7 nevertheless, you shall die like men,
  and fall like any prince."*p*

p Or *fall as one man, O princes*

8 Arise, O God, judge the earth;
  for to thee belong all the nations!

Psalm 83

A Song.
A Psalm of
Asaph.

O God, do not keep silence;
  do not hold thy peace or be still, O God!
2 For lo, thy enemies are in tumult;
  those who hate thee have raised their heads.
3 They lay crafty plans against thy people;
  they consult together against thy protected ones.
4 They say, "Come, let us wipe them out as a nation;
  let the name of Israel be remembered no more!"
5 Yea, they conspire with one accord;
  against thee they make a covenant—
6 the tents of Edom and the Ish'maelites,
  Moab and the Hagrites,
7 Gebal and Ammon and Am'alek,
  Philistia with the inhabitants of Tyre;
8 Assyria also has joined them;
  they are the strong arm of the children of Lot. *Selah*

9 Do to them as thou didst to Mid'ian,
  as to Sis'era and Jabin at the river Kishon,
10 who were destroyed at En-dor,
  who became dung for the ground.
11 Make their nobles like Oreb and Zeeb,
  all their princes like Zebah and Zalmun'na,
12 who said, "Let us take possession for ourselves
  of the pastures of God."

q Or a
tumbleweed

13 O my God, make them like whirling dust,*q*
  like chaff before the wind.
14 As fire consumes the forest,
  as the flame sets the mountains ablaze,
15 so do thou pursue them with thy tempest
  and terrify them with thy hurricane!
16 Fill their faces with shame,
  that they may seek thy name, O Lord.
17 Let them be put to shame and dismayed for ever;
  let them perish in disgrace.
18 Let them know that thou alone,
  whose name is the Lord,
  art the Most High over all the earth.

Psalm 84

To the
choirmaster:
according to the
Gittith. A Psalm
of the Sons of
Korah.

How lovely is thy dwelling place,
  O Lord of hosts!
2 My soul longs, yea, faints
  for the courts of the Lord;
my heart and flesh sing for joy
  to the living God.
3 Even the sparrow finds a home,
  and the swallow a nest for herself,
  where she may lay her young,
at thy altars, O Lord of hosts,
  my King and my God.
4 Blessed are those who dwell in thy house,
  ever singing thy praise! *Selah*

r Heb lacks *to*
Zion

5 Blessed are the men whose strength is in thee,
  in whose heart are the highways to Zion.*r*
6 As they go through the valley of Baca
  they make it a place of springs;
  the early rain also covers it with pools.
7 They go from strength to strength;
  the God of gods will be seen in Zion.

8 O Lord God of hosts, hear my prayer;
  give ear, O God of Jacob! *Selah*
9 Behold our shield, O God;
  look upon the face of thine anointed!

10 For a day in thy courts is better
  than a thousand elsewhere.
I would rather be a doorkeeper in the house of my God
  than dwell in the tents of wickedness.
11 For the Lord God is a sun and shield;

he bestows favor and honor.
No good thing does the LORD withhold
from those who walk uprightly.
12 O LORD of hosts,
blessed is the man who trusts in thee!

Psalm 85

To the
choirmaster.
A Psalm of the
Sons of Korah.

LORD, thou wast favorable to thy land;
thou didst restore the fortunes of Jacob.
2 Thou didst forgive the iniquity of thy people;
thou didst pardon all their sin. *Selah*
3 Thou didst withdraw all thy wrath;
thou didst turn from thy hot anger.
4 Restore us again, O God of our salvation,
and put away thy indignation toward us!
5 Wilt thou be angry with us for ever?
Wilt thou prolong thy anger to all generations?
6 Wilt thou not revive us again,
that thy people may rejoice in thee?
7 Show us thy steadfast love, O LORD,
and grant us thy salvation.

8 Let me hear what God the LORD will speak,
for he will speak peace to his people,
to his saints, to those who turn to him in their hearts.[s]

s Gk: Heb *but let
them not turn
back to folly*

9 Surely his salvation is at hand for those who fear him,
that glory may dwell in our land.

10 Steadfast love and faithfulness will meet;
righteousness and peace will kiss each other.
11 Faithfulness will spring up from the ground,
and righteousness will look down from the sky.
12 Yea, the LORD will give what is good,
and our land will yield its increase.
13 Righteousness will go before him,
and make his footsteps a way.

Psalm 86

A Prayer of
David.

Incline thy ear, O LORD, and answer me,
for I am poor and needy.
2 Preserve my life, for I am godly;
save thy servant who trusts in thee.
Thou art my God; 3 be gracious to me, O Lord,
for to thee do I cry all the day.
4 Gladden the soul of thy servant,
for to thee, O Lord, do I lift up my soul.
5 For thou, O Lord, art good and forgiving,
abounding in steadfast love to all who call on thee.
6 Give ear, O LORD, to my prayer;
hearken to my cry of supplication.
7 In the day of my trouble I call on thee,
for thou dost answer me.
8 There is none like thee among the gods, O Lord,
nor are there any works like thine.
9 All the nations thou hast made shall come
and bow down before thee, O Lord,
and shall glorify thy name.
10 For thou art great and doest wondrous things,
thou alone art God.
11 Teach me thy way, O LORD,
that I may walk in thy truth;
unite my heart to fear thy name.
12 I give thanks to thee, O Lord my God, with my whole heart,
and I will glorify thy name for ever.
13 For great is thy steadfast love toward me;
thou hast delivered my soul from the depths of Sheol.

14 O God, insolent men have risen up against me;
a band of ruthless men seek my life,
and they do not set thee before them.
15 But thou, O Lord, art a God merciful and gracious,
slow to anger and abounding in steadfast love and faithfulness.

16 Turn to me and take pity on me;
    give thy strength to thy servant,
    and save the son of thy handmaid.
17 Show me a sign of thy favor,
    that those who hate me may see and be put to shame
    because thou, LORD, hast helped me and comforted me.

Psalm 87

A Psalm of the
Sons of Korah.
A Song.

On the holy mount stands the city he founded;
2   the LORD loves the gates of Zion
    more than all the dwelling places of Jacob.
3 Glorious things are spoken of you,
    O city of God. *Selah*

4 Among those who know me I mention Rahab and Babylon;
    behold, Philistia and Tyre, with Ethiopia—
    "This one was born there," they say.
5 And of Zion it shall be said,
    "This one and that one were born in her";
    for the Most High himself will establish her.
6 The LORD records as he registers the peoples,
    "This one was born there." *Selah*
7 Singers and dancers alike say,
    "All my springs are in you."

Psalm 88

A Song. A Psalm
of the Sons of
Korah. To the
choirmaster:
according to
Mahalath
Leannoth. A
Maskil of Heman
the Ezrahite.

*Cn: Heb O LORD,
God of my
salvation*

O LORD, my God, I call for help[f] by day;
    I cry out in the night before thee.
2 Let my prayer come before thee,
    incline thy ear to my cry!
3 For my soul is full of troubles,
    and my life draws near to Sheol.
4 I am reckoned among those who go down to the Pit;
    I am a man who has no strength,
5 like one forsaken among the dead,
    like the slain that lie in the grave,
like those whom thou dost remember no more,
    for they are cut off from thy hand.
6 Thou hast put me in the depths of the Pit,
    in the regions dark and deep.
7 Thy wrath lies heavy upon me,
    and thou dost overwhelm me with all thy waves. *Selah*

8 Thou hast caused my companions to shun me;
    thou hast made me a thing of horror to them.
I am shut in so that I cannot escape;
9   my eye grows dim through sorrow.
Every day I call upon thee, O LORD;
    I spread out my hands to thee.
10 Dost thou work wonders for the dead?
    Do the shades rise up to praise thee? *Selah*
11 Is thy steadfast love declared in the grave,
    or thy faithfulness in Abaddon?
12 Are thy wonders known in the darkness,
    or thy saving help in the land of forgetfulness?

13 But I, O LORD, cry to thee;
    in the morning my prayer comes before thee.
14 O LORD, why dost thou cast me off?
    why dost thou hide thy face from me?
15 Afflicted and close to death from my youth up,
    I suffer thy terrors; I am helpless.[g]

*[g] The meaning of
the Hebrew word
is uncertain*

16 Thy wrath has swept over me;
    thy dread assaults destroy me.
17 They surround me like a flood all day long;
    they close in upon me together.
18 Thou hast caused lover and friend to shun me;
    my companions are in darkness.

Psalm 89

A Maskil of
Ethan the
Ezrahite.

ᵛGk: Heb *the
steadfast love of
the* Lord

ʷOr *sons of gods*

ˣGk Syr: Heb
greatly terrible

ʸCn: Heb *are
exalted in*

ᶻCn: Heb *help*

I will sing of thy steadfast love, O Lord,ᵛ for ever;
    with my mouth I will proclaim thy faithfulness to all
        generations.
2 For thy steadfast love was established for ever,
    thy faithfulness is firm as the heavens.
3 Thou hast said, "I have made a covenant with my chosen one,
    I have sworn to David my servant:
4 'I will establish your descendants for ever,
    and build your throne for all generations.'" *Selah*

5 Let the heavens praise thy wonders, O Lord,
    thy faithfulness in the assembly of the holy ones!
6 For who in the skies can be compared to the Lord?
    Who among the heavenly beingsʷ is like the Lord,
7 a God feared in the council of the holy ones,
    great and terribleˣ above all that are round about him?
8 O Lord God of hosts,
    who is mighty as thou art, O Lord,
    with thy faithfulness round about thee?
9 Thou dost rule the raging of the sea;
    when its waves rise, thou stillest them.
10 Thou didst crush Rahab like a carcass,
    thou didst scatter thy enemies with thy mighty arm.
11 The heavens are thine, the earth also is thine;
    the world and all that is in it, thou hast founded them.
12 The north and the south, thou hast created them;
    Tabor and Hermon joyously praise thy name.
13 Thou hast a mighty arm;
    strong is thy hand, high thy right hand.
14 Righteousness and justice are the foundation of thy throne;
    steadfast love and faithfulness go before thee.
15 Blessed are the people who know the festal shout,
    who walk, O Lord, in the light of thy countenance,
16 who exult in thy name all the day,
    and extolʸ thy righteousness.
17 For thou art the glory of their strength;
    by thy favor our horn is exalted.
18 For our shield belongs to the Lord,
    our king to the Holy One of Israel.

19 Of old thou didst speak in a vision
    to thy faithful one, and say:
"I have set the crownᶻ upon one who is mighty,
    I have exalted one chosen from the people.
20 I have found David, my servant;
    with my holy oil I have anointed him;
21 so that my hand shall ever abide with him,
    my arm also shall strengthen him.

22 The enemy shall not outwit him,
    the wicked shall not humble him.
23 I will crush his foes before him
    and strike down those who hate him.
24 My faithfulness and my steadfast love shall be with him,
    and in my name shall his horn be exalted.
25 I will set his hand on the sea
    and his right hand on the rivers.
26 He shall cry to me, 'Thou art my Father,
    my God, and the Rock of my salvation.'
27 And I will make him the first-born,
    the highest of the kings of the earth.
28 My steadfast love I will keep for him for ever,
    and my covenant will stand firm for him.
29 I will establish his line for ever
    and his throne as the days of the heavens.
30 If his children forsake my law
    and do not walk according to my ordinances,
31 if they violate my statutes
    and do not keep my commandments,
32 then I will punish their transgression with the rod
    and their iniquity with scourges;

33 but I will not remove from him my steadfast love,
   or be false to my faithfulness.
34 I will not violate my covenant,
   or alter the word that went forth from my lips.
35 Once for all I have sworn by my holiness;
   I will not lie to David.
36 His line shall endure for ever,
   his throne as long as the sun before me.
37 Like the moon it shall be established for ever;
   it shall stand firm while the skies endure."[a] *Selah*

[a] Cn: Heb *the witness in the skies is sure*

38 But now thou hast cast off and rejected,
   thou art full of wrath against thy anointed.
39 Thou hast renounced the covenant with thy servant;
   thou hast defiled his crown in the dust.
40 Thou hast breached all his walls;
   thou hast laid his strongholds in ruins.
41 All that pass by despoil him;
   he has become the scorn of his neighbors.
42 Thou hast exalted the right hand of his foes;
   thou hast made all his enemies rejoice.
43 Yea, thou hast turned back the edge of his sword,
   and thou hast not made him stand in battle.

[b] Cn: Heb *removed his cleanness*

44 Thou hast removed the scepter from his hand,[b]
   and cast his throne to the ground.
45 Thou hast cut short the days of his youth;
   thou hast covered him with shame. *Selah*

46 How long, O Lord? Wilt thou hide thyself for ever?
   How long will thy wrath burn like fire?

[c] Cn: Heb *I*

47 Remember, O Lord,[c] what the measure of life is,
   for what vanity thou hast created all the sons of men!
48 What man can live and never see death?
   Who can deliver his soul from the power of Sheol? *Selah*

49 Lord, where is thy steadfast love of old,
   which by thy faithfulness thou didst swear to David?
50 Remember, O Lord, how thy servant is scorned;

[d] Cn: Heb *all of many*

   how I bear in my bosom the insults[d] of the peoples,
51 with which thy enemies taunt, O Lord,
   with which they mock the footsteps of thy anointed.

52   Blessed be the Lord for ever! Amen and Amen.

BOOK IV

Psalm 90

A Prayer of Moses, the man of God.

Lord, thou hast been our dwelling place[e]
   in all generations.
2 Before the mountains were brought forth,
   or ever thou hadst formed the earth and the world,
   from everlasting to everlasting thou art God.

[e] Another reading is *refuge*

3 Thou turnest man back to the dust,
   and sayest, "Turn back, O children of men!"
4 For a thousand years in thy sight
   are but as yesterday when it is past,
   or as a watch in the night.
5 Thou dost sweep men away; they are like a dream,
   like grass which is renewed in the morning:
6 in the morning it flourishes and is renewed;
   in the evening it fades and withers.

7 For we are consumed by thy anger;
   by thy wrath we are overwhelmed.
8 Thou hast set our iniquities before thee,
   our secret sins in the light of thy countenance.

[f] Syr: Heb *we bring our years to an end*

9 For all our days pass away under thy wrath,
   our years come to an end[f] like a sigh.

[g] Cn Compare Gk Syr Jerome Tg: Heb *pride*

10 The years of our life are threescore and ten,
   or even by reason of strength fourscore;
   yet their span[g] is but toil and trouble;
   they are soon gone, and we fly away.

11 Who considers the power of thy anger,
  and thy wrath according to the fear of thee?
12 So teach us to number our days
  that we may get a heart of wisdom.
13 Return, O LORD! How long?
  Have pity on thy servants!
14 Satisfy us in the morning with thy steadfast love,
  that we may rejoice and be glad all our days.
15 Make us glad as many days as thou hast afflicted us,
  and as many years as we have seen evil.
16 Let thy work be manifest to thy servants,
  and thy glorious power to their children.
17 Let the favor of the Lord our God be upon us,
  and establish thou the work of our hands upon us,
  yea, the work of our hands establish thou it.

Psalm 91

He who dwells in the shelter of the Most High,
  who abides in the shadow of the Almighty,
2 will say to the LORD, "My refuge and my fortress;
  my God, in whom I trust."
3 For he will deliver you from the snare of the fowler
  and from the deadly pestilence;
4 he will cover you with his pinions,
  and under his wings you will find refuge;
  his faithfulness is a shield and buckler.
5 You will not fear the terror of the night,
  nor the arrow that flies by day,
6 nor the pestilence that stalks in darkness,
  nor the destruction that wastes at noonday.
7 A thousand may fall at your side,
  ten thousand at your right hand;
  but it will not come near you.
8 You will only look with your eyes
  and see the recompense of the wicked.

h Cn: Heb *Because thou, LORD, art my refuge; you have made*

9 Because you have made the LORD your refuge,*h*
  the Most High your habitation,
10 no evil shall befall you,
  no scourge come near your tent.
11 For he will give his angels charge of you
  to guard you in all your ways.
12 On their hands they will bear you up,
  lest you dash your foot against a stone.
13 You will tread on the lion and the adder,
  the young lion and the serpent you will trample under foot.
14 Because he cleaves to me in love, I will deliver him;
  I will protect him, because he knows my name.
15 When he calls to me, I will answer him;
  I will be with him in trouble,
  I will rescue him and honor him.
16 With long life I will satisfy him,
  and show him my salvation.

Psalm 92

A Psalm. A Song for the Sabbath.

It is good to give thanks to the LORD,
  to sing praises to thy name, O Most High;
2 to declare thy steadfast love in the morning,
  and thy faithfulness by night,
3 to the music of the lute and the harp,
  to the melody of the lyre.
4 For thou, O LORD, hast made me glad by thy work;
  at the works of thy hands I sing for joy.
5 How great are thy works, O LORD!
  Thy thoughts are very deep!
6 The dull man cannot know,
  the stupid cannot understand this:
7 that, though the wicked sprout like grass
  and all evildoers flourish,

they are doomed to destruction for ever,
8   but thou, O LORD, art on high for ever.
9 For, lo, thy enemies, O LORD,
    for, lo, thy enemies shall perish;
    all evildoers shall be scattered.

ⁱSyr: Heb
uncertain

10 But thou hast exalted my horn like that of the wild ox;
    thou hast poured over meⁱ fresh oil.
11 My eyes have seen the downfall of my enemies,
    my ears have heard the doom of my evil assailants.

12 The righteous flourish like the palm tree,
    and grow like a cedar in Lebanon.
13 They are planted in the house of the LORD,
    they flourish in the courts of our God.
14 They still bring forth fruit in old age,
    they are ever full of sap and green,
15 to show that the LORD is upright;
    he is my rock, and there is no unrighteousness in him.

Psalm 93

The LORD reigns; he is robed in majesty;
    the LORD is robed, he is girded with strength.
Yea, the world is established; it shall never be moved;
2   thy throne is established from of old;
    thou art from everlasting.

3 The floods have lifted up, O LORD,
    the floods have lifted up their voice,
    the floods lift up their roaring.
4 Mightier than the thunders of many waters,

ʲCn: Heb *mighty
the waves*

    mightier than the wavesʲ of the sea,
    the LORD on high is mighty!

5 Thy decrees are very sure;
    holiness befits thy house,
    O LORD, for evermore.

Psalm 94

O LORD, thou God of vengeance,
    thou God of vengeance, shine forth!
2 Rise up, O judge of the earth,
    render to the proud their deserts!
3 O LORD, how long shall the wicked,
    how long shall the wicked exult?

4 They pour out their arrogant words,
    they boast, all the evildoers.
5 They crush thy people, O LORD,
    and afflict thy heritage.
6 They slay the widow and the sojourner,
    and murder the fatherless;
7 and they say, "The LORD does not see;
    the God of Jacob does not perceive."

8 Understand, O dullest of the people!
    Fools, when will you be wise?
9 He who planted the ear, does he not hear?
He who formed the eye, does he not see?
10 He who chastens the nations, does he not chastise?
He who teaches men knowledge,
11   the LORD, knows the thoughts of man,
    that they are but a breath.

12 Blessed is the man whom thou dost chasten, O LORD,
    and whom thou dost teach out of thy law
13 to give him respite from days of trouble,
    until a pit is dug for the wicked.
14 For the LORD will not forsake his people;
    he will not abandon his heritage;
15 for justice will return to the righteous,
    and all the upright in heart will follow it.

16 Who rises up for me against the wicked?
    Who stands up for me against evildoers?
17 If the LORD had not been my help,

my soul would soon have dwelt in the land of silence.
18 When I thought, "My foot slips,"
  thy steadfast love, O Lord, held me up.
19 When the cares of my heart are many,
  thy consolations cheer my soul.
20 Can wicked rulers be allied with thee,
  who frame mischief by statute?
21 They band together against the life of the righteous,
  and condemn the innocent to death.
22 But the Lord has become my stronghold,
  and my God the rock of my refuge.
23 He will bring back on them their iniquity
  and wipe them out for their wickedness;
  the Lord our God will wipe them out.

Psalm 95

O come, let us sing to the Lord;
  let us make a joyful noise to the rock of our salvation!
2 Let us come into his presence with thanksgiving;
  let us make a joyful noise to him with songs of praise!
3 For the Lord is a great God,
  and a great King above all gods.
4 In his hand are the depths of the earth;
  the heights of the mountains are his also.
5 The sea is his, for he made it;
  for his hands formed the dry land.
6 O come, let us worship and bow down,
  let us kneel before the Lord, our Maker!
7 For he is our God,
  and we are the people of his pasture,
  and the sheep of his hand.

O that today you would hearken to his voice!
8 Harden not your hearts, as at Mer'ibah,
  as on the day at Massah in the wilderness,
9 when your fathers tested me,
  and put me to the proof, though they had seen my work.
10 For forty years I loathed that generation
  and said, "They are a people who err in heart,
  and they do not regard my ways."
11 Therefore I swore in my anger
  that they should not enter my rest.

Psalm 96

O sing to the Lord a new song;
  sing to the Lord, all the earth!
2 Sing to the Lord, bless his name;
  tell of his salvation from day to day.
3 Declare his glory among the nations,
  his marvelous works among all the peoples!

4 For great is the Lord, and greatly to be praised;
  he is to be feared above all gods.
5 For all the gods of the peoples are idols;
  but the Lord made the heavens.
6 Honor and majesty are before him;
  strength and beauty are in his sanctuary.

7 Ascribe to the Lord, O families of the peoples,
  ascribe to the Lord glory and strength!
8 Ascribe to the Lord the glory due his name;
  bring an offering, and come into his courts!
9 Worship the Lord in holy array;
  tremble before him, all the earth!

10 Say among the nations, "The Lord reigns!
  Yea, the world is established, it shall never be moved;
  he will judge the peoples with equity."
11 Let the heavens be glad, and let the earth rejoice;
  let the sea roar, and all that fills it;
12 let the field exult, and everything in it!
Then shall all the trees of the wood sing for joy
13   before the Lord, for he comes,

for he comes to judge the earth.
He will judge the world with righteousness,
  and the peoples with his truth.

Psalm 97

The LORD reigns; let the earth rejoice;
  let the many coastlands be glad!
2 Clouds and thick darkness are round about him;
  righteousness and justice are the foundation of his throne.
3 Fire goes before him,
  and burns up his adversaries round about.
4 His lightnings lighten the world;
  the earth sees and trembles.
5 The mountains melt like wax before the LORD,
  before the Lord of all the earth.

6 The heavens proclaim his righteousness;
  and all the peoples behold his glory.
7 All worshipers of images are put to shame,
  who make their boast in worthless idols;
  all gods bow down before him.
8 Zion hears and is glad,
  and the daughters of Judah rejoice,
  because of thy judgments, O God.
9 For thou, O LORD, art most high over all the earth;
  thou art exalted far above all gods.

k Cn: Heb *You who love the* LORD *hate evil*

10 The LORD loves those who hate evil;*k*
  he preserves the lives of his saints;
  he delivers them from the hand of the wicked.

l Gk Syr Jerome: Heb *is sown*

11 Light dawns*l* for the righteous,
  and joy for the upright in heart.
12 Rejoice in the LORD, O you righteous,
  and give thanks to his holy name!

Psalm 98

A Psalm.

O sing to the LORD a new song,
  for he has done marvelous things!
His right hand and his holy arm
  have gotten him victory.
2 The LORD has made known his victory,
  he has revealed his vindication in the sight of the nations.
3 He has remembered his steadfast love and faithfulness
  to the house of Israel.
All the ends of the earth have seen
  the victory of our God.

4 Make a joyful noise to the LORD, all the earth;
  break forth into joyous song and sing praises!
5 Sing praises to the LORD with the lyre,
  with the lyre and the sound of melody!
6 With trumpets and the sound of the horn
  make a joyful noise before the King, the LORD!

7 Let the sea roar, and all that fills it;
  the world and those who dwell in it!
8 Let the floods clap their hands;
  let the hills sing for joy together
9 before the LORD, for he comes
  to judge the earth.
He will judge the world with righteousness,
  and the peoples with equity.

Psalm 99

The LORD reigns; let the peoples tremble!
  He sits enthroned upon the cherubim; let the earth quake!
2 The LORD is great in Zion;
  he is exalted over all the peoples.
3 Let them praise thy great and terrible name!
  Holy is he!

m Cn: Heb *and the king's strength*

4 Mighty King,*m* lover of justice,
  thou hast established equity;
thou hast executed justice
  and righteousness in Jacob.

5 Extol the LORD our God;
  worship at his footstool!
  Holy is he!

6 Moses and Aaron were among his priests,
  Samuel also was among those who called on his name.
  They cried to the LORD, and he answered them.

7 He spoke to them in the pillar of cloud;
  they kept his testimonies,
  and the statutes that he gave them.

8 O LORD our God, thou didst answer them;
  thou wast a forgiving God to them,
  but an avenger of their wrongdoings.

9 Extol the LORD our God,
  and worship at his holy mountain;
  for the LORD our God is holy!

Psalm 100

A Psalm for the thank offering.

n Heb *land* or *earth*
o Another reading is *and not we ourselves*

Make a joyful noise to the LORD, all the lands!*n*
2   Serve the LORD with gladness!
    Come into his presence with singing!

3 Know that the LORD is God!
  It is he that made us, and we are his;*o*
  we are his people, and the sheep of his pasture.

4 Enter his gates with thanksgiving,
  and his courts with praise!
  Give thanks to him, bless his name!

5 For the LORD is good;
  his steadfast love endures for ever,
  and his faithfulness to all generations.

Psalm 101

A Psalm of David.

I will sing of loyalty and of justice;
  to thee, O LORD, I will sing.
2 I will give heed to the way that is blameless.
  Oh when wilt thou come to me?

I will walk with integrity of heart
  within my house;
3 I will not set before my eyes
  anything that is base.

I hate the work of those who fall away;
  it shall not cleave to me.
4 Perverseness of heart shall be far from me;
  I will know nothing of evil.

5 Him who slanders his neighbor secretly
  I will destroy.
The man of haughty looks and arrogant heart
  I will not endure.

6 I will look with favor on the faithful in the land,
  that they may dwell with me;
he who walks in the way that is blameless
  shall minister to me.

7 No man who practices deceit
  shall dwell in my house;
no man who utters lies
  shall continue in my presence.

8 Morning by morning I will destroy
  all the wicked in the land,
cutting off all the evildoers
  from the city of the LORD.

Psalm 102

A prayer of one afflicted, when he is faint and

Hear my prayer, O LORD; let my cry come to thee!
2 Do not hide thy face from me
  in the day of my distress!
Incline thy ear to me;
  answer me speedily in the day when I call!

3 For my days pass away like smoke,
  and my bones burn like a furnace.

pours out his
complaint
before the LORD.

4 My heart is smitten like grass, and withered;
 I forget to eat my bread.
5 Because of my loud groaning
 my bones cleave to my flesh.

^pThe meaning of
the Hebrew word
is uncertain

6 I am like a vulture^p of the wilderness,
 like an owl of the waste places;
7 I lie awake,
 I am like a lonely bird on the housetop.
8 All the day my enemies taunt me,
 those who deride me use my name for a curse.
9 For I eat ashes like bread,
 and mingle tears with my drink,
10 because of thy indignation and anger;
 for thou hast taken me up and thrown me away.
11 My days are like an evening shadow;
 I wither away like grass.

12 But thou, O LORD, art enthroned for ever;
 thy name endures to all generations
13 Thou wilt arise and have pity on Zion;
 it is the time to favor her;
 the appointed time has come.
14 For thy servants hold her stones dear,
 and have pity on her dust.
15 The nations will fear the name of the LORD,
 and all the kings of the earth thy glory.
16 For the LORD will build up Zion,
 he will appear in his glory;
17 he will regard the prayer of the destitute,
 and will not despise their supplication.

18 Let this be recorded for a generation to come,
 so that a people yet unborn may praise the LORD:
19 that he looked down from his holy height,
 from heaven the LORD looked at the earth,
20 to hear the groans of the prisoners,
 to set free those who were doomed to die;
21 that men may declare in Zion the name of the LORD,
 and in Jerusalem his praise,
22 when peoples gather together,
 and kingdoms, to worship the LORD.

23 He has broken my strength in mid-course;
 he has shortened my days.
24 "O my God," I say, "take me not hence
 in the midst of my days,
thou whose years endure
 throughout all generations!"
25 Of old thou didst lay the foundation of the earth,
 and the heavens are the work of thy hands.
26 They will perish, but thou dost endure;
 they will all wear out like a garment.
Thou changest them like raiment, and they pass away;
27 but thou art the same, and thy years have no end.
28 The children of thy servants shall dwell secure;
 their posterity shall be established before thee.

Psalm 103

A Psalm of
David.

Bless the LORD, O my soul;
 and all that is within me, bless his holy name!
2 Bless the LORD, O my soul,
 and forget not all his benefits,
3 who forgives all your iniquity,
 who heals all your diseases,
4 who redeems your life from the Pit,
 who crowns you with steadfast love and mercy,

^qHeb uncertain

5 who satisfies you with good as long as you live^q
 so that your youth is renewed like the eagle's.

6 The LORD works vindication
 and justice for all who are oppressed.
7 He made known his ways to Moses,

his acts to the people of Israel.
8 The LORD is merciful and gracious,
    slow to anger and abounding in steadfast love.
9 He will not always chide,
    nor will he keep his anger for ever.
10 He does not deal with us according to our sins,
    nor requite us according to our iniquities.

11 For as the heavens are high above the earth,
    so great is his steadfast love toward those who fear him;
12 as far as the east is from the west,
    so far does he remove our transgressions from us.
13 As a father pities his children,
    so the LORD pities those who fear him.
14 For he knows our frame;
    he remembers that we are dust.

15 As for man, his days are like grass;
    he flourishes like a flower of the field;
16 for the wind passes over it, and it is gone,
    and its place knows it no more.
17 But the steadfast love of the LORD is from
        everlasting to everlasting
    upon those who fear him,
    and his righteousness to children's children,
18 to those who keep his covenant
    and remember to do his commandments.

19 The LORD has established his throne in the heavens,
    and his kingdom rules over all.
20 Bless the LORD, O you his angels,
    you mighty ones who do his word,
    hearkening to the voice of his word!
21 Bless the LORD, all his hosts,
    his ministers that do his will!
22 Bless the LORD, all his works,
    in all places of his dominion.
Bless the LORD, O my soul!

Psalm 104

Bless the LORD, O my soul!
    O LORD my God, thou art very great!
Thou art clothed with honor and majesty,
2   who coverest thyself with light as with a garment,
who hast stretched out the heavens like a tent,
3   who hast laid the beams of thy chambers on the waters,
who makest the clouds thy chariot,
    who ridest on the wings of the wind,
4 who makest the winds thy messengers,
    fire and flame thy ministers.

5 Thou didst set the earth on its foundations,
    so that it should never be shaken.
6 Thou didst cover it with the deep as with a garment;
    the waters stood above the mountains.
7 At thy rebuke they fled;
    at the sound of thy thunder they took to flight.
8 The mountains rose, the valleys sank down
    to the place which thou didst appoint for them.
9 Thou didst set a bound which they should not pass,
    so that they might not again cover the earth.

10 Thou makest springs gush forth in the valleys;
    they flow between the hills;
11 they give drink to every beast of the field;
    the wild asses quench their thirst.
12 By them the birds of the air have their habitation;
    they sing among the branches.
13 From thy lofty abode thou waterest the mountains;
    the earth is satisfied with the fruit of thy work.

Or fodder for the animals that serve man   14 Thou dost cause the grass to grow for the cattle,
    and plants for man to cultivate,*
    that he may bring forth food from the earth,

15   and wine to gladden the heart of man,
oil to make his face shine,
    and bread to strengthen man's heart.
16 The trees of the LORD are watered abundantly,
    the cedars of Lebanon which he planted.
17 In them the birds build their nests;
    the stork has her home in the fir trees.
18 The high mountains are for the wild goats;
    the rocks are a refuge for the badgers.
19 Thou hast made the moon to mark the seasons;
    the sun knows its time for setting.
20 Thou makest darkness, and it is night,
    when all the beasts of the forest creep forth.
21 The young lions roar for their prey,
    seeking their food from God.
22 When the sun rises, they get them away
    and lie down in their dens.
23 Man goes forth to his work
    and to his labor until the evening.

24 O LORD, how manifold are thy works!
    In wisdom hast thou made them all;
    the earth is full of thy creatures.
25 Yonder is the sea, great and wide,
    which teems with things innumerable,
    living things both small and great.
26 There go the ships,
    and Leviathan which thou didst form to sport in it.

27 These all look to thee,
    to give them their food in due season.
28 When thou givest to them, they gather it up;
    when thou openest thy hand, they are filled with good things.
29 When thou hidest thy face, they are dismayed;
    when thou takest away their breath, they die
    and return to their dust.
30 When thou sendest forth thy Spirit,[s] they are created;
    and thou renewest the face of the ground.

s Or breath

31 May the glory of the LORD endure for ever,
    may the LORD rejoice in his works,
32 who looks on the earth and it trembles,
    who touches the mountains and they smoke!
33 I will sing to the LORD as long as I live;
    I will sing praise to my God while I have being.
34 May my meditation be pleasing to him,
    for I rejoice in the LORD.
35 Let sinners be consumed from the earth,
    and let the wicked be no more!
Bless the LORD, O my soul!
Praise the LORD!

Psalm 105

O give thanks to the LORD, call on his name,
    make known his deeds among the peoples!
2 Sing to him, sing praises to him,
    tell of all his wonderful works!
3 Glory in his holy name;
    let the hearts of those who seek the LORD rejoice!
4 Seek the LORD and his strength,
    seek his presence continually!
5 Remember the wonderful works that he has done,
    his miracles, and the judgments he uttered,
6 O offspring of Abraham his servant,
    sons of Jacob, his chosen ones!
7 He is the LORD our God;
    his judgments are in all the earth.
8 He is mindful of his covenant for ever,
    of the word that he commanded, for a thousand generations,
9 the covenant which he made with Abraham,
    his sworn promise to Isaac,
10 which he confirmed to Jacob as a statute,

to Israel as an everlasting covenant,
11 saying, "To you I will give the land of Canaan
as your portion for an inheritance."

12 When they were few in number,
of little account, and sojourners in it,
13 wandering from nation to nation,
from one kingdom to another people,
14 he allowed no one to oppress them;
he rebuked kings on their account,
15 saying, "Touch not my anointed ones,
do my prophets no harm!"

16 When he summoned a famine on the land,
and broke every staff of bread,
17 he had sent a man ahead of them,
Joseph, who was sold as a slave.

18 His feet were hurt with fetters,
his neck was put in a collar of iron;
19 until what he had said came to pass
the word of the LORD tested him.
20 The king sent and released him,
the ruler of the peoples set him free;
21 he made him lord of his house,
and ruler of all his possessions,
22 to instruct[t] his princes at his pleasure,
and to teach his elders wisdom.

^tGk Syr Jerome:
Heb *to bind*

23 Then Israel came to Egypt;
Jacob sojourned in the land of Ham.
24 And the LORD made his people very fruitful,
and made them stronger than their foes.
25 He turned their hearts to hate his people,
to deal craftily with his servants.

26 He sent Moses his servant,
and Aaron whom he had chosen.
27 They wrought his signs among them,
and miracles in the land of Ham.
28 He sent darkness, and made the land dark;
they rebelled[u] against his words.

^uCn Compare Gk
Syr: Heb *they did
not rebel*

29 He turned their waters into blood,
and caused their fish to die.
30 Their land swarmed with frogs,
even in the chambers of their kings.
31 He spoke, and there came swarms of flies,
and gnats throughout their country.
32 He gave them hail for rain,
and lightning that flashed through their land.
33 He smote their vines and fig trees,
and shattered the trees of their country.
34 He spoke, and the locusts came,
and young locusts without number;
35 which devoured all the vegetation in their land,
and ate up the fruit of their ground.
36 He smote all the first-born in their land,
the first issue of all their strength.
37 Then he led forth Israel with silver and gold,
and there was none among his tribes who stumbled.
38 Egypt was glad when they departed,
for dread of them had fallen upon it.
39 He spread a cloud for a covering,
and fire to give light by night.
40 They asked, and he brought quails,
and gave them bread from heaven in abundance.
41 He opened the rock, and water gushed forth;
it flowed through the desert like a river.
42 For he remembered his holy promise,
and Abraham his servant.
43 So he led forth his people with joy,
his chosen ones with singing.

44 And he gave them the lands of the nations;
   and they took possession of the fruit of the peoples' toil,
45 to the end that they should keep his statutes,
   and observe his laws.
Praise the LORD!

Psalm 106

Praise the LORD!
O give thanks to the LORD, for he is good;
   for his steadfast love endures for ever!
2 Who can utter the mighty doings of the LORD,
   or show forth all his praise?
3 Blessed are they who observe justice,
   who do righteousness at all times!

4 Remember me, O LORD, when thou showest favor to thy people;
   help me when thou deliverest them;
5 that I may see the prosperity of thy chosen ones,
   that I may rejoice in the gladness of thy nation,
   that I may glory with thy heritage.

6 Both we and our fathers have sinned;
   we have committed iniquity, we have done wickedly.
7 Our fathers, when they were in Egypt,
   did not consider thy wonderful works;
   they did not remember the abundance of thy steadfast love,
   but rebelled against the Most High[v] at the Red Sea.
8 Yet he saved them for his name's sake,
   that he might make known his mighty power.
9 He rebuked the Red Sea, and it became dry;
   and he led them through the deep as through a desert.
10 So he saved them from the hand of the foe,
   and delivered them from the power of the enemy.
11 And the waters covered their adversaries;
   not one of them was left.
12 Then they believed his words;
   they sang his praise.

13 But they soon forgot his works;
   they did not wait for his counsel.
14 But they had a wanton craving in the wilderness,
   and put God to the test in the desert;
15 he gave them what they asked,
   but sent a wasting disease among them.

16 When men in the camp were jealous of Moses
   and Aaron, the holy one of the LORD,
17 the earth opened and swallowed up Dathan,
   and covered the company of Abi'ram.
18 Fire also broke out in their company;
   the flame burned up the wicked.

19 They made a calf in Horeb
   and worshiped a molten image.
20 They exchanged the glory of God
   for the image of an ox that eats grass.
21 They forgot God, their Savior,
   who had done great things in Egypt,
22 wondrous works in the land of Ham,
   and terrible things by the Red Sea.
23 Therefore he said he would destroy them—
   had not Moses, his chosen one,
stood in the breach before him,
   to turn away his wrath from destroying them.

24 Then they despised the pleasant land,
   having no faith in his promise.
25 They murmured in their tents,
   and did not obey the voice of the LORD.
26 Therefore he raised his hand and swore to them
   that he would make them fall in the wilderness,
27 and would disperse[w] their descendants among the nations,
   scattering them over the lands.

[v] Cn Compare 78. 17, 56: Heb *at the sea*

[w] Syr Compare Ezek 20.23: Heb *cause to fall*

28 Then they attached themselves to the Ba'al of Pe'or,
  and ate sacrifices offered to the dead;
29 they provoked the LORD to anger with their doings,
  and a plague broke out among them.
30 Then Phin'ehas stood up and interposed,
  and the plague was stayed.
31 And that has been reckoned to him as righteousness
  from generation to generation for ever.

32 They angered him at the waters of Mer'ibah,
  and it went ill with Moses on their account;
33 for they made his spirit bitter,
  and he spoke words that were rash.

34 They did not destroy the peoples,
  as the LORD commanded them,
35 but they mingled with the nations
  and learned to do as they did.
36 They served their idols,
  which became a snare to them.
37 They sacrificed their sons
  and their daughters to the demons;
38 they poured out innocent blood,
  the blood of their sons and daughters,
  whom they sacrificed to the idols of Canaan;
  and the land was polluted with blood.
39 Thus they became unclean by their acts,
  and played the harlot in their doings.

40 Then the anger of the LORD was kindled against his people,
  and he abhorred his heritage;
41 he gave them into the hand of the nations,
  so that those who hated them ruled over them.
42 Their enemies oppressed them,
  and they were brought into subjection under their power.
43 Many times he delivered them,
  but they were rebellious in their purposes,
  and were brought low through their iniquity.

44 Nevertheless he regarded their distress,
  when he heard their cry.
45 He remembered for their sake his covenant,
  and relented according to the abundance of his steadfast love.
46 He caused them to be pitied
  by all those who held them captive.

47 Save us, O LORD our God,
  and gather us from among the nations,
that we may give thanks to thy holy name
  and glory in thy praise.

48 Blessed be the LORD, the God of Israel,
  from everlasting to everlasting!
And let all the people say, "Amen!"
  Praise the LORD!

BOOK V

Psalm 107

O give thanks to the LORD, for he is good;
  for his steadfast love endures for ever!
2 Let the redeemed of the LORD say so,
  whom he has redeemed from trouble
3 and gathered in from the lands,
  from the east and from the west,
  from the north and from the south.

4 Some wandered in desert wastes,
  finding no way to a city to dwell in;
5 hungry and thirsty,
  their soul fainted within them.
6 Then they cried to the LORD in their trouble,
  and he delivered them from their distress;
7 he led them by a straight way,

till they reached a city to dwell in.
8 Let them thank the LORD for his steadfast love,
  for his wonderful works to the sons of men!
9 For he satisfies him who is thirsty,
  and the hungry he fills with good things.

10 Some sat in darkness and in gloom,
  prisoners in affliction and in irons,
11 for they had rebelled against the words of God,
  and spurned the counsel of the Most High.
12 Their hearts were bowed down with hard labor;
  they fell down, with none to help.
13 Then they cried to the LORD in their trouble,
  and he delivered them from their distress;
14 he brought them out of darkness and gloom,
  and broke their bonds asunder.
15 Let them thank the LORD for his steadfast love,
  for his wonderful works to the sons of men!
16 For he shatters the doors of bronze,
  and cuts in two the bars of iron.

*Cn: Heb *fools*

17 Some were sick* through their sinful ways,
  and because of their iniquities suffered affliction;
18 they loathed any kind of food,
  and they drew near to the gates of death.
19 Then they cried to the LORD in their trouble,
  and he delivered them from their distress;
20 he sent forth his word, and healed them,
  and delivered them from destruction.
21 Let them thank the LORD for his steadfast love,
  for his wonderful works to the sons of men!
22 And let them offer sacrifices of thanksgiving,
  and tell of his deeds in songs of joy!

23 Some went down to the sea in ships,
  doing business on the great waters;
24 they saw the deeds of the LORD,
  his wondrous works in the deep.
25 For he commanded, and raised the stormy wind,
  which lifted up the waves of the sea.
26 They mounted up to heaven, they went down to the depths;
  their courage melted away in their evil plight;
27 they reeled and staggered like drunken men,
  and were at their wits' end.
28 Then they cried to the LORD in their trouble,
  and he delivered them from their distress;
29 he made the storm be still,
  and the waves of the sea were hushed.
30 Then they were glad because they had quiet,
  and he brought them to their desired haven.
31 Let them thank the LORD for his steadfast love,
  for his wonderful works to the sons of men!
32 Let them extol him in the congregation of the people,
  and praise him in the assembly of the elders.

33 He turns rivers into a desert,
  springs of water into thirsty ground,
34 a fruitful land into a salty waste,
  because of the wickedness of its inhabitants.
35 He turns a desert into pools of water,
  a parched land into springs of water.
36 And there he lets the hungry dwell,
  and they establish a city to live in;
37 they sow fields, and plant vineyards,
  and get a fruitful yield.
38 By his blessing they multiply greatly;
  and he does not let their cattle decrease.

39 When they are diminished and brought low
  through oppression, trouble and sorrow,
40 he pours contempt upon princes
  and makes them wander in trackless wastes;

41 but he raises up the needy out of affliction,
   and makes their families like flocks.
42 The upright see it and are glad;
   and all wickedness stops its mouth.
43 Whoever is wise, let him give heed to these things;
   let men consider the steadfast love of the LORD.

Psalm 108

A Song.
A Psalm of
David.

My heart is steadfast, O God, my heart is steadfast!
I will sing and make melody!
   Awake, my soul!
2 Awake, O harp and lyre!
   I will awake the dawn!
3 I will give thanks to thee, O LORD, among the peoples,
   I will sing praises to thee among the nations.
4 For thy steadfast love is great above the heavens,
   thy faithfulness reaches to the clouds.

5 Be exalted, O God, above the heavens!
   Let thy glory be over all the earth!
6 That thy beloved may be delivered,
   give help by thy right hand, and answer me!

y Or *by his
holiness*

7 God has promised in his sanctuary:[y]
   "With exultation I will divide up Shechem,
   and portion out the Vale of Succoth.
8 Gilead is mine; Manas'seh is mine;
   E'phraim is my helmet;
   Judah my scepter.
9 Moab is my washbasin;
   upon Edom I cast my shoe;
   over Philistia I shout in triumph."

10 Who will bring me to the fortified city?
   Who will lead me to Edom?
11 Hast thou not rejected us, O God?
   Thou dost not go forth, O God, with our armies.
12 O grant us help against the foe,
   for vain is the help of man!
13 With God we shall do valiantly;
   it is he who will tread down our foes.

Psalm 109

To the
choirmaster.
A Psalm of
David.

Be not silent, O God of my praise!
2 For wicked and deceitful mouths are opened against me,
   speaking against me with lying tongues.
3 They beset me with words of hate,
   and attack me without cause.
4 In return for my love they accuse me,
   even as I make prayer for them.[z]
5 So they reward me evil for good,
   and hatred for my love.

z Syr: Heb
I prayer
a Heb *stand at his
right hand*

6 Appoint a wicked man against him;
   let an accuser bring him to trial.[a]
7 When he is tried, let him come forth guilty;
   let his prayer be counted as sin!
8 May his days be few;
   may another seize his goods!
9 May his children be fatherless,
   and his wife a widow!
10 May his children wander about and beg;
   may they be driven out of[b] the ruins they inhabit!

b Gk: Heb *and
seek*

11 May the creditor seize all that he has;
   may strangers plunder the fruits of his toil!
12 Let there be none to extend kindness to him,
   nor any to pity his fatherless children!
13 May his posterity be cut off;
   may his name be blotted out in the second generation!
14 May the iniquity of his fathers be remembered before the LORD,
   and let not the sin of his mother be blotted out!
15 Let them be before the LORD continually;

c Gk: Heb *their*

   and may his[c] memory be cut off from the earth!

16 For he did not remember to show kindness,
  but pursued the poor and needy
  and the brokenhearted to their death.
17 He loved to curse; let curse come on him!
  He did not like blessing; may it be far from him!
18 He clothed himself with cursing as his coat,
  may it soak into his body like water,
  like oil into his bones!
19 May it be like a garment which he wraps round him,
  like a belt with which he daily girds himself!
20 May this be the reward of my accusers from the LORD,
  of those who speak evil against my life!
21 But thou, O GOD my Lord,
  deal on my behalf for thy name's sake;
  because thy steadfast love is good, deliver me!
22 For I am poor and needy,
  and my heart is stricken within me.
23 I am gone, like a shadow at evening;
  I am shaken off like a locust.
24 My knees are weak through fasting;
  my body has become gaunt.
25 I am an object of scorn to my accusers;
  when they see me, they wag their heads.
26 Help me, O LORD my God!
  Save me according to thy steadfast love!
27 Let them know that this is thy hand;
  thou, O LORD, hast done it!
28 Let them curse, but do thou bless!

d Gk: Heb they
have arisen and
have been put to
shame

  Let my assailants be put to shame;*d* may thy servant be glad!
29 May my accusers be clothed with dishonor;
  may they be wrapped in their own shame as in a mantle!
30 With my mouth I will give great thanks to the LORD;
  I will praise him in the midst of the throng.
31 For he stands at the right hand of the needy,
  to save him from those who condemn him to death.

Psalm 110

A Psalm of
David.

e Another reading
is *in holy array*
f Cn: Heb *the dew*
of your youth

g Or *the head*

The LORD says to my lord: "Sit at my right hand,
till I make your enemies your footstool."
2 The LORD sends forth from Zion your mighty scepter.
  Rule in the midst of your foes!
3 Your people will offer themselves freely
  on the day you lead your host
  upon the holy mountains.*e*
From the womb of the morning
  like dew your youth*f* will come to you.
4 The LORD has sworn
  and will not change his mind,
"You are a priest for ever
  after the order of Melchiz'edek."
5 The Lord is at your right hand;
  he will shatter kings on the day of his wrath.
6 He will execute judgment among the nations,
  filling them with corpses;
he will shatter chiefs*g* over the wide earth.
7 He will drink from the brook by the way;
  therefore he will lift up his head.

Psalm 111

Praise the LORD.
I will give thanks to the LORD with my whole heart,
  in the company of the upright, in the congregation.
2 Great are the works of the LORD,
  studied by all who have pleasure in them.
3 Full of honor and majesty is his work,
  and his righteousness endures for ever.
4 He has caused his wonderful works to be remembered;
  the LORD is gracious and merciful.
5 He provides food for those who fear him;
  he is ever mindful of his covenant.

6 He has shown his people the power of his works,
  in giving them the heritage of the nations.
7 The works of his hands are faithful and just;
  all his precepts are trustworthy,
8 they are established for ever and ever,
  to be performed with faithfulness and uprightness.
9 He sent redemption to his people;
  he has commanded his covenant for ever.
  Holy and terrible is his name!
10 The fear of the LORD is the beginning of wisdom;
  a good understanding have all those who practice it.
  His praise endures for ever!

Psalm 112

Praise the LORD.
Blessed is the man who fears the LORD,
  who greatly delights in his commandments!
2 His descendants will be mighty in the land;
  the generation of the upright will be blessed.
3 Wealth and riches are in his house;
  and his righteousness endures for ever.
4 Light rises in the darkness for the upright;
  the LORD[h] is gracious, merciful, and righteous.
5 It is well with the man who deals generously and lends,
  who conducts his affairs with justice.
6 For the righteous will never be moved;
  he will be remembered for ever.
7 He is not afraid of evil tidings;
  his heart is firm, trusting in the LORD.
8 His heart is steady, he will not be afraid,
  until he sees his desire on his adversaries.
9 He has distributed freely, he has given to the poor;
  his righteousness endures for ever;
  his horn is exalted in honor.
10 The wicked man sees it and is angry;
  he gnashes his teeth and melts away;
  the desire of the wicked man comes to nought.

[h] Gk: Heb lacks
the LORD

Psalm 113

Praise the LORD!
Praise, O servants of the LORD,
  praise the name of the LORD!
2 Blessed be the name of the LORD
  from this time forth and for evermore!
3 From the rising of the sun to its setting
  the name of the LORD is to be praised!
4 The LORD is high above all nations,
  and his glory above the heavens!
5 Who is like the LORD our God,
  who is seated on high,
6 who looks far down
  upon the heavens and the earth?
7 He raises the poor from the dust,
  and lifts the needy from the ash heap,
8 to make them sit with princes,
  with the princes of his people.
9 He gives the barren woman a home,
  making her the joyous mother of children.
Praise the LORD!

Psalm 114

When Israel went forth from Egypt,
  the house of Jacob from a people of strange language,
2 Judah became his sanctuary,
  Israel his dominion.
3 The sea looked and fled,
  Jordan turned back.
4 The mountains skipped like rams,
  the hills like lambs.
5 What ails you, O sea, that you flee?
  O Jordan, that you turn back?

6 O mountains, that you skip like rams?
O hills, like lambs?

7 Tremble, O earth, at the presence of the LORD,
at the presence of the God of Jacob,

8 who turns the rock into a pool of water,
the flint into a spring of water.

Psalm 115

Not to us, O LORD, not to us,
but to thy name give glory,
for the sake of thy steadfast love and thy faithfulness!

2 Why should the nations say,
"Where is their God?"

3 Our God is in the heavens;
he does whatever he pleases.

4 Their idols are silver and gold,
the work of men's hands.

5 They have mouths, but do not speak;
eyes, but do not see.

6 They have ears, but do not hear;
noses, but do not smell.

7 They have hands, but do not feel;
feet, but do not walk;
and they do not make a sound in their throat.

8 Those who make them are like them;
so are all who trust in them.

9 O Israel, trust in the LORD!
He is their help and their shield.

10 O house of Aaron, put your trust in the LORD!
He is their help and their shield.

11 You who fear the LORD, trust in the LORD!
He is their help and their shield.

12 The LORD has been mindful of us; he will bless us;
he will bless the house of Israel;
he will bless the house of Aaron;

13 he will bless those who fear the LORD,
both small and great.

14 May the LORD give you increase,
you and your children!

15 May you be blessed by the LORD,
who made heaven and earth!

16 The heavens are the LORD's heavens,
but the earth he has given to the sons of men.

17 The dead do not praise the LORD,
nor do any that go down into silence.

18 But we will bless the LORD
from this time forth and for evermore.
Praise the LORD!

Psalm 116

I love the LORD, because he has heard
my voice and my supplications.

2 Because he inclined his ear to me,
therefore I will call on him as long as I live.

3 The snares of death encompassed me;
the pangs of Sheol laid hold on me;
I suffered distress and anguish.

4 Then I called on the name of the LORD:
"O LORD, I beseech thee, save my life!"

5 Gracious is the LORD, and righteous;
our God is merciful.

6 The LORD preserves the simple;
when I was brought low, he saved me.

7 Return, O my soul, to your rest;
for the LORD has dealt bountifully with you.

8 For thou hast delivered my soul from death,
my eyes from tears,
my feet from stumbling;

9 I walk before the LORD
  in the land of the living.
10 I kept my faith, even when I said,
  "I am greatly afflicted";
11 I said in my consternation,
  "Men are all a vain hope."

12 What shall I render to the LORD
  for all his bounty to me?
13 I will lift up the cup of salvation
  and call on the name of the LORD,
14 I will pay my vows to the LORD
  in the presence of all his people.
15 Precious in the sight of the LORD
  is the death of his saints.
16 O LORD, I am thy servant;
  I am thy servant, the son of thy handmaid.
  Thou hast loosed my bonds.
17 I will offer to thee the sacrifice of thanksgiving
  and call on the name of the LORD.
18 I will pay my vows to the LORD
  in the presence of all his people,
19 in the courts of the house of the LORD,
  in your midst, O Jerusalem.
Praise the LORD!

Psalm 117

Praise the LORD, all nations!
  Extol him, all peoples!
2 For great is his steadfast love toward us;
  and the faithfulness of the LORD endures for ever.
Praise the LORD!

Psalm 118

O give thanks to the LORD, for he is good;
  his steadfast love endures for ever!

2 Let Israel say,
  "His steadfast love endures for ever."
3 Let the house of Aaron say,
  "His steadfast love endures for ever."
4 Let those who fear the LORD say,
  "His steadfast love endures for ever."

5 Out of my distress I called on the LORD;
  the LORD answered me and set me free.
6 With the LORD on my side I do not fear.
  What can man do to me?
7 The LORD is on my side to help me;
  I shall look in triumph on those who hate me.
8 It is better to take refuge in the LORD
  than to put confidence in man.
9 It is better to take refuge in the LORD
  than to put confidence in princes.

10 All nations surrounded me;
  in the name of the LORD I cut them off!
11 They surrounded me, surrounded me on every side;
  in the name of the LORD I cut them off!
12 They surrounded me like bees,
  they blazed[i] like a fire of thorns;
  in the name of the LORD I cut them off!
13 I was pushed hard,[j] so that I was falling,
  but the LORD helped me.
14 The LORD is my strength and my song;
  he has become my salvation.

15 Hark, glad songs of victory
  in the tents of the righteous:
"The right hand of the LORD does valiantly,
16   the right hand of the LORD is exalted,
  the right hand of the LORD does valiantly!"
17 I shall not die, but I shall live,
  and recount the deeds of the LORD.

[i] Gk: Heb were extinguished

[j] Gk Syr Jerome: Heb thou didst push me hard

18 The LORD has chastened me sorely,
 but he has not given me over to death.

19 Open to me the gates of righteousness,
 that I may enter through them
 and give thanks to the LORD.

20 This is the gate of the LORD;
 the righteous shall enter through it.

21 I thank thee that thou hast answered me
 and hast become my salvation.

22 The stone which the builders rejected
 has become the head of the corner.

23 This is the LORD's doing;
 it is marvelous in our eyes.

24 This is the day which the LORD has made;
 let us rejoice and be glad in it.

25 Save us, we beseech thee, O LORD!
 O LORD, we beseech thee, give us success!

26 Blessed be he who enters in the name of the LORD!
 We bless you from the house of the LORD.

27 The LORD is God,
 and he has given us light.
Bind the festal procession with branches,
 up to the horns of the altar!

28 Thou art my God, and I will give thanks to thee;
 thou art my God, I will extol thee.

29 O give thanks to the LORD, for he is good;
 for his steadfast love endures for ever!

**Psalm
119**

Blessed are those whose way is blameless,
 who walk in the law of the LORD!

2 Blessed are those who keep his testimonies,
 who seek him with their whole heart,

3 who also do no wrong,
 but walk in his ways!

4 Thou hast commanded thy precepts
 to be kept diligently.

5 O that my ways may be steadfast
 in keeping thy statutes!

6 Then I shall not be put to shame,
 having my eyes fixed on all thy commandments.

7 I will praise thee with an upright heart,
 when I learn thy righteous ordinances.

8 I will observe thy statutes;
 O forsake me not utterly!

9 How can a young man keep his way pure?
 By guarding it according to thy word.

10 With my whole heart I seek thee;
 let me not wander from thy commandments!

11 I have laid up thy word in my heart,
 that I might not sin against thee.

12 Blessed be thou, O LORD;
 teach me thy statutes!

13 With my lips I declare
 all the ordinances of thy mouth.

14 In the way of thy testimonies I delight
 as much as in all riches.

15 I will meditate on thy precepts,
 and fix my eyes on thy ways.

16 I will delight in thy statutes;
 I will not forget thy word.

17 Deal bountifully with thy servant,
 that I may live and observe thy word.

18 Open my eyes, that I may behold
 wondrous things out of thy law.

19 I am a sojourner on earth;
 hide not thy commandments from me!

20 My soul is consumed with longing
 for thy ordinances at all times.
21 Thou dost rebuke the insolent, accursed ones,
 who wander from thy commandments;
22 take away from me their scorn and contempt,
 for I have kept thy testimonies.
23 Even though princes sit plotting against me,
 thy servant will meditate on thy statutes.
24 Thy testimonies are my delight,
 they are my counselors.

25 My soul cleaves to the dust;
 revive me according to thy word!
26 When I told of my ways, thou didst answer me;
 teach me thy statutes!
27 Make me understand the way of thy precepts,
 and I will meditate on thy wondrous works.
28 My soul melts away for sorrow;
 strengthen me according to thy word!
29 Put false ways far from me;
 and graciously teach me thy law!

30 I have chosen the way of faithfulness,
 I set thy ordinances before me.
31 I cleave to thy testimonies, O LORD;
 let me not be put to shame!
32 I will run in the way of thy commandments
 when thou enlargest my understanding!

33 Teach me, O LORD, the way of thy statutes;
 and I will keep it to the end.
34 Give me understanding, that I may keep thy law
 and observe it with my whole heart.
35 Lead me in the path of thy commandments,
 for I delight in it.
36 Incline my heart to thy testimonies,
 and not to gain!
37 Turn my eyes from looking at vanities;
 and give me life in thy ways.
38 Confirm to thy servant thy promise,
 which is for those who fear thee.
39 Turn away the reproach which I dread;
 for thy ordinances are good.
40 Behold, I long for thy precepts;
 in thy righteousness give me life!

41 Let thy steadfast love come to me, O LORD,
 thy salvation according to thy promise;
42 then shall I have an answer for those who taunt me,
 for I trust in thy word.
43 And take not the word of truth utterly out of my mouth,
 for my hope is in thy ordinances.
44 I will keep thy law continually,
 for ever and ever;
45 and I shall walk at liberty,
 for I have sought thy precepts.
46 I will also speak of thy testimonies before kings,
 and shall not be put to shame;
47 for I find my delight in thy commandments,
 which I love.
48 I revere thy commandments, which I love,
 and I will meditate on thy statutes.

49 Remember thy word to thy servant,
 in which thou hast made me hope.
50 This is my comfort in my affliction
 that thy promise gives me life.
51 Godless men utterly deride me,
 but I do not turn away from thy law.
52 When I think of thy ordinances from of old,
 I take comfort, O LORD.
53 Hot indignation seizes me because of the wicked,
 who forsake thy law.

54 Thy statutes have been my songs
  in the house of my pilgrimage.
55 I remember thy name in the night, O LORD,
  and keep thy law.
56 This blessing has fallen to me,
  that I have kept thy precepts.

57 The LORD is my portion;
  I promise to keep thy words.
58 I entreat thy favor with all my heart;
  be gracious to me according to thy promise.
59 When I think of thy ways,
  I turn my feet to thy testimonies;
60 I hasten and do not delay
  to keep thy commandments.
61 Though the cords of the wicked ensnare me,
  I do not forget thy law.
62 At midnight I rise to praise thee,
  because of thy righteous ordinances.
63 I am a companion of all who fear thee,
  of those who keep thy precepts.
64 The earth, O LORD, is full of thy steadfast love;
  teach me thy statutes!

65 Thou hast dealt well with thy servant,
  O LORD, according to thy word.
66 Teach me good judgment and knowledge,
  for I believe in thy commandments.
67 Before I was afflicted I went astray;
  but now I keep thy word.
68 Thou art good and doest good;
  teach me thy statutes.
69 The godless besmear me with lies,
  but with my whole heart I keep thy precepts;
70 their heart is gross like fat,
  but I delight in thy law.
71 It is good for me that I was afflicted,
  that I might learn thy statutes.
72 The law of thy mouth is better to me
  than thousands of gold and silver pieces.

73 Thy hands have made and fashioned me;
  give me understanding that I may learn thy commandments.
74 Those who fear thee shall see me and rejoice,
  because I have hoped in thy word.
75 I know, O LORD, that thy judgments are right,
  and that in faithfulness thou hast afflicted me.
76 Let thy steadfast love be ready to comfort me
  according to thy promise to thy servant.
77 Let thy mercy come to me, that I may live;
  for thy law is my delight.
78 Let the godless be put to shame,
  because they have subverted me with guile;
  as for me, I will meditate on thy precepts.
79 Let those who fear thee turn to me,
  that they may know thy testimonies.
80 May my heart be blameless in thy statutes,
  that I may not be put to shame!

81 My soul languishes for thy salvation;
  I hope in thy word.
82 My eyes fail with watching for thy promise;
  I ask, "When wilt thou comfort me?"
83 For I have become like a wineskin in the smoke,
  yet I have not forgotten thy statutes.
84 How long must thy servant endure?
  when wilt thou judge those who persecute me?
85 Godless men have dug pitfalls for me,
  men who do not conform to thy law.
86 All thy commandments are sure;
  they persecute me with falsehood; help me!

87 They have almost made an end of me on earth;
 but I have not forsaken thy precepts.
88 In thy steadfast love spare my life,
 that I may keep the testimonies of thy mouth.

89 For ever, O Lord, thy word
 is firmly fixed in the heavens.
90 Thy faithfulness endures to all generations;
 thou hast established the earth, and it stands fast.
91 By thy appointment they stand this day;
 for all things are thy servants.
92 If thy law had not been my delight,
 I should have perished in my affliction.
93 I will never forget thy precepts;
 for by them thou hast given me life.
94 I am thine, save me;
 for I have sought thy precepts.
95 The wicked lie in wait to destroy me;
 but I consider thy testimonies.
96 I have seen a limit to all perfection,
 but thy commandment is exceedingly broad.

97 Oh, how I love thy law!
 It is my meditation all the day.
98 Thy commandment makes me wiser than my enemies,
 for it is ever with me.
99 I have more understanding than all my teachers,
 for thy testimonies are my meditation.
100 I understand more than the aged,
 for I keep thy precepts.
101 I hold back my feet from every evil way,
 in order to keep thy word.
102 I do not turn aside from thy ordinances,
 for thou hast taught me.
103 How sweet are thy words to my taste,
 sweeter than honey to my mouth!
104 Through thy precepts I get understanding;
 therefore I hate every false way.

105 Thy word is a lamp to my feet
 and a light to my path.
106 I have sworn an oath and confirmed it,
 to observe thy righteous ordinances.
107 I am sorely afflicted;
 give me life, O Lord, according to thy word!
108 Accept my offerings of praise, O Lord,
 and teach me thy ordinances.
109 I hold my life in my hand continually,
 but I do not forget thy law.
110 The wicked have laid a snare for me,
 but I do not stray from thy precepts.
111 Thy testimonies are my heritage for ever;
 yea, they are the joy of my heart.
112 I incline my heart to perform thy statutes
 for ever, to the end.

113 I hate double-minded men,
 but I love thy law.
114 Thou art my hiding place and my shield;
 I hope in thy word.
115 Depart from me, you evildoers,
 that I may keep the commandments of my God.
116 Uphold me according to thy promise, that I may live,
 and let me not be put to shame in my hope!
117 Hold me up, that I may be safe
 and have regard for thy statutes continually!
118 Thou dost spurn all who go astray from thy statutes;
 yea, their cunning is in vain.
119 All the wicked of the earth thou dost count as dross;
 therefore I love thy testimonies.
120 My flesh trembles for fear of thee,
 and I am afraid of thy judgments.

121 I have done what is just and right;
 do not leave me to my oppressors.
122 Be surety for thy servant for good;
 let not the godless oppress me.

123 My eyes fail with watching for thy salvation,
 and for the fulfilment of thy righteous promise.
124 Deal with thy servant according to thy steadfast love,
 and teach me thy statutes.
125 I am thy servant; give me understanding,
 that I may know thy testimonies!
126 It is time for the LORD to act,
 for thy law has been broken.
127 Therefore I love thy commandments
 above gold, above fine gold.
Gk Jerome: Heb uncertain 128 Therefore I direct my steps by all thy precepts;*k*
 I hate every false way.

129 Thy testimonies are wonderful;
 therefore my soul keeps them.
130 The unfolding of thy words gives light;
 it imparts understanding to the simple.
131 With open mouth I pant,
 because I long for thy commandments.
132 Turn to me and be gracious to me,
 as is thy wont towards those who love thy name.
133 Keep steady my steps according to thy promise,
 and let no iniquity get dominion over me.
134 Redeem me from man's oppression,
 that I may keep thy precepts.
135 Make thy face shine upon thy servant,
 and teach me thy statutes.
136 My eyes shed streams of tears,
 because men do not keep thy law.

137 Righteous art thou, O LORD,
 and right are thy judgments.
138 Thou hast appointed thy testimonies in righteousness
 and in all faithfulness.
139 My zeal consumes me,
 because my foes forget thy words.
140 Thy promise is well tried,
 and thy servant loves it.
141 I am small and despised,
 yet I do not forget thy precepts.
142 Thy righteousness is righteous for ever,
 and thy law is true.
143 Trouble and anguish have come upon me,
 but thy commandments are my delight.
144 Thy testimonies are righteous for ever;
 give me understanding that I may live.

145 With my whole heart I cry; answer me, O LORD!
 I will keep thy statutes.
146 I cry to thee; save me,
 that I may observe thy testimonies.
147 I rise before dawn and cry for help;
 I hope in thy words.
148 My eyes are awake before the watches of the night,
 that I may meditate upon thy promise.
149 Hear my voice in thy steadfast love;
 O LORD, in thy justice preserve my life.
150 They draw near who persecute me with evil purpose;
 they are far from thy law.
151 But thou art near, O LORD,
 and all thy commandments are true.
152 Long have I known from thy testimonies
 that thou hast founded them for ever.

153 Look on my affliction and deliver me,
 for I do not forget thy law.
154 Plead my cause and redeem me;

give me life according to thy promise!
155 Salvation is far from the wicked,
for they do not seek thy statutes.
156 Great is thy mercy, O LORD;
give me life according to thy justice.
157 Many are my persecutors and my adversaries,
but I do not swerve from thy testimonies.
158 I look at the faithless with disgust,
because they do not keep thy commands.
159 Consider how I love thy precepts!
Preserve my life according to thy steadfast love.
160 The sum of thy word is truth;
and every one of thy righteous ordinances endures for ever.

161 Princes persecute me without cause,
but my heart stands in awe of thy words.
162 I rejoice at thy word
like one who finds great spoil.
163 I hate and abhor falsehood,
but I love thy law.
164 Seven times a day I praise thee
for thy righteous ordinances.
165 Great peace have those who love thy law;
nothing can make them stumble.
166 I hope for thy salvation, O LORD,
and I do thy commandments.
167 My soul keeps thy testimonies;
I love them exceedingly.
168 I keep thy precepts and testimonies,
for all my ways are before thee.

169 Let my cry come before thee, O LORD;
give me understanding according to thy word!
170 Let my supplication come before thee;
deliver me according to thy word.
171 My lips will pour forth praise
that thou dost teach me thy statutes.
172 My tongue will sing of thy word,
for all thy commandments are right.
173 Let thy hand be ready to help me,
for I have chosen thy precepts.
174 I long for thy salvation, O LORD,
and thy law is my delight.
175 Let me live, that I may praise thee,
and let thy ordinances help me.
176 I have gone astray like a lost sheep; seek thy servant,
for I do not forget thy commandments.

**Psalm
120**

A Song of
Ascents.

In my distress I cry to the LORD,
that he may answer me:
2 "Deliver me, O LORD,
from lying lips,
from a deceitful tongue."

3 What shall be given to you?
And what more shall be done to you,
you deceitful tongue?
4 A warrior's sharp arrows,
with glowing coals of the broom tree!

5 Woe is me, that I sojourn in Meshech,
that I dwell among the tents of Kedar!
6 Too long have I had my dwelling
among those who hate peace.
7 I am for peace;
but when I speak,
they are for war!

Psalm 121

A Song of Ascents.

I lift up my eyes to the hills.
From whence does my help come?
2 My help comes from the LORD,
who made heaven and earth.

3 He will not let your foot be moved,
he who keeps you will not slumber.
4 Behold, he who keeps Israel
will neither slumber nor sleep.

5 The LORD is your keeper;
the LORD is your shade
on your right hand.
6 The sun shall not smite you by day,
nor the moon by night.

7 The LORD will keep you from all evil;
he will keep your life.
8 The LORD will keep
your going out and your coming in
from this time forth and for evermore.

Psalm 122

A Song of Ascents.
Of David.

I was glad when they said to me,
"Let us go to the house of the LORD!"
2 Our feet have been standing
within your gates, O Jerusalem!

3 Jerusalem, built as a city
which is bound firmly together,
4 to which the tribes go up,
the tribes of the LORD,
as was decreed for Israel,
to give thanks to the name of the LORD.
5 There thrones for judgment were set,
the thrones of the house of David.

6 Pray for the peace of Jerusalem!
"May they prosper who love you!
7 Peace be within your walls,
and security within your towers!"
8 For my brethren and companions' sake
I will say, "Peace be within you!"
9 For the sake of the house of the LORD our God,
I will seek your good.

Psalm 123

A Song of Ascents.

To thee I lift up my eyes, O thou who art enthroned in the
heavens!
2 Behold, as the eyes of servants
look to the hand of their master,
as the eyes of a maid
to the hand of her mistress,
so our eyes look to the LORD our God,
till he have mercy upon us.

3 Have mercy upon us, O LORD, have mercy upon us,
for we have had more than enough of contempt.
4 Too long our soul has been sated
with the scorn of those who are at ease,
the contempt of the proud.

Psalm 124

A Song of Ascents.
Of David.

If it had not been the LORD who was on our side,
let Israel now say—
2 If it had not been the LORD who was on our side,
when men rose up against us,
3 then they would have swallowed us up alive,
when their anger was kindled against us;
4 then the flood would have swept us away,
the torrent would have gone over us;
5 then over us would have gone the raging waters.

6 Blessed be the LORD,
who has not given us
as prey to their teeth!

7 We have escaped as a bird
    from the snare of the fowlers;
the snare is broken,
    and we have escaped!
8 Our help is in the name of the LORD,
    who made heaven and earth.

Psalm 125

A Song of
Ascents.

Those who trust in the LORD are like Mount Zion,
    which cannot be moved, but abides for ever.
2 As the mountains are round about Jerusalem,
    so the LORD is round about his people,
    from this time forth and for evermore.
3 For the scepter of wickedness shall not rest
    upon the land allotted to the righteous,
lest the righteous put forth
    their hands to do wrong.
4 Do good, O LORD, to those who are good,
    and to those who are upright in their hearts!
5 But those who turn aside upon their crooked ways
    the LORD will lead away with evildoers!
    Peace be in Israel!

Psalm 126

A Song of
Ascents.

l Or brought back
those who
returned to Zion

When the LORD restored the fortunes of Zion,*l*
    we were like those who dream.
2 Then our mouth was filled with laughter,
    and our tongue with shouts of joy;
then they said among the nations,
    "The LORD has done great things for them."
3 The LORD has done great things for us;
    we are glad.
4 Restore our fortunes, O LORD,
    like the watercourses in the Negeb!
5 May those who sow in tears
    reap with shouts of joy!
6 He that goes forth weeping,
    bearing the seed for sowing,
shall come home with shouts of joy,
    bringing his sheaves with him.

Psalm 127

A Song of
Ascents.
Of Solomon.

m Another
reading is *so*

Unless the LORD builds the house,
    those who build it labor in vain.
Unless the LORD watches over the city,
    the watchman stays awake in vain.
2 It is in vain that you rise up early and go late to rest,
eating the bread of anxious toil;
    for*m* he gives to his beloved sleep.
3 Lo, sons are a heritage from the LORD,
    the fruit of the womb a reward.
4 Like arrows in the hand of a warrior are the sons of one's youth.
5 Happy is the man who has
    his quiver full of them!
He shall not be put to shame
    when he speaks with his enemies in the gate.

Psalm 128

A Song of
Ascents.

Blessed is every one who fears the LORD,
    who walks in his ways!
2 You shall eat the fruit of the labor of your hands;
    you shall be happy, and it shall be well with you.
3 Your wife will be like a fruitful vine
    within your house;
your children will be like olive shoots
    around your table.
4 Lo, thus shall the man be blessed
    who fears the LORD.
5 The LORD bless you from Zion!
    May you see the prosperity of Jerusalem
    all the days of your life!

6 May you see your children's children!
   Peace be upon Israel!

Psalm 129

A Song of
Ascents.

"Sorely have they afflicted me from my youth,"
   let Israel now say—
2 "Sorely have they afflicted me from my youth,
   yet they have not prevailed against me.
3 The plowers plowed upon my back;
   they made long their furrows."
4 The LORD is righteous;
   he has cut the cords of the wicked.
5 May all who hate Zion
   be put to shame and turned backward!
6 Let them be like the grass on the housetops,
   which withers before it grows up,
7 with which the reaper does not fill his hand
   or the binder of sheaves his bosom,
8 while those who pass by do not say,
   "The blessing of the LORD be upon you!
   We bless you in the name of the LORD!"

Psalm 130

A Song of
Ascents.

Out of the depths I cry to thee, O LORD!
2   Lord, hear my voice!
Let thy ears be attentive
   to the voice of my supplications!
3 If thou, O LORD, shouldst mark iniquities,
   Lord, who could stand?
4 But there is forgiveness with thee,
   that thou mayest be feared.
5 I wait for the LORD, my soul waits,
   and in his word I hope;
6 my soul waits for the LORD
   more than watchmen for the morning,
   more than watchmen for the morning.
7 O Israel, hope in the LORD!
   For with the LORD there is steadfast love,
   and with him is plenteous redemption.
8 And he will redeem Israel
   from all his iniquities.

Psalm 131

A Song of
Ascents.
Of David.

O LORD, my heart is not lifted up,
   my eyes are not raised too high;
I do not occupy myself with
   things too great and too marvelous for me.
2 But I have calmed and quieted my soul,
   like a child quieted at its mother's breast;
   like a child that is quieted is my soul.
3 O Israel, hope in the LORD
   from this time forth and for evermore.

Psalm 132

A Song of
Ascents.

Remember, O LORD, in David's favor,
   all the hardships he endured;
2 how he swore to the LORD
   and vowed to the Mighty One of Jacob,
3 "I will not enter my house
   or get into my bed;
4 I will not give sleep to my eyes
   or slumber to my eyelids,
5 until I find a place for the LORD,
   a dwelling place for the Mighty One of Jacob."
6 Lo, we heard of it in Eph'rathah,
   we found it in the fields of Ja'ar.
7 "Let us go to his dwelling place;
   let us worship at his footstool!"
8 Arise, O LORD, and go to thy resting place,
   thou and the ark of thy might.
9 Let thy priests be clothed with righteousness,

and let thy saints shout for joy.
10 For thy servant David's sake
   do not turn away the face of thy anointed one.

11 The LORD swore to David a sure oath
   from which he will not turn back:
"One of the sons of your body
   I will set on your throne.
12 If your sons keep my covenant
   and my testimonies which I shall teach them,
their sons also for ever shall sit upon your throne."

13 For the LORD has chosen Zion;
   he has desired it for his habitation:
14 "This is my resting place for ever;
   here I will dwell, for I have desired it.
15 I will abundantly bless her provisions;
   I will satisfy her poor with bread.
16 Her priests I will clothe with salvation,
   and her saints will shout for joy.
17 There I will make a horn to sprout for David;
   I have prepared a lamp for my anointed.
18 His enemies I will clothe with shame,
   but upon himself his crown will shed its luster."

Psalm 133

A Song of
Ascents.

Behold, how good and pleasant it is
   when brothers dwell in unity!
2 It is like the precious oil upon the head,
   running down upon the beard,
upon the beard of Aaron,
   running down on the collar of his robes!
3 It is like the dew of Hermon,
   which falls on the mountains of Zion!
For there the LORD has commanded the blessing,
   life for evermore.

Psalm 134

A Song of
Ascents.

Come, bless the LORD, all you servants of the LORD,
   who stand by night in the house of the LORD!
2 Lift up your hands to the holy place,
   and bless the LORD!
3 May the LORD bless you from Zion,
   he who made heaven and earth!

Psalm 135

Praise the LORD.
Praise the name of the LORD,
   give praise, O servants of the LORD,
2 you that stand in the house of the LORD,
   in the courts of the house of our God!
3 Praise the LORD, for the LORD is good;
   sing to his name, for he is gracious!
4 For the LORD has chosen Jacob for himself,
   Israel as his own possession.

5 For I know that the LORD is great,
   and that our Lord is above all gods.
6 Whatever the LORD pleases he does,
   in heaven and on earth,
   in the seas and all deeps.
7 He it is who makes the clouds rise at the end of the earth,
   who makes lightnings for the rain
   and brings forth the wind from his storehouses.
8 He it was who smote the first-born of Egypt,
   both of man and of beast;
9 who in thy midst, O Egypt,
   sent signs and wonders
   against Pharaoh and all his servants;
10 who smote many nations
   and slew mighty kings,
11 Sihon, king of the Amorites,
   and Og, king of Bashan,

and all the kingdoms of Canaan,
12 and gave their land as a heritage,
  a heritage to his people Israel.

13 Thy name, O LORD, endures for ever,
  thy renown, O LORD, throughout all ages.
14 For the LORD will vindicate his people,
  and have compassion on his servants.
15 The idols of the nations are silver and gold,
  the work of men's hands.
16 They have mouths, but they speak not,
  they have eyes, but they see not,
17 they have ears, but they hear not,
  nor is there any breath in their mouths.
18 Like them be those who make them!—
  yea, every one who trusts in them!

19 O house of Israel, bless the LORD!
  O house of Aaron, bless the LORD!
20 O house of Levi, bless the LORD!
  You that fear the LORD, bless the LORD!
21 Blessed be the LORD from Zion,
  he who dwells in Jerusalem!
Praise the LORD!

Psalm 136

O give thanks to the LORD, for he is good,
  for his steadfast love endures for ever.
2 O give thanks to the God of gods,
  for his steadfast love endures for ever.
3 O give thanks to the Lord of lords,
  for his steadfast love endures for ever;

4 to him who alone does great wonders,
  for his steadfast love endures for ever;
5 to him who by understanding made the heavens,
  for his steadfast love endures for ever;
6 to him who spread out the earth upon the waters,
  for his steadfast love endures for ever;
7 to him who made the great lights,
  for his steadfast love endures for ever;
8 the sun to rule over the day,
  for his steadfast love endures for ever;
9 the moon and stars to rule over the night,
  for his steadfast love endures for ever;

10 to him who smote the first-born of Egypt,
  for his steadfast love endures for ever;
11 and brought Israel out from among them,
  for his steadfast love endures for ever;
12 with a strong hand and an outstretched arm,
  for his steadfast love endures for ever;
13 to him who divided the Red Sea in sunder,
  for his steadfast love endures for ever;
14 and made Israel pass through the midst of it,
  for his steadfast love endures for ever;
15 but overthrew Pharaoh and his host in the Red Sea,
  for his steadfast love endures for ever;
16 to him who led his people through the wilderness,
  for his steadfast love endures for ever;
17 to him who smote great kings,
  for his steadfast love endures for ever;
18 and slew famous kings,
  for his steadfast love endures for ever;
19 Sihon, king of the Amorites,
  for his steadfast love endures for ever;
20 and Og, king of Bashan,
  for his steadfast love endures for ever;
21 and gave their land as a heritage,
  for his steadfast love endures for ever;
22 a heritage to Israel his servant,
  for his steadfast love endures for ever.

23 It is he who remembered us in our low estate,
  for his steadfast love endures for ever;
24 and rescued us from our foes,
  for his steadfast love endures for ever;
25 he who gives food to all flesh,
  for his steadfast love endures for ever.
26 O give thanks to the God of heaven,
  for his steadfast love endures for ever.

Psalm 137

°Heb streams
ᵖOr poplars

By the waters° of Babylon, there we sat down and wept,
  when we remembered Zion.
2 On the willowsᵖ there
  we hung up our lyres.
3 For there our captors
  required of us songs,
and our tormentors, mirth, saying,
  "Sing us one of the songs of Zion!"

4 How shall we sing the LORD's song
  in a foreign land?
5 If I forget you, O Jerusalem,
  let my right hand wither!
6 Let my tongue cleave to the roof of my mouth,
  if I do not remember you,
if I do not set Jerusalem
  above my highest joy!

7 Remember, O LORD, against the Edomites
  the day of Jerusalem,
how they said, "Rase it, rase it!
  Down to its foundations!"

*qOr you who are
devastated*

8 O daughter of Babylon, you devastator!q
  Happy shall he be who requites you
  with what you have done to us!
9 Happy shall he be who takes your little ones
  and dashes them against the rock!

Psalm 138

*A Psalm of
David.*

I give thee thanks, O LORD, with my whole heart;
  before the gods I sing thy praise;
2 I bow down toward thy holy temple
  and give thanks to thy name for thy steadfast love and thy
    faithfulness;
for thou hast exalted above everything
  thy name and thy word.ʳ

*ʳCn: Heb thou
hast exalted thy
word above all thy
name*
*ˢSyr Compare Gk
Tg: Heb thou
didst make me
arrogant in my
soul with strength*

3 On the day I called, thou didst answer me,
  my strength of soul thou didst increase.ˢ
4 All the kings of the earth shall praise thee, O LORD,
  for they have heard the words of thy mouth;
5 and they shall sing of the ways of the LORD,
  for great is the glory of the LORD.
6 For though the LORD is high, he regards the lowly;
  but the haughty he knows from afar.

7 Though I walk in the midst of trouble,
  thou dost preserve my life;
thou dost stretch out thy hand against the wrath of my enemies,
  and thy right hand delivers me.
8 The LORD will fulfil his purpose for me;
  thy steadfast love, O LORD, endures for ever.
  Do not forsake the work of thy hands.

Psalm 139

*To the
choirmaster.
A Psalm of
David.*

O LORD, thou hast searched me and known me!
2 Thou knowest when I sit down and when I rise up;
  thou discernest my thoughts from afar.
3 Thou searchest out my path and my lying down,
  and art acquainted with all my ways.
4 Even before a word is on my tongue,
  lo, O LORD, thou knowest it altogether.
5 Thou dost beset me behind and before,
  and layest thy hand upon me.

6 Such knowledge is too wonderful for me;
  it is high, I cannot attain it.

7 Whither shall I go from thy Spirit?
  Or whither shall I flee from thy presence?
8 If I ascend to heaven, thou art there!
  If I make my bed in Sheol, thou art there!
9 If I take the wings of the morning
  and dwell in the uttermost parts of the sea,
10 even there thy hand shall lead me,
  and thy right hand shall hold me.
11 If I say, "Let only darkness cover me,
  and the light about me be night,"
12 even the darkness is not dark to thee,
  the night is bright as the day;
  for darkness is as light with thee.

13 For thou didst form my inward parts,
  thou didst knit me together in my mother's womb.

t Cn Compare Gk Syr Jerome: Heb fearful things I am wonderful

14 I praise thee, for thou art fearful and wonderful.*t*
  Wonderful are thy works!
Thou knowest me right well;
15   my frame was not hidden from thee,
when I was being made in secret,
  intricately wrought in the depths of the earth.
16 Thy eyes beheld my unformed substance;
  in thy book were written, every one of them,
the days that were formed for me,
  when as yet there was none of them.
17 How precious to me are thy thoughts, O God!
  How vast is the sum of them!
18 If I would count them, they are more than the sand.
  When I awake, I am still with thee.*u*

u Or were I to come to the end I would still be with thee

19 O that thou wouldst slay the wicked, O God,
  and that men of blood would depart from me,
20 men who maliciously defy thee,
  who lift themselves up against thee for evil!*v*

v Cn: Heb uncertain

21 Do I not hate them that hate thee, O LORD?
  And do I not loathe them that rise up against thee?
22 I hate them with perfect hatred;
  I count them my enemies.
23 Search me, O God, and know my heart!
  Try me and know my thoughts!

w Heb hurtful
x Or the ancient way. Compare Jer. 6.16

24 And see if there be any wicked*w* way in me,
  and lead me in the way everlasting!*x*

Psalm 140

To the choirmaster. A Psalm of David.

Deliver me, O LORD, from evil men;
  preserve me from violent men,
2 who plan evil things in their heart,
  and stir up wars continually.
3 They make their tongue sharp as a serpent's,
  and under their lips is the poison of vipers. *Selah*
4 Guard me, O LORD, from the hands of the wicked;
  preserve me from violent men,
  who have planned to trip up my feet.
5 Arrogant men have hidden a trap for me,
  and with cords they have spread a net,*y*
  by the wayside they have set snares for me. *Selah*

y Or they have spread cords as a net

6 I say to the LORD, Thou art my God;
  give ear to the voice of my supplications, O LORD!
7 O LORD, my Lord, my strong deliverer,
  thou hast covered my head in the day of battle.
8 Grant not, O LORD, the desires of the wicked;
  do not further his evil plot! *Selah*

z Cn Compare Gk: Heb those who surround me are uplifted in head

9 Those who surround me lift up their head,*z*
  let the mischief of their lips overwhelm them!
10 Let burning coals fall upon them!
  Let them be cast into pits, no more to rise!
11 Let not the slanderer be established in the land;

let evil hunt down the violent man speedily!
12 I know that the LORD maintains the cause of the afflicted,
and executes justice for the needy.
13 Surely the righteous shall give thanks to thy name;
the upright shall dwell in thy presence.

Psalm 141

A Psalm of David.

I call upon thee, O LORD; make haste to me!
Give ear to my voice, when I call to thee!
2 Let my prayer be counted as incense before thee,
and the lifting up of my hands as an evening sacrifice!
3 Set a guard over my mouth, O LORD,
keep watch over the door of my lips!
4 Incline not my heart to any evil,
to busy myself with wicked deeds
in company with men who work iniquity;
and let me not eat of their dainties!

a Gk: Heb obscure
b Cn: Heb *for continually and my prayer*

c The Hebrew of verses 5–7 is obscure

5 Let a good man strike or rebuke me in kindness,
but let the oil of the wicked never anoint my head;*a*
for my prayer is continually*b* against their wicked deeds.
6 When they are given over to those who shall condemn them,
then they shall learn that the word of the LORD is true.
7 As a rock which one cleaves and shatters on the land,
so shall their bones be strewn at the mouth of Sheol.*c*
8 But my eyes are toward thee, O LORD God;
in thee I seek refuge; leave me not defenseless!
9 Keep me from the trap which they have laid for me,
and from the snares of evildoers!
10 Let the wicked together fall into their own nets,
while I escape.

Psalm 142

A Maskil of David, when he was in the cave. A Prayer.

d Or *Look to the right and watch*

I cry with my voice to the LORD,
with my voice I make supplication to the LORD,
2 I pour out my complaint before him,
I tell my trouble before him,
3 When my spirit is faint,
thou knowest my way!

In the path where I walk
they have hidden a trap for me.
4 I look to the right and watch,*d*
but there is none who takes notice of me;
no refuge remains to me,
no man cares for me.

5 I cry to thee, O LORD;
I say, Thou art my refuge,
my portion in the land of the living.
6 Give heed to my cry;
for I am brought very low!

Deliver me from my persecutors;
for they are too strong for me!
7 Bring me out of prison,
that I may give thanks to thy name!
The righteous will surround me;
for thou wilt deal bountifully with me.

Psalm 143

A Psalm of David.

Hear my prayer, O LORD; give ear to my supplications!
In thy faithfulness answer me, in thy righteousness!
2 Enter not into judgment with thy servant;
for no man living is righteous before thee.

3 For the enemy has pursued me;
he has crushed my life to the ground;
he has made me sit in darkness like those long dead.
4 Therefore my spirit faints within me;
my heart within me is appalled.
5 I remember the days of old,
I meditate on all that thou hast done;
I muse on what thy hands have wrought.

6 I stretch out my hands to thee;
    my soul thirsts for thee like a parched land. *Selah*

7 Make haste to answer me, O LORD!
    My spirit fails!
Hide not thy face from me,
    lest I be like those who go down to the Pit.

8 Let me hear in the morning of thy steadfast love,
    for in thee I put my trust.
Teach me the way I should go,
    for to thee I lift up my soul.

9 Deliver me, O LORD, from my enemies!
    I have fled to thee for refuge!*e*

10 Teach me to do thy will,
    for thou art my God!
Let thy good spirit lead me
    on a level path!

11 For thy name's sake, O LORD, preserve my life!
    In thy righteousness bring me out of trouble!

12 And in thy steadfast love cut off my enemies,
    and destroy all my adversaries,
for I am thy servant.

e One Heb Ms Gk: Heb *to thee I have hidden*

Psalm 144

A Psalm of David.

Blessed be the LORD, my rock,
who trains my hands for war,
    and my fingers for battle;

2 my rock*f* and my fortress,
    my stronghold and my deliverer,
my shield and he in whom I take refuge,
    who subdues the peoples under him.*g*

3 O LORD, what is man that thou dost regard him,
    or the son of man that thou dost think of him?

4 Man is like a breath,
    his days are like a passing shadow.

5 Bow thy heavens, O LORD, and come down!
    Touch the mountains that they smoke!

6 Flash forth the lightning and scatter them,
    send out thy arrows and rout them!

7 Stretch forth thy hand from on high,
    rescue me and deliver me from the many waters,
    from the hand of aliens,

8 whose mouths speak lies,
    and whose right hand is a right hand of falsehood.

9 I will sing a new song to thee, O God;
    upon a ten-stringed harp I will play to thee,

10 who givest victory to kings,
    who rescuest David thy*h* servant.

11 Rescue me from the cruel sword,
    and deliver me from the hand of aliens,
whose mouths speak lies,
    and whose right hand is a right hand of falsehood.

12 May our sons in their youth
    be like plants full grown,
our daughters like corner pillars
    cut for the structure of a palace;

13 may our garners be full,
    providing all manner of store;
may our sheep bring forth thousands
    and ten thousands in our fields;

14 may our cattle be heavy with young,
    suffering no mischance or failure in bearing;
may there be no cry of distress in our streets!

15 Happy the people to whom such blessings fall!
    Happy the people whose God is the LORD!

f With 18.2 2 Sam. 22.2: Hob *my steadfast love*
g Another reading is *my people under me*

h Heb *his*

Psalm 145

A Song of
Praise.
Of David.

I will extol thee, my God and King,
and bless thy name for ever and ever.
2 Every day I will bless thee,
and praise thy name for ever and ever.
3 Great is the Lord, and greatly to be praised,
and his greatness is unsearchable.

4 One generation shall laud thy works to another,
and shall declare thy mighty acts.
5 On the glorious splendor of thy majesty,
and on thy wondrous works, I will meditate.
6 Men shall proclaim the might of thy terrible acts,
and I will declare thy greatness.
7 They shall pour forth the fame of thy abundant goodness,
and shall sing aloud of thy righteousness.

8 The Lord is gracious and merciful,
slow to anger and abounding in steadfast love.
9 The Lord is good to all,
and his compassion is over all that he has made.

10 All thy works shall give thanks to thee, O Lord,
and all thy saints shall bless thee!
11 They shall speak of the glory of thy kingdom,
and tell of thy power,

[h] Heb *his*

12 to make known to the sons of men thy[h] mighty deeds,
and the glorious splendor of thy[h] kingdom.
13 Thy kingdom is an everlasting kingdom,
and thy dominion endures throughout all generations.

The Lord is faithful in all his words,
and gracious in all his deeds.[i]

[i] These two lines
are supplied by
one Hebrew Ms,
Gk and Syr

14 The Lord upholds all who are falling,
and raises up all who are bowed down.
15 The eyes of all look to thee,
and thou givest them their food in due season.
16 Thou openest thy hand,
thou satisfiest the desire of every living thing.
17 The Lord is just in all his ways,
and kind in all his doings.
18 The Lord is near to all who call upon him,
to all who call upon him in truth.
19 He fulfils the desire of all who fear him,
he also hears their cry, and saves them.
20 The Lord preserves all who love him;
but all the wicked he will destroy.

21 My mouth will speak the praise of the Lord,
and let all flesh bless his holy name for ever and ever.

Psalm 146

Praise the Lord!
Praise the Lord, O my soul!
2 I will praise the Lord as long as I live;
I will sing praises to my God while I have being.

3 Put not your trust in princes,
in a son of man, in whom there is no help.
4 When his breath departs he returns to his earth;
on that very day his plans perish.

5 Happy is he whose help is the God of Jacob,
whose hope is in the Lord his God,
6 who made heaven and earth,
the sea, and all that is in them;
who keeps faith for ever;
7   who executes justice for the oppressed;
who gives food to the hungry.

The Lord sets the prisoners free;
8   the Lord opens the eyes of the blind.
The Lord lifts up those who are bowed down;
the Lord loves the righteous.
9 The Lord watches over the sojourners,
he upholds the widow and the fatherless;
but the way of the wicked he brings to ruin.

10 The LORD will reign for ever,
    thy God, O Zion, to all generations.
Praise the LORD!

Psalm 147

Praise the LORD!
For it is good to sing praises to our God;
    for he is gracious, and a song of praise is seemly.
2 The LORD builds up Jerusalem;
    he gathers the outcasts of Israel.
3 He heals the brokenhearted,
    and binds up their wounds.
4 He determines the number of the stars,
    he gives to all of them their names.
5 Great is our LORD, and abundant in power;
    his understanding is beyond measure.
6 The LORD lifts up the downtrodden,
    he casts the wicked to the ground.

7 Sing to the LORD with thanksgiving;
    make melody to our God upon the lyre!
8 He covers the heavens with clouds,
    he prepares rain for the earth,
    he makes grass grow upon the hills.
9 He gives to the beasts their food,
    and to the young ravens which cry.
10 His delight is not in the strength of the horse,
    nor his pleasure in the legs of a man;
11 but the LORD takes pleasure in those who fear him,
    in those who hope in his steadfast love.

12 Praise the LORD, O Jerusalem!
    Praise your God, O Zion!
13 For he strengthens the bars of your gates;
    he blesses your sons within you.
14 He makes peace in your borders;
    he fills you with the finest of the wheat.
15 He sends forth his command to the earth;
    his word runs swiftly.
16 He gives snow like wool;
    he scatters hoarfrost like ashes.
17 He casts forth his ice like morsels;
    who can stand before his cold?
18 He sends forth his word, and melts them;
    he makes his wind blow, and the waters flow.
19 He declares his word to Jacob,
    his statutes and ordinances to Israel.
20 He has not dealt thus with any other nation;
    they do not know his ordinances.
Praise the LORD!

Psalm 148

Praise the LORD!
Praise the LORD from the heavens,
    praise him in the heights!
2 Praise him, all his angels,
    praise him, all his host!

3 Praise him, sun and moon,
    praise him, all you shining stars!
4 Praise him, you highest heavens,
    and you waters above the heavens!

5 Let them praise the name of the LORD!
    For he commanded and they were created.
6 And he established them for ever and ever;
    he fixed their bounds which cannot be passed.[j]

jOr he set a law which cannot pass away

7 Praise the LORD from the earth,
    you sea monsters and all deeps,
8 fire and hail, snow and frost,
    stormy wind fulfilling his command!
9 Mountain and all hills,
    fruit trees and all cedars!

10 Beasts and all cattle,
   creeping things and flying birds!
11 Kings of the earth and all peoples,
   princes and all rulers of the earth!
12 Young men and maidens together,
   old men and children!
13 Let them praise the name of the LORD,
   for his name alone is exalted;
   his glory is above earth and heaven.
14 He has raised up a horn for his people,
   praise for all his saints,
   for the people of Israel who are near to him.
Praise the LORD!

Psalm 149

Praise the LORD!
Sing to the LORD a new song,
   his praise in the assembly of the faithful!
2 Let Israel be glad in his Maker,
   let the sons of Zion rejoice in their King!
3 Let them praise his name with dancing,
   making melody to him with timbrel and lyre!
4 For the LORD takes pleasure in his people;
   he adorns the humble with victory.
5 Let the faithful exult in glory;
   let them sing for joy on their couches.
6 Let the high praises of God be in their throats
   and two-edged swords in their hands,
7 to wreak vengeance on the nations
   and chastisement on the peoples,
8 to bind their kings with chains
   and their nobles with fetters of iron,
9 to execute on them the judgment written!
   This is glory for all his faithful ones.
Praise the LORD!

Psalm 150

Praise the LORD!
Praise God in his sanctuary;
   praise him in his mighty firmament!
2 Praise him for his mighty deeds;
   praise him according to his exceeding greatness!
3 Praise him with trumpet sound;
   praise him with lute and harp!
4 Praise him with timbrel and dance;
   praise him with strings and pipe!
5 Praise him with sounding cymbals;
   praise him with loud clashing cymbals!
6 Let everything that breathes praise the LORD!
Praise the LORD!